MULTICULTURAL PSYCHOLOGY

MULTICULTURAL PSYCHOLOGY

GORDON C. NAGAYAMA HALL
CHRISTY BARONGAN

Upper Saddle River, New Jersey 07458

Library of Congress Cataloging-in-Publication Data

Hall, Gordon C. Nagayama.
   Multicultural psychology / Gordon C. Nagayama Hall, Christy Barongan.
     p. cm.
   Includes bibliographical references and index.
   ISBN 0-13-019146-9
    1. Ethnopsychology—United States.   2. Minorities—United States—Psychology.
  I. Barongan, Christy. II. Title.
  GN502.H335   2001
  155.8′2′0973—dc21

                  2001032176

VP, Editorial Director: *Laura Pearson*
Managing Editor (editoral): *Sharon Rheinhardt*
Sr. Managing Editor (production): *Mary Rottino*
Production Liaison: *Fran Russello*
Project Manager: *Publications Development Company of Texas*
Prepress and Manufacturing Buyer: *Tricia Kenny*
Art director: *Jane Conte*
Cover Designer:
Cover Art:
AVP, Director of Marketing: *Beth Gillett Mejia*

This book was set in 10.5/14 Clearface by Publications Development
Company of Texas and was printed and bound by R. R. Donnelly & Sons Company.
The cover was printed by Phoenix Color Corp.

 © 2002 by Pearson Education, Inc.
Upper Saddle River, New Jersey 07458

Printed in the United States of America

10 9 8 7 6 5 4 3 2 1

ISBN 0-13-019146-9

Pearson Education Ltd., *London*
Pearson Education Australia Pty., Limited, *Sydney*
Pearson Education Singapore, Pte. Ltd.
Pearson Education North Asia Ltd., *Hong Kong*
Pearson Education Canada, Ltd., *Toronto*
Pearson Educación de Mexico, S.A. de C.V.
Pearson Education—Japan, *Tokyo*
Pearson Education Malaysia, Pte. Ltd.
Pearson Education, Upper Saddle River, New Jersey

Contents

3 Theory and Multicultural Psychology: Biological and Social Psychology 71

4 Theory and Multicultural Psychology: Developmental Psychology and Personality 113

SECTION II

PSYCHOLOGY IN THE CONTEXT OF MULTICULTURAL ISSUES

5   African Americans   157

6   Asian Pacific Americans   195

7 Latino/a Americans   235

8 American Indians   265

9 Emerging Issues

Preface

American society is rapidly changing. Within 50 years, persons of color will be the majority in the United States and already compose one-third of the U.S. population. In California, persons of color are now the majority. Thus, competence in cultural issues is a necessary life skill for full participation in society during the twenty-first century.

Psychology has been slow to embrace the study of multicultural issues. Cross-cultural psychology has been the primary area in which psychology has examined culture. This approach typically examines two national groups that are not in the same social context. Conversely, multicultural psychology is the study of multiple cultural groups in the same context. Cultural groups influence one another when they are in the same sociocultural context; the strength of this influence is largely dependent on the power and status that cultural groups have in society. All the cultural groups discussed in this textbook have ethnic minority status. Thus, multicultural psychology is the study not only of culture, but also of the sociopolitical issues that ethnic minority persons face in the United States. Although cross-national issues are of importance in psychology, issues of dealing with persons of multiple cultural backgrounds in the United States are more likely to affect the lives of most American students. There are several cross-cultural psychology textbooks, but very few that address multicultural psychology within a single national and sociopolitical context.

This textbook is an introduction to cultural and minority status issues in psychology. The first section of the book provides a general context for multicultural issues in psychology. The section begins with an overview and definition of multicultural psychology. Traditional research methods are reviewed in the second chapter and the strengths and limitations of such methods in conducting research with women and persons of color are discussed. In the third and fourth chapters, we review how multicultural issues are addressed in biological, social, personality, and developmental psychology.

The second section of the book focuses on specific issues involving women and ethnic minority groups, including African Americans, Asian Pacific Americans, Latino/a Americans, and American Indians. Issues of gender, class, and sexual orientation are integrated into the discussion of these groups. The traditional individual approach that has characterized much of Western psychology is inadequate to explain the multiple influences that impinge on persons of color in the United States. Thus, we use an ecological theoretical perspective in this book that examines individual, family, community, institutional, and societal influences on behavior. Each chapter in this section includes coverage of history, current demographics, cultural values and identity, developmental and family issues, and mental health. We review research that compares each ethnic group with European Americans and other groups in an effort to demonstrate that each of the groups covered has characteristics and experiences that are unique and unlike those of other groups. Although there are similarities between European Americans and each of the groups of color covered in this book, there are unique aspects of each group and much diversity within each group.

An important feature of this text is our attempt to make it relevant to "real-life" issues. At the end of each chapter, we include an "Issues for Discussion" section that raises contemporary issues relevant to the material covered in the chapter. Another unique feature of our book is that we include biographical profiles, including personal perspectives, of some of the most prominent psychologists of color. These persons are considered leaders in multicultural psychology and represent diverse ethnic and professional backgrounds.

Attempting to understand and to accurately represent the psychology of the many different groups and individuals covered in this text has been a daunting task. At various times, we have felt like outsiders trying to write about topics that are accessible only to insiders. We realize that it is difficult to accurately depict the diversity within our own Eurasian American and Filipino American groups, let alone other ethnic groups. Because this is a psychology textbook, we have primarily relied on the findings of empirical studies. However, there are many issues in multicultural psychology that have yet to be studied with an empirical approach. Moreover, there are many multicultural issues that may defy empirical study, such as traditional forms of spirituality. Many of our colleagues from many different ethnic backgrounds have been extremely helpful in reviewing drafts of this book, including Stan Sue, Fred Leong, James Jones, Tiffany Townsend, Ndiya Nkongho, and Gia Maramba. These colleagues have provided us with an insider's perspective on many of the groups and issues we discuss.

This textbook is an introduction to and an overview of multicultural psychology. Whole books and courses have been devoted to most of the individual topics covered here. A single textbook cannot comprehensively address all cultural groups and issues. The purpose of this book is to provide the reader with tools to understand sociocultural issues in psychology. It is our hope that this textbook will whet the appetite of the reader to pursue additional studies in multicultural issues.

Gordon C. Nagayama Hall
Christy Barongan

SECTION I

MULTICULTURAL ISSUES IN THE CONTEXT OF PSYCHOLOGY

O N E

WHAT IS MULTICULTURAL PSYCHOLOGY?

Who is an American? According to the African American writer Toni Morrison, in our national identity, "American" has been defined as "White." What evidence is there for this assertion? We might consider who our leaders are. For many people in our nation and others, the presidency probably symbolizes what is American. In the two centuries that the United States has had presidents, all have been European American men, as have all vice presidents. Thus, it could be inferred that European men symbolize who is an American.

Are women Americans? The answer is a resounding yes. Yet, American women have not enjoyed the status and privileges of American men. Can persons of color be fully regarded as Americans? Past and current history is replete with the oppression of minority groups in the United States that has denied them full American status. Implicit in the definition of an American being a European American man is that he is heterosexual. Similar to other minorities, gays, lesbians, and bisexuals have not been allowed to participate fully in American society. Nor have persons who are not at least middle class. Thus, the further a person deviates from the prototype of the European American heterosexual man, the less the person is regarded as an American.

As we enter a new millennium, an increasing number of Americans are not of European ancestry. According to the U.S. Census Bureau, ethnic minorities constituted 30 percent of the population in 2000, and will approach 50 percent within 50 years. Thus, virtually every American is or soon will be influenced by ethnic minority issues. One might expect the rapidly growing ethnic minority population to be of central interest in American psychology. After all, the psychology of ethnic minority persons is American psychology. However, the growing size of the ethnic minority population and the growing importance of ethnic minority issues are not reflected in the attention devoted to multicultural issues in American psychology. Yet, it appears that developing a multicultural psychology is one of the greatest challenges that faces us at the beginning of this millennium.

The rapidly changing demographics of the United States do not ensure that cultural changes will automatically follow. Even if ethnic minority persons become a numerical majority, this does not mean that they will gain a commensurate amount of societal power. Women constitute 50 percent of the population but are not equally represented in positions of power. South Africa during apartheid is another sad reminder of how a powerful White minority controlled and dominated a numerical Black majority. Cultural change is not inevitable. The skills to thrive in a multicultural society are something that all Americans will need to make a conscious effort to learn.

In this chapter, we discuss why gender and cultural issues have been neglected in American psychology. We also discuss the kind of research that is conducted when gender and culture are considered, making a distinction between cross-cultural and multicultural approaches. We review definitions of the terms gender, race, culture, ethnicity, and class. The impact of acculturation is considered. Finally, we offer a definition of multiculturalism.

PSYCHOLOGY'S NEGLECT OF CULTURAL VARIABLES

Why is it that cultural variables have received so little attention in mainstream theory and research in psychology? One reason may be that over 90 percent of doctoral degree psychologists are European Americans (Bernal & Castro, 1994). Although 53 percent of the members of the American Psychological Association (APA) are men, 77 percent of the APA members who have the most distinguished status as Fellows are men. (Indeed, most Fellows are "fellows"!) Jean Phinney (1996), a European American psychologist, has contended that most European Americans do not think of themselves in terms of ethnicity. Rather than seeing themselves as European Americans or "White people," European Americans, more than other ethnic groups, simply see themselves as people or as Americans (Sears, Citrin, Cheleden, & van Laar, 1999). This relative lack of attention to culture may be because European Americans have been taught that "color blindness" is politically correct (Judd, Park, Ryan, Brauer, & Kraus, 1995). Therefore, culture may be a transparent issue for many European American psychologists (cf. Segall, Lonner, & Berry, 1998). Often, one's own culture becomes salient when one comes into contact with another culture. Lack of experience and contact with cultural groups other than one's own may lead to a neglect of cultural variables (Albert, 1988).

Most psychological research is conducted with European American participants (Graham, 1992). The African American psychologist Robert Guthrie reminded us that even the rat was white in experimental psychology research. In the same way that many European Americans see themselves simply as people, psychological research conducted with European American participants is seen simply as psychology, rather than European American psychology. Although the assumption may be that psychological principles revealed in research with European American participants are applicable to non-European American groups, this assumption usually is not tested.

The same criticisms apply to women's participation. Most of the theories and research in psychology have been proposed and conducted by men, and at times on participants who were all male. For example, according to Kohlberg's (1981) stages of moral development, boys tended to score higher than girls, suggesting that males are able to attain a higher level of moral development than females. Carol Gilligan (1982) criticized this model for not taking into consideration the different ways in which males and females decide on moral issues: Males tend to emphasize justice and females tend to emphasize care and responsibility to self and others. Thus, women who do not live up to this male norm have been interpreted as being morally inferior. Similarly, research in the medical field on risk factors for coronary heart disease have been conducted largely on male European Americans, assuming that the risk factors for this group generalize to women and to other ethnic groups. Only recently has it been recognized that the same risk factors are not as universal as previously thought. For example, because of the higher levels of estrogen in women prior to menopause, women are less likely to have strokes and heart attacks than men. However, after menopause, when estrogen levels drop, strokes and heart attacks increase in women. The role that estrogen plays as a protective factor in coronary heart disease would obviously not have been realized if participants in medical research consisted only of men.

Gender, culture, and ethnicity are often viewed as nuisance variables that complicate work rather than as variables that contribute to the basic understanding of psychological principles (Albert, 1988; Betancourt & Lopez, 1993). Even when researchers concede that culture and ethnicity are important constructs, validation of theories and research in different cultural contexts is not viewed as a necessary component of good research. There is much more emphasis in psychological science on internal validity than on external validity (S. Sue, 1999). Internal validity refers to research design issues, such as adequate measurement and experimental precision, whereas external validity refers to the generalizability of the research. Both types of validity are important, but there is a need for a greater emphasis on external validity if a balance is to be achieved.

For a person who does not view the world from a cultural framework, the consideration of cultural differences may be equated with discrimination (cf. Albert, 1988). This attitude is expressed in such statements as "All humans share the same experiences" and "We've all felt different at some time in our lives." Because all humans are created equal, isn't it almost un-American to study how some Americans may be different from others? However, the experiences of people of color in the United States are qualitatively different from those of European Americans (Clark, Anderson, Clark, & Williams, 1999). Unfortunately, any differences between European Americans and others have typically been associated with disadvantage (Jones, 1988). Another deterrent for some researchers to studying cultural differences is the fear of stereotyping particular groups (Albert, 1988). The belief seems to be that to ignore or to not assess potential differences will make them disappear.

Federal funding agencies recently have implemented a requirement that grant applicants include ethnic minority populations and women in their research samples or justify not including these populations. This is a huge step in the right direction toward research that is more culturally inclusive. However, this is only a first step. Grant applicants are not required to do anything other than attempt to include ethnic minority populations and women. Applicants are not required to include theories or measures that would examine unique aspects of these groups (G. Hall, 2001). Therefore, a grant applicant could comply with the letter of the law by including some ethnic minority participants, but not examine these participants as a separate group. The end result of this approach might not be much different than if ethnic minority participants had been excluded from the research.

CROSS-CULTURAL VERSUS MULTICULTURAL PSYCHOLOGY

Some psychologists have considered culture as a variable of interest. Cultural psychology emphasizes that psychological processes are shaped by cultural context (Fiske, Kitayama, Markus, & Nisbett, 1998; Shweder, 1991). An infant is not preprogrammed to function in a particular cultural context, but has the capacity to process information to learn via social interactions what is appropriate in a particular cultural context (Fiske et al., 1998). The contingencies of the social and cultural context will shape a person's behavior. For example, if the cultural context rewards independence, most persons will become independent. Conversely, if the cultural context rewards fitting in with a group, most persons will become interdependent. Learning the social norms in a cultural context is essential to survival and effective functioning (Fiske et al., 1998).

Quite often, persons in a particular cultural context are not aware that the cultural context exists until they come into contact with a different cultural context (Fiske et al., 1998). For example, if you have grown up exclusively in a particular region with people similar to yourself and have never left that area, you may not recognize that you have a particular cultural background. Once you leave the area, however, you may begin to recognize that your own characteristics are not universal. Cross-cultural psychology has brought much-needed attention to similarities and differences across cultural groups (Segall et al., 1998). Cross-cultural psychology usually involves the study of at least two cultures in nations that do not usually have direct contact with one another. For example, cultural characteristics in the United States may be contrasted with cultural characteristics in Japan. Cross-cultural research often uses an *etic* approach, which involves a search for universal behavior patterns by comparing two or more cultures; for example, some practices exist across most cultures, including marriage, kinship, ritual, rites of passage, and gift giving (Fiske et al., 1998). Another approach is to develop and measure a psychological construct in one culture and study it in a second culture; for example, the Five Factor Model of personality was developed in the United States and has been replicated in several other cultures worldwide (McCrae & Costa, 1997).

There are limitations to the etic approach. The etic perspective may fail to detect what is unique about a particular culture. For example, an analysis of marriage across cultures that is developed from an individualist perspective and examines a married couple and their nuclear family may overlook important influences in cultures in which the individual is but one of many influences in marriage; there may be other, equally important influences, including the extended family and nonrelatives in a community. Similarly, if one uses a Five Factor approach to personality, what if there are more than five personality factors in another culture? A model that considers only five factors would miss the others; for example, seven personality factors have been identified in Filipino (Church, Katigbak, & Reyes, 1998) and Spanish samples (Benet & Waller, 1995).

The etic approach is comparative, which often necessitates the description of a modal (most common) personality for each of the cultures being studied. But the modal personality approach may fail to capture many, if not most individuals. Many Americans are quite different from the president, for example. Perhaps a better example of a modal American is someone who is more "average." What would you list as characteristics of the "average" college student? When thinking of these characteristics, how many college students differ from this person in their values, cultural background, religion, and so on? Clearly, members of a particular group do not all look or act alike. Because there exists so much within-group cultural variability, Phinney (1996) has gone so far as to contend that between-group studies should not be conducted.

Another difficulty with the comparative approach is that it tends to favor the culture in which the approach has been developed. For example, if a theory and measure of psychopathology is developed in one culture and tested in other cultures, any cross-cultural differences from the normative data in the culture in which the theory and measure were developed will likely be viewed as deviant. A person may not be depressed by local standards, but may appear depressed relative to the norms of another culture. Because many psychological theories and tests have been developed by European American men, European American men are often the standard by which others are evaluated (Bem, 1993).

An alternative cultural approach is the *emic* perspective, a culture-specific orientation. An assumption of this approach is that there are unique aspects of particular cultures that may not universally occur; therefore, constructs and measures are developed within a particular culture. This focus on a single culture may allow more attention to variability within the culture. A limitation in the emic study of a single culture is that it is unknown whether the findings of a study actually are culturally unique without examining whether they exist in other cultures. Although most psychological research in the United States has not directly examined culture, it is emic in the sense that a single culture has been studied. An example of this is what is known in clinical psychology as empirically validated treatments. None of the treatments has been empirically validated on groups other than European Americans (S. Sue, 1999); thus, it is unknown whether these treatments are effective with African Americans, Asian Americans, Latino Americans, or American Indians, who, collectively, constitute nearly one-third of the U.S. population.

Missing from most cross-cultural approaches is the analysis of the effects of more than one cultural group living in the same context, which is characteristic of the United States. Exposure to more than one culture often results in a bicultural identity (LaFromboise, Coleman, & Gerton, 1993). Thus, an Asian American is not fully Asian because of Western influences, nor fully American because of Asian influences. Asian Americans who travel to Asia often feel very American because of their lifestyle and beliefs. Yet in America, Asian Americans often do not feel included in the mainstream because of their Asian characteristics and values. The group that many Asian Americans identify with the most is neither Asians nor mainstream Americans, but Asian Americans.

The cross-cultural approach usually does not address the issue of bicultural or multicultural identity. The assumption is that being an American means having a lot in common. There may not be enough perceived variability within the United States to consider that within-culture differences might exist. If our theory and research applies to one group of Americans (usually European Americans), then they must apply to other Americans, because Americans are more similar than different. Such a view may represent a failure to acknowledge the existence of cultural groups in the United States other than European Americans. Implicit in this view is that European American culture is American culture, and that non-European American groups have or should have assimilated.

Multicultural psychology is the study of the influences of multiple cultures in a single context on human behavior. The consideration of both cultural and sociopolitical issues becomes important when multiple cultural groups coexist in a single context (Jones, 1999; D. W. Sue, Ivey, & Pedersen, 1996; S. Sue, Ito, & Bradshaw, 1984). Each group in a multicultural context brings traditions and values that influence their own group as well as the other groups in the context. A common occurrence in multicultural contexts is that the most powerful group dominates or oppresses other groups (LaFromboise et al., 1993). Thus, group differences are not only cultural, they are also sociopolitical. For example, persons of color in the United States often are influenced by non-Western cultures and are also influenced by their status as minority persons. Thus, a sole focus on the cultural characteristics of persons of color in the United States would miss the effects of ethnic minority status, including discrimination and other forms of oppression by the majority group.

A common problem in cross-cultural and multicultural psychology is that cultural variables are often poorly defined or not defined at all (Betancourt & Lopez, 1993). Two or more cultural groups are compared and it is often assumed that any differences are cultural differences. For example, if African Americans and Latino Americans differ on a personality characteristic, is this difference culturally based? The answer to this question is unknown without directly measuring what is thought to be the basis of a cultural difference (Betancourt & Lopez, 1993). Not all African Americans or Latino Americans have the same degree of identification with African, Latino, or American culture. There may be many reasons other than cultural ones why the groups differ. Thus, the definition of culture and related constructs is necessary.

SEX, GENDER, RACE, CULTURE, ETHNICITY, AND CLASS

Sex, gender, race, culture, ethnicity, and class are terms that are central to multicultural psychology. In this section, we define each and discuss relevant issues.

Sex and Gender

The term sex is used to refer to biological differences between males and females; the term gender is used to refer to psychological and social differences between males and females. Although this distinction appears clear-cut, in practice it is sometimes difficult to distinguish between a gender and a sex difference. If we were to say, for example, that males tend to be more physically aggressive than females, this could be construed as either a gender or a sex difference, depending on whether we believed the difference was due to socialization (males are encouraged to behave aggressively and females are not) or testosterone, respectively. Thus, the distinction between what can be attributed to biology and what can be attributed to psychological and social factors is in itself a point of debate; as a result, many texts use the terms interchangeably.

In fact, gender differences that are assumed to be based on biology are often the findings that cause the greatest controversy in psychology, usually because such evidence is used to justify the status quo. For example, evolutionary theories argue that women are attracted to older, higher-status men and men are attracted to younger, attractive women because these are the partners that will give them the most potential for reproduction (Buss, 1989). Similarly, men are more likely than women to become involved in violent conflicts with other men for biological reasons; those males who in our evolutionary history defeated their rivals for the best mates were more likely to produce offspring than their less aggressive counterparts (Wilson & Daly, 1985).

Arguments such as these suggest that biology is destiny. However, environmental factors must also be taken into consideration. Take, for example, Michael Jordan, an athlete with superb skills in basketball. To some degree, these skills appear to be specific to the sport of basketball, given his unsuccessful career in minor league baseball, and this basketball ability may indeed be genetically determined. Nevertheless, even this talent must be cultivated through environmental factors such as exercise, practice, and participating in competitive games. This was apparent when Jordan returned at the end of the 1995 basketball season without having played or trained and was a mediocre player at best—a shadow of the athlete he was before, and the player he was to become again in the following years, with practice and training. Thus, Jordan can serve as a reminder to us all that genes and environment work together in determining who we are and what we do.

Gender is an important concept in terms of how we define and identify ourselves. By the age of 3, children know whether they are male or female; between ages 3 and 5 they know that being male or female is based on one's genitals; and by the age of 5 or 6, children begin to classify information in terms of gender. For example, girls wear dresses and play with dolls; boys wear ties and play with trucks. One negative consequence of making such generalizations about males and females is the risk of gender stereotypes. We have already encountered this risk in our discussion of biological sex differences. For example, if men are more physically aggressive than women, perhaps this finding might be used to justify why women should not be in the military; or, if women are better followers than leaders, then they would not make very good candidates for president. At times, differences between the sexes are almost glamorized in our culture, evident in such popular psychology books as *Men Are from Mars, Women Are from Venus.* However, such stereotyping is

not without negative consequences for both men and women. Gender stereotypes often lead to biased expectations of how we believe males and females
should act. Men may feel uncomfortable expressing their feelings, particularly
those feelings that denote weakness, such as sadness or grief. Women may feel
uncomfortable being assertive and competitive, which may make it difficult
for them to succeed in a work environment where those qualities are rewarded. Fortunately, there is a growing recognition in our culture of the impact that such gender-loaded messages can have. For example, Nike's latest
campaign slogan features females who play traditionally masculine sports
such as boxing and hockey, yet still maintain traditionally feminine interests,
such as knitting and preference for the color pink. Thus, these commercials
emphasize the idea that one can defy gender stereotypes by exemplifying
characteristics that are both masculine and feminine.

Attention to gender in psychology can sometimes lead to different assumptions about personality and development, psychopathology, and therapy. Such
assumptions can also lead to gender stereotyping, as we saw earlier in
Kohlberg's and Gilligan's differing views of moral development. Such assumptions can also affect what we consider to be normal and abnormal behavior. For
example, empathy, warmth, and expressiveness are usually considered to be
more characteristic of females, and assertiveness, independence, and competitiveness are usually considered more characteristic of males. However, the
characteristics that mental health professionals use to describe ideal mental
health are the same characteristics that are associated with masculinity
(Broverman, Broverman, Clarkson, Rosenkrantz, & Vogel, 1970). Research examining the benefits of androgny versus masculinity and femininity also supports the finding that masculine rather than feminine qualities are associated
with mental health (Taylor & Hall, 1982; Whitley, 1988). If our perception of
what is healthy is synonymous with masculinity, then females have a clear disadvantage in terms of mental health (Kaplan, 1983).

Persons do not need to be consciously or intentionally sexist to perpetu-
ate gender role stereotypes. Mere participation in a social system that has
been developed to favor males may inadvertently facilitate the sexist status
quo (Bem, 1993). Even when persons are aware of gender role stereotypes,
they may have difficulty dispelling them in a society that supports these
stereotypes. For example, parents may attempt to socialize their sons not to
be aggressive, but may come to believe that aggression is a necessary survival mechanism because many other boys are aggressive.

Psychology as a whole is still a young field, and the emphasis on the importance of gender in psychology is younger still, which is evident in

the number of female theorists in any given topic in psychology, as well as in the number of female psychologists today. Although there are increasing numbers of women entering the field of psychology, unfortunately this has been interpreted as a devaluing of the field as a whole (often referred to as the feminization of psychology) rather than as a positive change. Nevertheless, feminist psychologists have done much to promote theories, research, and practice in psychology that represent the concerns of women. These changes are apparent in the greater attention paid to issues such as domestic violence, rape, and eating disorders, both in the academic arena and in popular culture. Treatments that are more sensitive to gender issues, such as feminist therapy, have also been developed.

Although the feminist movement has had an impact in the field of psychology, one negative outcome has been the feeling of many women of color that feminism represents the concerns of middle-class, European American women specifically. For example, historically, feminists have fought for the right to work outside the home, something that African American women had been doing for some time as a necessity, not as a luxury. Not only were feminists not representing the needs of African American women, but they also discriminated against them (E. Brown, 1989; Dill, 1983). Furthermore, when minority women were encouraged to participate in the feminist movement, they were often placed in a double bind in which they were forced to choose which identity they considered more important—their race or their sex—and which movement they were going to support (Reid, 1984). More recently, feminists have attempted to represent the needs of all groups of people who have been denied rights and privileges as a result of discrimination, whether on the basis of sex, color, or sexual preference (L. Brown & Root, 1990). For example, L. Brown (1988) discusses a feminist therapy approach with gays and lesbians who are working with "coming out" issues. Childs (1990) incorporates both gender and race in her work with African American female clients.

Race

Race is a biological concept that refers to gene frequencies in a population. Races are differentiated by inherited characteristics, and this is often based on physical appearance. For example, one's skin color, facial features, and hair may suggest that one belongs to a particular racial group.

How many races are there? Major groupings have included those of East Asian, African, and European ancestry. However, these groupings are not adequate to categorize all groups. For example, in which of these three groups would Latinos be? How would a person with mixed-race background be classified? Gordon Nagayama Hall has commonly been misidentified as Latino, even by some Latinos; another common misidentification is that he is Jewish. Rarely has he been identified correctly as Eurasian. Thus, physical appearance is not always the best clue to a person's racial group.

Physical anthropologists even disagree on how many races there are; the range is from 3 to 37 (Yee, Fairchild, Weizmann, & Wyatt, 1993). Moreover, there is more variability within groups than between groups (Yee et al., 1993; Zuckerman, 1990). As discussed earlier in this chapter, a between-groups comparative approach obscures within-group differences. Thus, differences between the modal characteristics of two groups does not mean that there are no similarities among individual members of the two groups. For example, an African American girl and a European American girl who are the same age and have lived in the same neighborhood, have the same peer group, have attended the same schools, and have attended the same church are likely to be more similar than two African American girls or two European American girls who do not share such similar experiences.

What may be of more interest to multicultural psychologists is not race per se, but the social and cultural issues that are associated, in part, with race (Betancourt & Lopez, 1993). The meaning of race is socially constructed, in that it has been used to define people's roles in society (Jones, 1997). Race for some signifies that a person possesses certain psychological characteristics that are presumed to be, but are not necessarily, biologically based. Differences that distinguish racial outgroups from ingroups that are in positions of power are often deemed undesirable. For example, assertive behavior is likely to be conditioned according to what is acceptable in a particular sociocultural context, and is less likely to be biologically determined. A person from a racial outgroup whose behavior is more assertive than that of the ingroup may be labeled "aggressive"; similarly, an outgroup person whose behavior is less assertive than that of the ingroup may be labeled "passive." If it is assumed that psychological characteristics have a biological basis, then it follows that all members of a racial group should share these characteristics. If all members of racial groups are assumed to share certain deviant characteristics, race can be used as a proxy to determine who is superior and who is inferior (Jones, 1997). Moreover, a biological basis of psychological characteristics assumes that such characteristics are immutable. Thus, social hierarchies can be justified as permanent and as having a biological basis.

One's genetic heritage may have some bearing on one's sociocultural identity, but is not a perfect predictor. An Asian American may be very assimilated into mainstream American society and feel a very limited identification with Asian American culture or ethnicity. Conversely, a European American may grow up in an African American community and may have more of an identification with African Americans and African American culture and political issues than with other cultures. Most ethnic groups have "honorary" members of their groups who are not biologically part of the group but are considered members nonetheless. For example, European American actor Jim Carrey got his start on the television program, *In Living Color,* which had a primarily African American cast. Perhaps Carrey's acceptance by this group was related to his ability to poke fun at his own European American culture.

Culture

More central to the study of multicultural psychology than race is culture. Harry Triandis (1996) has defined culture as shared attitudes, beliefs, norms, roles, and self-definitions. According to Triandis, the elements of culture include familial roles, communication patterns, affective styles, and values regarding personal control, individualism, collectivism, spirituality, and religiosity. Stanley Sue (1991), who is profiled in this book as a prominent Asian American psychologist, has defined culture as the variability that exists between groups and societies. Culture, according to Sue, also involves the products of society or a group, such as behavioral patterns, knowledge, attitudes, values, and achievements. These products are transmitted from generation to generation through norms, rules, institutions, communication patterns, and socialization practices. Another definition of culture has been offered by Hope Landrine (1992, p. 17): "Culture is the unwritten social and psychiatric dictionary that we have each memorized and then repressed." This is consistent with the idea discussed earlier in this chapter that many persons are not aware that they possess cultural characteristics. It may be more likely for people to be unaware of their cultural characteristics if they live in a monocultural context where cultural differences are usually not apparent. Landrine (1992) also suggests that to increase understanding of cultural groups other than our own, we need to bring our own dictionary to the level of full conscious awareness, and memorize the dictionaries of others.

A real-life example of cultural differences is illustrated by a third-generation Japanese American woman who had moved with her Japanese American husband from Hawaii to the Pacific Northwest. She had developed a network of European American friends who often went out to lunch together. A common Japanese American custom is to offer to pay for everyone's lunch, with the assumption that each person will eventually take a turn at paying. The Japanese American woman paid for the lunch the first time, and her friends assured her that they would pay the next time. However, my friend discovered that when the next time came, she was the one paying again. She was upset with her European American friends' "rudeness," but would never directly communicate this to them. Think about the times when you go out to eat with friends. Do you offer to pay or expect someone to pay for the whole group? My wife and I (Hall), who are also third-generation Japanese Americans, tried to explain to the woman that many European Americans expect everyone to pay for his or her own meal. If someone else offers to pay, they may accept this as a gift, but may not feel obligated to reciprocate, even if they say that they will. Unfortunately, our friend could not understand this as a cultural difference and continued to view her European American friends as "rude." She and her husband eventually returned to Hawaii, where they are probably happily treating their friends, and being treated by their friends, to lunch.

The difference between this Hawaiian Japanese American woman and her European American friends involves what has variously been referred to as individualism-collectivism (Triandis, 1996), independence-interdependence (Markus & Kitayama, 1991), or the referential-indexical self (Landrine, 1992). In Western cultures, there is a strong emphasis on the self as an individual. Being unique and independent are valued; therefore, self-awareness, self-criticism, self-consciousness, self-reflection, self-determination, self-actualization, self-fulfillment, and self-change are goals in Western societies (Landrine, 1992). People are ultimately expected to take care of themselves, and one's responsibilities to others go only so far.

Persons of color in the United States tend to espouse collectivist values more than European Americans do, and women tend to espouse these values more than men do (Greenfield, 1994; Hill, Soriano, Chen, & LaFromboise, 1994; D. W. Sue & Sue, 1999). In cultures where social context is important, there tends to be a strong group identity. The goal in collectivist cultures is not to compete with others, but to cooperate. When all are in the same boat, rowing faster than the others will not facilitate group progress; on the other hand, if you are swimming in the water alone, as in individualist cultures, your own progress is all that matters.

Cultural patterns are broad groupings that apply to large numbers of people. For example, approximately two-thirds of the world's population would be considered collectivist (Triandis, 1996). Moreover, collectivism and individualism are but two of the many components of culture discussed above. Recognition of broad cultural differences is a necessary first step in understanding that behavior may have a cultural basis and that there are important cultural differences (S. Sue, 1991). However, there is much variability within cultural groups. This is why the concept of ethnicity is useful.

Ethnicity

Ethnicity is more specific to a particular social context than is culture, which is a broader concept. Ethnicity has been defined as a social psychological sense of peoplehood in which members of a group share a unique social and cultural heritage that is transmitted from one generation to another (Phinney, 1996; S. Sue, 1991). Individuals in a particular ethnic group may share common behaviors, attitudes, and values. Although Italian Americans, Japanese Americans, and Puerto Rican Americans are all Americans and may share some common cultural characteristics, each ethnic group has some specific characteristics that distinguish it from the others. For example, all three groups may value democracy and many persons in all three groups may speak English, which could be described as American cultural practices. However, the language, food, family, community, and other practices of each group may be unique to its ethnicity.

An important aspect of ethnicity is an interdependence of fate or struggles with others in the group (Phinney, 1996; S. Sue, 1991). This sense of interdependence is particularly salient for those having minority status. Thus, if you are a member of an ethnic minority group, the success or failure of someone in your ethnic group may be viewed as having some bearing on your own sense of well-being. A personal example (Hall) is when Kristi Yamaguchi won the Olympic gold medal in ice skating. I experienced a strong sense of pride that a Japanese American had won the gold medal. My sense of identification with Yamaguchi was stronger than my sense of identification with any other skaters from the United States, including other non-Japanese Asian Americans, or from Japan. I also felt a sense of unfairness when I saw another European American skater who had not won the gold medal apparently receiving more publicity and commercial endorsements than Yamaguchi.

Just because one belongs to a particular ethnic group does not mean that one will be the same as any other member of that ethnic group. Level of identification with one's ethnic group may vary across individuals. An African American who is attempting to assimilate into the mainstream will be very different from one who is immersing himself or herself in African culture. Yet, both are African Americans.

African American psychologist William Cross (1971) developed one of the earliest models of racial/ethnic identity that has influenced subsequent models. Cross's model was developed in an African American context, but this model has implications for other groups as well, including Asian Americans and Latino/a Americans (D. Sue & Sue, 1999). Cross conceptualized racial identity as a process involving different stages. The first stage, known as *Pre-Encounter,* is one in which African Americans view the world as non-Black or anti-Black. Because African Americans in this stage view European Americans as superior to African Americans, the goal is assimilation into European American society. African American identity is devalued.

The second stage of the Cross (1971) model is the *Encounter* stage, in which African Americans become aware of what it means to be African American and begin to validate themselves in terms of that ethnic identity. Movement into this stage is often precipitated by some encounter with discrimination. For example, an African American who is attempting to succeed in a corporation realizes that there are no African Americans in upper management. Moreover, he or she may be passed over for an upper management position by a European American with the same credentials and seniority. Because the person cannot escape that the status as an African American makes him or her different from others, the person actively searches for new and different interpretations of self-identity.

Immersion-Emersion is the third stage of the Cross (1971) model. African Americans in this stage immerse themselves in African American culture and may reject all values that are not African American. Rejection of European American values may be viewed as necessary to prove that one is African American. Such a person on a college campus might be an activist in African American student organizations and be considered a "radical" or a "militant." A person emerges from this stage with a strong African American identity.

The final stage of the Cross (1971) model is *Internalization*. In this stage, African Americans develop a self-confident and secure African American identity and are also comfortable expressing interests and preferences for experiences from other cultures. Anti-European American feelings decline. Persons in the Internalization stage identify with the oppression of all people and often become involved in social activism.

Ethnic identity may be associated with other identities. The Pre-Encounter and Encounter stages were associated with traditional attitudes toward women among African American women in New York City (Martin & Hall, 1992). Although the Immersion-Emersion stage was not associated with attitudes toward women, the Internalization stage was associated with feminist attitudes. Higher scores on measures of self-evaluation, sense of mastery, family relations, and social relations have been associated with stronger ethnic identity among African American, Asian American, and Mexican American adolescents (Phinney, 1991).

Do European Americans have an ethnic identity? Phinney (1996) has contended that most European Americans do not think of themselves in terms of ethnicity. However, some European Americans do become aware of their ethnic identity and its impact on others. One group of White Americans who may think of themselves in terms of ethnic identity is Jews. Perhaps this is because, like women and other minority groups, Jews have suffered from discrimination because of their differences. Janet Helms (1990) has developed a model of White racial identity that is analogous to the Cross (1971) model. As with the Cross model, there are a series of stages (see Table 1.1). The *Contact* stage is one in which race is not a distinguishing factor in psychological development. A person in this stage sees all people as having much in common. The second stage is *Disintegration,* and involves a confusion and perplexity about being White. A European American in this stage may face moral dilemmas about what it means to be White in a society that denigrates persons who are not White. The third stage, *Reintegration,* is an attempt to deal with the sense of disintegration by asserting racial superiority. For persons in this stage, African Americans and other minorities are viewed as inferior. *Pseudo-Independence* is the fourth stage, in which a person gains a broader understanding of impact of race, ethnicity, and culture on psychological development. However, race issues become important only during interactions with persons of color. A person in the Pseudo-independence stage may develop generalized, sometimes stereotypic, assumptions about various ethnic groups. The next stage, *Immersion/Emersion,* is an attempt to develop a personal and moral definition of Whiteness. A person in this stage may also encourage other Whites to redefine Whiteness. The final stage, *Autonomy,*

TABLE 1.1   *Stages of African American and White Identity*

African American Identity (Cross, 1971)	White Identity (Helms, 1990)
Pre-Encounter African American identity is devalued.	*Contact* Race is not a distinguishing factor.
	Disintegration Confusion about being White.
Encounter Validation of African American Identity.	*Reintegration* White racial superiority.
	Pseudo-Independence Broader understanding of race.
Immersion-Emersion African American culture only.	*Immersion-Emersion* Whiteness is redefined.
Internalization Identification with all people.	*Autonomy* Nonracist White identity.

involves the development of a nonracist White identity. A person in this stage gains an awareness of both the strengths and weaknesses of European American culture.

Class

Socioeconomic status (SES) is an important factor to discuss as it applies to gender and culture because both women and minorities are overrepresented in the lower class. Women are more likely to live in poverty because they are more likely than men to be the head of a single-parent family and are more likely to outlive men. Many factors related to ethnicity can also contribute to the overrepresentation of minorities in the lower class, such as acculturation issues, familiarity with the English language, and differences in education.

Another factor that can contribute to the number of women and minorities in the lower class is the prejudice and discrimination that both groups face because of stereotypes and a desire by those in power to maintain the status quo. Women currently earn 74 cents for every dollar that men earn, a statistic that supports the idea that women are not perceived as being as competent as men, even when they are doing the same job. Similarly, a competent minority applicant may appear less intelligent if she does not speak

English fluently, which may contribute to an employer's selecting another equally qualified candidate.

Being of low SES is associated with both physical and psychological liabilities. In addition to being associated with poorer health, a lower employment rate, poorer education, and an increased risk for violence, poverty is also associated with prejudice and discrimination (e.g., lazy bums on welfare) and with a higher risk for mental illness, perhaps because of the stressors associated with poverty. In fact, we will see in future chapters that often, differences between European Americans and ethnic minorities in terms of level of psychopathology can be accounted for by class rather than ethnicity.

Although social class has a bearing on psychological functioning, ethnic minority status has effects beyond social class. For example, African American children have lower standardized achievement scores than European American children regardless of family income level (Pungello, Kupersmidt, Burchinal, & Patterson, 1996). Similarly, ethnic disparities in quality of life are not explained by SES (Hughes & Thomas, 1998). Controlling for SES, African Americans have lower life satisfaction, lower happiness, and greater mistrust than European Americans. One important difference between ethnic minority persons and European Americans across levels is experiences of discrimination. It is possible that the effects of discrimination beyond the effects of social class may create disparities between persons of color and European Americans across class levels.

ACCULTURATION

All the models of ethnic identity involve a multicultural context in which different ethnic groups interact with one another. There are likely to be multiple cultural influences on a person, particularly when that person is a member of a minority group. The changes that groups and individuals undergo when they come into contact with another culture have been defined as acculturation (Williams & Berry, 1991). Acculturation is usually assumed to be applicable to ethnic groups whose immigration to the United States is relatively recent, such as Latino Americans and Asian Americans. Although we may not usually think of African Americans or American Indians as undergoing acculturation, as they have been in the United States for centuries, acculturation may also occur in these groups to the extent that there are cultural differences between these groups and the dominant mainstream European American culture.

American Indian psychologist Teresa LaFromboise and her colleagues (LaFromboise et al., 1993) have proposed models of acculturation that are applicable to American ethnic minority groups (see Table 1.2). One model of acculturation is *assimilation,* which involves absorption into the dominant or more desirable culture. Immigrants who voluntarily come to the United States are more likely to desire to assimilate than those who have been forced to immigrate (e.g., slaves, refugees; Ogbu, 1986). Similarly, you are more likely to identify with a college that you are attending if you have chosen it than if your parents have chosen for you. In a sense, you are an "involuntary immigrant" if your choice of college is restricted for economic or geographic reasons, whereas you are a "voluntary immigrant" if you are able to attend the college of your choice. However, not all who desire to assimilate into a culture are able to assimilate. The cultural distance between one's culture of origin and the second culture may affect one's ability to assimilate (Williams & Berry, 1991). For example, an Asian Indian who is Hindu will probably have a more difficult time assimilating into mainstream American culture than a person from England who is a Christian. The dangers of assimilation involve loss of one's original cultural identity and rejection by the members of one's culture of origin (LaFromboise et al., 1993). Each ethnic group has its pejorative terms for persons of color who are White on the inside, including "Oreo" (African Americans), "coconut" (Latinos), "banana" (Asian Americans), and "apple" (American Indians).

A second model of acculturation is actually known as *acculturation* (LaFromboise et al., 1993). This involves a person who is competent in a second culture but always will be identified as a member of the minority culture. This person may be relegated to a lower status within the second culture and not completely accepted. An example is Asian Indian physicians who have had residency training in the United States and are competent in

TABLE 1.2	*Models of Acculturation (LaFromboise, Coleman, & Gerton, 1993)*
Assimilation	Absorption into the dominant culture.
Acculturation	Competence in a second culture without complete acceptance.
Fusion	A combination of cultures to form a new culture.
Alternation	Bicultural competence.
Multicultural	Distinct cultural identities are maintained within a single multicultural social structure.

medicine. Yet, these physicians are viewed by many Americans as somehow "foreign." Such an experience may result in marginalization from both cultures. One reaction to such marginalization is separatism, which involves the formation of one's own group with the creation of the group's own standards. Rather than compete for acceptance in mainstream American culture, Asian Indian physicians might form their own group and associate exclusively with other Asian Indians. Difficulties with separatism are that some interaction with other groups is usually necessary unless one is in a large community of others similar to oneself. Another difficulty is that the mainstream can more easily ignore a separatist group than a group that attempts to interact with the mainstream.

Another model of acculturation is *fusion* (LaFromboise et al., 1993). Fusion involves cultures sharing an economic, political, or geographic space fusing together until they are indistinguishable and form a new culture. This is the idea behind the melting pot theory. The fusion model differs from the assimilation model because aspects of multiple cultures are integrated into the new culture. It differs from the multicultural model because cultures of origin are not distinctively maintained. There is evidence that greater percentages of European Americans, African Americans, Asian Americans, and Latino/a Americans prefer a melting pot than a society in which ethnic groups maintain distinct cultures (Sears et al., 1999). However, what typically occurs when multiple cultures share the same space is that the cultural minority groups become assimilated into the majority group at the price of their cultural identity (LaFromboise et al., 1993). It is unlikely that most ethnic minority persons would prefer a society in which one group is perpetually dominant (Gaertner, Dovidio, Nier, Ward, & Banker, 1999). Moreover, younger, better-educated ethnic minority persons who may question the dominance of the majority group may value identification with their own ethnic group more strongly than those who are older and less educated (Sears et al., 1999).

A fourth model of acculturation is *alternation,* which involves competence in two cultures (LaFromboise et al., 1993). The two cultures are regarded as equal, and a person maintains positive relationships with both cultures without having to choose between them. Biculturally competent individuals alter their behavior to fit a particular sociocultural context. For example, if one's cultural background values restraint, one is restrained in contexts where restraint is valued. In settings where free expression is valued, such as in many European American settings, a biculturally competent person is able to shift to a more expressive mode. Alternation is regarded as an optimal mode of functioning by LaFromboise and her colleagues. Ethnic minority high school students who have a bicultural identity have been found to feel a greater sense of unity with other ethnic groups than those who identify themselves only in terms of their ethnic minority group (Gaertner et al., 1999). However, American society does not value all cultures equally, and alternation may be difficult to maintain in practice. A truly biculturally competent person may have to overemphasize the non-European American culture to balance the emphasis of European American culture in society. In other words, it may require an overemphasis on a minority culture to actually regard the minority culture as equal to European culture and to achieve positive relationships with both cultures.

The *multicultural* model of acculturation involves distinct cultural identities that are maintained while cultures are tied together within a single multicultural social structure (LaFromboise et al., 1993). Individuals from one culture cooperate with those of other cultures to serve common needs. An example of this might be ethnic communities that have intergroup contact but at the same time maintain their culture of origin; a city might have Little Tokyo, Little Saigon, and Little Italy neighborhoods that are in geographic proximity and work cooperatively as part of the larger city structure. However, in real-life situations, separation of cultural groups is more common than interaction and cooperation. When there is interaction, there also tends to be mutual influence and cultures of origins tend not to be distinctly maintained. Thus, the multicultural model is difficult to achieve in practice (LaFromboise et al., 1993).

MULTICULTURALISM

According to the models of acculturation, multiculturalism may be an ideal rather than something that is very feasible. American psychology is far from being multicultural. European Americans have been the dominant group in American psychology and American psychology has primarily been monocultural. Asian American psychologist Derald Wing Sue and his colleagues (1998) have defined *monoculturalism* as having the following characteristics:

1. Belief in the superiority of one's own group.

2. Belief in the inferiority of other groups.

3. Having power over other groups.

4. The imposition of one's values and beliefs on others.

5. The unconscious assumption of universality.

In sharp contrast, *multiculturalism* emphasizes:

1. Cultural pluralism.

2. Social justice.

3. Learning to function effectively in a diverse world.

4. A broad definition of diversity, encompassing ethnicity, gender, sexual orientation, and physical challenge.

5. Celebrating the contributions of all groups.

6. Analytic thinking involving multiple perspectives.

7. An activist orientation, realizing that multiculturalism will remain an ideal without sociopolitical change.

8. Change at the individual, organizational, and societal levels.

9. Facing painful realities about ourselves, our group, and our society.

10. Cooperation.

To many of us, most of the emphases of multiculturalism would seem difficult to object to. For example, who wouldn't value social justice and cooperation? However, American psychology and, more generally, American society have been slow to understand and accept multicultural approaches. Because we all have been indoctrinated into an American society that is so centered on European American men, it may be difficult to perceive ourselves as monocultural.

D. Sue and his colleagues (1998) suggest seven resistances to multiculturalism that we have adapted for a discussion of multicultural psychology. The first resistance is that current theories are universal. However, this is an untested assumption in that the generalizability of many psychological theories has not been investigated with non-European American groups. A second resistance is the argument that there is a lack of multicultural theories.

This is simply untrue, as you will discover in this book. A third resistance is that multicultural models are too vague. We hope that by reading this book you will learn about sound theories and research on multicultural psychology. A fourth resistance is that multicultural models are too complex. This is the opposite of the too-vague criticism. The too-complex resistance often comes from those who would rather not have to go the "extra mile" to consider cultural factors in their research. Some psychologists in this group are not necessarily opposed to cultural considerations, but do not view them as germane to theory and research. A fifth resistance is the argument that there is a lack of research to support multicultural psychology. This is another resistance that should be put to rest by reading this book. A sixth resistance is that we must first consider all types of cultural diversity, such as gender, physical challenge, and sexual orientation, before we consider ethnic diversity. D. Sue and colleagues have described this as a "divide and conquer" strategy. Certainly, all forms of cultural diversity are important, but requiring that all be considered at once is to prevent progress in any of the areas. To the extent that we are able to, we espouse a broad definition of diversity in this book. The final resistance is that multiculturalism is anti-White. Multiculturalism is not against any group or approach but seeks to allow all groups and approaches to have a voice.

The resistance to multicultural psychology reflects a field that does not want to change. Yet, the cultural world in which psychology exists is rapidly changing. Multiethnic psychologist Christine Iijima Hall (1997), who is profiled in this book, has contended that psychology will become obsolete unless it undergoes cultural changes. We believe that the multicultural approach has the promise to make the field viable and relevant for a new generation of multicultural Americans.

REFERENCES

Albert, R. D. (1988). The place of culture in modern psychology. In P. A. Bronstein & K. Quina (Eds.), *Teaching a psychology of people: Resources for gender and sociocultural awareness* (pp. 12–18). Washington, DC: American Psychological Association.

Bem, S. L. (1993). *The lenses of gender: Transforming the debate on sexual inequality.* New Haven, CT: Yale University Press.

Benet, V., & Waller, N. G. (1995). The Big Seven factor model of personality description: Evidence for its cross-cultural generality in a Spanish sample. *Journal of Personality and Social Psychology, 69,* 701–718.

Bernal, M., & Castro, F. (1994). Are clinical psychologists prepared for service and research with ethnic minorities? *American Psychologist, 49,* 797–805.

Betancourt, H., & Lopez, S. R. (1993). The study of culture, ethnicity, and race in American psychology. *American Psychologist, 48,* 629–637.

Broverman, I. K., Broverman, D. M., Clarkson, F. E., Rosenkrantz, P., & Vogel, S. R. (1970). Sex-role stereotypes and clinical judgments of mental health. *Journal of Consulting and Clinical Psychology, 34,* 1–7.

Brown, E. B. (1989). Women's consciousness: Maggie Lena Walker and the independent order of Saint Luke. *Signs, 14,* 610–633.

Brown, L. S. (1988). Feminist therapy with lesbians and gay men. In M. Dutton-Douglas & L. E. Walker (Eds.), *Feminist psychotherapies: Integration of therapeutic and feminist systems* (pp. 206–277). Norwood, NJ: Ablex.

Brown, L. S., & Root, M. P. P. (1990). *Diversity and complexity in feminist therapy.* New York: Haworth Press.

Buss, D. M. (1989). Sex differences in human mate preferences: Evolutionary hypotheses tested in 37 cultures. *Behavioral and Brain Sciences, 12,* 1–49.

Childs, E. K. (1990). Therapy, feminist ethics, and the community of color with particular emphasis on the treatment of Black women. In H. Lerman & N. Porter (Eds.), *Feminist ethics in psychotherapy* (pp. 195–203). New York: Springer.

Church, A. T., Katigbak, M. S., & Reyes, J. A. S. (1998). Further exploration of Filipino personality structure using the lexical approach: Do the Big-Five or Big-Seven dimensions emerge? *European Journal of Personality, 12,* 249–269.

Clark, R., Anderson, N. B., Clark, V. R., & Williams, D. R. (1999). Racism as a stressor for African Americans: A biosocial model. *American Psychologist, 54,* 805–816.

Cross, W. E. (1971). Negro-to-Black conversion experience. *Black World, 20,* 13–27.

Dill, B. T. (1983). Race, class, and gender: Prospects for an all-inclusive sisterhood. *Feminist Studies, 9,* 131–150.

Fiske, A. P., Kitayama, S., Markus, H. R., & Nisbett, R. E. (1998). The cultural matrix of social psychology. In D. T. Gilbert, S. T. Fiske, & G. Lindzey (Eds.), *The handbook of social psychology* (4th ed., pp. 915–981). New York: McGraw-Hill.

Gaertner, S. L., Dovidio, J. F., Nier, J. A., Ward, C. M., & Banker, B. S. (1999). Across cultural divides: The value of a superordinate identity. In D. A. Prentice & D. T.

Miller (Eds.), *Cultural divides: Understanding and overcoming group conflict* (pp. 173–212). New York: Russell Sage Foundation.

Gilligan, C. (1982). *In a different voice: Psychological theory and women's development*. Cambridge, MA: Harvard University Press.

Graham, S. (1992). Most of the subjects were White and middles class: Trends in published research on African Americans in selected APA journals, 1970–1989. *American Psychologist, 47,* 629–639.

Greenfield, P. M. (1994). Independence and interdependence as developmental scripts: Implications for theory, research, and practice. In P. M. Greenfield & R. R. Cocking (Eds.), *Cross-cultural roots of minority child development* (pp. 1–37). Hillsdale, NJ: Erlbaum.

Hall, C. C. I. (1997). Cultural malpractice: The growing obsolescence of psychology with the changing U.S. population. *American Psychologist, 52,* 642–651.

Hall, G. C. N. (2001). Psychotherapy research with ethnic minorities: Empirical, ethical, and conceptual issues. *Journal of Consulting and Clinical Psychology, 69,* 502–510.

Helms, J. E. (1990). *Black and White racial identity: Theory, research, and practice.* New York: Greenwood Press.

Hill, H. M., Soriano, F. I., Chen, S. A., & LaFromboise, T. D. (1994). Sociocultural factors in the etiology and prevention of violence among ethnic minority youth. In L. D. Eron, J. H. Gentry, & P. Schegel (Eds.), *Reason to hope: A psychosocial perspective on violence and youth* (pp. 59–97). Washington, DC: American Psychological Association.

Hughes, M., & Thomas, M. E. (1998). The continuing significance of race revisited: A study of race, class, and quality of life in America, 1972 to 1996. *American Sociological Review, 63,* 785–795.

Jones, J. M. (1988). Racism in Black and White: A bicultural model of reaction and evolution. In P. A. Katz & D. A. Taylor (Eds.), *Eliminating racism: Profiles in controversy* (pp. 117–135). New York: Plenum Press.

Jones, J. M. (1997). *Prejudice and racism* (2nd ed.). New York: McGraw-Hill.

Jones, J. M. (1999). Cultural racism: The intersection of race and culture in intergroup conflict. In D. A. Prentice & D. T. Miller (Eds.), *Cultural divides: Understanding and overcoming group conflict* (pp. 465–490). New York: Russell Sage Foundation.

Judd, C. M., Park, B., Ryan, C. S., Brauer, M., & Kraus, S. (1995). Stereotypes and ethnocentrism: Diverging interethnic perceptions of African American and White American youth. *Journal of Personality and Social Psychology, 69,* 460–481.

Kaplan, M. (1983). A woman's view of the *DSM-III*. *American Psychologist, 38,* 786–792.

Kohlberg, L. (1981). *The philosophy of moral development* (Vols. 1–2). San Francisco: Harper & Row.

LaFromboise, T. D., Coleman, H. L. K., & Gerton, J. (1993). Psychological impact of biculturalism: Evidence and theory. *Psychological Bulletin, 114,* 395–412.

Landrine, H. (1992). Clinical implications of cultural differences: The referential versus the indexical self. *Clinical Psychology Review, 12,* 401–415.

Markus, H. R., & Kitayama, S. (1991). Culture and the self: Implications for cognition, emotion, and motivation. *Psychological Review, 98,* 224–253.

Martin, J. K., & Hall, G. C. N. (1992). Thinking Black, thinking internal, thinking feminist. *Journal of Counseling Psychology, 39,* 509–514.

McCrae, R. R., & Costa, P. T. (1997). Personality trait structure as a human universal. *American Psychologist, 52,* 509–516.

Ogbu, J. U. (1986). The consequences of the American caste system. In U. Neisser (Ed.), *The school achievement of minority children: New perspectives* (pp. 19–56). Hillsdale, NJ: Erlbaum.

Phinney, J. S. (1991). Ethnic identity and self-esteem: A review and integration. *Hispanic Journal of Behavioral Sciences, 13,* 193–208.

Phinney, J. S. (1996). When we talk about American ethnic groups, what do we mean? *American Psychologist, 51,* 918–927.

Pungello, E. P., Kupersmidt, J. B., Burchinal, M. R., & Patterson, C. J. (1996). Environmental risk factors and children's achievement from middle childhood to early adolescence. *Developmental Psychology, 32,* 755–767.

Reid, P. T. (1984). Women of color have no "place." *Focus, 7,* 2.

Sears, D. O., Citrin, J., Cheleden, S. V., & van Laar, C. (1999). Cultural diversity and multicultural politics: Is ethnic balkanization psychologically inevitable? In D. A. Prentice & D. T. Miller (Eds.), *Cultural divides: Understanding and overcoming group conflict* (pp. 35–79). New York: Russell Sage Foundation.

Segall, M. H., Lonner, W. J., & Berry, J. W. (1998). Cross-cultural psychology as a scholarly discipline: On the flowering of culture in behavioral research. *American Psychologist, 53,* 1101–1110.

Shweder, R. A. (1991). *Thinking through cultures: Expeditions in cultural psychology.* Cambridge, MA: Harvard University Press.

Sue, D. W., Carter, R. T., Casas, J. M., Fouad, N. A., Ivey, A. E., Jensen, M., LaFromboise, T. D., Manese, J. E., Ponterotto, J. G., & Vasquez-Nuttall, E. (1998). *Multicultural counseling competencies: Individual and organizational development.* Thousand Oaks, CA: Sage.

Sue, D. W., Ivey, A. E., & Pedersen, P. B. (1996). *A theory of multicultural counseling and therapy.* Pacific Grove, CA: Brooks/Cole.

Sue, D. W., & Sue, D. (1999). *Counseling the culturally different: Theory and practice* (3rd ed.). New York: Wiley.

Sue, S. (1991). Ethnicity and culture in psychological research and practice. In J. D. Goodchilds & D. Jacqueline (Eds.), *Psychological perspectives on human diversity in America* (pp. 51–85). Washington, DC: American Psychological Association.

Sue, S. (1999). Science, ethnicity, and bias: Where have we gone wrong? *American Psychologist, 54,* 1070–1077.

Sue, S., Ito, J., & Bradshaw, C. (1984). Ethnic minority research: Trends and directions. In E. E. Jones & S. J. Korchin (Eds.), *Minority mental health* (pp. 41–56). New York: Praeger.

Taylor, M. C., & Hall, J. A. (1982). Psychological androgyny: A review and reformulation of theories, methods, and conclusions. *Psychological Bulletin, 92,* 347–366.

Triandis, H. C. (1996). The psychological measurement of cultural syndromes. *American Psychologist, 51,* 407–415.

Whitley, B. E., Jr. (1988). Masculinity, femininity, and self-esteem: A multitrait, multimethod analysis. *Sex Roles, 18,* 419–431.

Williams, C. L., & Berry, J. W. (1991). Primary prevention of acculturative stress among refugees: Application of psychological theory and practice. *American Psychologist, 46,* 632–641.

Wilson, M., & Daly, M. (1985). Competitiveness, risk-taking, and violence: The young male syndrome. *Ethology and Sociobiology, 6,* 59–73.

Yee, A. H., Fairchild, H. H., Weizmann, F., & Wyatt, G. E. (1993). Addressing psychology's problems with race. *American Psychologist, 48,* 1132–1140.

Zuckerman, M. (1990). Some dubious premises in research and theory on racial differences: Scientific, social, and ethical issues. *American Psychologist, 45,* 1297–1303.

ISSUES FOR DISCUSSION

Who Is an American?

1. When you think of the prototypical American, whom do you think of? The writer Toni Morrison contends that "American" usually means

White male. Did you think of a European American man as the proto-typical American?

2. How does a researcher determine whether a difference between members of ethnic groups is based on cultural differences between the groups?

3. The "melting pot" or fusion model of acculturation has been contrasted with the "cultural mosaic" or multicultural model of acculturation. What are advantages and disadvantages of these two models? Which of the models is most likely to become a reality?

TWO

MULTICULTURAL RESEARCH AND ASSESSMENT

Psychology is a scientific field of study. Consequently, psychologists cannot rely solely on their intuition or long-held beliefs and assumptions when they draw conclusions about people; they must also rely on research. Researchers in psychology assume that science can lead to universal truths about human nature. This view is different from other fields, such as anthropology, which assumes that what is true about people often varies from culture to culture, or from philosophy, which utilizes introspection to understand human nature. However, it is becoming increasingly apparent in the field of psychology that the application of the scientific method does not always lead to universal truths. As a result, researchers have begun to question the basic assumptions of science as well as the way psychologists conduct their empirical investigations.

Psychological assessment is closely related to research. In assessment, research is conducted for the purpose of discovering specific information about an individual, such as his or her level of intelligence, personality traits, the presence of a psychological disorder, or readiness for treatment. Often, assumptions are made in assessment about universal constructs such as intelligence. It is also assumed that our assessment tools will be appropriate for all individuals and that the interpretations that we make will be consistent across groups. However, there are many reasons to question these assumptions, as well.

The purpose of this chapter is to review some of the relevant information pertaining to research and assessment. In the first part of the chapter, we review the assumptions of science as well as some of the most commonly used research methods, and then discuss the criticisms of the theory and practice of the scientific method. In the second part, we review some of the major tools used in assessment and the psychometric properties used to evaluate tests, and discuss some of the major problems with the assessment of diverse populations.

MULTICULTURAL RESEARCH

The Scientific Method

At the beginning of every psychology course, you have probably been exposed to the assumptions and advantages of science as opposed to other fields of study, such as art and humanities. Although these assumptions are probably familiar by now, it is worth reviewing them because they will be critical in our discussion of the limitations of the scientific method. These assumptions include objectivity, an unbiased approach, quantification of data, systematic and precise procedures, and the discovery of universal principles.

Objectivity.   First, science is assumed to be objective. By objective, we mean that science is *empirical,* or based on observation. The topics of investigation must be clearly identifiable to observers. Thus, science relies heavily on *operational definitions* of its *constructs* or concepts to ensure that observations are reliable. Operational definitions are statements about what observable phenomena are used as evidence of a particular construct. For example, if we are interested in operationally defining the construct of ethnicity, we must include in our definition aspects that are observable, such as physical characteristics like skin and hair color. It should be noted, however, that the use of operational definitions does not necessarily guarantee that everyone will agree on the criteria, even when they are objective. In fact, using physical characteristics to define ethnicity is particularly controversial. For example, it has often been argued that any person who has even "one drop" of African American ancestry should identify as being African American, although the person's physical appearance and personal identification may indicate otherwise.

Bias.   There is another meaning that is implied by the term objective: that science is unbiased. The scientific method is based on reason and logic, not emotion and opinion. Regardless of what the researcher's hypothesis may be in a particular study, the empirical evidence, rather than one's own personal interest in the outcome, will determine whether the hypothesis is supported or refuted. Often, research is designed in such a way as to increase the like-lihood that a researcher will not let his or her biases affect the results, such as making the researcher blind to the condition the participant is in. For example, researchers might not be told whether a client in therapy has been given an active drug, such as an antidepressant, or a placebo, such as a sugar pill, so that they will not base their observations on any precon-ceived notions about the effects of medication. It is not always possible, however, for a researcher to be blind to all variables of interest. It would not always be possible, for example, to prevent a researcher from knowing whether a participant was an ethnic minority or whether the participant was male or female, and researchers may have preconceived notions about ethnic minorities and women that could potentially affect the interpreta-tion of their behavior.

Quantification.   Another aspect of science is that it relies on quantifica-tion to understand data. Unlike in philosophy, in which introspection is used to search for answers to important questions, psychology and other scien-tific fields rely on data collection and statistical procedures to draw conclu-sions. The reliance on statistical procedures also ensures that findings reflect truth rather than opinion.

System and Precision.   Finally, science is assumed to be systematic and precise. Many of the other assumptions of science, such as the reliance on op-erational definitions and quantification and the reliance on reason and logic, all contribute to the assumption that science is systematic and precise.

Universal Principles.   It is often assumed that the scientific method can be used to discover universal principles of behavior. Therefore, the scientific method is a way of determining truth, a way of distinguishing fact from opin-ion. This assumption follows from all of the other assumptions about science.

Research Methods

Psychologists use different types of research methods to draw conclusions. Each method has its strengths and limitations and some are more useful in some situations than in others. These methods include case studies, correla-tional studies, experimental studies, quasi-experimental studies, and single-subject designs.

Case Studies.   A case study is an intensive investigation of a single individual. Often, the events of the person's life from childhood to adulthood are explored to understand that person's life circumstances, such as the existence of a mental disorder or the development of personality over time. Biographies of well-known individuals are examples of case studies. Clinical psychologists often utilize case studies in evaluating the effectiveness of therapy or to portray the characteristics of a particular disorder in more detail.

There are several advantages to case studies. First, an in-depth view of the person is provided, which is not typically the case in research. Thus, it is possible to track changes in the person over time or in response to specific events. For example, it would be possible to determine whether someone's temperament during infancy was consistent throughout childhood, adolescence, and adulthood. Second, case studies are often useful when studying unusual or rare events. For example, if a researcher were interested in examining the effects of being raised by gay parents who are also minorities, it may be difficult to gather a large sample of participants who share these experiences; thus, the researcher may wish to study a few individuals more intensely. Third, case studies may be able to reveal new and surprising findings that may not be under investigation. Relatedly, case studies are useful in generating hypotheses. For example, a clinician might note that in private practice, several Asian American clients appear to be suffering from depression, although they present primarily with somatic complaints; such an observation may lead to more controlled research on the assessment, diagnosis, and treatment of depression in Asian American clients. Indeed, there is evidence that Asian Americans may express depression via somaticization (Kuo, 1984).

There are also several limitations of case studies. One problem is that because case studies are uncontrolled, they do not prevent the biases of the researcher from interfering with the investigation. A researcher who believes that masked depression may be a manifestation unique to Asian Americans may not look for evidence to disconfirm this hypothesis. Perhaps there are many groups of people who present with somatic complaints rather than feelings of depression, or perhaps there are many Asian Americans who do, in fact, report feelings of depression. Relatedly, persons under investigation may also present information in a biased manner, perhaps out of a need to present themselves in a positive or negative light, because they have poor memory, or because they lack insight into their problems. Finally, case studies involve only observation: Because nothing is manipulated or analyzed, it is difficult to test specific hypotheses.

Correlational Studies. In correlational studies, researchers attempt to empirically demonstrate an association between two variables of interest. For example, a researcher may be interested in determining whether there is a correlation between SES and intelligence. The researcher may proceed by selecting a group of people, administering an IQ test, and obtaining information about their annual income. In this example, the researcher would be interested in a positive correlation between SES and IQ. In a positive correlation, as one variable increases, the other variable also increases; thus, in this example, the hypothesis is that as one's SES increases, one's level of intelligence also increases. It is also possible to have a negative correlation. In a negative correlation, as one variable increases, the other variable decreases. For example, we might predict that there is a negative correlation between IQ and truancy: As level of intelligence increases, the likelihood of truancy decreases.

There are several advantages to correlational studies. First, unlike case studies, statistical procedures are used to demonstrate a relationship between two variables. Because a correlation coefficient is calculated, we can empirically determine the degree to which the variables of interest are associated. Second, correlational studies are useful in examining variables that are not possible to manipulate in an experimental study. For example, studies examining the IQ scores of different ethnic groups are correlational because it is not possible to manipulate or change a person's ethnicity. In fact, many variables of interest in multicultural psychology cannot be manipulated, such as gender, SES, and sexual orientation. Finally, correlational studies are fairly economical. Correlational studies can be conducted with paper and pencil, many participants can be examined at once, and many variables can be examined at one time.

In spite of the numerous advantages of correlational studies, they are not without their drawbacks. The major limitation of correlational studies is that the researcher cannot determine causality, and establishing a causal relationship is usually the goal of most research. To illustrate, let us assume that we are interested in demonstrating that our culture's thin ideal of beauty for women leads to an increased risk of eating disorders. We could conduct a study in which we interview participants and ask them how often they watch television programming that promotes this thin ideal. In addition, we could give the participants a measure such as the Eating Disorders Inventory 2 (EDI-2; Gardner & Olmsted, 1991) to determine the extent to which they manifest symptomatology characteristic of an eating disorder.

Studies similar to our hypothetical study have actually been conducted and suggest that media portrayals may, indeed, contribute to body image concerns (Botta, 1999; Harrison & Cantor, 1997).

Can these researchers claim that a thin ideal of beauty causes eating disorders? Unfortunately, the answer is no. Although a significant correlation between viewing thin models and body image concerns was established, one of three interpretations is possible: (1) a thin ideal of beauty causes an increase in eating disorders; (2) people who are already predisposed to develop eating disorders seek out thin ideals of beauty; or (3) a third variable, such as ethnicity, is responsible for both the thin ideal of beauty and the risk for developing eating disorders. For example, although African American girls are also exposed to a thin ideal of beauty, they tend to have fewer body image concerns than European American girls do (Flynn & Fitzgibbon, 1998). Although the researchers' aim was to provide evidence for the first interpretation, the correlational method does not allow one to discern which of these interpretations is the correct one.

Finally, the last limitation of the correlational method is that even a small correlation can be statistically significant when the number of participants is large, and statistical significance is not synonymous with importance. A correlation of .2, for example, may be statistically significant in some situations, but accounts for only 4 percent of the variance, leaving 96 percent of the variance unaccounted for. This illustrates the difference between statistical significance and *clinical significance*. Sometimes, a finding may be statistically significant, but it has no practical significance.

Experimental Studies.   The only method that allows us to determine causality is the *experimental method*. To illustrate the experimental method, we will design an experimental study to test the hypothesis that a thin ideal of beauty causes body image concerns in women. In the experimental method, two criteria must be met. First, the factor hypothesized to cause the behavior being studied is systematically varied. This factor is called the *independent variable*. In this case, the amount of exposure to a thin ideal of beauty would be the factor that is systematically varied. Typically, one group, called the *experimental group*, will be exposed to the independent variable, and another group, called the *control group*, will not be exposed to the independent variable. In our example, the experimental group could view thin models from magazines or television, and the control group could view average-weight models (which are often difficult to find in magazines and on television).

There must be a minimum of two groups in an experiment, although there can be more than two groups, with more than one level of the independent variable. For example, we could have an experiment in which we include three groups: a group that is exposed to thin models, a group that is exposed to overweight models, and a group that is exposed to average-weight models. The next step in our experiment is to determine whether the two groups differed on a dependent variable, such as the EDI-2. We would hypothesize that participants who are exposed to thin models (the experimental group) will express greater body image concern (as indicated by higher scores on the EDI-2) than participants who are exposed to average-weight models (the control group).

The second criterion that must be met in an experimental study is that all other possible causative factors must be held constant. This means that the experimental and control groups are treated in the same respect in all other ways *except* for their exposure to the independent variable. If this criterion is not met, we cannot conclude that the manipulation of the independent variable caused a change in the dependent variable. Without the assurance that groups are treated identically in all other respects, it is possible that some *confounding factor* may potentially be responsible for a change in the dependent variable rather than the variable we are interested in. Let's assume, for example, that the experimental group was made up solely of European American women and that our control group was made up of African American women. In the experimental condition, the European American women view thin models, and in the control condition, the African American women view average-weight models; both are then given the EDI-2. Let us also assume that, as predicted, the experimental group reports more body image concerns than the control group. Although this finding would be consistent with our predictions, we cannot conclude that exposure to the thin models caused an increase in body image concerns because the experimental and control groups differed in the number of African American and European American women in each group. It is possible that the difference in body image concerns between the experimental group and control group is actually due to the fact that European American women are more concerned about being thin than are African American women because of the exposure to the thin models.

One way we try to ensure that participants in both groups are treated identically in all respects other than their exposure to the independent variable is through *random assignment*. In random assignment, each participant has an equal chance of being in either the experimental group or the control group. Therefore, if we randomly assign participants to each condition, any preexisting differences among the participants will most likely be evenly distributed across groups. For example, random assignment would increase the likelihood that the same number of African American and European American women would be in the experimental and control groups. Random assignment is considered the hallmark of experimental studies. Unfortunately, many of the variables of interest to psychologists make it difficult to randomly assign participants to groups. If we were interested in examining the effects of child abuse, for example, it would not be permissible to randomly assign parents to groups and to instruct the parents in the experimental group to abuse their child, while instructing the parents in the control group to refrain from verbal or physical abuse. In these situations, we must examine groups that are already predetermined: parents who abuse their children versus parents who do not abuse their children. We discuss this variation of the experimental method in more detail in the next section.

Another way that researchers attempt to control for confounding factors is by *matching* participants on variables that they believe may have an effect on the dependent variable, particularly when random assignment is not possible. For example, SES is a variable that is often controlled for in research. In our study, the effect of SES may be important to consider because eating disorders, unlike most other disorders, are more prevalent in high SES groups. Thus, an equal number of participants at each SES level could be distributed across both groups to rule out the possibility that differences in SES account for differences in body image concerns between groups. However, it would not be possible to control for all the possible factors that may be influencing the dependent variable, given that the researchers may not have identified some of those factors yet.

Incidentally, experimental studies similar to our hypothetical study on body image concerns have been conducted. In experimental studies in which participants are exposed for a short period of time to models of thin women from print ads (Irving, 1990; Kalonder, 1997; Ogden & Mundray, 1996; Pinhas, Toner, Ali, Garfinkel, & Stuckless, 1999; Posavac, Posavac, & Posavac, 1998; Stice & Shaw, 1994) and commercials (Heinberg & Thompson, 1995), exposure to thin models negatively affected body image satisfaction, mood, and self-esteem.

The major strength of experimental studies is that the experimental method is the only method that allows us to make causal inferences. Experimental studies are high on *internal validity,* meaning that the results from experimental studies are produced by the manipulation of the independent variable. Consequently, the experimental method is the gold standard in research and is preferred over case studies and correlational studies whenever possible.

Although experimental studies are considered the gold standard in research, they are not without their limitations. The experimental method allows us to have the most control over the variables in question and thus higher internal validity, but greater control often results in situations that may no longer be applicable to the behavior under investigation. For example, let's assume that we are conducting a study examining whether or not being exposed to a thin ideal of beauty leads to disordered eating. We decide to measure disordered eating by giving participants the opportunity to eat as many cookies as they wish during the experiment. We predict that participants who are exposed to a thin ideal of beauty will eat fewer cookies than participants who are not exposed to a thin ideal of beauty. Let us also assume that our hypothesis is confirmed in this study. Have we proven that the media's portrayal of a thin ideal of beauty leads to eating disorders? Perhaps not. After all, how similar is eating a few cookies in an experiment to what one finds in eating disordered individuals? Such individuals may starve themselves, binge, purge, exercise excessively, and engage in many other behaviors that are not captured by our measure of disordered eating. In addition, can the findings of our study, which focuses primarily on college women, be applied to adolescents? Older women? Women with less or more education?

This example illustrates the problem of *generalizability* in experimental studies. Generalizability refers to how readily we can use experimental findings to understand real-life behavior in related situations. Thus, although experiments are high on internal validity, they may be low on *external validity*, or generalizability of findings to other populations and other settings. Whereas internal validity relies on random assignment, external validity relies on *random sampling,* or *randomization.* In random sampling, every individual in the population has an equal chance of either being in the study or not being in the study. Unfortunately, in most research, obtaining a random sample is more often the exception than the rule for practical reasons; researchers rarely have the entire population to choose from in selecting participants. There is often an inverse relationship between internal and external validity: As internal validity increases, external validity often decreases. The reason for this inverse relationship is that to conduct experiments that have high internal validity, we must often conduct research in contrived situations to have sufficient control over the independent variable. However, as we exert more control, we also limit the extent to which the variables of interest are being studied in a way that represents real life.

Psychological studies as a whole are often criticized for questionable generalizability for many reasons. Most experimental studies are conducted on introductory college students who are different from the general population in numerous ways, such as their age and years of education (Kazdin, 1999; Sears, 1985). Experimental studies are also criticized for generalizing findings to all people when usually White, middle-class males are used as participants. In *analogue* studies, sometimes animals are used to understand important psychological concepts such as intelligence and depression, but what looks like depression or intelligence in an animal may not be analogous to depression and intelligence in humans.

Finally, another problem with the experimental method is that it is not possible to experimentally manipulate many of the variables of interest in psychology. We cannot systematically vary someone's gender, ethnicity, and age, and we cannot ethically manipulate variables such as child abuse and aggression. Thus, the experimental method is not an option for many of our research questions.

Variations in the Experimental Design

Because it is not always possible, practical, or ethical to test hypotheses through experiments, often, variations of the experimental design must be used. In this section, we review some of these variations.

Quasi-Experimental Designs.   Recall that in experimental studies, participants are randomly assigned to either the experimental group or the control group to ensure that any existing characteristics that may affect the dependent variable are distributed evenly across groups. Random assignment ensures that causal inferences can be made about the effects of the independent variable on the dependent variable. However, there are often situations in which we cannot randomly assign participants to conditions. In some cases, researchers may wish to examine differences between groups that already differ on the variable of interest but analyze the results as if they were from a true experiment. Examples of the quasi-experimental design are studies examining differences in IQ among ethnic groups because the participants were not randomly assigned to groups; they already differed in terms of their ethnicity. We cannot conclude from these studies that being African American leads to a lower IQ because many factors other than ethnicity could have contributed to the lower IQ score, such as low SES, experiences with prejudice and discrimination, or differential academic expectations from teachers. However, important information can still be obtained from such a study.

Single-Subject Designs.   Single-subject designs are experiments that have only one participant. However, they are not case studies. The difference between the two methodologies is that, whereas a case study is uncontrolled in that variables are not manipulated, in single-subject designs, the researcher systematically manipulates a variable and observes the result. Thus, in a single-subject design, the participant serves as his or her own control.

An example of a single-subject design is an ABAB design. In this method, the researcher first gathers baseline data (A). Then the researcher introduces the independent variable and observes any changes in the participant (B). The researcher then removes the independent variable and observes any changes, particularly whether there is a return to baseline (A). Finally, the researcher implements the independent variable again (B). This method might be useful to a parent who is interested in determining whether giving his child praise increases the likelihood of helpful behavior (e.g., cleaning her room, setting the table, taking out the trash). The parent would first observe the child for a week to determine how often she engages in helpful behavior (A). Then, he would verbally praise the child whenever she engages in helpful behavior and observe whether this leads to an increase in helpful behavior (B). He would then return to simply observing her behavior to see if the lack of praise results in a return to baseline (A). Finally, he would reinstate the verbal praise for helpful behavior to determine whether it again results in an increase in helpful behavior (B).

Single-subject designs are particularly useful in situations in which a researcher may not have access to a large number of participants, such as in a study examining the effects of therapy. Single-subject designs may also be useful from a multicultural perspective, particularly when a researcher may not have access to large samples of different ethnic minority groups. However, there are several problems with the single-subject design. First, lack of a return to baseline in A after treatment is withdrawn does not necessarily indicate that the treatment was unsuccessful. For example, if a therapist used a single-subject design to assess the effectiveness of cognitive-behavioral treatment for depression, we might expect a high level of depressive symptomatology in A, followed by a reduction in depressive symptomatology in B. But withdrawal of the treatment may not lead to a reemergence of depressive symptomatology again in A because the goal of treatment is to teach the client skills that he or she can use after therapy has been discontinued. Another problem with the ABAB design is that withdrawal of treatment may be unethical in certain situations. For example, if a behavioral treatment were implemented to reduce self-destructive behaviors, withdrawal of treatment would be undesirable. Thus, although withdrawal of the treatment may lead to further evidence that the intervention was successful, it may not always be advisable to do so. Finally, the single-subject design may have limited generalizability. As with case studies, single-subject designs are limited in the extent to which we can draw conclusions about other people in other situations.

Research in Multicultural Psychology

At the beginning of this chapter, we discussed the value of research in all scientific fields, including psychology. However, the current state of research pertaining to multicultural issues has been criticized on many grounds. Many of these criticisms pertain to the assumptions of science discussed at the beginning of the chapter. In general, the problem with many of these assumptions is that they run counter to the assumptions of a multicultural view of the world. Others argue that the problem is not with the assumptions of science, but rather with the way research is carried out. In the following sections, we review some of the major criticisms of research from a multicultural perspective.

Objectivity.   Recall that science is defined by its goal of objectivity. The personal views of the researcher should not influence an empirical investigation if the research conducted adequately follows the scientific method. Such objectivity allows us to distinguish what is truth from what is opinion. However, many researchers question the level of objectivity that occurs in much of the research conducted in psychology. Research examining both gender and cultural differences has been criticized for being biased in a manner that favors European American males, most likely because most researchers are European American males. For example, in the nineteenth century, the brains of both women and African Americans were assumed to be underdeveloped (Fee,

1979). Often, such "evidence" was used to justify the subordinate roles that women and minorities have in society (Gould, 1981). Such an argument might seem outdated, yet as recently as 1994, Herrnstein and Murray made a similar argument in *The Bell Curve* about minorities. In reviewing the research on intelligence, these researchers concluded that European Americans are innately intellectually superior to minorities. Furthermore, they argued that the programs designed to eradicate these discrepancies, such as Affirmative Action, remedial programs, and welfare, are of little use because differences in intelligence are due to genetics rather than to social injustice. Research of this nature calls into question the assumed objectivity in science.

Even the way scientific research is disseminated to the scientific community may reflect a lack of objectivity. Many researchers have pointed out that journal reviewers are biased toward accepting studies that have significant findings because nonsignificant findings are less interesting. From an objective scientific perspective, however, nonsignificant findings in a well-conducted study should hold the same weight as significant findings if we assume that the purpose of research is to discover truth rather than to confirm our own hypotheses. This bias in accepting significant findings creates a misrepresentation of the research examining the hypothesis in question. For example, if 100 studies are conducted examining personality differences between American Indians and European Americans and only 5 of these studies find a significant difference, then only these 5 studies will be published. In terms of the studies that are published, 5 studies supporting the existence of personality differences may seem fairly convincing, but 5 studies out of 100 is not very strong evidence. Thus, the bias toward publishing articles with significant differences may lead to a high rate of *false positives,* or reporting that there is a significant difference between groups when there is not.

Bias.   One of the assumptions that follows from the objectivity of the scientific method is that research is unbiased. However, we have already seen that researchers are not always objective and that their biases can affect the scientific process. Hare-Mustin and Marecek (1988) discuss two types of bias that occur in research on differences between groups: alpha bias and beta bias. *Alpha bias* refers to the tendency to exaggerate differences. Stereotypes that make sweeping generalizations about groups of people, such as that women are emotional and men are rational, are examples of alpha bias. Such discrepancies between men and women are prevalent in our culture, as illustrated by the popular self-help book, *Men Are from Mars, Women Are from Venus.*

Beta bias is the tendency to minimize or ignore differences. Beta bias is evident in medical research in which conclusions about the risk of coronary heart disease are generalized from studies conducted primarily on European American, middle-class males because researchers assume that what is true for European American men is true for everyone. However, more recent research indicates that this assumption is often inaccurate. For example, women are at a decreased risk of coronary heart disease prior to menopause, and being African American is a risk factor for heart disease.

The problem with most of the bias that occurs in psychological research is that it reflects a particular value system, namely, White, male, and middle class (Fee, 1986). At times, bias may be motivated for political reasons, such as justifying the subordination of certain groups of people. This is most apparent in research that has been used to demonstrate the intellectual inferiority of minority groups and theories that blame the victim for negative outcomes, such as "battered woman syndrome." Some researchers go so far as to argue that the scientific method itself recapitulates our patriarchal society in its value of the objective and the rational, as well as in the unequal relationship between the all-powerful, knowledgeable, and controlling experimenter and the subject who is deceived and manipulated, at times against his or her will (Landrine, Klonoff, & Brown-Collins, 1992).

However, at times, bias may simply reflect the inability to look beyond one's own value system. Science assumes that researchers can be detached from their subject, but researchers who study psychology may be so much a part of their own culture that they may not be able to study psychological processes objectively. This problem is often referred to as *ethnocentrism* by anthropologists, but is not usually used to describe psychologists' work because their findings are supposedly more universal (Ingleby, 1995). To illustrate, we examine the importance of autonomy in our culture: Most people consider a lack of autonomy to be indication of psychological problems that may even lead to the development of a disorder. In fact, Frederick and Grow (1996) argue that eating disorders develop as a result of being raised in an environment in which autonomy is discouraged. As a result, one develops poor self-esteem. One then attempts to feel good about oneself by satisfying the needs of others rather than one's own needs because one does not feel that one is a worthwhile individual. A manifestation of this pattern of behavior is the focus on being thin so that others will find one attractive.

Part of the reason that lack of autonomy and a focus on others' needs over one's own are often interpreted negatively is that our culture is an individualistic culture. Recall from Chapter One that in individualistic cultures, the accomplishments of the individual are valued; thus, independence, uniqueness, and competition are valued because these qualities reflect an ability to be self-reliant. Such a view is in direct contrast to cultures that are characterized by collectivism, and most minority groups are collectivist cultures. In collectivist cultures, individual goals are secondary to the goals of the group as a whole; conformity is valued because it creates harmony among members, and drawing attention to oneself is looked down on. Thus, behavior that is acceptable in a collectivistic culture may not be valued in an individualistic culture, and vice versa. For example, in many collectivistic cultures, it is not uncommon for grown children to live with their parents and extended relatives for both social and financial support. In mainstream American culture, grown children who continue to live with their parents are evaluated unfavorably because it suggests that they are unable to take care of themselves on their own. In fact, excessive reliance on one's parents in adulthood may even be interpreted as a personality disorder. One may appear to be developmentally arrested at a stage in which one continues to be dependent on one's parents, rather than becoming independent and self-reliant, as all adults are supposed to do. Thus, because of our value of individualism, we may inadvertently over-pathologize people from collectivist cultures, interpreting their behavior as a sign of unhealthy dependence on others, rather than viewing their behavior in the appropriate cultural context.

Quantitative Methods.   Although statistical analyses of data have advantages in terms of providing a more objective way of evaluating hypotheses, they are not without their limitations. One idea that is often lost when results of a study are reported is that a significant finding represents the average response of a group of people. For example, if we were to conduct a study examining the correlation between sitting in the front of the classroom and grades, we may find a significant positive correlation between these two variables. Aside from the possibility of misinterpreting this correlational study in a manner that suggests causality (it may be that good students choose to sit in the front rather than that sitting in the front row causes good grades), another problem is that this finding may be interpreted to mean that the association between these two variables always occurs. In fact, even in the data set from which the result was derived, there will be some individuals for whom sitting in the front seat was not associated with high grades, unless the correlation is perfect, which is rarely the case.

In some ways, an average finding in research is like a stereotype (although there are usually fewer negative ramifications for using research findings inappropriately). If you were forced to make a guess about a person, the average finding would be your best guess, but it does not guarantee that you will be correct. For example, if you were to guess the height of a particular female, your best guess would be 5'5", which is the average height for most females. However, there are many females who are not exactly this height. Thus, although an average may represent what is generally true for a group of people, it is not always very useful in understanding a particular individual.

Stereotypes often work in the same way. One stereotype of African Americans is that they have exceptional athletic ability. If you were forced to choose people for a sports team and knew nothing about the person other than ethnicity, choosing someone who is African American might be your strategy. However, there are many African Americans who do not fit this stereotype. Thus, averages, like stereotypes, can often be limited when we use them to understand a particular individual because there are some people who will not be accounted for. Both averages and stereotypes can also be problematic because they may lead people to believe that they know more about someone than they actually do; therefore, they may not attempt to verify their impression with evidence. Such assumptions potentially can have serious consequences, such as not admitting an African American student to a particular university because on average, African Americans score lower on tests of intelligence. (We discuss some of the problems with stereotypes in more detail in Chapter Three.)

A related misinterpretation that often occurs when differences between groups are found is that such differences do not take into account the fact that, in general, within-group differences tend to be larger than between-group differences. To illustrate, we use the often-quoted difference in IQ scores between African Americans and European Americans: Let us assume that the mean score for the African American group is 90 and the mean score of the European American group is 100; thus, there is a 10-point difference between the average IQ score for the two groups. However, let's also assume that the range of scores in the African American group are from 85 to 120, and the range of scores for the European American group are from 90 to 125. Consequently, there are members of the African American group who outscore members of the European American group. So, even though the average finding would lead us to believe that European Americans always perform better on IQ tests than African Americans, this is not the case. This is an example of the kind of misperception that can occur from examining only the average group finding.

Another potential misinterpretation in research findings is the assumption that all findings are of clinical or practical significance. Recall that some findings may be statistically significant but small, and therefore of no practical value. This is often the case in many of the gender differences reported in psychology. For example, while gender differences in cognitive ability may be statistically significant, they often account for only 1 to 5 percent of the variability (Hyde, 1997). Thus, 95 to 99 percent of the variance in cognitive ability is not accounted for by gender. Although gender accounts for only a small proportion of the variance, differences such as these are often emphasized in textbooks (an example of alpha bias) and may consequently be interpreted as being larger than they actually are.

System and Precision.   Some researchers have also challenged the assumption that science is conducted in a systematic manner. Kuhn (1962) argues that rather than proceeding in a systematic fashion, science progresses in spurts. When a particular paradigm or theory is predominant, evidence to refute that paradigm will actually be suppressed. Researchers are resistant to the development of a new theory until the evidence that is not accounted for by the old theory becomes too great; then, researchers formulate a new theory and reject the old theory at once. This process, Kuhn argues, follows a noncumulative development, rather than a logical, systematic one. In fact, researchers deny evidence, resist change, and do not acknowledge errors until they are forced to do so.

Universal Principles.   Another assumption of the scientific method is that it can be used to discover truth or reality. This assumption is often referred to as *logical positivism*, which assumes that truth can be discovered through careful application of the scientific method. The perspective that best characterizes multicultural psychology, however, is that of *social constructionism*, which assumes that our beliefs affect the way research is conducted; therefore, research is affected by the values of our culture and by history. This position is in direct contrast to the assumption of logical positivism. Because reality is influenced by the social context, truth is relative rather than absolute; what is true for one group of people at one point in time may not be true for another group of people at another point in time.

Social constructionism is often used in other fields of study such as literature, but it can also be used in psychology. For example, Freud's personality theory is often criticized by contemporary psychologists for its lack of generalizability, its presumed universality, and its sexist implications. Freud based his theory on case studies of primarily European, middle- to upper-middle-class young women in the Victorian era. From a scientific perspective, case studies are low on internal validity, and the lack of a representative sample also compromises the external validity of his theory. However, the theory that Freud formulated was relevant to the population of patients that he saw. Freud was a product of the Victorian era, which was a time in which forbidden aggressive and sexual impulses were not acknowledged, much less acted on. Women who exposed their ankles at that time were equivalent to women who pose for *Playboy* today. Thus, Freud's theory about the importance of forbidden impulses conflicting with moral ideals was quite applicable to the people who lived during that era. The applicability of Freud's theory is one example of how truth is relative depending on the situation.

The focus on social constructionism is implicit in the distinction made in multicultural psychology between etic and emic research (Landrine et al., 1992). Recall from Chapter One that etic refers to the focus on the outsider's or researcher's perspective. Such research emphasizes the scientific method in its emphasis on quantitative methods, standardized procedures, controlled studies, and operational definitions. Emic refers to the focus on the insider's or participant's perspective. Such research is more qualitative in nature, uncontrolled, nonstandardized, and more open-ended. Typically, traditional research emphasizes the former, whereas multicultural research emphasizes the latter. However, Jahoda (1995) argues that even researchers who are interested in examining cross-cultural differences and think that they are conducting emic research often take an etic approach in that they still employ Western concepts and research methods and assume that findings will be true for all group members.

It is worth noting that not all multicultural researchers find fault with the assumptions of science. Sue (1999) argues that the problem with multicultural psychology research is not with science or our scientific methods, but rather that scientific methods are not adhered to when we draw conclusions about research findings. Sue argues that psychological science favors internal validity over external validity; as a result, studies are more likely to get published when they utilize the experimental method, but little attention is paid to the nature of the sample. In research, we adopt a position of skepticism in which we assume that the null hypothesis is true unless the data suggest otherwise. However, we do not have the same skepticism in generalizing our findings to other groups of people; we assume that the results are true for other groups unless research demonstrates otherwise. A recent literature review of research on ethnic minority issues supports Sue's criticism of psychology. Hall and Maramba (2001) found a limited number of articles published in psychology journals on multicultural issues. Sue argues that when applying the scientific method in determining external validity, it behooves researchers to demonstrate that their findings can be generalized to other groups of people in other settings, rather than to assume that this is the case.

Conclusion

Because psychology involves the scientific study of behavior and mental processes, an emphasis on research and the scientific method are paramount. However, we have seen that with respect to multicultural psychology, there are numerous problems not only with the assumptions of the scientific method, but also with the application of the scientific method. Given these difficulties, what can be done to improve multicultural research? Although there is no clear-cut answer to this problem, there are steps that can be taken.

First, whenever possible, researchers should try to include both emic and etic approaches when testing hypotheses. Thus, rather than abandoning the scientific method, other methods that reflect sensitivity to participants' perspectives should be valued as well and used to supplement traditional research. Landrine et al. (1992) illustrate how such research can be conducted and argue that combining research methods leads to a more complete understanding of the meaning of differences between groups of people when they occur.

Second, when a multimethod approach cannot be used in research, psychologists should acknowledge the limitations of their study and be cautious in overgeneralizing their results. Although these recommendations are not new and are in fact made explicit in the ethical standards for psychologists, some researchers make statements about their findings that are at minimum misleading and at worst not supported by their study (Bleier, 1986). In following these recommendations, most psychological studies should, for example, indicate that a limitation of the study is that it was conducted on introductory psychology students, who may differ from the general population in many ways. Other studies would most likely have to acknowledge a limitation in terms of generalizability to people of different ethnic backgrounds as well.

Third, researchers should make an attempt to be aware of their biases and to acknowledge what their point of view is rather than presenting a stance of neutrality when this is not the case. In doing so, those who are evaluating their work can use this knowledge in determining the validity of the results. For example, the obvious bias in this text is one that values cultural diversity and the belief that different value systems can be equally valid. Thus, everything that you read in this text should be read with the knowledge of the value system under which we are operating.

Finally, researchers should include females, ethnic minority research participants, and other diverse groups whenever possible to ensure the generalizability of their findings. This final recommendation is included in the research guidelines put forth by the National Institute of Mental Health (Hohmann & Parron, 1996). Relatedly, Sue (1999) argues that when differences are found between people of different groups, rather than attributing that difference to distal concepts like gender and ethnicity, attempts should be made to provide more proximal explanatory concepts such as individualism versus collectivism to give meaning to these differences.

In general, it is ultimately the responsibility of the individual researcher to ensure that research is conducted, reported, and disseminated in a manner that will be useful and representative of diverse groups of people. The traditional scientific method implies certain values, and values change over time. As our population becomes more diverse, the way psychology research is conducted must also be reevaluated and change.

MULTICULTURAL ASSESSMENT

Assessment is the process of evaluation that psychologists use to draw conclusions about individuals. Assessments are conducted for many purposes, such as determining level of intelligence, personality structure, presence of psychopathology, treatment recommendations, and appropriateness for employment. Because so many important decisions are made on the basis of psychological assessments, there has been considerable controversy over the instruments used and the interpretations that have been made based on the assessment of various minority groups. As a result, many legal policies have been created for the sole purpose of protecting these disenfranchised groups from negative ramifications of the assessment process. In 1975, the case of *Larry P. v. Wilson Riles* resulted in the prohibition of IQ tests for determining eligibility for placement in special education programs because of the concern that African Americans were overrepresented in remedial classes (Lambert, 1981). Similarly, the Equal Opportunity Employment Act of 1991 and the Americans with Disabilities Act of 1990 banned the use of tests or procedures used for hiring employees that result in discrimination on the basis of race, religion, sex, national origin, or disability. The implementation of such laws suggests that the general public is keenly aware of the potential for the misuse of assessment. How can assessment result in discrimination? In the following sections, we discuss the most common types of tests used in assessments, the methods used to evaluate these tests, and some of the major criticisms of assessment from a multicultural perspective.

Types of Tests

There are many types of tests that can be included in the assessment process. Because we are particularly interested in assessment of diverse populations, we limit our discussion to those measures that have created the most controversy in how they have been used. In particular, these measures include intelligence tests, personality tests, and measures of psychopathology.

Intelligence Tests.   Intelligence tests are designed to assess a person's general cognitive ability or aptitude. They are usually denoted by a global measure of intelligence, such as an IQ score, although other measures of cognitive ability may also be obtained from these tests. Intelligence tests are often used as aptitude tests that presumably reflect a person's innate intellectual potential. They are often distinguished from achievement tests that reflect a person's mastery level in a particular area, which is influenced by learning. In practice, however, it is difficult to create test items that distinguish between innate and learned abilities, and some tests are characterized as being both aptitude and achievement tests, such as the SAT. Intelligence tests can be administered individually or in a group format. For precise measurement of cognitive abilities, individualized tests of intelligence are preferred, although group intelligence tests may be useful for screening purposes.

Of all the tests that are utilized in the assessment process, intelligence tests are the most controversial. One reason for the controversy is that most minority groups score lower than European Americans on standardized intelligence tests. There is considerable debate over whether group differences in intelligence are due to biological factors, environmental differences such as prejudice and discrimination, or bias in testing. (We explore the nature-nurture debate in Chapter Three, and the potential for bias in testing is discussed in a later section.) In addition, knowing a person's level of intelligence may be important for class placement. A student with exceptional abilities may qualify for a gifted program, and a student with a below-average IQ might be placed in remedial classes. This is one of the uses of intelligence tests that has been the most problematic because of concern that this practice discriminates against minorities: African American and Latino/a American students tend to be overrepresented in educable mentally retarded (EMR) classrooms. It is because of this concern that the judge in the *Larry P.* case ruled that intelligence tests could no longer be used for determining EMR placement. Intelligence tests are sometimes used to screen for potential employees, although this practice is controversial as well. Given that most minority groups score lower than European Americans on most intelligence tests, an employer who uses an intelligence test as a screening device will exclude many minorities for consideration for employment. Moreover, intelligence tests are designed to predict academic achievement, and the extent to which they can accurately predict occupational success is unclear (McClelland, 1994).

Personality Tests.   Personality tests are often used to assess individual personality characteristics. Some personality measures, such as the 16 Personality Factors questionnaire (16PF), measure multiple traits. Some measure specific personality traits, such as Type A versus Type B personality. Personality tests are usually classified as being either objective or projective in nature. Objective personality tests involve standardized procedures, structured responses (e.g., yes/no), and unambiguous tasks such as questionnaires. These tests lend themselves more readily to empirical investigation and therefore tend to have better psychometric properties. The Minnesota Multiphasic Personality Inventory 2 (MMPI-2) is an example of an objective personality test. Projective personality tests are more unstructured in nature (e.g., tell me a story), utilize ambiguous stimuli such as inkblots or pictures, and are often based on psychodynamic theory. Projective tests usually are not standardized and are more difficult to score and therefore tend to have poorer psychometric properties than objective tests. The Rorschach Inkblot Test and the Thematic Apperception Test (TAT) are examples of projective tests.

Measures of Psychopathology.   Personality tests such as the MMPI-2 and Rorschach may also be used to assess psychopathology. In addition to personality tests, clinicians may utilize clinical interviews to make a diagnosis. In structured interviews, questions are asked in a specific order, and there are specific follow-up questions based on the person's initial response. An example of a structured interview is the Diagnostic Interview Schedule (DIS). In unstructured interviews, the clinician uses his or her clinical judgment and expertise in deciding which questions to ask and which responses require further inquiry. Although unstructured interviews are more commonly used, structured interviews are favored in research because the investigator is often interested in making a precise diagnosis. In addition, structured interviews often have better psychometric properties than unstructured interviews.

Clinicians also rely on the *Diagnostic and Statistical Manual of Mental Disorders,* fourth edition (*DSM-IV;* APA, 1994) in determining whether a person meets the specific criteria for a mental illness. The *DSM-IV* is an improvement over earlier versions of the *DSM,* in that the current version is atheoretical (rather than psychodynamic) and can therefore be used by clinicians and researchers of all theoretical orientations. The current version also focuses on operational criteria, thereby making the diagnostic process more amenable to research. Finally, the criteria for the disorders are based on empirical evidence.

Psychometrics

Psychometrics pertain to the science of psychological measurement. The psychometric properties of a test refer to how scientifically sound the test is. Because research is an important component of the assessment process, the psychometric properties of a test are one of the major criteria that researchers use in evaluating whether any assessment tool is appropriate or not. In the following, we discuss the importance of norms, reliability, validity, methods, and bias in evaluating the psychometric properties of a test.

Norms.   To evaluate how an individual performs on a test, that person's score must be compared to normative data that indicate the average score for the test. For example, in most IQ tests, the average score is set at 100. Thus, a high or low level of intelligence will be indicated by a score considerably above or below 100, respectively. Norms are determined by giving the test to a standardization sample that represents the population for which the test will be used. For example, an IQ test designed for adults should not be normed on children, and vice versa. Generally speaking, the larger the standardization sample and the closer the match between the standardization sample and the test takers, the more useful the test will be.

Reliability.   Reliability refers to repeatability or consistency of results. One form of reliability that is of particular interest in diagnosing psychopathology is *interrater reliability,* which refers to the consistency among raters or observers. To illustrate, the *DSM-IV* outlines specific criteria that must be met to warrant a particular diagnosis, such as specific symptoms, duration of symptoms, and other disorders that should be ruled out. To determine the interrater reliability of the *DSM-IV, reliability coefficients* are calculated. Because reliability coefficients are correlation coefficients, the higher the correlation, the better the reliability of the measure. Thus, if we wanted to evaluate whether the *DSM-IV* is associated with high interrater reliability, we may ask two different clinicians to make a diagnosis of the same individual and calculate the results. For example, if an African American male presented with symptoms such as delusions, irritable mood, and disturbances in thinking and one clinician gave this individual a diagnosis of Bipolar Disorder but the other clinician gave him a diagnosis of Schizophrenia, this finding might suggest poor interrater reliability in using the *DSM-IV.*

Validity.   Validity refers to whether a test measures what it purports to measure. Reliability and validity are related in that reliability is a necessary but not sufficient criterion for validity. In other words, a test must be reliable to be valid, but reliability does not guarantee validity. For example, bathroom scales tend to be less reliable measures of weight than the scales used in your doctor's office; however, even the most reliable scale will not be valid for measuring height, which requires a different instrument altogether. Similarly, a highly reliable test of intelligence for Americans may not be a valid test of intelligence for people in Africa.

Two types of validity that are particularly important to consider in multicultural psychology are criterion-related validity and construct validity. *Criterion-related validity* refers to the statistical relationship between a set of test scores and a set of criterion scores. There are two types of criterion-related validity: *concurrent validity,* in which two sets of scores are available at the same time, and *predictive validity,* in which a test is evaluated against some score or behavior that will become available in the future. If you have just constructed a new test of intelligence, you would determine its concurrent validity by administering your new test and an existing IQ test to individuals concurrently and calculating a correlation coefficient between the two scores. You would determine your test's predictive validity by correlating IQ scores on your test with the person's GPA for the following school year to determine whether people with higher IQ scores obtain higher grades.

The second type of validity that is important to consider is *construct validity*. Many of the characteristics that we attempt to measure in psychology are hypothetical constructs—concepts that help to make human behavior more understandable but cannot be observed directly. For example, we cannot observe intelligence directly, but we infer it when we observe behaviors that we believe are indicative of intelligence, such as making good grades, having good problem-solving skills, and comprehending new information easily. Construct validity refers to the extent to which a test is successful in measuring a hypothetical construct. In testing construct validity, our test must be related to observable behaviors to be useful. Because constructs are used to explain a variety of related behaviors, it is not possible to determine the construct validity of a test with a single statistic or study.

Methods.   The methods used to test the construct in question are also important to consider. The tools of assessment can include behavioral observations, interviews, and questionnaires. Behavioral observations can be made informally during the interview, or can be made in the person's natural setting, such as observing a student interacting with other students during recess. Interviews can be structured or unstructured. Questionnaires can have specific responses (e.g., checklists, multiple choice) or more open-ended responses (fill in the blank, stories). The methods used in assessment can affect the psychometric properties of the test. For example, individually administered intelligence tests, objective personality tests, and structured interviews tend to be preferred over group intelligence tests, projective personality tests, and unstructured tests.

The methods used in assessment also can have important implications for construct validity. To illustrate, let us use college exams as an example. Your score on an exam is used to evaluate your understanding of the material learned in the course. Let us pretend that you perform much better on essay tests than you do on multiple-choice tests and that your professor's exams are all multiple choice. As a result, you may perform more poorly on her tests than if she had used an essay format. However, if the professor includes some multiple-choice questions and some essay questions, there is less likelihood that your performance will be negatively affected by the method used. The same holds true for the tests that are used in assessment: In general, we can have more faith that we are tapping the construct in question when different methods of measuring the same construct are highly correlated (Campbell & Fiske, 1959).

Bias.   Assessment tools are subject to several sources of bias. All sources of bias call into question the reliability and validity of test results and should therefore be minimized. Bias can emerge on the part of the examinee or the examiner or from the test itself. Examinees' responses can be biased for several reasons. Examinees may be affected by internal factors such as motivation, hunger, and fatigue; they may have particular response biases such as always responding in the affirmative (yea-sayers), always responding in the negative (nay-sayers), always responding in the middle of a Likert-type scale, or randomly responding to test items. Examinees may also be affected by coaching; for example, students often take courses designed to help them perform better on SAT and GRE tests.

Many of the same sources of bias can also apply to the examiner, such as mood, motivation, hunger, and fatigue. Examiners may also vary in how familiar they are with certain tests, which can affect administration, scoring, and interpretation. Examiners may vary in terms of how well they are able to establish rapport with examinees; this may be of particular concern when examinee and examiner are of different ethnic or cultural backgrounds. Examiners may also be influenced by stereotypes based on race, gender, sexual orientation, and so on and may harbor negative or positive feelings toward particular groups, which can influence the assessment process.

Yet another source of bias is test bias. *Test bias* is a statistical term referring to whether a test results in different predictions for different groups and is evaluated by examining factors such as the validity coefficients for the test, the slope, and the y-intercept. If the same test results in different slopes or y-intercepts for different groups, then the test systematically predicts differently for different groups, indicating that the test is biased. If a test is biased, the same test will overpredict the performance of one group and underpredict the performance of another group. Whenever researchers are concerned about test bias, it is usually because of the possibility that a test may be underpredicting the performance of ethnic minority groups. This is of particular concern with aptitude tests, which are often used to predict future performance in school.

Assessment from a Multicultural Perspective

As mentioned at the beginning of this section, both the general public and researchers have expressed concern over the way assessment has been used with diverse populations. One of the areas in which this debate is most heated is in the use of intelligence tests, in which minority groups tend to score lower than European Americans. However, differences in tests that measure personality characteristics and psychopathology are also often interpreted in a manner suggesting that minorities are inferior or more pathological. In the following, we review some of the problems with the assessment of diverse populations.

Norms.   One of the major problems with most of the tests used in assessment is that the standardization samples used to create these tests tend to include small numbers of minority groups. Consequently, generalizability of such tests to various minority groups has not been empirically validated. At first glance, it may seem that the solution to this problem is fairly simple: Include more minority groups in the standardization sample. However, this is not as easy to carry out as it seems. First, there is the issue of identifying the desired minority groups (Okazaki & Sue, 2000). One of the most common methods is self-identification, in which participants indicate their ethnicity through self-report. This method requires researchers to determine the number of ethnic categories they wish to include, which can be broad (e.g., Asian) or specific (e.g., Chinese, Japanese). On the one hand, broad categories allow a researcher to obtain larger sample sizes, but they will also be fairly heterogeneous. The more heterogeneous the category is, the less precise it will be in making predictions. Even if the researcher decides to use narrow categories, individuals from the same ethnic group can vary in factors, such as acculturation and fluency in English, which can influence their understanding of test items as well as their response. Often, it is those ethnic minorities who are least acculturated that are interpreted as being the most pathological (Okazaki & Sue, 2000). The researcher will also have to decide how to classify multiracial individuals. Should persons who are half Japanese American and half European American be analyzed with other Japanese Americans? Or should they be analyzed with other biracial/multiracial individuals, who may have different ethnic backgrounds (e.g., half African American and half European American)? Another complication in the identification process is that multiracial individuals may identify as biracial, as an ethnic minority, or as European American (Brown, 1995).

Another problem is in recruiting ethnic minorities for participation in the standardization sample. In the research section, we noted that college populations are often utilized because they are samples of convenience, but these individuals may not be representative of the general population. Researchers may include community samples through the *snowballing technique*, in which they start with a known group of participants and recruit other participants through contacts. However, these individuals may be friends or family members who share certain characteristics that may not generalize to other ethnic minorities. For example, they may all live in an urban setting or have similar SES levels. Researchers may recruit individuals from clinical settings, but different ethnic minority groups vary in the extent to which they utilize mental health services: African Americans and American Indians tend to overutilize them, and Asian Americans and Latino/a Americans tend to underutilize them (Sue, Zane, & Young, 1994). In addition, those minorities who seek treatment may differ from other ethnic minorities in factors such as level of acculturation and psychopathology that may also make generalizability difficult.

Reliability.   There are several problems relating to reliability in the assessment of minority groups. First, test manuals and articles examining the psychometric properties of tests do not always provide reliability statistics for different minority groups. Reliability statistics for different minority groups are sometimes conducted for some of the most commonly used psychological tests, such as IQ tests and the MMPI-2, but are less frequently reported for other measures. The lack of reliability statistics may result in part from the difficulty of finding adequate samples of different groups. Even when minority groups are sampled, low reliability may result from assuming that groups will be homogeneous. As mentioned earlier, members from the same ethnic minority group may vary in numerous ways, including differing levels of acculturation, understanding of English, and experience with assessment.

The 2000 presidential election is a good example of the way unfamiliarity with the assessment procedure can contribute to an unreliable measurement. Considerable controversy was generated over the reliability of the votes in Florida because of the "butterfly" format that was used to list the candidates. The ballot was a two-page form in which candidates' names were listed on both the right and left side of the form. Voters signified the candidate they endorsed by marking a corresponding bubble next to the candidate's name. However, the bubbles for different candidates were very close together, and some voters complained that although they intended to vote for Al Gore, they had inadvertently marked the bubble for Pat Buchanan instead. As a result, many Democrats were concerned that the votes obtained under this system were unreliable and did not represent the intent of the voters. Recent research suggests that the error rate associated with the butterfly ballot format was higher than it was for other methods of voting, suggesting that the butterfly format itself may have contributed to poor reliability (Sinclair, Mark, Moore, Lavis, & Soldat, 2000). The same difficulties could arise in psychological testing for individuals who are not familiar with the testing format (e.g., pencil/paper, computer) or who do not speak English as their first language.

Another factor that may affect the reliability of the test is the match between examiner and examinee in terms of ethnicity and language (Okazaki & Sue, 2000). If the examiner is European American and the examinee is an ethnic minority, there is always the possibility that the examiner may misinterpret information based on lack of familiarity with the language and culture of the examinee. Even if the examiner is an ethnic minority, both examiner and examinee may differ in terms of their acculturation level and understanding of English. Consequently, the match between examiner and examinee can potentially affect the interpretation of test and interview results.

Validity. Recall that validity refers to the extent to which a test is truly measuring what it was intended to measure. Given that reliability of instruments is minimally necessary for validity, it is clear that the problems associated with reliability can then contribute to instruments with questionable validity. If we cannot be certain that the test taker adequately understood the methods, questions, or responses of the test, then we cannot be certain that we have accurately measured the construct in question.

Even the translation of an instrument to someone's native language is no guarantee that a measure will be more valid. To illustrate, let us assume that we are interested in assessing depression in different ethnic groups. One question that is commonly asked on such measures is the extent to which someone feels "sad" or "blue." However, a strict translation of this type of question may have little meaning for someone from a non-Western culture (Kleinman, 1995). In fact, it is not uncommon for many groups within the United States, such as minority groups, children, and older adults, to present with somatic and/or cognitive symptoms rather than mood symptoms when they are depressed.

This example brings up an important issue in determining the construct validity of psychological measures. Researchers must determine the extent to which the construct that their test is supposed to measure has the same meaning for other groups of people. To illustrate, Rotter's (1966) Locus of Control (LOC) scale is designed to measure the extent to which people believe that they exercise control over their lives. An internal LOC suggests that a person believes that his or her behavior can contribute to success. For example, a person with an internal LOC who performs poorly on an exam might believe that meeting with the professor, getting a tutor, and spending more time studying will improve his or her grade in the course. A student with an external LOC might believe that there is nothing that can be done to improve his or her grade because it is determined by factors outside of his or her control, such as an unfair professor. Research suggests that having an internal LOC is associated with many positive outcomes (Jones & Thorne, 1987). LOC is often studied in minority populations to determine whether disenfranchised groups feel less in control over their lives, and there is some research to support this perspective. However, having an external LOC does not always translate into poorer outcomes for these individuals, as the theory would predict (Jones & Thorne, 1987). This example illustrates that the constructs our tests are supposed to be measuring may not always be universal.

Methods.   Earlier, we discussed the fact that the experimental method is often the gold standard because it allows the researcher to have the most control over the variables of interest. The same principle holds true in assessment: In general, the tests that are most often examined from a multicultural perspective are the standardized instruments such as IQ tests and objective personality tests such as the MMPI-2. These tests are also the instruments that are based on quantitative rather than qualitative data and, consequently, the ones that have the most empirical support. In contrast, there has been limited research investigating other assessment tools, such as behavioral observation, qualitative assessment, and projective tests (Okazaki & Sue, 2000). This is unfortunate, as these methods are best suited for small sample sizes because they involve more in-depth analysis of the data. Given the difficulties in finding representative samples of minority groups, these more in-depth methods would be one way of being sensitive to both individual and cultural factors in assessment. In addition, including several methods of testing the same concept is important in establishing construct validity. For example, assessing personality with both the MMPI-2 and a projective test may be a more valid measure of personality than using the MMPI-2 alone.

There have been a few attempts to include some of these less utilized forms of assessment in testing minority groups. Jones and Thorne (1987) outline an interviewing technique that focuses on the subject's viewpoint by emphasizing a narrative account of the person's experience. They argue that this method gives the examiner a better idea of the examinee's understanding of individual test items, which is useful in interpreting test results. One example of a projective test that has been adapted to different groups is the TAT, in which the examinee is instructed to tell a story about the picture shown as well as what the characters in the story are thinking and feeling. This test has been modified for use with Latino/a children (Tell-Me-a-Story, or TEMAS), African Americans (Bailey & Green, 1977), and American Indians (Monopoli & Alworth, 2000).

Bias.   One of the major criticisms of the tools used in assessment is that they are biased against minority groups, specifically in diagnosing psychopathology. This is evident in research indicating that African Americans are more likely to be diagnosed with Schizophrenia and European Americans are more likely to be diagnosed with Bipolar Disorder when they present with similar symptoms (Adebimpe, 1981). Many researchers argue that this difference is actually due to bias in diagnosis rather than to a difference in prevalence rates for the disorders. In particular, African Americans are more likely to appear suspicious, mistrustful, and paranoid compared to European Americans. Because of experiences with prejudice and discrimination, being a minority can create a sensitivity to the reaction of others that may seem like paranoia but is actually appropriate and even adaptive at times (Ridley, 1984). However, this behavior may be misinterpreted negatively by clinicians, resulting in a diagnosis of Paranoid Schizophrenia rather than Bipolar Disorder.

Some of the assessment tools used by psychologists have also been criticized for being biased against minorities, such as the MMPI and MMPI-2. Researchers have argued that these instruments tend to overpathologize minority test takers (Butcher, Braswell, & Raney, 1983; Dana, 1988). However, a recent meta-analysis conducted by Hall, Bansal, and Lopez (1999) suggests that the MMPI/MMPI-2 does not unfairly portray African Americans and Latino/a Americans as pathological, lending some empirical support for the use of this personality measure with minority groups.

Bias is of particular concern in intelligence tests. Because these tests are written by and standardized on European Americans, they reflect the beliefs and values of the dominant culture. For example, intelligence tests presume that the examinee will have an understanding of English. Consequently, if English is not one's first language, one will likely perform worse on an intelligence test than if the test were in one's native language. There are a few translated versions of the Wechsler Adult Intelligence Scale (WAIS), but these versions are often unavailable in the United States and do not always have updated norms (Okazaki & Sue, 2000).

The content of test items may also reflect the values of the dominant culture. For example, one type of item that intelligence tests often utilize is knowledge of proverbs or expressions common to our culture, such as "Better late than never." It is assumed that someone who is intelligent will know the meaning of such proverbs. But what if you live in a culture where the common expressions are different from the ones used on intelligence tests? My mother (Barongan) never used this expression, but she has often used her own translation of this expression, which is "Better late than dead"; in other words, it is better to show up late for something than to drive recklessly to your destination and end up in an accident. Unfortunately, this expression is not likely to be found on any test of intelligence. This example humorously illustrates how much of what we assume to be general knowledge on IQ tests may not be common for someone who grows up in a culture other than the dominant one.

Relatedly, intelligence tests often reflect a particular aspect of intelligence, mainly "book smarts," but may not reflect other aspects of intelligence that might be more important to ethnic minorities, such as "street smarts" or the ability to work well with others. In addition, scores on intelligence tests are based on verbal responses, fine motor skills such as manipulating small objects, and the ability to provide a response within a specified time limit. The fact that verbal and timed responses are often included reflect an implicit value of the ability to express oneself verbally and to complete tasks quickly—both qualities that may not be universally valued by all cultures. Moreover, a person with a physical disability who may know the answer to a particular question may not get credit because of the way he or she was required to respond. Thus, intelligence tests may also be biased against people who have disabilities.

In an effort to address some of these problems, many researchers have attempted to create culture-free tests by eliminating or minimizing test items that are culturally loaded. Often, such tests eliminate verbal responses, emphasize nonverbal items involving novel stimuli, avoid the use of time limits, and require minimal physical responses, such as pointing. Examples of such tests include Raven's (1976) Progressive Matrices and the Culture Fair Test of Intelligence (Cattell, 1940). However, there are problems with these tests, as well. First, they often are not as psychometrically sound as are traditional intelligence tests. Second, they are less commonly used for purposes of screening. Third, most researchers now agree that there is no such thing as a culture-free test, in that it is impossible to eliminate all influences of culture in creating test items. Finally, it has not been proven that the difference in intelligence scores between European Americans and other minority groups is due to test bias (Linn, 1978).

This last point requires further clarification. Recall that test bias from a psychometric perspective is a statistical question of whether a test predicts differentially for different groups of people. Intelligence tests are not biased in that they do not result in differential predictions between European Americans and other minority groups. In other words, intelligence tests predict that European American children will achieve higher academic performance than African American children, and this is an accurate prediction. Given that the criterion used to evaluate intelligence tests (i.e., our school system) also reflects the values of the majority group, it should not be surprising that European Americans would be more likely to excel in this environment.

It is important to keep in mind, however, that a test that is not biased may still be inappropriate to use with certain groups of people. Helms (1995) makes an important distinction between cultural (or what we have referred to as test) bias, which is determined through statistical procedures, and cultural equivalence, which reflects the extent to which the construct the test is measuring has the same meaning for a specific group. Although researchers often use the terms interchangeably, they actually pertain to different but related aspects of measurement. Cultural/test bias pertains more specifically to predictive validity; cultural equivalence addresses construct validity. Although research suggests that differences in IQ tests are not due to cultural/test bias, Helms argues that bias may, in fact, be involved because many of the statistical assumptions that are necessary for those analyses are often violated. She further argues that even if tests are not biased in a statistical sense, the tests may still lack cultural equivalence because of the difficulty delineating universal criteria for something as complex as intelligence.

It is also important to distinguish between the concepts of test bias and the fair use of tests. Test bias refers to whether the same test predicts differently for different groups of people. Fairness, on the other hand, refers to the way tests are used and is more subjective and open to interpretation. Thus, even if IQ tests are not statistically biased, society may still conclude that they are used in an unfair manner. For example, an employer may wish to exclude African Americans from a particular job position without appearing to be racist. The employer may decide to use an IQ test as a screening device for employment, knowing that African Americans attain lower scores on this test. Thus, use of the IQ test allows the employer to exclude minorities from consideration for the job without appearing to discriminate on the basis of race. In this situation, the test may not be biased, but it clearly is used in an unfair and inappropriate manner.

Conclusion

Many of the concerns involving multicultural research relate to multicultural assessment. These issues include overreliance on samples of convenience that do not necessarily represent the population at large, overemphasis on between-group differences and underemphasis on within-group differences, and ways in which our values dictate the variables we choose to study and the methods used to study them. Consequently, many of the suggestions for multicultural assessment are similar to those given for multicultural research. First, researchers should include minority groups in standardization samples to ensure that the test results can be applied to diverse populations. Second, researchers should determine that tests are psychometrically sound when applied to minority groups: that they are reliable, valid, and unbiased. Third, researchers should include more qualitative, subjective methods of assessment in addition to the standardized, objective tests that are traditionally employed. In doing so, researchers may wish to borrow from the methods often used by anthropologists in studying different cultures and from therapists working with clients, in which the investigator develops a close relationship with the individual and attempts to capture the subjective experience of the person as accurately as possible (Ingleby, 1995). Fourth, when making interpretations, researchers should be sensitive to factors such as within-group differences, language barriers, level of acculturation, and the match between examiner and examinee and indicate when these factors call into question the certainty of one's interpretations. Finally, researchers should be sensitive to the way their data may be used and misused by others by making explicit the limitations of their findings, by making statements in terms of probability, and by refraining from generalizations that are not empirically supported.

REFERENCES

Adebimpe, V. R. (1981). Overview: White norms and psychiatric diagnosis of Black patients. *American Journal of Psychiatry, 138,* 279–284.

American Psychiatric Association. (1994). *Diagnostic and statistical manual of mental disorders* (4th ed.). Washington, DC: Author.

Bailey, B. E., & Green, J. (1977). Black Thematic Apperception Test stimulus material. *Journal of Personality Assessment, 41,* 25–30.

Bleier, R. (1986). Sex differences research: Science or belief? In R. Bleier (Ed.), *Feminist approaches to science* (pp. 147–164). New York: Pergamon Press.

Botta, R. A. (1999). Television images and adolescent girls' body image disturbance. *Journal of Communication, 49,* 22–41.

Brown, U. M. (1995). Black/White interracial young adults: Quest for a racial identity. *American Journal of Orthopsychiatry, 65,* 125–130.

Butcher, J. N., Braswell, L., & Raney, D. (1983). A cross-cultural comparison of American Indian, Black, and White inpatients on the MMPI and presenting symptoms. *Journal of Consulting and Clinical Psychology, 51,* 587–594.

Campbell, D. T., & Fiske, D. W. (1959). Convergent and discriminant validity by the multitrait-multimethod matrix. *Psychological Bulletin, 56,* 81–105.

Cattell, R. B. (1940). A culture free intelligence test: Part 1. *Journal of Educational Psychology, 31,* 161–179.

Dana, R. H. (1988). Culturally diverse groups and MMPI interpretation. *Professional Psychology: Research and Practice, 19,* 490–495.

Fee, E. (1979). Nineteenth century crainology: The study of the female skull. *Bulletin of the History of Medicine, 53,* 415–433.

Fee, E. (1986). Critiques to modern science: The relationship of feminism to other radical epistemologies. In R. Bleier (Ed.), *Feminist approaches to science* (pp. 24–56). New York: Pergamon Press.

Flynn, K. J., & Fitzgibbon, M. F. (1998). Body images and obesity risk among Black females: A review of the literature. *Annals of Behavioral Medicine, 20,* 13–24.

Frederick, C. M., & Grow, V. M. (1996). A meditional model of autonomy, self-esteem, and eating disorders attitudes and behaviors. *Psychology of Women Quarterly, 20,* 217–266.

Gardner, D. M., & Olmsted, M. P. (1991). *Eating Disorders Inventory* (2nd ed.). Odessa, FL: Psychological Assessment Resources.

Gould, S. J. (1981). *The mismeasure of man.* New York: Norton.

Hall, G. C. N., Bansal, A., & Lopez, I. R. (1999). Ethnicity and psychopathology: A meta-analytic review of 31 years of comparative MMPI/MMPI-2 research. *Psychological Assessment, 11,* 186–197.

Hall, G. C. N., & Maramba, G. G. (2001). In search of cultural diversity: Recent literature in cross-cultural and ethnic minority psychology. *Cultural Diversity and Ethnic Minority Psychology, 7,* 12–26.

Hare-Mustin, R. T., & Marecek, J. (1988). The meaning of difference. *American Psychologist, 43,* 455–464.

Harrison, K., & Cantor, J. (1997). The relationship between media consumption and eating disorders. *Journal of Communication, 47,* 40–67.

Heinberg, L. J., & Thompson, J. K. (1995). Body image and televised images of thinness and attractiveness: A controlled laboratory investigation. *Journal of Social and Clinical Psychology, 14,* 325–338.

Helms, J. (1995). Why is there no study of cultural equivalence in standardized cognitive ability testing? In N. R. Goldberger & J. B. Veroff (Eds.), *The culture and psychology reader* (pp. 674–719). New York: New York University Press.

Herrnstein, R. J., & Murray, C. (1994). *The Bell Curve: Intelligence and class structure in American life.* New York: Free Press.

Hohmann, A. A., & Parron, D. L. (1996). How the new NIH guidelines on inclusion of women and minorities apply: Efficacy trials, effectiveness trials, and validity. *Journal of Consulting and Clinical Psychology, 64,* 851–855.

Hyde, J. (1997). Gender differences in cognition: Results from meta-analyses. In P. J. Caplan, M. Crawford, J. S. Hyde, & J. T. E. Richardson (Eds.), *Gender differences in human cognition* (pp. 30–51). New York: Oxford University Press.

Ingleby, D. (1995). Problems in the study and of the interplay between science and culture. In N. R. Goldberger & J. B. Veroff (Eds.), *The culture and psychology reader* (pp. 108–123). New York: New York University Press.

Irving, L. M. (1990). Mirror images: Effects of the standard of beauty on self- and body-esteem of women exhibiting various levels of bulimic symptoms. *Journal of Social and Clinical Psychology, 9,* 230–242.

Jahoda, G. (1995). In pursuit of the emic-etic distinction: Can we ever capture it? In N. R. Goldberger & J. B. Veroff (Eds.), *The culture and psychology reader* (pp. 128–138). New York: New York University Press.

Jones, E. E., & Thorne, A. (1987). Rediscovery of the subject: Intercultural approaches to clinical assessment. *Journal of Consulting and Clinical Psychology, 55,* 488–495.

Kalonder, C. R. (1997). Media influences on male and female non-eating disordered college students: A significant issue. *Eating Disorders, 5,* 47–57.

Kazdin, A. E. (1999). Overview of research design issue in clinical psychology. In P. C. Kendall, J. N. Butcher, & G. N. Holmbeck (Eds.), *Handbook of research methods in clinical psychology* (pp. 3–30). New York: Wiley.

Kleinman, A. (1995). Do psychiatric disorders differ in different cultures? The methodological questions. In N. R. Goldberger & J. B. Veroff (Eds.), *The culture and psychology reader* (pp. 631–651). New York: New York University Press.

Kuhn, T. S. (1962). *The structure of scientific revolutions.* Chicago: University of Chicago Press.

Kuo, W. H. (1984). Prevalence of depression among Asian-Americans. *Journal of Nervous and Mental Disease, 172,* 449–457.

Lambert, N. M. (1981). Psychological evidence in *Larry P. v. Wilson Riles:* An evaluation by a witness for the defense. *American Psychologist, 36,* 937–952.

Landrine, H., Klonoff, E. A., & Brown-Collins, A. (1992). Cultural diversity and methodology in feminist psychology. *Psychology of Women Quarterly, 16,* 145–163.

Linn, R. L. (1978). Single-group validity, differential validity, and differential prediction. *Journal of Applied Psychology, 63,* 507–512.

McClelland, D. C. (1994). The knowledge-testing-educational complex strikes back. *American Psychologist, 49,* 66–69.

Monopoli, J., & Alworth, L. L. (2000). The use of the Thematic Apperception Test in the study of Native American psychological characteristics: A review and archival study of Navaho men. *Genetic, Social, and General Psychology Monographs, 126,* 43–78.

Ogden, J., & Mundray, K. (1996). The effect of the media on body satisfaction: The role of gender and size. *European Eating Disorders Review, 4,* 171–182.

Okazaki, S., & Sue, S. (2000). Implications of test revisions for assessment with Asian Americans. *Psychological Assessment, 12,* 272–280.

Pinhas, L., Toner, B. B., Ali, A., Garfinkel, P., & Stuckless, N. (1999). The effects of the ideal of female beauty on mood and body satisfaction. *International Journal of Eating Disorders, 25,* 223–226.

Posavac, H. D., Posavac, S. S., & Posavac, E. J. (1998). Exposure to media images of female attractiveness and concern with body weight among young women. *Sex Roles, 38,* 187–201.

Raven, J. C. (1976). *Standard Progressive Matrices.* Oxford, England: Oxford Psychologists.

Ridley, C. R. (1984). Clinical treatment of the nondisclosing Black client. *American Psychologist, 39,* 1234–1244.

Rotter, J. (1966). Generalized expectancies for internal vs. external control of reinforcement. *Psychological Monographs, 80,* 1–28.

Sears, D. O. (1985). College sophomores in the laboratory: Influences of a narrow data base on social psychology's view of human nature. *Journal of Personality and Social Psychology, 51,* 515–530.

Sinclair, R. C., Mark, M. M., Moore, S. E., Lavis, C. A., & Soldat, A. S. (2000, December 7). An electoral butterfly effect. *Nature, 408,* 665–666.

Stice, E., & Shaw, H. E. (1994). Adverse effects of the media portrayed thin ideal on women and linkages to bulimic symptomatology. *Journal of Social and Clinical Psychology, 13,* 288–308.

Sue, S. (1999). Science, ethnicity, and bias. *American Psychologist, 54,* 1070–1077.

Sue, S., Zane, N., & Young, K. (1994). Research on psychotherapy with culturally diverse groups. In A. E. Bergin & S. L. Garfield (Eds.), *Handbook of psychotherapy and behavior change* (4th ed., pp. 783–817). New York: Wiley.

ISSUES FOR DISCUSSION

1. Find a research article in a journal that pertains to diversity in psychology. Describe the purpose of the study (hypotheses, methodology, and results) and critique this study based on information discussed in this chapter.

2. Interview someone you know who is a nonmajority group member. How has his or her experience of being a minority (e.g., different value systems, experiences with prejudice and discrimination, acculturation, language differences) shaped his or her understanding of self and others? In what ways might his or her behavior be misunderstood by others?

THREE

THEORY AND MULTICULTURAL PSYCHOLOGY: BIOLOGICAL AND SOCIAL PSYCHOLOGY

Psychology is a diverse field, encompassing many different facets of behavior. Historically, many of the principles of psychology were believed to apply to all individuals because discovering universal principles is one of the goals of science, as we saw in Chapter Two. Consequently, the study of psychology has been fairly ethnocentric, reflecting the worldview of researchers who were primarily European American, middle class, and male. More recently, however, researchers are becoming increasingly aware of the fact that many of the findings that were once thought to be universal do not always generalize to other groups of people. Thus, it is important for psychologists to consider the sociocultural context of their research.

The purpose of Chapters Three and Four is to review some of the multicultural aspects of the major fields of psychology. We review the fields of biological psychology and social psychology in this chapter; in the next chapter, we discuss developmental psychology and personality. Research studies from other countries, as well as on ethnic minorities in the United States, are included. However, it is important to keep in mind that cultural beliefs and value systems may differ for these two groups; someone living in Japan, for example, may share similarities with Japanese immigrants and Japanese Americans born in the United States, but these individuals may also have important differences in their worldview based on level of acculturation, experiences with prejudice and discrimination, and other factors.

BIOLOGICAL PSYCHOLOGY

Biological psychology examines the biological processes that can impact our cognitions, emotions, and behavior. Biological theories of psychological processes have become increasingly common, in part due to the advances in technology that have allowed researchers to isolate biological factors more effectively. Biological theories are pitted against environmental explanations of behavior in almost every field of psychology. This controversy is often referred to as the nature-nurture debate, which often takes on political as well as scientific ramifications, as we will see.

The emphasis in this book is on ethnicity, culture, and minority status. As discussed in Chapter One, there is not a consensus on the definition of race, which is a biological variable. It is unlikely that biological differences exist across ethnic and cultural groups because these variables are psychosocial rather than biological variables. Nevertheless, we contend that psychosocial variables are what distinguish our species from others. Sexual attraction is an area that illustrates this issue. Nonhuman primate sexual intercourse is driven primarily by biological variables, including sexual drive and the estrus cycle. Sexual attraction in humans is a much more complex process. Biological drives may create the basis for human sexual attraction; however, sexual attraction is not sufficient for sexual intercourse to occur. The establishment of some form of a relationship between the two persons is usually a prerequisite for sexual contact. In other words, most humans are more selective in whom they have sex with than are other nonhuman primates. Ethnic and cultural variables may also influence one's choice of a sexual partner. Beyond being attracted or not being attracted to persons from particular cultural groups based on the person's physical appearance, styles of courtship may differ across and within cultural groups; one's courtship style (e.g., aggressive) may determine how attractive one is. Such psychosocial variables have a relatively limited influence on nonhuman primate sexual mating, other than in a primitive manner. Thus, knowledge of a person's biological sexuality would tell us little about who his or her sexual partner would most likely be. Conversely, psychosocial variables could provide better insight into whom the person might be attracted to and into who might be attracted to this person.

In this section, we review some of the most frequently examined biological factors in psychology, including genetics, neurotransmitters and hormones, structure of the brain, and sociobiology. We also discuss the implications of the nature-nurture debate in more detail and illustrate its impact on multicultural psychology.

Genetics

Genetics refers to the study of how traits are transmitted from one generation to the next. Genetic transmission of traits, or *heritability,* is assumed to be responsible for many aspects of behavior, including physical characteristics, personality characteristics, intelligence, and some mental disorders. In fact, when most people say that a particular characteristic is biologically determined, such as depression, they usually mean that it is inherited from one's parents.

There are several ways that researchers attempt to determine whether certain behaviors are genetically determined. These research methods include family studies, twin studies, and adoption studies. The greater the genetic similarity among family members, the more likely that the behavior in question is inherited. If we were trying to determine whether Schizophrenia is inherited, we would predict that the greatest similarity in schizophrenic symptoms would be between monozygotic or identical twins and that the least similarity in symptoms would be between an adopted child and the adoptive parent. Although none of these methods alone rules out environmental causes of behavior, when used in combination, they provide stronger evidence of genetic transmission. In other words, if family studies, twin studies, and adoption studies all support the hypothesis that a particular trait is genetically transmitted, then the limitations of any particular method are minimized and the case for genetic transmission is strengthened. This is certainly the case with Schizophrenia: Family studies (Brunner, Nelen, Breakfield, & Ropers, 1993), twin studies (Gottesman, 1991), and adoption studies (Kety, 1988) all support the hypothesis that Schizophrenia is genetically transmitted.

Genetic differences are often assumed to be responsible for racial differences. For example, the classification of people into Caucasoid, Mongoloid, and Negroid is based on presumed genetic differences (Rushton, 1988). Such classification systems are often based on differences in physical characteristics, such as skin color, shape of facial features, and hair type. However, these physical characteristics vary considerably among members of the same race (Betancourt & Lopez, 1993), and there are usually more similarities between groups of people from different races than there are differences (a good example of the alpha bias discussed in Chapter Two). It is important to keep in mind that many of the physical characteristics that are used to distinguish among ethnic groups are arbitrary. We could classify races in terms of shared blood type, susceptibility to allergies, or lactose intolerance, all of which would lead to different classification systems. Although there is still considerable debate on the best way to define race, many researchers argue that race is more a political and cultural concept than a biological one (Fairchild, 1991; Jones, 1999).

Genetic differences are presumed to be the cause of group differences other than physical characteristics, such as intelligence. Genetic differences in intelligence have historically been used as evidence for the superiority of certain ethnic groups over others. However, some researchers have found little evidence to suggest that average differences in IQ among ethnic groups are genetic in origin and more evidence to suggest that such differences may arise from social circumstances (Mackintosh, 1986; Nisbett, 1998). We will return to the nature-nurture debate over intelligence later in this chapter.

Neurotransmitters and Hormones

Another common biological factor examined in psychology is neurotransmitters. Neurotransmitters are chemicals in the brain that are responsible for the communication between brain and behavior. For example, the neurotransmitter dopamine plays a role in inhibiting emotions and behavior. Neurotransmitters are thought to be important in the development of several mental illnesses; for example, there is evidence to suggest that Schizophrenia may be related to high levels of dopamine. Antipsychotic medications decrease the level of dopamine in the brain, which has the effect of reducing some of the psychotic symptoms commonly seen in Schizophrenia; thus, these medications appear to work by lowering dopamine levels.

To date, there is limited research indicating cultural differences in neurotransmitter levels. Such research would be useful in determining whether differences in neurotransmitters affect the prevalence rate of disorders, symptoms, or medications that are effective for different groups. Because most medications are tested on European American males, information regarding side effects, most effective dosage, and other important factors may not generalize to other groups. For example, there is some evidence to suggest that the recommended dosage for antipsychotic drugs used to treat

Schizophrenia may be too high for Asian Americans (Ajir et al., 1997; Lin, Poland, Fleishaker, & Phillips, 1993).

Hormones are chemicals that are also important in regulating behavior. Whereas neurotransmitters primarily operate in the brain, hormones usually operate in the body. Hormones are important in regulating the fight-or-flight response; this is the response that occurs when you encounter a dangerous or seemingly dangerous experience, such as a car accident, a bear in the woods, or, for some people, an exam in psychology. In the fight-or-flight response, the hormone adrenaline is operating to prepare your body for action by causing your heart to race, your pupils to dilate, your sweat glands to activate, and so on.

Research suggests that hormones may account for differences in health across diverse populations (Schooler & Baum, 2000). It is possible that differences in neuroendocrine activity may affect one's stress response, such as the fight-or-flight response, which can have implications for one's risk for both physical and psychological disorders. Tischenkel et al. (1989) found that African Americans showed greater diastolic blood pressure (DBP) responses to behavioral challenge tests than European Americans, and African American women showed greater DBP responses than both African American men and European American women.

In addition, encountering prejudice may be both an acute and a chronic stressor for some minorities and women that may lead to an increased risk for physical and psychological problems (Allison, 1998). In fact, Clark, Anderson, Clark, and Williams (1999) suggest that even perceiving racism in interactions, whether or not the perception is correct, may cause physiological reactions such as increased heart rate and blood pressure that can lead to increased susceptibility to physical and psychological disorders. To illustrate: Denial of one's experience with racism could lead to physiological changes that put one at greater risk for hypertension, for example, by affecting prolonged activation of the sympathetic nervous system, which leads to higher resting systolic blood pressure levels. Moreover, experience with racism will most likely be a chronic stressor for many minorities, and chronic stress may affect the functioning of one's immune system in such a way that increases one's susceptibility to disease.

This idea is consistent with much of the research in the area of stress and health. First, there is recognition that psychological and physical processes can lead to both psychological and physical problems, rather than viewing the mind and body as being separate. Second, the idea that experiences with both acute and chronic stress can create psychological and physical problems is integral to the field of stress and health. Finally, it is also well documented that denial of one's feelings has detrimental effects on both psychological problems and physical problems, such as high blood pressure. Although the idea that we can study the consequences of prejudice and discrimination through biological mechanisms is a fairly new concept, it is receiving increasing acceptance (Belcourt-Dittloff & Stewart, 2000; Ocampo, 2000).

Although most theories for how we respond to stress utilize the fight-or-flight response, more recent evidence suggests that this reaction may be more characteristic of the way males respond to stress (Taylor et al., 2000). Females are more likely to respond to stress with what has been labeled a "tend-and-befriend" response, in which they engage in nurturing behaviors and form alliances with other people. This response is consistent with the woman's role as caregiver and has adaptive value from an evolutionary perspective, in that her offspring will be more likely to survive in times of stress if her response is to tend to her children. We discuss evolutionary theory in more detail in the sociobiology section.

Sex hormones are also important in contributing to the different physical characteristics between males and females, such as hair, voice, and reproductive organs. Sex hormones such as testosterone are also thought to play an important role in aggression. Although males and females have both androgens and estrogens, the androgens are more prominent in males, and the estrogens are more prominent in females. Testosterone is a type of androgen that may be associated with aggression, possibly explaining why males are more aggressive than females (Julian & McHenry, 1989). However, some researchers have challenged the idea that males are more aggressive, suggesting that, whereas males may express their aggression in more direct and physical ways, females may be just as aggressive, although their aggression is expressed in more indirect and verbal ways (Harris, 1992). Furthermore, there is also evidence to suggest that the difference in aggressive behavior between males and females is a product of learning rather than hormones (Baron & Richardson, 1994). Males are socialized to be more aggressive than females; consequently, aggressive behavior is tolerated and reinforced in males, but it is discouraged and punished in females. Nevertheless, gender role expectations concerning aggression behavior may be changing. Recent data suggest that women's and men's aggression against opposite-gender partners is approximately equal (Archer, 2000; Magdol, Moffitt, Caspi, & Silva, 1998). This may be a function of values in egalitarian societies in which punishment for men's aggression against women is more severe than punishment for women's aggression against men (Archer, 2000).

Structure of the Brain

The structure of the brain is another biological factor that is thought to be responsible for many of the behaviors of interest to psychologists. There are parts of the brain that are important in the fight-or-flight response, such as the amygdala and the septum, which suggests that this response is innate. Structural abnormalities in the brain have been associated with certain mental disorders, such as Schizophrenia. Research suggests that Schizophrenia is associated with enlarged ventricles and other abnormal brain structures such as impaired blood flow to certain brain regions (Kim et al., 2000). Unfortunately, there has been limited research examining race differences in brain morphology and neuropsychological functioning in Schizophrenia, although more research is needed in this area (Lewine & Caudle, 1999).

Sex differences in brain structure have been used to explain differences in cognitive abilities between males and females. The most often cited sex difference involves *lateralization* of brain functioning. Lateralization refers to the fact that the left and right hemispheres of the brain control different types of cognitive activities. Typically, the left hemisphere is responsible for activities such as language and logical reasoning, and the right hemisphere is responsible for spatial skills and nonverbal reasoning. Males and females differ in lateralization: Males' cognitive processing tends to be more focused in the right hemisphere for visual-spatial skills, whereas females process visual-spatial information more equally, in both the left and right hemispheres. This difference in cognitive processing is often used to explain why males are superior at visual-spatial abilities (Bleier, 1986). Thus, some researchers have interpreted this finding to mean that females are innately inferior in visual-spatial processing because they must use their entire brain to understand something, whereas males need to use only their right hemisphere. An alternative explanation is that females have a more complete understanding of problems because they utilize both left and right hemispheres in a task, whereas males utilize their right hemisphere only. But because the majority of researchers have been male, interpretations of research findings usually reflect the assumption of male superiority.

Another structural difference often noted is that of brain size among ethnic groups. Rushton (1996) argues that on average, Asians have larger brains than

Europeans, who have larger brains than African Americans. Rushton argues that this difference in brain size is the basis of differences in IQ scores among the three groups, as well as many other characteristics such as sexual behavior, crime, and family stability. This research has caused considerable controversy. Researchers have criticized the methodology used to measure brain size (Peters, 1995) and have questioned the assumption that brain size is necessarily related to IQ (Kamin & Omari, 1998).

Sociobiology

Sociobiology is the study of the evolutionary basis of social behavior. Whereas genetics is aimed at explaining individual differences, sociobiology is aimed at explaining differences among groups of people. Because sociobiology is based on evolutionary theory, we will briefly review Darwin's (1958) theory of evolution and natural selection.

Many people associate the phrase "survival of the fittest" with Darwin's theory, although they sometimes misinterpret what this phrase means. It does not imply that species compete and the winners have the privilege of passing their genes on to the next generation. Instead, the "fight" occurs at the cellular level. Darwin believed that species gradually evolve in a way that optimizes their suitability to the environment. The ultimate goal of any species is to make sure that its genes are passed on to the next generation, thereby ensuring survival of the species. By chance, genetic mutations occur that sometimes give some species an advantage of surviving; for example, long necks in giraffes allow giraffes to reach food that other animals are not able to access. Not all genetic mutations lead to a survival advantage, but when they do, the organism's offspring are also more likely to survive because they, too, will have this characteristic. As long as this characteristic leads to a survival advantage, it will be passed on from generation to generation.

Sociobiology is often used to explain why people continue to engage in behaviors that no longer seem adaptive. Because biological evolution proceeds at a much slower pace than cultural evolution, it takes a long time for a change in genetic makeup to occur, but not a very long time for changes in culture to occur. It may take thousands of years for changes in the gene pool to take place, but cultural changes can occur in a matter of years. To illustrate: Behaviors such as rape are sometimes explained using sociobiology theory. It is often argued that the use of force in sexual behavior can be seen as being biologically adaptive in that it increases the chances of reproductive success (Ellis, 1991; Malamuth, 1996). As long as the behavior leads to the continued survival of the species, that behavior will be passed on to one's offspring, and rape is a behavior that accomplishes this goal. Clearly, rape would not be considered a viable option for passing on one's genetic makeup in our society today, yet the behavior persists. However, it has only been within the past 30 years or so that we have held a more sympathetic view of rape victims; historically, sexual aggression against women was tolerated. In the rare instances in which rape cases were brought to court, often the victims were the subjects of the trial, for questions regarding their promiscuity and implied consent were of more concern than was the perpetrator's behavior. In some situations, rape was even endorsed; for example, it was believed that a wife had a duty to pleasure her husband, and therefore husbands could not be accused of raping their wives. Thus, although the cultural change in our views about rape has occurred fairly recently, the biological changes are much slower to follow.

Sociobiologists often argue that many sex differences in characteristics such as aggressive behavior, interest in childrearing and domestic tasks, and spatial abilities are based on our evolutionary history as hunters and gatherers. Men's continued interest in hunting, despite the need not to do so, is also used as evidence for the discrepancy between cultural and biological evolution. Implicit in the hunter-gatherer argument is the assumption that the skills required for hunting and gathering are mutually exclusive and that men possess the skills necessary for hunting (e.g., physical strength) and women possess the skills necessary for gathering (e.g., better memory for specific locations). However, there is some evidence to suggest that this is not always the case. Goodman, Griffin, Estioko-Griffin, and Grove (1999) describe a hunting-and-gathering society in the Philippines in which mothers are also competent hunters. Such exceptions are important because evolutionary theory is presumably universal. Goodman and colleagues conclude that women's ability to hunt depends on features of the social and physical environment rather than a biological incompatibility between hunting and mothering.

Hunter-gatherer differences have also been used to explain the cross cultural differences in aggressive behavior between men and women such that men are more aggressive (DeVos & Hippler, 1969). Such cross-cultural evidence strengthens the evolutionary perspective because it demonstrates that these behaviors are not affected by different value systems. However, Lepowsky (1999) also cites an exception to the men-are-more-aggressive norm. Among the Vanatinai, a hunting-and-gathering society of New Guinea, violence in general is very rare. In addition, relationships between men and women are fairly egalitarian and there is no formal social hierarchy among group members. Lepowsky argues that these differences in social structure contribute to the low levels of violence against women and between groups. Even in the United States, there are cultures (such as among the Quakers) in which aggression is considered inappropriate (A. Fiske, Kitayama, Markus, & Nisbett, 1998).

Feminists usually disagree with the evolutionary explanation of sex differences because it discounts the impact of social factors that also contribute to our behavior. For example, in most cultures, boys are encouraged to engage in more physical activity, and such physical activity often includes aggression. Boys' greater participation in sports is an example of this; although females are increasingly participating in sports, it is still rare for sports such as football to have a girls'/women's team. There is also a substantial body of literature supporting evidence that aggression may result from social, personal, and environmental causes (Baron & Richardson, 1994).

One of the most controversial areas in which sociobiology is applied is in explaining mating strategies. Darwin's theory is based on the assumption of random mating, but in reality, people rarely randomly choose their partners; they usually look for certain characteristics in the other person that they find desirable. *Assortative mating* reflects the idea that people actively choose their mates. Assortative mating can be affected by many factors. For instance, genetic similarity theory argues that the purpose of assortative mating is to assure the survival of one's own specific genes (Rushton, 1989); thus, people are attracted to those with similar genetic makeup. Genetic similarity theory may explain why people are often attracted to someone of the same ethnicity.

Assortative mating can be used to explain why males and females may adopt different mating strategies (A. Buss, 1989). Two of the common attraction patterns of interest to sociobiologists are that women tend to choose men who are high in status and financially secure, and men tend to choose women who are young and attractive (Sprecher, Sullivan, & Hatfield, 1994). According to evolutionary theory, this attraction pattern is also associated with the survival of the species. Women and men must choose different strategies in mating because they differ in terms of their survival strategies. For women, it is more advantageous to be attracted to older and financially secure men because a female can bear only one offspring at a time (with the exception of twins and other multiple births). Thus, her best strategy for ensuring survival of their offspring is to ensure that each child has the best chance of survival; one way of ensuring this is to find a male who is stable and will be able to provide for her children. Men choose women who are young and attractive because men are unable to bear offspring themselves; consequently, their best strategy for ensuring the survival of their offspring is to be certain that the females they impregnate will be able to bear children. Men tend to find women in their early to mid-twenties the most attractive, and this is the age at which women are at the height of their childbearing years.

Evolutionary theory is also used to explain many other behaviors related to mating and offspring, such as why men compete with one another over women, why men are more concerned about fidelity than women are, why partners are unfaithful to one another, and why women are more suitable for child rearing. This theory is appealing in its comprehensiveness and its depth; it can explain so many different aspects of human behavior, and biological factors cannot be reduced to any other causal factor. However, this perspective is also controversial because it implies that the parts of human nature that we find undesirable (aggressiveness, infidelity, superficiality in relationships) are inevitable. Feminists disagree with these explanations of mating strategies for the same reasons they disagree with biological explanations for sex differences: Such explanations maintain the status quo and minimize the importance of social factors. Moreover, evolutionary theory is criticized for implying that we have no free will. In some ways, evolutionary theory is criticized for the same reasons that Freud's theory is criticized: It is sexist, reductive, biological, and presents a negative view of human nature.

The current thin ideal of beauty for women is one example of attraction that is not accounted for by evolutionary theory. Many of the models and actresses seen in the media are much thinner than the average woman, and the preponderance of diet articles in magazines and products designed to promote weight loss suggests that women want to be thinner. Although men, too, are becoming more concerned about their weight, the pressure to be thin is much greater for women, as evidenced by the fact that 90 percent of people with eating disorders are women (APA, 1994). This thin ideal of beauty is in contrast to what evolutionary theory would predict to be desirable because the boylike figure of many of the models and actresses that results from being underweight is not ideal for bearing children. In fact, being underweight can interfere with a woman's ability to become pregnant.

Barber (1998) argues that the thin ideal of beauty may be better accounted for by sociocultural than biological factors. He found evidence to suggest that the amount of body fat that is desirable in a culture is inversely correlated with the value of women's work, the degree of political power that women have, and the amount of control they have over economic resources. For women who have little economic wealth, who do not work outside the home, and who do not have political power, body fat energy may be advantageous because it is more feminine; consequently, women who are more curvaceous are more likely to attract a mate and bear offspring, as evolutionary theory predicts. In addition, the ability to store body fat is advantageous in times when food may not be plentiful because it increases the likelihood of survival. For women who are career-oriented, body fat may be a disadvantage because highly feminized women may be seen as being less competent. In addition, because women who work outside the home are not dependent on a husband for economic resources, it is not as necessary for them to have more body fat for survival and to attract a mate.

The idea that mate selection is based more on social roles than on evolved mechanisms is referred to as social structural theory (Eagly & Wood, 1999). Proponents of this view argue that men have held positions of power and women have attended to domestic tasks in part due to physical sex differences, such as females' ability to bear and nurse children and males' greater physical strength, although these characteristics are less important in postindustrial societies. In addition, positions of power lead to behavior that is more often associated with men, such as dominance and assertiveness, whereas lower positions lead to more submissive behavior. Thus, the fact that women are likely to engage in child rearing behavior and men are more likely to provide financial support for the family is more a function of the social roles that have evolved rather than of genetic evolution. Similarly, Silverstein and Phares (1996) argue that the traditional family structure is a by-product of industrialization, which forced fathers to spend more time away from the family; as a result, mothering became more central to the lives of children than it had been previously. This position, however, is not without its critics (Friedman, Bleske, & Scheyd, 2000; Kendrick & Li, 2000; Kleyman, 2000).

The sociobiological perspective is also criticized for promoting racist ideology. Research citing biological differences in IQ, personality, and other characteristics among different groups of people are often attributed to evolutionary theory. These biological differences are interpreted to suggest that some groups of people are more highly developed than others. Rushton

(1996) argues that people of Asian, European, and African ancestry differ in their reproductive strategies: Mongoloids emphasize higher levels of parental investment than do Caucasoids, who are more committed to parental investment than are Negroids. As mentioned earlier, this research has been criticized on many grounds, including Rushton's definition of race, methodologies used in determining differences in brain size, questionable evidence that these differences are biologically based, and the presumed objectivity of the research.

Sociobiological theories have also been used by some gay rights activists to argue that homosexuality is biologically determined rather than immoral; consequently, homosexuals should not be discriminated against (Brookey, 2000). This conclusion follows from the assumption that biologically determined behavior cannot be changed. If biology is destiny, and homosexuality is biologically determined, then one cannot choose to be gay, nor can one choose to be heterosexual. However, Brookey argues that biological theories about homosexuality may not be beneficial to the gay rights movement and are vulnerable to political manipulation.

A. Fiske et al. (1998) argue that the best way to resolve the issues of biological universals on the one hand and the idea that culture affects our behavior on the other hand is to recognize that biology and culture both influence one another. Just as psychologists increasingly recognize that dualistic concepts such as the mind-body split may be inappropriate in understanding behavior, they must also accept the idea that biological and cultural theories are not mutually exclusive, for the purpose of evolution is to make the organism fit its environment. Because what is adaptive in one culture may not be adaptive in another, universals in human behavior may not always be found. Thus, evolutionary theory cannot be understood without understanding the context of human behavior that is culture. Culture, like biology, is capable of affecting our behavior in ways of which we are not always conscious. Although this position makes logical sense and can account for the supportive body of literature in both areas, it is not a view held by all researchers.

Biological Bases of Behavior

Of all the hotly debated topics in the field of psychology, the nature-nurture debate is most certainly one of the top contenders. In almost any field of psychology, the conclusion of most research is usually that both biology and environment contribute to behavior, often in about equal proportions. However, our research methods are not precise enough yet to pinpoint exactly which factors are due to biology and which are due to environment. Nevertheless, researchers continue to fuel this debate, arguing that one side is more important than the other.

Perhaps one reason that scientists often seem unscientific in their alliance to a particular side of the nature-nurture debate is that this debate often goes beyond the realm of scientific investigation. Those who are in favor of environmental explanations of behavior view biological evidence as a threat to our free will and an attempt to maintain the status quo. Biological explanations of behavior have been used as evidence that male European Americans are superior, thereby justifying their privileged place in society. In contrast, proponents of the biological perspective argue that mental illnesses such as depression, schizophrenia, and alcoholism have benefited greatly from an increased understanding of their biological causes. Prior to the evidence that these disorders were biologically based, society viewed the victims of these disorders as being weak-willed, difficult, and immoral, and treatment for the disorders was difficult and sometimes nonexistent. Similarly, gays and lesbians were viewed as immoral people who chose to be attracted to members of their own sex.

One of the reasons the nature-nurture debate often leads to political debates is because it is assumed that what is biological cannot be changed, but what is environmental can be. However, biology is not necessarily destiny, and what is learned in our environment is not always easily unlearned (Angoff, 1988). To illustrate, let us consider Bipolar Disorder and Schizophrenia, two of the disorders that appear to have a strong biological basis. In the past, someone with Bipolar Disorder or Schizophrenia would likely have been hospitalized for life. However, with the advent of medications that can be used to treat these disorders, people with Bipolar Disorder and Schizophrenia are better able to respond to other forms of treatment such as psychotherapy and can at times live independently or with minimal support. Thus, the improved treatment of people with these biologically based disorders is a clear example that biology is not always destiny.

It is also the case that what is learned is not so easily unlearned. It has been more than 30 years since the beginning of the civil rights movement, the women's movement, and the gay rights movement. Much has been done to educate people about the value of diversity and the importance of treating people who are different from ourselves as equal rather than lesser.

Nevertheless, acts of prejudice, though less blatant, still abound in our culture; examples of this fact are abundant in the news, such as the continued existence of the KKK and the recent controversy over homosexuality in the Boy Scouts and in the military.

Given that important political implications are often drawn from the nature-nurture debate, it is worth illustrating how the research examining nature-nurture questions is often interpreted (and misinterpreted). In the following section, we review the research on biological versus environmental bases of intelligence.

Intelligence

Is intelligence inherited or is it learned? The answer to this question has important implications for differences among ethnic groups. Historically, the widely accepted belief was that European Americans were innately intellectually superior to other ethnic groups. In a highly controversial article, Arthur Jensen (1969) cited scientific evidence indicating that African Americans are less intelligent than European Americans and that this difference is due to biological factors. More recently, Herrnstein and Murray (1994) made similar claims about the genetic superiority of European Americans in their controversial book *The Bell Curve*. The authors also conclude that because these differences are innate, society should stop trying to eradicate differences among ethnic groups.

Although most people think of intelligence as being biologically determined, there is evidence to support the influence of environmental factors on intelligence. One of the most important environmental factors is providing a stimulating environment. Research on animals has demonstrated that it is possible to breed "maze-bright" and "maze-dull" rats, which supports the belief the intelligence is inherited (Cooper & Zubek, 1958). However, when maze-dull rats are placed in a stimulating environment with toys and other objects and maze-bright rats placed in plain surroundings, differences in ability to get through the maze disappear. This finding suggests that, although intelligence may be inherited, it is also affected by environmental factors such as providing an enriched environment.

This finding holds true for people, too: When children with low IQ scores are provided with an enriched environment, their cognitive performance increases (Baumrind, 1993; Connolly, 1978; Marfo & Kysela, 1985). The idea that an enriched environment can increase a person's level of intelligence has been the basis for the development of Head Start programs. Head Start programs are designed to give preschoolers from low-income families a head start in those abilities they will need in school. Outcome research on such programs find short-term improvements on IQ tests, but the effects on intelligence do not seem to be long-lasting. However, children still benefit from the program in other ways: They tend to stay in school longer, they are less likely to drop out of school, and they are more likely to continue their education after high school (Zigler, 1994; Zigler & Styfco, 1994).

Another cultural difference in cognitive abilities that receives much attention is that Asian Americans tend to have better academic performance than European Americans (Fuligni, 1997; Hsia & Peng, 1998). As with other differences among minority groups, this difference is often interpreted as evidence that Asians are innately superior to European Americans in math. However, there is research evidence to suggest that this difference may reflect differences in school systems and attitudes toward math. For example, European Americans do not believe that studying will improve their ability in math because they believe that mathematical abilities are biologically determined (Chen & Stevenson, 1995). In contrast, Asian Americans believe that studying is very important. Asian American parents and children place a high value on education and, more than other groups, fear that school failure will lead to negative consequences (Fuligni, 1997; Steinberg, Dornbusch, & Brown, 1992). Asian American students do 40 to 50 percent more homework than other students from elementary school on (Steinberg et al., 1992). These factors contribute to a better learning environment, which may lead to a better education for Asian American students. Asian American academic achievement is discussed further in Chapter Six.

Conclusion

As we have seen, the field of psychology is fraught with heated debates about whether differences in psychology are biologically or environmentally based. This argument often has political and social ramifications because biological differences are often interpreted as evidence that certain people are innately inferior to other groups of people, and differences in social standings are therefore justified. Because the idea that biological differences may exist among people often leads to arguments that maintain the status quo, the trend in psychology has been to downplay the biological evidence of differences. This is unfortunate because such an attitude reinforces the notion that biological differences are undesirable and unchangeable. Clearly, there are biological differences among groups of people: African Americans do have darker skin than European Americans; males and females differ in anatomy. However, these differences are not what lead to prejudice and discrimination. The real problem is not that differences exist, but that people use these differences to make unsubstantiated claims about certain groups of people, such as that European Americans should be in positions of power, or that women are not suitable for certain jobs. Thus, our goal should not be to prove that differences do not exist among people, but rather that those differences are not an excuse for prejudice and discrimination.

SOCIAL PSYCHOLOGY

Social psychology is the scientific study of how we think about, influence, and relate to one another. Whereas sociobiology assumes that behavior is rooted in biological processes, social psychology examines societal and personality influences on behavior. In fact, the field of social psychology arose in part as a reaction to sociobiological theories (Jones, 1997). Ironically, it has only been within recent years that social psychology has examined the impact of cultural factors on behavior, although cultural factors are clearly social in nature. More often, the study of social factors has involved social influence on individual behavior (A. Fiske et al., 1998). In the following sections, we review some of the areas of social psychology that are particularly relevant to multicultural psychology: attribution, prejudice, love and aggression, and social influence.

Attribution

We are constantly making interpretations about why people behave as they do, as well as why we do the things that we do. For example, if a friend tells you that he did not pass the last psychology exam, you may attribute his failure to a lack of studying or to an unfair professor. The kinds of judgment that we make about behavior are fairly predictable, and the study of these judgments is the focus of *attribution theory* (Heider, 1958).

There are two types of attributions we can make: internal and external. Internal attributions are inferences about a person's behavior that are due to factors within the person. Often, these factors are personality characteristics, such as when we assume that someone is not talking at a party because she is shy. External attributions are inferences about a person's behavior that are due to external factors such as the weather, peer pressure, or luck; for example, you may attribute your bad mood to a rainy day.

Generally speaking, making attributions helps us to make sense of other people's behavior. However, we are often subject to certain types of bias in making attributions. One such bias is the *fundamental attribution error:* When making judgments about someone else's behavior, we tend to attribute behavior to causes within the person (Ross & Nisbett, 1991). For example, if you say hello to someone and the person does not say hello in return, you may attribute that person's behavior to rudeness, an internal factor, rather than to the fact that the person did not see you, an external factor.

Psychology researchers are often criticized for committing the fundamental attribution error in that they tend to find the source of behavior within the person rather than in the situation. For instance, to explain why some women stay in abusive relationships, researchers looked for personality characteristics associated with a battered woman syndrome rather than attributing their behavior to external factors such as lack of economic independence or fear of retaliation by the husband. Similarly, in attempting to understand why African Americans are overrepresented in the lower SES groups, some people may attribute their behavior to internal factors such as laziness or lack of ambition rather than to external factors such as the effects of prejudice and discrimination.

Although the fundamental attribution error has been assumed to be a universal bias, more recent research suggests that it may actually be specific to individualistic cultures (A. Fiske et al., 1998). Several studies have found that in collectivist cultures, people are more likely to attribute someone's behavior to situational factors rather than to personality characteristics. Recall that individualistic cultures focus on the individual; as a result, it makes sense that European Americans would be more likely to have a bias in which they assume that behavior is produced by factors within the person. In fact, such a view is implicit in most of our theories of personality, as we will see in Chapter Four. Collectivist cultures, on the other hand, place greater emphasis on the group rather than the individual. People in collectivist cultures do not expect people to be consistent in their behavior; different behaviors may be necessary, depending on what the situation calls for. Consequently, it makes sense that people from collectivist cultures would be more sensitive to contextual cues.

Another common error in judgment is the *self-serving bias* (Schlenker, Weigold, & Hallam, 1990), the tendency to attribute personal failure to external factors and personal success to internal factors. For example, both students (Davis & Stephan, 1980) and teachers (Arkin, Cooper, & Kolditz, 1980) are more likely to attribute students' good grades to internal factors and poor grades to external factors. A student may attribute her A to being intelligent, whereas the teacher may attribute the student's A to the fact that he is a good teacher. In contrast, a student may attribute her D to external factors such as having an unfair professor, and the teacher may attribute the student's poor grade to having a poor student. We engage in the self-serving bias because we are motivated to present ourselves in a positive light; taking responsibility for our successes and disavowing our failures allows us to maintain our self-esteem.

As with the fundamental attribution error, the self-serving bias does not hold true for all people. For example, people who are depressed appear to have the opposite pattern of attributions: They attribute their successes to external factors and attribute their failures to internal factors. Consequently, people who are depressed tend to have low self-esteem. The self-serving bias has also not been found in cross-cultural studies that focus on Asian research participants. In these studies, Asian participants were more likely to attribute their successes to external factors such as luck and their failures to internal factors such as a lack of effort (Kitayama & Markus, 1995). This pattern results because of a bias toward self-effacement, which is more likely to maintain one's self-esteem in collectivist cultures, in which the accomplishments of the individual are minimized. This strategy for maintaining self-esteem is often used by women, whose belief system can also be characterized as collectivist in nature in that they value relationships, put other people's needs before their own, and define themselves in terms of their connectedness to others. For example, women often bond with one another by making derogatory comments about their own appearance and praising the appearance of others. If a woman were to announce that she was absolutely satisfied with her weight during a conversation in which other women were commiserating over how they wish they could lose 10 pounds, she would probably disrupt the harmony of the group. Thus, self-effacement is a useful mechanism for maintaining self-esteem for women as well.

In addition to the self-serving bias, there are other social psychological processes that appear to maintain self-esteem in Western cultures but are not found in collectivist cultures. For example, having insufficient justification for performing an unpleasant behavior often produces discomfort (dissonance) that leads people to believe that the task was in fact enjoyable (Festinger, 1957). Similarly, when people experience dissonance because they possess two incongruent beliefs and/or behaviors, they are motivated to change one of the beliefs/behaviors to be more consistent. These tendencies reflect a need to view behavior as being derived from internal factors such as preferences, intentions, and reasons and the need to be consistent in one's behavior. Individuals from collectivist cultures do not demonstrate these tendencies because self-esteem is not about behaving consistently or intrinsic motivations; they are willing to sacrifice consistency to maintain a sense of harmony with others. It may even be perceived as selfish to act according to one's own desires or to express one's attitudes if they make other people uncomfortable (A. Fiske et al., 1998).

Another common error in judgment that people make is the *just world theory,* an attribution error based on the assumption that people get what they deserve (Lerner, 1980). In other words, bad things happen to bad people, good things happen to good people. This bias is apparent when people blame a rape victim for her victimization because of the way she is dressed or because she is a "bad" girl. These types of causal attribution are referred to as rape myths (Burt, 1980). Because of the feminist movement, attributions for rape more recently have focused on external factors, such as living in a society in which rape is condoned. Another example of the just world theory is the blaming of AIDS victims for contracting their illness, whether it is from being gay, using drugs, or being promiscuous.

The just world theory occurs because it helps us to preserve the belief that the world is an orderly place and we can remain safe if we just do the right thing. It follows from this assumption that if something bad happens to someone, he or she must have done something to deserve it. Unfortunately, this type of thinking has negative consequences: It often leads to blaming the victim and a lack of empathy for those who are suffering. When the just world theory is used to explain why groups of people suffer, such thinking may lead to prejudice. An example of this type of thinking is implicit in anti-Semitism, in which people may blame Jews for their own misfortune because they believe that the Jews are responsible for the crucifixion of Jesus Christ.

Prejudice

Prejudice is a kind of attitude, usually a negative attitude toward a particular group of people. Prejudice occurs when an interpersonal encounter between two individuals turns into an intergroup encounter (Jones, 1997). The literal meaning of prejudice is prejudgment, and prejudgments about others are often a basis of prejudice. Prejudice not only includes our beliefs about others, but also involves emotions and behavior.

Prejudice involves beliefs or stereotypes about other people. Examples of common stereotypes are that women are emotional, men always want sex, African Americans are good at sports, and Asians excel in math and science. A stereotype is a type of *schema*. Schemas are heuristics that allow us to organize information more quickly. For example, we have a schema for male and female; although individual schemas may vary, a typical schema for a female may include a high-pitched voice, breasts, and long hair, and a schema for a male may include a low-pitched voice, facial hair, and a penis. Schemas help us to save time in processing information. However, when we overutilize schemas as a way of understanding someone, as is often the case with stereotypes, we may misunderstand the person's actual characteristics.

There are several problems with the use of stereotypes as a guide for understanding others (Jones, 1997). First, stereotypes are often factually incorrect. All members of a group do not share the same characteristics, and stereotyping underestimates the actual amount of variability in a stereotyped group. Second, stereotypes are resistant to contradictory information. Counter-stereotypic information may be regarded as an exception to the rule that can be disregarded. For example, although the presentation of competent African American children reduced stereotyping in most European American children, this information actually increased the amount of stereotyping among highly prejudiced children (Bigler & Liben, 1993). Third, stereotypes are typically ethnocentric, utilizing ingroup standards (Jones, 1997). Any departure from these standards is regarded as deviant. Fourth, stereotypes can lead to a self-fulfilling prophecy in which we encourage the appearance of the behaviors that will reinforce our stereotype. For example, if a teacher believes that African American students are not intelligent, she may call on African American students less and put less effort into helping them improve their grades, which may consequently lead to poor academic achievement. Studies have demonstrated that teachers' expectations can, indeed, become a self-fulfilling prophecy (Brophy, 1986; Rosenthal & Jacobson, 1966). Finally, and perhaps most important, stereotypes exert control over the powerless by forcing them to conform to a particular image. S. Fiske (1995) argues that because stereotypes are about power, the majority group is rarely stereotyped; those who are powerless must pay close attention to the powerful to predict their behavior, and the superficial information gained from a stereotype cannot serve this purpose. Even when minority groups have stereotypes of the majority group, it is more an irritation than a threat because they have no power to enforce the stereotype.

Targets of stereotypes may also behave in ways that fulfill stereotypes. For example, anxiety about negative stereotypes of their group may interfere with the academic performance of ethnic minority students, whether they believe the stereotypes or not. This phenomenon is known as *stereotype threat* (J. Aronson, Quinn, & Spencer, 1998; Steele, 1997); it is further discussed in Chapter Four. In addition, being rejected by the dominant group as a result of prejudice has a direct and negative effect on well-being (Branscombe, Schmitt, & Harvey, 1999; Crocker & Lawrence, 1999).

Prejudice also involves emotions. These emotions are usually negative, such as fear, anger, and envy. Negative emotions are often apparent in hate crimes against people of a different race or sexual orientation. Today, openly displaying one's negative emotions about groups of people is not as acceptable as it once was, as evidenced in John Rocker's case. John Rocker is a pitcher for the Atlanta Braves who made negative remarks about minority groups and quickly became very unpopular to most Americans as a result. Although Rocker's expressions might be regarded as extreme, expressions of prejudice are not uncommon in everyday life. In a study involving African American students at Pennsylvania State University, nearly 90 percent had heard disparaging remarks about African Americans, and 59 percent had been targets of remarks during the prior week (D'Augelli & Hersheberger, 1993). Swim, Cohen, and Hyers (1998) also found that it was fairly common for African Americans and women to report being the target of racist and sexist behaviors. Only 11 percent of African Americans surveyed reported that they had never heard disparaging remarks about African Americans on campus. Seventy-one percent of the women surveyed reported experiences in which they were treated in a sexist manner, whereas only 27 percent of men reported sexist experiences.

Negative emotions about other groups of people also appear in covert forms, sometimes referred to as *symbolic racism* (Sears, 1988), which reflects racism based on moral abstractions concerning minorities as a threat to the American way. Symbolic racism is often expressed in more subtle ways, such as opposing Affirmative Action because one feels that African Americans already have equal opportunities for employment (Jacobson, 1985). Symbolic racism has also been used to explain other forms of prejudice, including negative attitudes toward women (Swim, Aikin, Hall, & Hunter, 1995) and the obese (Crandall, 1994).

Minority group members can also have negative feelings toward one another, a situation that is sometimes referred to as horizontal hostility (White & Langer, 1999). For example, African Americans may feel that light-skinned or biracial individuals are not Black enough; gays and lesbians may not wish to include bisexuals as part of their group; the deaf community may not consider individuals who use oral English rather than American Sign Language deaf enough; conservative Jews may have negative feelings toward reform Jews. White and Langer argue that horizontal hostility occurs because more mainstream members are perceived as a threat to the group's distinctiveness, and thus inclusion of such members may weaken the position of the group. In this respect, minority groups take a stance similar to that of exclusive country clubs: You can't let just anyone join.

Although prejudice usually involves negative emotions such as anger, fear, and envy, it can also involve positive emotions, such as the belief that women need to be protected and cared for by men. Glick and Fiske (2001) have referred to these attitudes toward women as benevolent sexism. These attitudes can be distinguished from what they call benevolent sexism, which includes men's negative attitudes toward women who present a threat, such as feminists, career women, or women as seductresses. They argue, however, that even stereotypes that are based on positive emotions can still lead to prejudice and discrimination. In the case of benevolent sexism, these views also contribute to unequal status between men and women in that women must rely on men for survival. Furthermore, they argue that women in sexist societies tend to agree with statements denoting benevolent sexism, perhaps as a way to protect themselves from the potential of hostile backlash on the part of men. The same criticisms may apply to positive stereotypes of minority groups, such as with Asian Americans and Jews. For example, if these groups are perceived as being successful, then they may not appear to be victims of prejudice and discrimination and may not appear to warrant the benefits of programs such as Affirmative Action.

Finally, prejudice involves discrimination, and this is the area in which prejudice is the most detrimental. Examples of discrimination include not hiring people or not allowing people to live in your neighborhood because they are African American or assaulting someone because he is gay. There can also be more subtle forms of discrimination, such as not allowing those under a certain height to become a police officer, or not hiring someone with a low IQ. In the first scenario, such a restriction may rule out women more often than men without seeming to discriminate against women. In the latter scenario, this screening process would lead to fewer ethnic minorities being hired because ethnic minorities obtain lower scores on most IQ tests, as we discussed earlier.

Why does prejudice occur? Several theories have been proposed. One theory argues that prejudice results from the social inequalities among groups of people (Allport, 1954). When some people have money, power, and prestige and others do not, those who are privileged may try to justify why things are distributed so unequally. Thus, they may conclude that those who have little deserve little because they do not work as hard (a good example of the just world theory). As mentioned earlier, such statements can become a self-fulfilling prophecy: If you tell people they are not worthwhile, they may begin to believe it. Those in power may also act in a way to help these sentiments become a self-fulfilling prophecy. For example, employers may not promote a woman because they expect her to quit her job once she marries and starts a family; consequently, few women attain positions of power in their jobs, a phenomenon often referred to as the glass ceiling.

Prejudice may also be a function of the ingroup bias. Regardless of what the basis is for grouping people, whether it is gender, ethnicity, sexual preference, or religious beliefs, we tend to favor members of our own group over members of the outgroup. Even when individuals are randomly split into groups, the ingroup bias occurs (Sherif, Harvey, White, Hood, & Sherif, 1961). Consequently, we may become biased against those who are different from ourselves. Khmelkov and Hallinan (1999) argue that many of the organizational practices in schools encourage prejudice; these include curriculum tracking, ability grouping, ESL programs, and extracurricular activities. For example, ESL programs are usually separated from the rest of the school and consist of primarily minority students. In contrast, sports that require expensive equipment such as golf and tennis consist primarily of European American students. Ingroup bias can be magnified by situational factors, such as encouraging competition among groups, as Sherif demonstrated when he randomly split boys at camp into separate groups who then competed against one another in several activities. (Conversely, prejudice can also be decreased by encouraging cooperation between group members, as we will see.)

Another explanation for prejudice and discrimination is that these may be by-products of *scapegoating*. Scapegoating refers to the tendency to blame others for our problems. Like the self-serving bias, scapegoating also helps to boost our self-esteem because it allows us to avoid taking responsibility for our problems and gives us another outlet for our distress. Scapegoating is similar to the psychodynamic concept of displacement, in which one expresses his or her anger toward a safer target. For example, people may blame a suffering economy on the influx of immigrants as a way to avoid taking responsibility for the problem. Family therapy also focuses on scapegoating in that the family member who presents with the disorder, or the symptom bearer, becomes the embodiment of everything that is wrong in the family. In other words, one family member becomes the embodiment of everything that is wrong in the family. If, for example, the daughter of the family develops an eating disorder, then the family can focus their energy on helping her rather than on the marital problems that are also disrupting the family. Alice Walker, the well-known African American writer, uses the concept of scapegoating to explain the abuse of African American women by African American men. Through her writing, she often conveys the sentiment that African American men are abusive to African American women as a way to take out their frustration over their mistreatment by European Americans. Thus, African American women serve as scapegoats because it would be dangerous for African American men to express their anger toward the appropriate target.

Another theory suggests that prejudice is a product of our cognitive processes. We have discussed this perspective in demonstrating how stereotypes are a type of schema about particular groups of people, and the formation of schemas is a type of cognitive process. Even when stereotypes are correct (and many of them are not), they are similar to the mean of a particular group. As we discussed in Chapter Two, averages are not always useful when attempting to understand a particular individual because some people will not fit this value. Consequently, even when some stereotypes may have a grain of truth to them, they often lead to biases in our perceptions of others. Categorization can also bias our interpretations because we may assume that other groups of people are more similar than our own. People tend to be very sensitive to differences within their own group, but they tend to be less sensitive to differences outside their group—another ramification of the ingroup bias. For example, European Americans may feel that all Asians look alike but that they themselves are very diverse in their appearance.

Other cognitive abilities can also contribute to prejudice. Cognitive abilities such as perspective taking, a need for cognition, attributional complexity, perceiving similarities between groups, and perceiving differences within the same group make it less likely that a person will rely on stereotypes to understand others (Levy, 1999). Intolerance of ambiguity, concrete thinking, and inability to use logical reasoning, on the other hand, contribute to prejudice (Harding, Proshansky, Kutner, & Ghein, 1969).

Social and personality factors can also contribute to prejudice. Personality characteristics such as authoritarianism (e.g., conventionalism, aggression toward social deviants, and belief in submission to authority figures), social dominance (needing to believe one's own group is superior), and the Protestant work ethic (believing that people can pull themselves up by their bootstraps) can foster prejudice (Levy, 1999). In addition, people who suffer from narcissistic personality disorders may subject others to racism because of their grandiosity, insecurity, and lack of empathy (C. Bell, 1978).

Situational factors can also contribute to prejudice. We have already discussed the way in which factors such as homogeneous grouping of individuals, competition, and status differences can foster prejudiced beliefs. In addition to these situational factors, the media can also play a role in prejudice. Graves (1999) suggests that television is a major socializing factor, particularly in children. Given that on average children watch three hours of television a day and that television provides a source of vicarious experience for race relations, particularly for individuals who do not have exposure to diverse groups, television can be an important factor in contributing to prejudice. Graves indicates that there are very few portrayals of minorities on television and almost no portrayals of certain minority groups, such as Latinos and American Indians. In addition, when minorities are shown, they are usually portrayed in a stereotypical way. For example, they are likely to be criminals or crime victims, they are often in low-status occupational roles, and their characters are fairly superficial. Moreover, interactions among members of different races is limited. Graves argues that these limited portrayals of minority groups convey the groups' lack of power to children.

Several methods have been proposed for reducing prejudice and discrimination. Allport (1954) recognized that prejudice is caused by many factors and therefore cannot be eliminated by focusing on only one facet of the problem. He also believed that laws prohibiting discrimination, such as Affirmative Action, can be effective even before changes in attitudes have taken place.

Another method for reducing prejudice is based on the contact hypothesis, which suggests that contact with members of different groups will decrease stereotypes of groups. The contact hypothesis is the basis for school desegregation. Unfortunately, research on desegregation suggests that contact alone is not sufficient to reduce prejudice (Stephan, 1987). In fact, sometimes contact alone can lead to increased conflict rather than social harmony (Amir, 1994). Contact with other groups can improve racial attitudes under some conditions: (1) when there is prolonged, personal contact between group members; (2) when group members have equal status; and (3) when group members must work cooperatively against an external threat. The last finding was one of the conclusions of Sherif et al.'s (1961) study, in which competition produced animosity between two groups of boys; however, when both groups were introduced to a third group that served as the common enemy, they were able to work cooperatively to achieve superordinate goals.

The movie *Remember the Titans* is a good example of how these factors can contribute to more positive intergroup relations. *Titans* is based on a true story in which Black students were being integrated into a predominantly White high school in Virginia. The movie focuses primarily on the relationships between Black and White members of the school's football team (equal-status members). Initially, members self-segregate and associate only with members of the same ethnicity, as is often the case in school settings (Khmelkov & Hallinan, 1999). However, the Black football coach (played by Denzel Washington) takes the players on a retreat during which they are forced to room with members of the outgroup. In addition, they are instructed to find out personal information about one another (prolonged, personal contact). Finally, the racially mixed football team must compete against other schools who are still segregated and band together to defeat their competitors (working cooperatively against an external threat).

Cooperative learning techniques also appear to reduce prejudice (Slavin & Cooper, 1999). These techniques often are employed in academic settings and usually involve students working collaboratively in multiracial groups. In these groups, competition among individual group members is discouraged and all members are encouraged to make contributions to the group. Overall, research on cooperative learning suggests that these techniques improve both intergroup relations and academic performance. Moreover, students in a cooperative learning environment are more likely to form strong friendships with one another rather than superficial relationships.

Changing the situational factors that contribute to prejudice may also be necessary. For example, school systems could encourage a more diverse composition of students by supporting heterogeneous groupings of students in the classroom (Khmelkov & Hallinan, 1999). Teachers could be better trained in utilizing cooperative learning techniques (Slavin & Cooper, 1999). Television programmers could be encouraged to portray a greater number of ethnic minority characters in diverse roles and who have well-developed characters. In addition, television programs can be specifically designed for children to educate them on the value of diversity (Graves, 1999).

Finally, prejudice can also be reduced by encouraging empathy toward others (Stephan & Finlay, 1999). Prejudice often occurs when individuals neglect to take the other person's perspective; consequently, encouraging people to pay closer attention to others can be useful in reducing prejudice (S. Fiske, 1995). Sometimes, this can be accomplished simply by reminding people of their sense of responsibility, because this appeals to one's self-concept of being fair-minded. Stephan and Finlay indicate that teaching empathy skills is often used in training therapists and medical students, and it is also a component of many multicultural programs. Empathy training is also used in the treatment of sex offenders and people with antisocial tendencies, and as a way of resolving conflicts between groups of people. Techniques such as role playing can be used to facilitate the process of perspective taking. In addition, Levy (1999) recommends teaching people other cognitive skills such as perceiving similarities between groups and differences within the same group, insight training, and capitalizing on cognitive dissonance by creating positive interactions with minority members (which may cause persons to change their beliefs/stereotypes to be consistent).

Love and Aggression

Love and aggression are influenced by many factors, including personality, individual experiences, and learning history. Social psychologists, however, focus on the impact of the social context on the expression of love and aggression. We review the components of both concepts and discuss important differences in the expression of love and aggression from a multicultural perspective.

Hatfield (1988) distinguishes between two types of love: passionate love and compassionate love. Passionate love often involves intense emotions and sexual attraction; compassionate love involves feelings of warmth, trust, and respect. Passionate love often characterizes the way we feel about someone at the beginning of a romantic relationship; compassionate love better characterizes the way we feel toward a good friend. Sometimes our feelings of love for a person change over time; often, relationships that begin with passionate love evolve into compassionate love after years of being with the person.

One of the reasons that passionate love is particularly important in our culture is that we believe that marriage should be based in part on passionate love for the other person. This expectation may help to explain why 50 percent of marriages in the United States end in divorce: If we are no longer feeling passionate love for our partner, we may become dissatisfied with the relationship. This dissatisfaction may even lead us to become unfaithful to our partner, as we may want to find passionate love once again.

It is important to keep in mind, however, that in some cultures, and even in our culture in the past, marriages were arranged by parents and were based on factors such as money, religion, and social status. In such marriages, the two parties may not have even known one another very well, if at all, and their feelings of passionate love for one another were much less important because it was assumed that they could grow to love one another. For this reason, people in arranged marriages are less likely to get divorced. This type of marriage arrangement may seem strange to us because it goes against what we value in an individualistic culture: our own personal happiness. However, arranged marriages are consistent with the values of collectivist cultures (Dion & Dion, 1993, Levine, Sato, Hashimoto, & Verma, 1995). In other cultures, romantic love is rated as less important than in Western countries (Simmons, Vomkolke, & Shimizu, 1986). However, this does not mean that passion and attraction are not important to members of collectivist cultures. Research suggests that passionate love is correlated with marital satisfaction, even in cultures that have a more pragmatic view of marriage (Contreras, Hendrick, & Hendrick, 1996). Nevertheless, it does suggest that our view of romantic love as the ideal is certainly not the only basis of a successful marriage.

Aggression can be defined as any form of behavior that is intended to injure someone physically or psychologically (Berkowitz, 1993). Aggression includes many components, such as feelings, cognitions, and behavior. The feelings underlying aggression may include anger, jealousy, and fear. Cognitions may involve negative beliefs about others. In research, aggression is most often defined by behavior. In determining whether a particular behavior constitutes an act of aggression, researchers often examine the intention of the perpetrator and whether the response was unwanted by the recipient.

Intention refers to whether or not the person wanted to harm the other person. For example, if you yell at someone with the intent of hurting that person's feelings, or if you hit someone with the intent of hurting that person physically, these behaviors would constitute acts of aggression. The problem with evaluating intentions, however, is that intention is an internal process that cannot be determined by empirical means. A person may claim to have good intentions, but others may perceive his or her behavior as being aggressive. In addition, a person may not realize that his or her behavior is hurting someone else because the behavior is culturally sanctioned. At one time in our own history, abusing one's slaves was not considered an act of aggression because slaves were considered property, and one cannot aggress against one's property. Similarly, acts of sexual harassment and rape do not always involve conscious intent on the part of the perpetrator; for example, perpetrators may argue that they thought the other person would find the sexually oriented joke humorous. Perpetrators of rape often engage in cognitive distortions that may keep them from believing that they intended to harm the person; for example, perpetrators often believe rape myths such as the idea that even when women say no they actually mean yes (Burt, 1980). In these examples, the slave owners/perpetrators may claim that their intentions were not malicious, but the victim often perceives their actions as aggressive.

In determining whether a particular behavior constitutes an aggressive act, it is also important to assess whether the response of the perpetrator is unwanted by the recipient. In the case of both slavery and acts of rape, the recipients of the behavior would most likely concur that the perpetrator's actions were unwanted. On the other hand, acts of sadomasochism, in which a person enjoys being subjected to pain, would not constitute aggressive behavior, according to this definition. (Interestingly, at one point in time, women who repeatedly became involved in abusive relationships were thought to be sadomasochists, which suggests that they were not actually victims of aggression because they enjoyed the abuse.) An act of suicide likewise would not be considered an act of aggression against the self, in that the person has willingly taken his or her own life. However, sometimes suicide can be a form of aggression against others when the person commits suicide to hurt other people.

There are several factors that contribute to aggressive behavior. First, aversive factors such as pain (Berkowitz, 1983), heat (P. Bell, 1980), and being attacked (Taylor & Pisano, 1971) increase the likelihood of aggression. Second, disinhibiting factors such as anonymity (Zimbardo, 1969), alcohol (Taylor & Leonard, 1983), physiological arousal (Schachter & Singer, 1962), and violent pornography (Donnerstein & Berkowitz, 1981) also make aggression more likely. Third, role expectations can lead to aggressive behavior. Zimbardo and his colleagues (Haney, Banks, & Zimbardo, 1973) demonstrated that randomly assigning people to the roles of prisoner and guard resulted in aggressive behavior on the part of the guards, so much so that the study had to be terminated. Finally, personality characteristics such as disagreeableness, suspiciousness, hostility, and emotional reactivity are associated with aggressive behavior (Caprara, Barbaranelli, Pastorelli, & Perugini, 1994).

Aggression can be directed toward groups of people as well as toward individuals. Group forms of violence are of particular interest in multicultural psychology because often, group violence is aimed at people who are different in some way from the perpetrators. *Genocidal violence* refers to acts of aggression that are aimed at eliminating particular groups of people, such as the killing of Jews during the Holocaust.

Staub (1996) has identified several factors that lead to group violence. One factor is difficult life conditions. When people encounter difficult life conditions, they become more self-focused and less concerned about the needs of others; as a result, they may employ scapegoating as a way to blame other people for their difficulties and then engage in acts of aggression against those individuals. This perspective is consistent with the frustration-aggression hypothesis (Dollard, Doob, Miller, Mowrer, & Sears, 1939), which states that frustration always leads to aggression and aggression is always a product of frustration. In addition, people may try to devalue those they hold responsible for their troubles by portraying them as lazy or inferior to make their own acts of aggression seem more justified.

Green, Abelson, and Garnett (1999) found that the correlation between one difficult life condition, economic hardship, and hate crimes against minorities is not as robust as once believed, in part because the effects of frustration dissipate over time, especially in the absence of a proximal target. However, political leaders and organizations may play a mediating role in aggressive behavior through the process of scapegoating. This finding is consistent with Berkowitz's (1978) reformulation of the frustration-aggression hypothesis, in which frustration must also be accompanied by an aggressive cue before aggressive behavior occurs. In addition, Green et al. argue that the mind-set of individuals who commit hate crimes is more useful in explaining their behavior than economic factors are. In particular, people who are uncomfortable with social change, such as race mixing, immigration, and the blurring of gender roles, are more likely to commit hate crimes.

People with an authoritarian personality (Levy, 1999) may be more likely to condone group violence. Recall that individuals with this personality constellation tend to hold conventional beliefs, engage in child-rearing practices that focus on punishment and respect for authority, and hold prejudiced and stereotypical views of others. Such individuals may be more likely to follow leaders who endorse acts of aggression against others, particularly in times of economic hardship.

Cultures differ in the extent to which they condone violence. Even within the United States, there are differences in the number of homicides in geographic regions, with the southern states having a higher rate of homicide than the northern states (A. Fiske et al., 1998). Although murder rates for felony-related crimes in northern and southern states do not differ, the South has higher rates of crimes related to insults. This finding suggests that it is the value system of European Americans in the South, in which aggressive retaliation to assaults on one's honor are acceptable, that contributes to an increased homicide rate for that geographic region.

Social Influence

Social influence refers to the impact others have on our behavior. For many behaviors, we follow implicit norms for how to behave. For example, we know, often without being told to do so, that we should take turns speaking in a conversation. Other times, we may behave in certain ways because someone tells us to do so, such as when a restaurant has a dress code that requires a jacket and tie for males. Conformity, compliance, and obedience are all examples of social influence that vary in degree.

Conformity involves voluntarily yielding to social norms, even at the expense of one's own preferences. This type of social influence was illustrated in an experiment by Asch (1956), in which participants were asked to take turns judging the length of a line. In this experiment, only one person in the room was actually a participant; the other members were confederates. On some trials, all confederates deliberately gave the same wrong answer; Asch found that the participants often conformed to the implicit group norm by giving the incorrect answer. Thus, under some conditions, we may conform to other people's behavior, even when we think that it is wrong. This is often the case when adolescents succumb to peer pressure by engaging in sexual intercourse, alcohol use, and other behaviors.

Compliance refers to a change of behavior in response to an explicit request. Compliance differs from conformity, in which the behavioral norms are often unstated. One method of inducing compliance is the foot-in-the-door technique (Freedman & Fraser, 1966). In this method, you would ask persons to comply with a small request, and after they agreed, ask them to comply with a larger request. For example, a researcher might ask you to participate in a survey on drinking on college campuses, and if you agreed to participate, the researcher may then ask you to participate in a drug and alcohol awareness program. A similar technique for inducing compliance is the door-in-the-face technique (Cialdini et al., 1975). In this procedure, you would first make a very large request from someone that is likely to be turned down; then you would make a smaller request. This strategy is often used by alumni associations when they request that you make a donation to your college or university. Often, callers first ask you to make a donation of $500 and then ask if you would at least be willing to make a small donation of $20. Generally, the door-in-the-face technique is more effective than the foot-in-the-door technique.

Obedience refers to compliance with a demand. Here, the person's response is to an explicit message, as it is in compliance, but the message in this case is a direct order. One of the most well-known studies on obedience is Milgram's (1963) classic study. Milgram became interested in obedience after World War II, when officers who worked under Hitler performed inhumane acts against Jews in the name of duty. Milgram wanted to find out under what conditions people would be willing to hurt someone else because they were ordered to do so. Much to the surprise of Milgram and others, many people were willing to obey orders in his studies, even when they believed that the other person was suffering.

In individualistic cultures, we are often disconcerted about the fact that other people can influence our behavior against our will because we prefer to believe that we are in control of our destiny. Even the terms used to describe social influences on our behavior, such as obedience, compliance, and conformity, have a negative connotation. Thus, much of the research in social psychology is aimed at identifying factors that can minimize the likelihood of conformity, compliance, and obedience. However, in collectivist cultures, adjusting one's behavior to fit the requests or expectations of others is highly valued and is sometimes even a moral imperative (A. Fiske et al., 1998). In these cultures, conformity is seen as being necessary for social functioning, rather than a sign of weakness.

CONCLUSION

In this chapter, we focused on multicultural considerations in the fields of biological and social psychology. Historically, the examination of multicultural factors was considered a source of error variance and was therefore avoided in the search for universal principles of human behavior. However, as we have seen, inclusion of multicultural factors has sometimes called into question scientific findings that were once considered universal. In addition, attention to multicultural factors has revealed that political factors and cultural biases sometimes influence the research conducted, as well as the conclusions that are drawn. Biological explanations for differences among groups of people often lead to interpretations supporting the idea of inferior and superior races. Major findings in social psychology are actually more relevant for individualistic cultures than collectivist cultures. These examples are only the beginning of many such findings that are likely to be discovered as diversity becomes an important consideration in research. The field of psychology can also be useful in elucidating the nature of these biases and what we can do to prevent them, as we learned in the examination of prejudice in the social psychology section. These considerations in the various fields of psychology are important to keep in mind in future chapters that focus on specific ethnic groups.

REFERENCES

Ajir, K., Smith, M., Lin, K. M., Fleishaker, J. C., Chambers, J. H., Anderson, D., Nuccio, I., Zheng, Y., & Poland, R. E. (1997). The pharmacokinetics and pharmacodynamics of adinazolam: Multi-ethnic comparisons. *Psychopharmacology, 129,* 265–270.

Allison, K. W. (1998). Stress and oppressed social category membership. In J. K. Swim & C. Stangor (Eds.), *Prejudice: The target's perspective* (pp. 145–170). San Diego, CA: Academic Press.

Allport, G. W. (1954). *The nature of prejudice.* Reading, MA: Addison-Wesley.

American Psychiatric Association. (1994). *Diagnostic and statistical manual of mental disorders* (4th ed.). Washington, DC: Author.

Amir, Y. (1994). The contact hypothesis in intergroup relations. In W. J. Lonner & R. S. Malpass (Eds.), *Psychology and culture* (pp. 231–237). Boston: Allyn & Bacon.

Angoff, W. H. (1988). The nature-nurture debate, aptitudes, and group differences. *American Psychologist, 43,* 713–720.

Archer, J. (2000). Sex differences in aggression between heterosexual partners: A meta-analytic review. *Psychological Bulletin,126,* 651–680.

Arkin, R. M., Cooper, H., & Kolditz, T. (1980). A statistical review of literature concerning the self-serving attribution bias in interpersonal influence situations. *Journal of Personality, 48,* 435–448.

Aronson, E., Blaney, N., Stephan, C., Sikes, J., & Snapp, M. (1978). *The jigsaw classroom.* Beverly Hills, CA: Sage.

Aronson, J., Quinn, D. M., & Spencer, S. J. (1998). Stereotype threat and the academic underperformance of minorities and women. In J. K. Swim & C. Stangor (Eds.), *Prejudice: The target's perspective* (pp. 83–103). San Diego, CA: Academic Press.

Asch, S. E. (1956). Studies of independence and conformity: I. A minority of one against a unanimous majority. *Psychological Monographs, 70* (No. 416), 70.

Barber, N. (1998). Secular changes in standards of bodily attractiveness in women: Tests of a reproductive model. *International Journal of Eating Disorders, 23,* 449–453.

Baron, R. A., & Richardson, D. R. (1994). *Human aggression* (2nd ed.). New York: Plenum Press.

Baumrind, D. (1993). The average expectable environment is not good enough: A response to Scarr. *Child Development, 64,* 1299–1317.

Belcourt-Dittloff, A., & Stewart, J. (2000). Historical racism: Implications for Native Americans. *American Psychologist, 55,* 1166–1167.

Bell, C. C. (1978). Racism, narcissism, and integrity. *Journal of the National Medical Association, 70,* 89–92.

Bell, P. A. (1980). Effects of heat, noise, and provocation on retaliatory evaluative behavior. *Journal of Social Psychology, 110,* 97–100.

Berkowitz, L. (1978). Whatever happened to the frustration-aggression hypothesis? *American Behavioral Scientist, 21,* 691–708.

Berkowitz, L. (1983). Aversively stimulated aggression: Some parallels and differences in research with animals and humans. *American Psychologist, 38,* 1135–1144.

Berkowitz, L. (1993). *Aggression: Its causes, consequences, and control.* New York: McGraw-Hill.

Betancourt, H., & Lopez, S. R. (1993). The study of culture, ethnicity, and race in American psychology. *American Psychologist, 48,* 629–637.

Bigler, R. S., & Liben, L. S. (1993). A cognitive-developmental approach to racial stereotyping and reconstructive memory in Euro-American children. *Child Development, 64,* 1507–1518.

Bleier, R. (1986). Sex differences research: Science or belief? In R. Bleier (Ed.), *Feminist approaches to science* (pp. 147–164). New York: Pergamon Press.

Branscombe, N. R., Schmitt, M. T., & Harvey, R. D. (1999). Perceiving pervasive discrimination among African Americans: Implications for group identification and well-being. *Journal of Personality and Social Psychology, 77,* 135–149.

Brookey, R. A. (2000). Saints or sinners: Sociobiological theories of male homosexuality. *International Journal of Sexuality and Gender Studies, 5,* 37–58.

Brophy, J. (1986). Teacher influences on student achievement. *American Psychologist, 41,* 1069–1077.

Brunner, H. G., Nelen, M., Breakfield, X. O., & Ropers, H. H. (1993). Abnormal structures associated with a point mutation in the structural gene for monoamine oxidase A. *Science, 262,* 578–580.

Burt, M. R. (1980). Cultural myths and supports for rape. *Journal of Personality and Social Psychology, 38,* 62–83.

Buss, A. H. (1989). Personality as traits. *American Psychologist, 44,* 1378–1388.

Buss, D. M., Shackelford, T. K., Kirkpatrick, L. A., Choe, J. C., Lim, H. K., Hasegawa, M., Hasegawa, T., & Bennett, K. (1999). Jealousy and the nature of beliefs about infidelity: Tests of competing hypotheses about sex differences in the United States, Korea, and Japan. *Personal Relationships, 6,* 125–150.

Caprara, G. V., Barbaranelli, C., Pastorelli, C., & Perugini, M. (1994). Individual differences in the study of human aggression. *Aggressive Behavior, 20,* 291–303.

Chen, C., & Stevenson, H. W. (1995). Motivation and mathematics achievement: A comparative study of Asian-American, Caucasian-American, and East Asian high school students. *Child Development, 66,* 1215–1234.

Cialdini, R. B., Vincent, J. E., Lewis, S. K., Catalan, J., Wheeler, D., & Darby, B. L. (1975). A reciprocal concessions procedure for inducing compliance: The door-in-the-face technique. *Journal of Personality and Social Psychology, 21,* 206–215.

Clark, R., Anderson, N. B., Clark, V. R., & Williams, D. R. (1999). Racism as a stressor for African Americans. *American Psychologist, 54,* 805–816.

Connolly, J. A. (1978). Intelligence levels of Down's syndrome children. *American Journal of Mental Deficiency, 83,* 193–196.

Contreras, R., Hendrick, S. S., & Hendrick, C. (1996). Perspectives on marital love and satisfaction in Mexican American and Anglo-American couples. *Journal of Counseling and Development, 74,* 408–415.

Cooper, R., & Zubek, J. (1958). Effects of enriched and restricted early environments on the learning ability of bright and dull rats. *Canadian Journal of Psychology, 12,* 159–164.

Crandall, C. S. (1994). Prejudice against fat people. *Journal of Personality and Social Psychology, 66,* 882–894.

Crocker, J., & Lawrence, J. S. (1999). Social stigma and self-esteem: The role of contingencies of worth. In D. A. Prentice & D. T. Miller (Eds.), *Cultural divides: Understanding and overcoming group conflict* (pp. 364–392). New York: Russell Sage.

Darwin, C. (1958). *The origin of species* (6th ed.). New York: New American Library.

D'Augelli, A. R., & Hershberger, S. L. (1993). African American undergraduates on a predominantly White campus: Academic factors, social networks, and campus climate. *Journal of Negro Education, 62,* 67–81.

Davis, M. H., & Stephan, W. G. (1980). Attributions for exam performance. *Journal of Applied Social Psychology, 10,* 235–248.

DeVos, G., & Hippler, A. A. (1969). Cultural psychology: Comparative studies of human behavior. In G. Lindzey & E. Aronson (Eds.), *The handbook of social psychology* (2nd ed., pp. 323–417). New York: McGraw-Hill.

Dion, K. L., & Dion, K. K. (1993). Gender and ethnocultural comparisons in styles of love. *Psychology of Women Quarterly, 17,* 463–473.

Dollard, J., Doob, L., Miller, N. E., Mowrer, O. H., & Sears, R. R. (1939). *Frustration and aggression.* New Haven, CT: Yale University Press.

Donnerstein, E., & Berkowitz, L. (1981). Victim reactions in aggressive erotic films as a factor in violence against women. *Journal of Personality and Social Psychology, 41,* 710–724.

Eagly, A. H., & Wood, W. (1999). Origins of sex differences in human behavior: Evolved dispositions versus social roles. *American Psychologist, 54,* 408–423.

Ellis, L. (1991). A synthesized (biosocial) theory of rape. *Journal of Consulting and Clinical Psychology, 59,* 631–642.

Fairchild, H. (1991). Scientific racism: The cloak of objectivity. *Journal of Social Issues, 47,* 101–115.

Festinger, L. (1957). *A theory of cognitive dissonance.* Evanston, IL: Row, Peterson.

Fiske, A. P., Kitayama, S., Markus, H. R., & Nisbett, R. E. (1998). The cultural matrix of social psychology. In D. T. Gilbert, S. T. Fiske, & G. Lindzey (Eds.), *The handbook of social psychology* (4th ed., pp. 915–981). New York: McGraw-Hill.

Fiske, S. T. (1995). Controlling other people: The impact of power on stereotyping. In N. R. Goldberger & J. B. Veroff (Eds.), *The culture and psychology reader* (pp. 438–456). New York: New York University Press.

Freedman, J., & Fraser, S. (1966). Compliance without pressure: The foot-in-the-door technique. *Journal of Personality and Social Psychology, 4,* 195–202.

Friedman, B. X., Bleske, A. L., & Scheyd, G. J. (2000). Incompatible with evolutionary theorizing. *American Psychologist, 55,* 1059–1060.

Fuligni, A. J. (1997). The academic achievement of adolescents from immigrant families: The roles of family background, attitudes, and behavior. *Child Development, 68,* 351–363.

Goodman, M. J., Griffin, P. B., Estioko-Griffin, A. A., & Grove, J. S. (1999). The compatibility of hunting and mothering among the agta hunter-gatherers of the Philippines. In L. A. Peplau, S. C. DeBro, R. C. Veniegas, & P. L. Taylor (Eds.), *Gender, culture, and ethnicity* (pp. 62–69). Mountain View, CA: Mayfield.

Gottesman, I. I. (1991). *Schizophrenia genesis: The origins of madness.* New York: Freeman.

Graves, S. B. (1999). Television and prejudice reduction: When does television as a vicarious experience make a difference? *Journal of Social Issues, 55,* 707–725.

Green, D. P., Abelson, R. P., & Garnett, M. (1999). The distinctive political views of hate-crime perpetrators and white supremacists. In D. A. Prentice & D. T. Miller (Eds.), *Cultural divides: Understanding and overcoming group conflict* (pp. 429–464). New York: Russell Sage.

Hamilton, V. L. (1980). Intuitive psychologist or intuitive lawyer? Alternative models of the attribution process. *Journal of Personality and Social Psychology, 39,* 767–772.

Haney, C., Banks, C., & Zimbardo, P. (1973). Interpersonal dynamics in a simulated prison. *International Journal of Criminology and Penology, 1,* 69–97.

Harding, J., Proshansky, H., Kutner, B., & Ghein, I. (1969). Prejudice and ethnic relations. In G. Lindzey & E. Aronson (Eds.), *The handbook of social psychology* (2nd ed., pp. 1–76). New York: McGraw-Hill.

Harris, N. B. (1992). Sex, race, and experiences of aggression. *Aggressive Behavior, 18,* 201–217.

Hatfield, E. (1988). Passionate and companionate love. In R. J. Sternberg & M. L. Barnes (Eds.), *The psychology of love* (pp. 191–217). New Haven, CT: Yale University Press.

Heider, F. (1958). *The psychology of interpersonal relations.* New York: Wiley.

Herrnstein, R. J., & Murray, C. (1994). *The bell curve: Intelligence and class structure in American life.* New York: Free Press.

Hsia, J., & Peng, S. S. (1998). Academic achievement and performance. In L. C. Lee & N. W. S. Zane (Eds.), *Handbook of Asian American psychology* (pp. 325–357). Thousand Oaks, CA: Sage.

Jacobson, C. K. (1985). Resistance to affirmative action: Self-interest or racism? *Journal of Conflict Resolution, 29,* 306–329.

Jensen, A. R. (1969). How much can we boost IQ and scholastic achievement? *Harvard Educational Review, 39,* 1–123.

Jones, J. M. (1997). *Prejudice and racism* (2nd ed.). New York: McGraw-Hill.

Jones, J. M. (1999). Cultural racism: The intersection of race and culture in intergroup conflict. In D. A. Prentice & D. T. Miller (Eds.), *Cultural divides: Understanding and overcoming group conflict* (pp. 465–490). New York: Russell Sage.

Julian, T., & McHenry, P. C. (1989). Relationship of testosterone to men's family functioning at mid-life: A research note. *Aggressive Behavior, 15,* 281–289.

Kamin, L. J., & Omari, S. (1998). Race, head size, and intelligence. *South African Journal of Psychology, 28,* 119–128.

Kendrick, D. T., & Li, N. (2000). The Darwin is in the details. *American Psychologist, 55,* 1060–1061.

Kety, S. S. (1988). Schizophrenic illness in the families of schizophrenic adoptees: Findings from the Danish national sample. *Schizophrenic Bulletin, 14,* 217–222.

Khmelkov, V. T., & Hallinan, M. T. (1999). Organizational effects on race relations in schools. *Journal of Social Issues, 55,* 627–645.

Kim, J. J., Mohamed, S., Andreasen, N. C., O'Leary, D. S., Watkins, G. L., Ponto, L. L. B., & Hichwa, R. D. (2000). Regional neural dysfunctions in chronic schizophrenia studied with positron emission tomography. *American Journal of Psychiatry, 157,* 542–548.

Kitayama, S., & Markus, H. R. (1995). Culture and self: Implications for internationalizing psychology. In N. R. Goldberger & J. B. Veroff (Eds.), *The culture and psychology reader* (pp. 366–383). New York: New York University Press.

Kleyman, E. (2000). From allies to adversaries? *American Psychologist, 55,* 1061–1062.

Lepowsky, M. (1999). Women, men and aggression in an egalitarian society. In L. A. Peplau, S. C. DeBro, R. C. Veniegas, & P. L. Taylor (Eds.), *Gender, culture, and ethnicity* (pp. 284–290). Mountain View, CA: Mayfield.

Lerner, M. J. (1980). *The belief in a just world: A fundamental delusion.* New York: Plenum Press.

Levine, R., Sato, S., Hashimoto, T., & Verma, J. (1995). Love and marriage in eleven cultures. *Journal of Cross-Cultural Psychology, 26,* 554–571.

Levy, S. R. (1999). Reducing prejudice: Lessons from social-cognitive factors underlying perceiver differences in prejudice. *Journal of Social Issues, 55,* 745–765.

Lewine, R. R., & Caudle, J. (1999). Race in the "decade of the brain." *Schizophrenia Bulletin, 25,* 1–5.

Lin, K. M., Poland, R. E., Fleishaker, J. C., & Phillips, J. P. (1993). Ethnicity and differential responses to benzodiazepines. In K. M. Lin, R. E. Poland, & G. Nakasaki (Eds.), *Psychopharmacology and psychobiology of ethnicity* (pp. 91–105). Washington, DC: American Psychiatric Press.

Mackintosh, N. J. (1986). The biology of intelligence? *British Journal of Psychology, 77,* 1–18.

Magdol, L., Moffitt, T. E., Caspi, A., & Silva, P. A. (1998). Developmental antecedents of partner abuse: A prospective-longitudinal study. *Journal of Abnormal Psychology, 107,* 375–389.

Malamuth, N. M. (1996). The confluence model of sexual aggression: Feminist and evolutionary perspectives. In D. M. Buss & N. M. Malamuth (Eds.), *Sex, power, conflict: Evolutionary and feminist perspectives* (pp. 269–295). New York: Oxford University Press.

Marfo, K., & Kysela, G. M. (1985). Early intervention with mentally handicapped children: A critical appraisal of applied research. *Journal of Pediatric Psychology, 10,* 305–324.

Milgram, S. (1963). Behavioral study of obedience. *Journal of Abnormal and Social Psychology, 67,* 371–378.

Nisbett, R. E. (1998). Race, genetics, and I.Q. In C. Jencks & M. Phillips (Eds.), *The Black–White test score gap* (pp. 86–102). Washington, DC: Brookings Institution.

Ocampo, C. (2000). Physiology and racism. *American Psychologist, 55,* 1164–1165.

Peters, M. (1995). Race differences in brain size. *American Psychologist, 50,* 947–948.

Rosenthal, R., & Jacobson, L. (1966). Teachers' expectancies: Determinates of pupils' I.Q. gains. *Psychological Reports, 19,* 115–118.

Ross, L., & Nisbett, R. E. (1991). *The person and the situation: Perspectives of social psychology.* New York: McGraw-Hill.

Rushton, J. P. (1988). Race differences in behaviour: A review and evolutionary analysis. *Personality and Individual Differences, 9,* 1009–1024.

Rushton, J. P. (1989). Genetic similarity, human altruism, and group selection. *Behavior and Brain Science, 12,* 503–559.

Rushton, J. P. (1996). Race, genetics, and human reproductive strategies. *Genetic, Social, and General Psychology Monographs, 122,* 21–53.

Schachter, S., & Singer, J. E. (1962). Cognitive, social and physiological determinants of emotional state. *Psychological Review, 69,* 379–399.

Schlenker, B. R., Weigold, M. F., & Hallam, J. R. (1990). Self-serving attributions in a social contexts: Effects of self-esteem and social pressure. *Journal of Personality and Social Psychology, 58,* 855–863.

Schooler, T., & Baum, A. (2000). Neuroendocrine influences on the health of diverse populations. In R. M. Eisler & M. Hersen (Eds.), *Handbook of gender, culture, and health* (pp. 3–19). Mahwah, NJ: Erlbaum.

Sears, D. O. (1988). Symbolic racism. In P. A. Katz & D. A. Taylor (Eds.), *Eliminating racism: Profiles in controversy* (pp. 53–84). New York: Plenum Press.

Sherif, M., Harvey, O. J., White, B. J., Hood, W. R., & Sherif, C. W. (1961). *The Robbers Cave experiment: Intergroup conflict and cooperation.* Middletown, CT: Wesleyan University Press.

Silverstein, L. B., & Phares, V. (1996). Fathering as a feminist issue. *Psychology of Women Quarterly, 20,* 3–38.

Simmons, C. H., Vomkolke, A., & Shimizu, H. (1986). Attitudes toward romantic love among American, German, and Japanese students. *Journal of Social Psychology, 126,* 327–336.

Slavin, R. E., & Cooper, R. (1999). Improving intergroup relations: Lessons learned from cooperative learning programs. *Journal of Social Issues, 55,* 647–663.

Sprecher, S., Sullivan, Q., & Hatfield, E. (1994). Mate selection preferences: Gender differences examined in a national sample. *Journal of Personality and Social Psychology, 66,* 1074–1080.

Staub, E. (1996). Cultural-societal roots of violence: The examples of genocidal violence and of contemporary youth violence in the United States. *American Psychologist, 51,* 117–132.

Steele, C. M. (1997). A threat in the air: How stereotypes shape intellectual identity and performance. *American Psychologist, 52,* 613–629.

Steinberg, L., Dornbusch, S. M., & Brown, B. B. (1992). Ethnic differences in adolescent achievement: An ecological perspective. *American Psychologist, 47,* 723–729.

Stephan, W. G. (1987). The contact hypothesis in intergroup relations. In C. Hendrick (Ed.), *Group processes and intergroup relations* (pp. 13–40). Newbury Park, CA: Sage.

Stephan, W. G., & Finlay, K. (1999). The role of empathy in improving intergroup relations. *Journal of Social Issues, 55,* 729–743.

Swim, J. K., Aikin, K. J., Hall, W. S., & Hunter, B. A. (1995). Sexism and racism: Old-fashioned and modern prejudices. *Journal of Personality and Social Psychology, 68,* 199–214.

Swim, J. K., Cohen, L. L., & Hyers, L. L. (1998). Experiencing everyday prejudice and discrimination. In J. K. Swim & C. Stangor (Eds.), *Prejudice: The target's perspective* (pp. 37–60). San Diego, CA: Academic Press.

Taylor, S., Klein, L. C., Lewis, B. P., Gruenewald, T. L., Gurung, R. A. R., & Updegraff, J. A. (2000). Biobehavioral responses to stress in females: Tend-and-befriend, not fight-or-flight. *Psychological Review, 107,* 411–429.

Taylor, S., & Leonard, K. E. (1983). Alcohol and human physical aggression. *Aggression, 2,* 77–101.

Taylor, S., & Pisano, R. (1971). Physical aggression as a function of frustration and physical attack. *Journal of Social Psychology, 84,* 261–267.

Tischenkel, N., Saab, P. G., Schneiderman, N., Nelesen, R. A., Pasin, R. D., Goldstein, D. A., Spitzer, S. B., Woo-Ming, R., & Weidler, D. J. (1989). Cardiovascular and neurohormonal responses to behavioral challenge as a function of race and sex. *Health Psychology, 8,* 503–524.

White, J. B., & Langer, E. J. (1999). Horizontal hostility: Relations between similar minority groups. *Journal of Social Issues,55,* 537–559.

Zigler, E. (1994). Reshaping early childhood intervention to be a more effective weapon against poverty. *American Journal of Community Psychology, 22,* 37–47.

Zigler, E., & Styfco, S. J. (1994). Head Start: Criticisms in a constructive context. *American Psychologist, 49,* 127–132.

Zimbardo, P. G. (1969). The human choice: Individuation, reason, and order versus deindividuation, impulse, and chaos. *Nebraska Symposium on Motivation, 17,* 237–307.

ISSUES FOR DISCUSSION

1. Think of some examples of news stories covered in the media that pertain to the nature-nurture debate (e.g., mental illness, parenting abilities). Were their conclusions based on scientific evidence? Are there sociopolitical ramifications to these findings?

2. Describe a time when you were discriminated against and/or someone made assumptions about you based on appearance or other characteristics (e.g., being young/old, attractive/unattractive; race, gender, intelligence). What was your reaction? How did this incident affect your behavior?

FOUR

THEORY AND MULTICULTURAL PSYCHOLOGY: DEVELOPMENTAL PSYCHOLOGY AND PERSONALITY

In Chapter Three, we demonstrated that the examination of multicultural factors in the fields of biological and social psychology led to reformulations of research findings that were once thought to be universal. In addition, we examined the way sociopolitical factors can influence the study of psychology and the way scientific findings are interpreted. In this chapter, we continue our review of multicultural factors, focusing on the fields of developmental psychology and personality. These fields are particularly relevant to clinical psychology because they have important implications for psychopathology and the treatment of mental disorders. Developmental psychology and personality focus primarily on healthy individuals, but in doing so, these fields suggest how abnormal behavior can arise. When abnormal development and personality formation occur, psychological disorders may result; these disorders may then require professional treatment. This straightforward pathway to pathology is deceiving, however, because it is not as easy as it may seem to define what is "normal" or "healthy" in development and personality. Is it normal to be raised by two parents? To be attached to one's mother? Is it normal to become increasingly independent as we get older? To be able to express a full range of emotions (e.g., happiness, sadness, anger)? If so, are we abnormal when these conditions are not met? These are just a few of the issues that we explore in the following sections.

DEVELOPMENTAL PSYCHOLOGY

Developmental psychology is the study of the physical, cognitive, social, moral, language, and personality changes that occur during the course of a person's life, from infancy to old age. As with other fields of psychology, many aspects of human growth and development were presumed to be universal without empirical evidence. More recently, researchers have investigated whether this is the case. The conclusion of a major review was that there are not substantial ethnic or racial differences in developmental processes (Rowe, Vazsonyi, & Flannery, 1994). However, there are several limitations with these studies. First, broad ethnic categories (i.e., Black, White, Hispanic, Asian) are often used that may obscure potential within-group differences. Second, the use of measures developed for European Americans with non-European Americans may have obscured developmental processes that are culturally unique (Hall, Bansal, & Lopez, 1999). As we discussed in Chapter Two, using ethnocentric assessment tools with diverse groups of people can lead to poor psychometric properties. Third, much developmental research involves an etic approach, which does not consider cultural specificity. Finally, Coll et al. (1996) argue that most developmental models do not take into consideration many important factors that affect development in minority children, such as prejudice and discrimination, social position variables, and family structure. Consequently, even though researchers are beginning to recognize the importance of multicultural factors in human development, the current research methodology in this area needs to be refined further. In the following, we review several of the major areas of developmental psychology: temperament, attachment, parenting, cognitive development, moral reasoning, and language development.

Temperament

Temperament refers to physical and emotional characteristics that are present early in life and that tend to remain relatively stable across the life span. It is often believed to be the raw material out of which personality evolves. Thomas and Chess (1977) describe three temperament types apparent in infancy: *easy, difficult,* and *slow to warm up.* Easy infants tend to be sociable; difficult infants tend to be more withdrawn; and slow-to-warm-up infants tend to be withdrawn initially but sociable after some time has passed. Three other common temperament types are sociability, emotionality, and activity level (Buss

& Plomin, 1984). *Sociability* refers to how the infant interacts with the environment; for example, some infants enjoy interacting with strangers and others do not. *Emotionality* refers to the tendency to become physiologically aroused in response to environmental stimuli; for example, some infants are light sleepers, and others can sleep through a party. *Activity level* refers to the sheer amount of response output of the individual; some infants crawl around, actively exploring their environment, and other infants are quiet and stay in one place. These characteristics tend to be stable from infancy onward and may have a biological basis. However, researchers also note that just because a child is born with a particular temperament does not necessarily mean that his or her personality is already predetermined. A person's temperament interacts with environmental experiences that can either inhibit or enhance the expression of particular traits.

There is some evidence for cultural differences in the types of temperament that infants are likely to posses. For example, Asian American and American Indian infants tend to be calmer and more placid than European American and African American babies (Chisholm 1984; Freedman, 1974). Cultural factors may also be important to consider in the assessment of temperament. For example, in measuring the temperament of sociability, it is important for the investigator to be aware of the fact that members of collectivist cultures may not be as effective in meeting strangers as members of individualistic cultures and that they may be less sociable toward outgroup members than ingroup members (Rothbaum, Weisz, Pott, Miyake, & Morelli, 2000; Triandis, 1995).

Attachment

One of the major tasks of development is learning to relate to other people. Many developmental and personality theories argue that our ability to relate to other people originates in our attachment to our parents. All infants form a strong bond with the people that care for them, and there is evidence to suggest that this bond is biologically based (Bowlby, 1969). In other words, infants are biologically wired to cry, smile, and vocalize to attract attention, and adults are wired to respond to such behaviors with a desire to care for the infant. This biological predisposition on the part of infants and parents makes it more likely that infants will survive. Freud presents another biological perspective for attachment: Psychoanalytic theory argues that infants form an attachment to the mother because she provides the milk that is necessary for life, thereby satisfying the biologically determined life instinct. However, research suggests that attachment does not depend on food alone; it also depends on having someone who will hold and rock the infant and provide a safe environment (Harlow & Zimmerman, 1959).

One of the assumptions underlying most attachment theories is that attachment to the mother must occur for normal development. This belief is made explicit in most psychodynamic theories of personality, as we will see later in this chapter. Most laypeople also believe that the bond between mother and child is both innate and necessary. Cross-cultural studies do suggest that fathers' interactions with their children tend to focus on play activities, whereas mothers' interactions with their children tend to be more nurturing, at least in terms of providing immediate physical needs (Bronstein, 1999). However, Silverstein and Phares (1996) argue that the rough-and-tumble play characteristic of fathers' interaction with children is an artifact resulting from lack of involvement; mothers also engage in more rough-and-tumble play when they do not get to spend as much time with their children.

Historically, this bond between mother and infant has taken place because men have traditionally worked outside the home while women tended to child care. However, this does not mean that attachment to the mother is a necessary prerequisite for healthy development. Silverstein and Phares (1996) argue that the traditional family structure is a by-product of industrialization, which forced fathers to spend more time away from the family. As a result, mothering became more central to the lives of children than it had been previously, and the ideological position developed in which mothers were thought to have a special bond with their children that is unique compared to any other relationship. This view was reinforced further by Bowlby's (1951) theory of attachment, which also argued that the mother-infant relationship is unique and necessary for healthy development. The authors of this article argue that, contrary to this popular myth, the ability to parent is not innate in mothers or fathers, either human and nonhuman; instead, individuals learn how to be a good parent through experience. They also argue that fathers' involvement in child rearing should be a feminist issue because it would allow women to have greater satisfaction in both the public and domestic spheres, in addition to benefiting children.

There is some research to support the idea that fathers' involvement is associated with more positive outcomes in their children's development (Coley, 1998). Moreover, when fathers are the primary caregivers, fathers report as much distress from being separated from their children as mothers do (Deater-Deckard, Scarr, McCartney, & Eisenberg, 1994), and infants whose fathers are involved in care giving are more empathic as adults (Koestner, Franz, & Weinberger, 1990). These findings suggest that fathers do form an attachment to their children and that this attachment leads to positive outcomes. Multicultural studies also challenge the notion that attachment to the mother is necessary for healthy development; in cultures in which infants are taken care of by people other than the mother, such as extended family members, these children also grow up to have secure and healthy relationships (Tronick, Morelli, & Ivey, 1992).

Other basic assumptions about attachment have been questioned as well. Rothbaum et al. (2000) indicate that there are three basic hypotheses of attachment theory: (1) the mother's sensitivity to the child's needs is important in the development of secure attachment; (2) children who are securely attached are more socially competent than children who are not securely attached; and (3) infants use mothers as a base from which they can safely explore their environment. Rothbaum and colleagues suggest that, contrary to the body of literature supporting the universality of attachment theory, these tenets are not universal. For example, in the United States, sensitivity to one's child means waiting for the child to express his or her needs and then responding to those needs appropriately. In Japan, being sensitive to a child's needs means anticipating what the child needs before he or she has to ask for it. In the United States, competence means autonomy, which reflects our value of individualism; in Japan, competence means not expressing your feelings if it will hurt other people, which reflects the value of collectivism. This difference in the value of autonomy is evident in other child rearing practices, as well. For example, in the United States, infants are often given their own room, whereas in other cultures, cosleeping and cobathing are common (Fiske, Kitayama, Markus, & Nisbett, 1998; Markus & Kitayama, 1991). Finally, exploring one's environment is also a manifestation of the value of individualism. Japanese infants are less likely to explore their environment and are more likely to focus their attention on the mother.

Parenting

Parenting style is also important in personality and social development. Baumrind (1989) has identified three main parenting styles. *Authoritarian* parents are high on control and low on warmth; they tend to be unsympathetic and demand obedience from their children. This parenting style leads to children who are unfriendly, distrustful, and withdrawn. *Permissive* parents are high on warmth but low on control; they are empathic toward their children but provide little discipline. This style leads to immature, dependent, and unhappy children. *Authoritative* parents are high on both control and warmth; they reason with their children, explain why they do what they do, and are firm but understanding. This parenting style leads to friendly, cooperative, responsible, and self-reliant children.

It is often assumed that the authoritative parenting style is the style that most often leads to healthy development. However, more recent research suggests that the effectiveness of a particular parenting style is affected by the child's temperament. Kochanska (1991) found that an authoritative parenting style is more predictive of positive outcomes when children are fearful and anxious. In addition, cultural factors are important to consider. In Asian American families, parents are more likely to utilize an authoritarian parenting style, but Asian American students still perform well academically (Chao, 1994). Moreover, there is some research to suggest that cultural differences in parenting styles may result from differences in perception rather than actual differences in parenting, in that ethnic minority children may not interpret authoritarian parenting in the same way that European Americans do. Sonnek (1999) found that parenting behaviors that were rated by European Americans as being authoritarian were rated more positively by Latino Americans. Although specific parental behaviors may be perceived differently, there is some cross-cultural evidence to suggest that positive outcomes are associated with parents who show warmth and affection toward their children and negative results are associated with parental rejection, however those behaviors are culturally defined (Rohner, 1994).

Ideal parenting is also presumed to take place in a nuclear family model, but many ethnic minority groups, including African Americans and Latino Americans, have an extended family model of child rearing (Levitt, Guacci-Franco, & Levitt, 1993; M. Wilson, 1989). Even in the United States, the ideal family of mother, father, and children is not always the norm; it is estimated that 15 percent of European Americans, 41 percent of African Americans, and 30 percent of Latino Americans have single-parent families with the mother as the single parent, and there has been an increase in lesbian parents and never-married mothers (Silverstein & Phares, 1996). Empirical studies suggest that these alternatives to the traditional nuclear family model are not placing children at greater risk for psychological problems. In a review of the literature on single-parent families, Blechman (1982) argues that research has not demonstrated an increased risk of psychopathology for these children. In addition, children of gay and lesbian parents are similar to children of heterosexual parents (Bailey, Bobrow, Wolfe, & Mikach, 1995; Flaks, Ficher, Masterpasqua, & Joseph, 1995), and the parenting skills of gay and lesbian parents do not differ from those of heterosexual parents (Victor & Fish, 1995).

Assumption of the importance of the nuclear family model in child development is also implicit in concerns about the effects of day care and divorce on children. Given the increasing number of dual-career families, it is not uncommon for parents to entrust the care of their children to someone else. Critics argue that mothers who place their children in day care are selfish and endangering the attachment bond between mother and child that is vital to personality and social development. Research on the effects of day care suggests that the quality of the day care facility are more important than the amount of time spent in day care, and that being in day care does not undermine the child's attachment to the parent (Field, 1991).

Similarly, the high divorce rate in the United States has created concern over whether children's experience of divorce leads to an increased risk for psychological problems. This problem may be of particular concern for African Americans, as there is some research to suggest that the divorce rate is even higher for these families (Kposowa, 1998). Although it is true that children and adolescents may suffer problems following divorce and/or separation (Fergusson, Horwood, & Lynske, 1994; Hoyt, Cowen, Pedro-Carroll, & Alpert-Gillis, 1990; Wallerstein, 1991), there is some research to suggest that parental discord before and after the divorce is more detrimental to children's well-being than divorce per se (Derdeyn, 1994; Shaw, Winslow, & Flanagan, 1999). Suggestions for minimizing the potentially negative impact of divorce include providing support to the children, communicating decisions to them, and maintaining a good relationship with the other parent (Caplan, 1989).

Cognitive Development

Cognitive development refers to changes in how children think about the world. The most influential theorist in the area of cognitive development is Jean Piaget. Piaget argued that cognitive development is our way of adapting to the environment. Unlike other animals, we do not have many built-in responses that guide our behavior; consequently, the ways we adapt to the environment can vary. Children's approach to exploring the world and understanding their environment proceeds through four stages of development:

(1) the sensorimotor stage, (2) the preoperational stage, (3) the concrete-operational stage, and (4) the formal-operational stage. The *sensorimotor stage* occurs from birth through the first two years of life. In this stage, children primarily explore the world through their senses (seeing, hearing, etc.) and through motor activities (crawling around, putting things in their mouths, etc.). For example, one of the first schemas that infants may create is objects that fit versus do not fit in one's mouth. One important outcome of this stage is *object permanence,* the awareness that objects continue to exist even when out of sight. Knowing that our parents continue to exist even when we do not see them is an example of object permanence. Thus, object permanence requires an ability to form mental representations of objects and to manipulate those objects in their minds. Infants also develop the capacity for self-recognition at this stage; for example, they can recognize themselves in a mirror, rather than respond to their reflection as if it were another baby.

The *preoperational stage* occurs from about 2 to 7 years of age. In this stage, children are increasingly able to use mental representations. It is usually at this age that language development improves dramatically, and acquiring language requires the ability to recognize that words represent objects. Children at this stage also play make-believe games such as having an imaginary friend, pretending to be a superhero, or pretending to have a tea party with their stuffed animals. However, because children at this stage are *egocentric,* they have difficulty seeing things from someone else's point of view, or what is called *perspective taking.* Children at this stage are also unable to *conserve,* meaning that they do not recognize that superficial changes in appearance do not change the basic amount of something. For example, if orange juice from a short, wide container is poured into a tall, thin container, children at this stage will say that the tall, thin container holds more juice.

The *concrete-operational stage* occurs at ages 7 to 11. At this stage, children can understand principles of conversation. Thus, if the same juice experiment were performed at this stage, children would recognize that both containers hold the same amount of juice. In addition, they also develop the ability to see things from someone else's perspective; thus, they can imagine how another child feels to be called names, which allows them to be more sensitive to other people's feelings. Children at this stage are also able to grasp complex classification schemes, such as grouping animals into dogs versus cats. However, they still engage in concrete rather than abstract thinking.

The *formal-operational stage* occurs after the age of 11. Children at this stage can engage in abstract thinking. In addition, children can think more scientifically, in that they can form hypotheses for how things work, test these hypotheses, and accept or reject them based on the evidence. Consequently, children at this stage can think about cause and effect, understanding how the past can influence the future, rather than thinking in the here and now; thus, they can develop general rules, principles, and theories to predict future events. Children at this stage can also engage in *metacognition,* meaning that they can reflect on their own thinking. However, not all adults reach this stage of cognitive development.

Piaget's theory is useful in understanding prejudice. As we discussed in Chapter Three, having empathy for others is one characteristic that can affect prejudice: Those with greater empathy are less likely to be prejudiced. The development of empathy is clearly related to the development of perspective taking because empathy requires persons to put themselves in someone else's position. Moreover, being less prejudiced requires the development of other cognitive abilities as well, such as being able to see similarities among different groups and differences among similar groups, having a need for cognition, and being able to think in more abstract and complex ways (Levy, 1999). Intolerance of ambiguity, concrete thinking, and inability to use logical reasoning, on the other hand, contribute to prejudice (Harding, Proshansky, Kutner, & Ghein, 1969).

One of the major critics of Piaget's theory was Lev Vygotsky (1979), and his criticisms are particularly important from a multicultural perspective. Piaget viewed the process of child development as being innate; therefore, he placed much less emphasis on social influences. In contrast, Vygotsky believed that structural differences in cognition arose from cultural differences that are transmitted to the child from parents, teachers, and others; thus, social influences are very important in shaping cognitive development. This perspective makes intuitive sense; if cognition develops to help us better adapt to our environment, as Piaget argues, then individuals from different cultures may develop different schemas, heuristics, and problem-solving strategies, given that adaptive behavior may vary from culture to culture.

For example, in Chapter Three we discussed the fact that many of the heuristics used in attribution theory were specific to individualistic cultures, as these strategies assumed that behavior is motivated internally and is expected to be consistent across situations. In collectivist cultures, behavior is expected to change according to situational factors. Thus, biases such as the fundamental attribution error may be more adaptive in an individualistic culture than they would be in a collectivist culture. In the personality section, we also explore the ways in which our schemas about the self are largely culturally determined (Norenzayan & Nisbett, 2000).

Another problem with Piaget's theory is that it assumes that all cultures value the principles of formal logic as the major way of understanding the world. However, there is some recent evidence to suggest that this assumption may be incorrect. Peng and Nisbett (1999) argue that American and other Western cultures favor nondialectical thinking, which is characterized by dualistic thinking and reasoning that is linear, logical, and moves in one direction. Thus, if a contradiction between two ideas occurs, we must figure out which statement is the correct statement. Asian cultures, however, favor dialectical thinking, which reflects a cognitive tendency toward acceptance of contradiction. Dialectical thinking is reflected in yin-yang reasoning, in which change and contradiction are inevitable; therefore, it is meaningless to discuss one event without considering the whole picture. This idea is similar to the Gestalt principle that the whole is more than the sum of its parts. Peng and Nisbett found this difference in thinking reflected in many ways. For example, Chinese participants moderated their views when confronted with opposing propositions, whereas Americans became more extreme (a phenomenon known as group polarization in social psychology). Although the view that basic cognitive processes differ across cultures is not accepted by all researchers (Chan, 2000; Ho, 2000; Hong, Morris, Chiu, & Benet-Martinez, 2000), anecdotal evidence of the consequences of our dualistic thinking abounds in this textbook. The need to resolve rather than accept contradictions is evident in the ongoing nature-nurture debate, the mind-body split, and the difficulty in accepting individuals with multiple minority statuses, such as being biracial, bisexual, and a woman of color (issues we address in more detail in Chapter Nine).

Moral Reasoning

The development of moral reasoning is also a major task in childhood and adolescence. Kohlberg (1981) identified three stages of moral reasoning. *Preconventional morality* characterizes children up to age 9; at this stage, children's sense of morality is guided by an attempt to avoid punishment and to obtain rewards. *Conventional morality* begins in early adolescence; at this stage, commonly accepted laws and rules determine children's conception of right and wrong. *Postconventional morality* develops in adolescence;

at this stage, one's conception of morality is more abstract, focusing more on individual rights and following one's own ethical principles. Some individuals never reach the postconventional stage of moral development, according to Kohlberg.

Kohlberg's (1981) model of moral development is often criticized for not taking into consideration gender and cultural differences in moral values. There is some evidence to suggest that the preconventional and conventional stage may be universal, but there are gender and cultural differences in moral reasoning for the postconventional stage. Gilligan (1982) argues that whereas boys are more likely to base moral judgments in this stage on justice, girls tend to base their moral judgments on caring and maintaining interpersonal relationships, and this emphasis should not be considered more immature, as Kohlberg suggests. F. Wilson (1995) examined the effects of gender, age, and ethnic/cultural variables on moral reasoning and found no significant differences between groups. However, consistent with Gilligan's findings, female participants were more likely to focus on ethics of care and males were more likely to emphasize justice in moral reasoning.

However, even Gilligan's (1982) view has been criticized for being ethnocentric. Gilligan emphasizes the conflict between one's own desires and one's responsibilities to others, but other cultures do not have this conflict: What is good for the other person is the best course of action (Fiske et al., 1998). This bias carries over into the assessment of morality. Eckensberger (1994) argues that Kohlberg's scoring system is difficult to utilize in non-Western groups. For example, in Israel, participants expressed a moral concern for collective happiness, which is not an objective in Western traditions; in addition, participants from Taiwan emphasized the importance of filial piety and collective utility.

Shweder, Much, Mahapatra, and Park (1997) argue that there are three major types of moral reasoning: a focus on autonomy, which characterizes Western countries; a focus on community, which characterizes East Asian countries; and a focus on divinity, which characterizes India. In our culture, we believe that people have basic rights (life, liberty, the pursuit of happiness) that cannot be violated; consequently, moral reasoning involves behaviors that help us to realize these rights (Fiske et al., 1998). In many Asian cultures, which are heavily influenced by Confucianism and Buddhist teachings, filial piety and concern for others are more important; consequently, obedience, especially to one's parents, is a moral imperative (Fiske et al., 1998). In India, suffering, personal responsibility, and Karma (in which every act of good or evil will affect others) are emphasized (Shweder et al., 1997). Thus, the best course of action from a moral standpoint may vary from culture to culture.

Language Development

The development of language allows us to communicate complex ideas to other people. Although all languages share some common features, they also differ in important ways. For example, they differ in number of *phonemes*, the smallest units or building blocks of language. The sounds c, th, b, and sh are examples of phonemes. The English language has about 40 phonemes; other languages have twice as many (Bourne, Dominowski, Loftus, & Healy, 1986). Initially, as infants are beginning to acquire language, they are able to babble many different phonemes. However, as they grow older, they lose the ability to distinguish sounds that are not in their native language (Werker & Desjardins, 1995). Research indicates that even deaf infants babble by making repetitive movements with their hands rather than sounds (Pettito & Marentetto, 1991).

It is often difficult to learn the phonemes from a different language because certain phonemes do not exist in our vocabulary. For example, in Japan, there is no distinction between r and l sounds, hence the common mispronunciation of *rice* as *lice*. In Tagalog, the national language of the Philippines, there is no distinction between the p and f sounds; consequently, words like *fish* are sometimes mispronounced in English as *pish*.

Grammatical rules also vary in different languages. In English, we occasionally use personal pronouns to describe objects, such as when we refer to a boat as she, but this is generally not the rule. In Spanish, however, all objects are denoted with a masculine or feminine pronoun, such as *el libro* (book, masc.) and *la casa* (house, fem.). In Tagalog, there is no differentiation between the pronouns he and she, even for males and females; thus, Filipinos often refer to females as he and males as she. Another difference in grammatical rules is that in English, adjectives come before nouns, but in Spanish and many other languages, the reverse is true; thus, white house becomes *casa blanca*.

Vocabularies of languages also differ. In fact, the number of words that a language has to describe a particular concept often reveals something about what that culture values. For example, there are more words for *camel* in Arabic than there are in English, and in English there are many words to describe *automobiles* (Triandis, 1995); this difference reflects the greater importance of automobiles as a mode of transportation in our society. Similarly, in English, there are many words pertaining to self-focused emotions such as anger, whereas in Japanese, there are many words for interpersonal emotions such as sympathy (Markus & Kitayama, 1991); this difference highlights the distinction between individualistic cultures, which focus more on the self, versus collectivist cultures, which focus more on the needs of others.

Although there are different theories for how language develops, there appears to be an ideal age range in which language develops much more rapidly and easily, usually before the age of 5. As children grow older, language acquisition becomes much more difficult. Unfortunately, in our culture, learning a second language usually does not occur until adolescence—long past the age at which such a task is mastered with ease. Even learning several languages at once is mastered fairly easily before the age of 5.

As our culture becomes more diverse, it becomes increasingly likely that people will be speaking another language in addition to English. However, some educators argue that bilingual education might confuse children; they might start mixing the languages together, causing them to perform poorly in school. Research does not support this fear. In fact, there is some evidence to suggest that bilingual children actually do better in reading, nonverbal logic, mental flexibility, and understanding of language (Diaz, 1983; Hakuta & Diaz, 1985). Bilingual education also leads to a better appreciation for cultural diversity (Lambert, Genesee, Holobow, & Chartrand, 1993).

Although research does not support the assumption that bilingualism leads to cognitive and academic difficulties, speaking a language other than English can lead to stigmatization, which can lead to poor academic achievement and other negative consequences (Yamamoto, Silva, Ferrari, & Nukariya, 1997). Some researchers argue that the movement to deny bilingual education is a denial of ethnic minority students' culture and an attempt to marginalize minorities in the low SES groups, in particular (Macedo, 1998). The controversy in Oakland, California, over the formal acceptance of Ebonics as a language also raised questions about the value of standard English versus African American identity (Ogbu, 1999).

Another important aspect of language development is concept formation. Different languages not only have different phonemes and structure, but they also reflect differences in the ways concepts are organized and perceived. Usually, these differences in concept represent differences in what is important to a particular culture. For example, the Dani of New Guinea have only two color terms corresponding to light and dark. This does not mean that the Dani cannot see the same colors that we do, however. In experiments in which they were shown prototypical colors, such as a true red, they were able to learn these concepts quickly (Rosch, 1973). This study illustrates that some aspects of categorization are universal, in that members from all cultures can easily learn categories for things like basic colors and shapes. However, this study also illustrates that the words and concepts that people use reflect what is important in their culture, which leads to differences in the number and organization of words conveying certain concepts.

One of the characteristics that reflects the value system of our culture is that English is a male-dominated language. It has been standard practice in English to use *man, mankind,* and *he* to refer to all people. You may assume that such usage has little if any effect, but research suggests otherwise: When reading passages, children are more likely to think of boys when the pronoun *he* is used rather than assuming that *he* refers to all people (Hyde, 1984). In addition, men and women process stimuli more quickly when they represent stereotypes of males and females, such as a female nurse and a male physician, even when they are opposed to gender stereotyping (Banaji & Hardin, 1996). In my own personal experience (Barongan), the use of the masculine pronoun had a profound effect on my understanding of the Bible. As a child, I used to argue to my parents that I was exempt from the teachings of the Bible because everything in it referred explicitly to man and mankind, and I was a girl! The use of male nouns and pronouns to represent all people reveals something about what is valued in our culture: masculinity. Not surprisingly, the characteristics that are associated with individualistic cultures, such as competitiveness, independence, and aggressiveness, are more typical of stereotypes of males than of females. Many texts currently try to rectify this problem by alternating the use of masculine and feminine pronouns or using the gender-inclusive *he or she,* as is the case in this textbook.

PERSONALITY

Personality, like developmental psychology, also examines the ways people change and grow over time. Research in personality is often criticized for focusing too much on group norms and not enough on individual differences. Because experimental studies are the gold standard in psychology, most personality research emphasizes a *nomothetic approach,* which attempts to find general laws that apply to all people. However, in a field that focuses on individual differences, case studies may actually be better suited for the study of personality. The problem with utilizing case studies is that they often lack the scientific rigor of experimental studies; consequently, *idiographic approaches* that focus on the uniqueness of the individual are often neglected, even in the field of personality.

Another criticism of the field of psychology in general and of personality in particular is the tendency to locate the source of the problem within the person. As we discussed in Chapter Three, this bias is known as the fundamental attribution error. It is particularly relevant in the field of personality because we assume that personality is something that resides within individuals and is the cause of their behavior. Because of this bias, we tend to make assumptions that have the effect of blaming the victim. For example, an African American who lives in poverty is assumed to be poor because he or she is lazy and lacks intelligence rather than because of factors related to prejudice and discrimination. A woman who stays in an abusive relationship is assumed to do so because she has battered woman syndrome rather than because she lacks the financial independence to leave or because her partner has threatened to kill her if she leaves. This bias highlights one of the negative consequences of living in an individualistic culture.

In the following, we first review several of the major personality theories and then discuss some of the strengths and limitations of these theories from a multicultural perspective. The following theories will be examined: psychodynamic theories, behavioral/social cognitive theories, humanistic/existential theories, trait theories, and self theories.

Psychodynamic Theories

Psychodynamic theories refer to those theories that are based on Sigmund Freud's (1920) theory of personality. All psychodynamic theories make certain assumptions about behavior. First, they argue that behavior is influenced by unconscious processes, or processes of which the person may be unaware. Second, they assume that adult behavior is shaped by childhood experiences, usually before the age of 5. Finally, they argue that lack of awareness of childhood conflicts leads to pathology.

Freud argued that psychopathology could develop in several ways. First, psychopathology can result from an imbalance among one of the three basic structures of personality: the id, the ego, and the superego. The *id* corresponds to our innate aggressive and sexual instincts, the *ego* to the rational part of our personality, and the *superego* to the moral aspect of our personality. An imbalance in which the id is strong and the superego is weak can result in Antisocial Personality Disorder, in which persons seek to gratify their sexual and aggressive urges with little regard for other people, rules, or authority.

Second, a person may become fixated at one of the psychosexual stages of development, either because of overgratification or undergratification of the child's needs during this period of development. The psychosexual stages are characterized by a concentration of sexual energy, or *libido*, on a particular erogenous zone. The infant moves from self-satisfying through autoeroticism to heterosexual relationships, which are necessary to function normally in society. The *oral stage* characterizes the first year of life, during which the infant's primary source of pleasure is the mouth. The *anal stage* occurs during ages 2 to 3, during which toilet training occurs. The *phallic stage* occurs during ages 3 to 5. It is during this stage that the *Oedipus/Electra complex* occurs, in which the child's sexual energy is focused on the opposite-sex parent. However, the child recognizes that the same-sex parent is a rival, and to avoid punishment by the same-sex parent, the child represses the conflict and identifies with the same-sex parent, which results in the development of the superego and traditional gender role development. The *latency stage* occurs during ages 6 to 12, during which the child's libidinal energy is focused on developing academic and social skills. The *genital stage* begins around adolescence and is characterized by sexual energy that is focused on the opposite sex; this results from the displacement of one's sexual desire for the parent onto a more appropriate love object. Inappropriate resolution of the conflicts that occur at these stages can result in *fixation* at that stage. Fixation at the oral stage of development, for example, leads to problems characterized by dependency and oral behaviors such as overeating and smoking.

Finally, psychological problems can result from the rigid and inappropriate application of defense mechanisms. *Defense mechanisms* are tools used by the ego to contain the expression of id instincts. For example, repression of the Oedipal conflict and displacement of sexual feelings in the genital stage are necessary for healthy development. Projection involves attributing one's own aggressive or sexual instincts to someone else. Although occasional use of projection and other defense mechanisms is normal, overuse and the indiscriminate use of the defense mechanisms can result in psychopathology. Paranoid disorders, in which individuals constantly perceive aggressive behavior in others, are examples of psychopathology resulting from the overuse of projection.

Psychodynamic theory assumes that psychological disorders result from repressed childhood conflicts. Thus, the goal of treatment is usually to make these unconscious conflicts conscious. This is accomplished by having persons talk about the events of their past in detail. The therapist helps clients uncover these conflicts by making interpretations about unconscious motives underlying the clients' behavior. The therapist makes use of (1) free association, in which clients are encouraged to say whatever comes to mind and the resulting associations without self-censoring; (2) dream analysis, in which clients describe the manifest content or remembered content of the dream, and the therapist makes interpretations about the latent content, or the symbols behind the dream, which will reveal the unconscious conflict; (3) transference, in which clients view the therapist as some significant person (usually a parent) from their past; and (4) resistance, in which clients unconsciously avoid the process of making the unconscious conscious by forgetting important information, missing sessions, or bringing up important information at the end of therapy sessions so that it cannot be discussed.

Freud's theory of personality has had an enormous impact on the field of psychology, for he developed the first theory of personality, the first psychological theory of psychopathology, and the first form of talking therapy. His theory is so pervasive that many concepts of psychodynamic theory, such as that behavior can be motivated by unconscious processes, that we can be influenced by our past, and the existence of defense mechanisms, are assumptions that most people have about personality—even those who have never taken a psychology course. Freud has also influenced many related fields, as well, including art, literature, and religion. In fact, every personality theory that has been developed since Freud is in some way a reaction to or a revision of his original theory.

Nevertheless, psychodynamic theories have been criticized on many grounds. One of the major criticisms is the lack of empirical evidence supporting many of their major assumptions. Part of the reason for this lack of empirical evidence is that many of the concepts in psychodynamic theory are difficult to operationally define. It is assumed that behavior is motivated by unconscious processes; therefore, examining behavior will be insufficient in understanding a person's motivations. Relatedly, many of the hypotheses in psychodynamic theory are untestable and so cannot be invalidated; in other words, there is often no null hypothesis to test in psychodynamic theory because any outcome can be used as evidence to support the theory. Finally, psychodynamic theory is based primarily on case studies rather than experiments, and the cases primarily consisted of young, middle-class women living in Vienna during the Victorian era.

Another criticism of psychodynamic theories is that they are biased against women. Freud has been criticized for his assumption of penis envy in girls, his assumption that traditional gender roles are biologically determined and are necessary for normal development, his belief that females have a weaker superego than males, his belief that the need for clitoral stimulation in the sexual act is a sign of pathology, and his insistence that mothers are responsible for producing pathology in their children. In addition, Freud has also been criticized for his excessive emphasis on id impulses and his lack of attention to social factors in the development of personality. Psychodynamic therapy has also been criticized for recapitulating a patriarchal model, in that the therapist (historically male) is the expert who interprets unconscious motivations, and the client (usually female) is the patient who is unaware of the motives of her own behavior.

More recent conceptualizations of psychodynamic theory have taken some of these criticisms into consideration. For example, Karen Horney (1967a, 1967b) did not believe that women suffered from penis envy. Instead, she believed that females wanted all the rights and privileges that men enjoy in our society for being men, rather than desiring their genitalia specifically. In addition, she focused more on cultural factors, arguing that gender roles were assigned by society rather than biology, and she focused more on psychological rather than sexual needs in the development of personality.

Object relations theory and self theories differ from Freud's original theory, in that they focus on interpersonal relationships rather than biological drives and on pre-Oedipal development rather than Oedipal conflicts. In object relations theory, infants move from complete dependence on the mother to interdependence, a healthy give and take in which persons can rely on others and others can rely on them (Liebert & Liebert, 1998). This view of healthy behavior is more consistent with the values of collectivist cultures, in which the goal of behavior is interdependence. According to this perspective, pathology results when the mother does not facilitate the development of interdependence in her child. Self psychology argues that the healthy individual develops a coherent sense of self through experiences with the parent that allows children to feel that they are worthwhile and to share in their parents' goodness (Kohut & Wolf, 1978). Children who do not have these experiences overcompensate for their lack of a coherent self by adhering to a grandiose version of the self and may develop Narcissistic characteristics as a result.

Although these theories are more often accepted by feminists because of the focus on connectedness and interpersonal relationships, they have also been criticized on several grounds. Okun (1992) argues that, similar to Freud's theory, these theories lack empirical support. She also questions the assumption that most of personality is formed in the first few years of life. In addition, these theories still contain many sexist assumptions: Women are accused of harming their children when they act in ways that satisfy their own needs rather than others', whereas men are not; the mother-child relationship is considered inevitable and necessary, whereas the father-child relationship is of even less importance than it was in Freud's theory; and there is no acknowledgment in these theories of the impact of sociocultural issues, such as the changing roles of women in society. Finally, therapy still involves an unequal power relationship between therapist and client.

Psychodynamic theories are also criticized from a cultural perspective. These theories assume that the patriarchal, nuclear family model is necessary for normal development, and anything that deviates from this model will lead to pathology. For example, in some cultures, wet nurses are used for breast-feeding and extended family members such as siblings and grandmothers take considerable responsibility for child rearing (Espin & Gawelek, 1992). Psychodynamic theories imply that these cultures, as well as matriarchal societies, gay and lesbian parents, single-parent families in which mothers or fathers are the primary caretakers, and extended family systems would all lead to unhealthy psychological development. As we discussed in the developmental psychology section, empirical evidence suggests that all of these variations of family structure can lead to healthy psychological adjustment.

Nevertheless, psychodynamic theory is used to explain some important concepts relevant to multicultural psychology. Theories developed to explain prejudice are often based on psychodynamic conceptualizations, such as the authoritarian personality and narcissistic personality, as we discussed in Chapter Three. In addition, the concept of defense mechanisms such as displacement (or scapegoating) has been useful in understanding discrimination, and defense mechanisms such as denial have been used to describe a strategy for dealing with prejudice and discrimination, albeit an unhealthy one. Clark, Anderson, Clark, and Williams (1999) argue that denial of one's experiences with prejudice may be associated with certain physiological symptoms that could lead to both physical and psychological problems. Thompson (1996) also argues that eating disorders in women of color develop as a coping strategy (defense mechanism) for dealing with racism, homophobia, classism, acculturation, and abuse rather than as a concern for one's appearance. Thus, living up to the thin ideal of beauty may be more relevant for European American women than it is for women of color as an etiological factor in eating disorders. Psychodynamic theory can also be used to understand therapists' reluctance to bring up issues related to race and ethnicity with their clients, in that they may unconsciously experience guilt over being from the majority culture, may overidentify with their clients, or may hold negative stereotypes about their clients (Holmes, 1992).

Behavioral/Social Cognitive Theories

Behavioral theories of personality developed in reaction to psychodynamic theories. Behavioral theorists' major criticism of psychodynamic theories is that mental processes such as unconscious conflicts and subjective experience are not acceptable scientific data because they are not open to verification by others. In congruence with the scientific method, behavioral theorists focus on the study of behavior because it is directly observable. As a result, behavioral theories tend to have more empirical support than dynamic theories. The three principles of learning theory are classical conditioning, operant conditioning, and modeling/observational learning.

Classical conditioning was originally discovered by accident by a Russian physiologist named Ivan Pavlov (1927). It involves the pairing of stimuli so that an automatic, reflexive response evoked by one stimulus can eventually be evoked by a previously neutral stimulus. Pavlov demonstrated that, after several paired presentations of food with the sound of a bell, dogs eventually salivated to the sound of the bell only. In Pavlov's study, food served as the *unconditioned stimulus* because it reflexively produced an *unconditioned response,* salivation. The bell represented the *conditioned stimulus:* Prior to its presentation with the food, the bell had no association for the dog; however, after pairing the presentation of the bell with the food, the bell also evoked a *conditioned response,* salivation, that was identical to the unconditioned response produced by the food. Classical conditioning operates in controlling human behavior, as well, such as when you get hungry around noon because that is the time that you normally associate with eating lunch. Classical conditioning is often the basis of emotional reactions that we develop toward new stimuli, such as the fear of elevators.

Whereas classical conditioning involves learning paired associations, *operant conditioning* involves learning the association between behavior and its consequences (Skinner, 1938). Operant conditioning occurs through reinforcement and punishment. Reinforcement can be positive or negative. *Positive reinforcement* occurs when a stimulus is presented or added after a behavior is performed, which increases the likelihood that the behavior will be performed again. For example, giving children $10 for every A on their report card increases the likelihood that they will get As again in the future. *Negative reinforcement* occurs when an aversive stimulus is removed after a behavior is performed, which also increases the likelihood that the behavior will be performed again. For example, some African American students underachieve academically to avoid being accused of acting too White (Fordham & Ogbu, 1986); underachievement is negatively reinforced because it removes the aversive stimulus of being called too White. Behavior that is controlled by negative reinforcement is often undesirable because it usually involves avoidance. *Punishment* occurs when something is added or removed after a behavior is performed that decreases the likelihood that the behavior will occur again. For example, a speeding ticket is a punishment for speeding; a fine is added after the behavior to deter you from speeding in the future. Time-out is a punishment for throwing temper tantrums; reinforcements such as friends, toys, and attention are removed to discourage temper tantrums in the future. Punishment is less often used in treatment because of ethical concerns, because it does not foster the development of adaptive behavior, and because it can lead to undesirable behaviors such as aggression and avoidance.

Observational learning or modeling is the process through which the behavior of one person, the observer, changes as a result of being exposed to the behavior of another, the model (Bandura, 1977). Social cognitive theories such as observational learning developed as a reaction to behavioral theories. Social cognitive theorists argue that it is too extreme to focus exclusively on behavior because thought processes affect the behaviors that we choose to perform. Consequently, we also have to examine mental processes such as observational learning.

Bandura empirically demonstrated the way observational learning can influence behavior in his famous Bobo doll studies (Bandura & Walters, 1963). In these studies, nursery school children observed a model on film interacting with an inflatable plastic doll. The model behaved aggressively with the doll by punching it, hitting it with a hammer, kicking it, throwing rubber balls at it, and saying aggressive things to it. After viewing this film, the children were then taken into a room with a Bobo doll and other toys and were observed behind a one-way mirror. They were encouraged to reproduce the behaviors they had observed, and the children were able to do so with surprising accuracy. Principles of modeling are the basis of commercials meant to scare you out of doing drugs, driving without a seat belt, and other potentially dangerous activities. Modeling also accounts for why television programs are now rated for violent content.

Social cognitive theorists also argue that behavioral theory is too deterministic and does not reflect our capacity for self-motivation (Bandura, 1986). Focusing on cognitions gives the individual more control, in that one's behavior is influenced not only by the situation but by one's beliefs as well. Bandura (1978) is also well-known for his theory of *triadic reciprocal determinism*. This theory suggests that our behavior is influenced by both environmental factors and person variables, which include thoughts and feelings. Each of these three factors—behavior, the environment, and person variables—can influence and be influenced by the other two factors. In other words, each factor can serve as both a cause and an effect of behavior. This position is a modification of classical behavioral theory; in which behavior is always caused by environmental factors. Bandura's perspective is also less deterministic than classical behavioral theory, for people are not just responding to their environment.

Behavior and social cognitive theories assume that maladaptive behavior is learned in the same manner that adaptive behavior is learned. For example, anorexia may be reinforced by the compliments persons receive when they begin to lose weight. A bad romantic breakup may be perceived as punishment for intimacy, which leads to the avoidance of relationships. Phobias may persist because avoidance of the feared object or situation, such as getting in an elevator, removes the aversive experience of anxiety. A boy may learn from observing his father that being aggressive often gets you what you want. Thus, the goal in behavioral treatments is to reduce the occurrence of maladaptive behaviors and to increase the occurrence of adaptive behaviors.

Aversion therapy is a form of behavior therapy that relies on principles of classical conditioning. It is often used with people who have behaviors that are deemed unacceptable, such as addictions, aggressive behavior, and sexual fetishes (Emmelkamp, 1994). In aversion therapy, the deviant behavior is paired with an aversive stimulus so that the behavior will be associated with negative consequences rather than pleasing ones. For example, one form of treatment for smoking cessation involves rapidly smoking many cigarettes consecutively. By doing so, cigarette smoking will acquire negative associations rather than the positive associations that were formerly associated with smoking. Parents who encourage their children to smoke a single cigarette (and consequently to feel sick afterwards) to discourage them from smoking in the future are also utilizing principles of classical conditioning and aversion therapy.

A token economy is a form of behavior therapy that is based on principles of operant conditioning. In a token economy, the person earns tokens for performing desirable behavior and may lose tokens for undesirable behavior. In children, desirable behaviors might include brushing their teeth, setting the table, and doing their homework; undesirable behaviors might include fighting with their siblings, throwing temper tantrums, and talking back to their parents. These tokens can later be exchanged for things that the child wants, such as a particular toy or going to the movies. Token economies use principles of operant conditioning because they attempt to encourage more adaptive behaviors through positive reinforcement and decrease maladaptive behaviors through punishment.

Social skills training is a type of behavioral therapy that is based on principles of modeling. In social skills training, the client is taught the skills that are necessary to interact with others. Social skills training can occur at many different levels, from teaching persons with autism how to make eye contact with another person to teaching depressed persons how to introduce themselves to someone new. Social skills training often involves role playing, in which the therapist models the behavior first, and then the client imitates the therapist's behaviors. For example, a therapist may role-play the part of the client, and the client may role-play the part of a stranger; therapist and client then switch roles and evaluate the role play.

Other theories of personality rely more heavily on cognitive factors in understanding personality. Cognitive theory assumes that people's beliefs, expectations, and interpretations of the world are important in influencing their thoughts, feelings, and behavior. These theories have been particularly important in the formation of empirically validated treatments for psychological disorders. Ellis's (1996) rational-emotive behavior theory (REBT) assumes that rational thinking leads to healthy behavior; consequently, maladaptive behavior results when people operate on irrational beliefs. Beck (1976) argues that psychological problems result from faulty learning; people with psychological disorders make incorrect inferences about the world on the basis of inadequate or incorrect information.

In both of these theories, treatment focuses on teaching people how to think more rationally, logically, and realistically. In REBT, the therapist accomplishes this by (1) identifying thoughts based on irrational beliefs, (2) challenging the irrational beliefs, and (3) replacing irrational beliefs with rational ones. For example, "Nobody likes me" might be an irrational belief that a client has. The therapist might challenge this belief by pointing out to the client that this conclusion was based on one example of a rude comment by an acquaintance. The client might then be encouraged to replace this belief with a statement such as "Everyone doesn't have to like me." Beck's (1976) approach is similar but focuses more on *collaborative empiricism,* in which therapist and client are coscientists who are testing hypotheses together, rather than emphasizing rational dispute on the part of the therapist. The goals of Beck's cognitive therapy include (1) correcting clients' faulty information processing, (2) modifying clients' dysfunctional beliefs, and (3) providing clients with skills and experiences that create adaptive thinking.

Behavioral and social cognitive theories are useful in understanding many concepts relevant to multicultural psychology. Classical conditioning can be used to explain how stereotypes are formed. For example, if you have had many experiences in which comments about Jews are associated with stinginess, you may associate stinginess with Jewish people that you encounter. These stereotypes can be further reinforced through modeling, in that media portrayals of minority members are often stereotypical in nature (Graves, 1999). Operant conditioning can be used to explain how minority groups end up in powerless positions. African Americans' attempts to do well in school, to move into a predominantly White neighborhood, or to apply for a job can all result in punishment (rejection), which makes it less likely that attempts will be made in the future. Negative reinforcement can be used to understand underachievement in African Americans, as we have seen. Moreover, the greater attention to environmental factors allows psychologists to study the impact of prejudice, discrimination, and social structure as potential influences on personality. In addition, cognitive therapy is amenable to people of different cultural backgrounds. Ellis (1991) has worked with clients of different Asian backgrounds and advocates attempting to understand cultural issues during therapy.

However, these theoretical perspectives have been criticized on several grounds. Espin and Gawelek (1992) argue that behavior and cognitive perspectives do not address how social structure itself might lead to unhealthy consequences. For example, cognitive theories assume that persons are incorrect in their assessment that positive outcomes are unlikely; however, experiences with prejudice and discrimination may actually make it likely that minority individuals will not obtain certain jobs, live in a particular neighborhood, or attend the school of their choosing. Moreover, although these theories are based heavily on research, most of the research has been conducted on European Americans. In addition, Krantrowitz and Ballou (1992) argue that implicit in cognitive behavioral theories is the value of logical positivism, with its focus on linear, cause-and-effect thinking. The thinking of many minority groups, on the other hand, is often better characterized as being nonlinear, circular, and interpersonal in nature. Moreover, the focus on self-sufficiency as the goal of treatment rather than depending on the support of others may be problematic and inconsistent with the values of clients from collectivist cultures (Haaga & Davison, 1986). In addition, the argumentative style used in REBT may not be well-suited for Asian American clients, and the assertiveness skills that are taught to clients usually reflect individualistic and characteristically masculine behaviors (Krantrowitz & Ballou, 1992). For example, clients are discouraged from apologizing when turning down someone's request because apologizing is not being assertive. However, for women and other collectivist-oriented individuals, assertiveness may be viewed as being less important than maintaining harmony, and even when one must turn down a request, apologizing may be necessary to preserve the relationship (Fiske et al., 1998).

Humanistic/Existential Theories

Humanistic theories developed as a reaction to psychodynamic and behavioral theories. Many theorists disagreed with the deterministic view of human nature presented in these theories, believing instead that people have more freedom to determine the outcome of their lives. Rather than reducing all human behavior to biological or environmental factors, humanistic theorists argue that people are unique. Thus, to understand personality, we must focus on the individual's phenomenological experience. Humanistic theorists also believe that people are innately good and naturally seek out experiences that will lead them to growth. This idea is reflected in the term *self-actualization,* which reflects the movement toward fully realizing one's potential. Existential theories attempt to combine psychoanalysis and existential philosophy. Like humanistic theory, existential theories focus on living a full life, or an authentic life. Existential theories focus on four universal human struggles: (1) the meaning of life, (2) taking responsibility for one's life, (3) the certainty of death, and (4) the fact that we are ultimately alone in the world. In the following, we briefly review the humanistic theories of Rogers and Maslow and the existential theory of Perls.

One of the most influential humanistic theorists was Carl Rogers (1961). Rogers believed that people are basically good and, given the proper environment, they will inherently strive for growth. All parents need to do to provide a child with the appropriate environment is to demonstrate *unconditional positive regard* for their child. In other words, parents should accept their children with all their faults and love them no matter what they do. If children grow up with unconditional positive regard, they will develop into self-actualized or fully functioning persons. Psychological problems result when conditions of worth are placed on the child. For example, if parents show encouragement and support for their children only when they are getting As on their report card, they are not showing unconditional positive regard for their children, who may learn that their parents love them only when they perform well academically. Because children want to be loved by their parents, they want to identify only those aspects of themselves of which their parents approve. As a result, children experience *incongruence,* or a discrepancy between their ideal self, what they wish to be like, and their real self, their true or actual qualities. Incongruence leads to maladjustment because people must distort and deny their experience to live up to the image of the ideal self. Such inaccurate perceiving of self leads people away from their natural tendencies toward growth.

Rogers developed client-centered therapy as an alternative to psychoanalysis. The goal of client-centered therapy is to help individuals become more congruent so that they can be fully functioning persons. The therapist accomplishes this by expressing unconditional positive regard for clients, being genuine in his or her response to clients, and being empathic. Like psychodynamic therapists, humanistic therapists are nondirective, but for different reasons. Because humanistic therapists value clients' phenomenological experience, they let the clients decide what is important to discuss. Unlike psychodynamic therapists, humanistic therapists do not make interpretations about the client's unconscious conflicts. Humanistic therapists also differ from psychodynamic therapists in that they discourage transference; they believe that it fosters dependence on the therapist rather than encouraging clients' own inherent tendencies toward self-actualization. In fact, unlike psychodynamic therapists, humanistic therapists may self-disclose personal information about themselves if they feel that it will be therapeutic.

Maslow's (1970) humanistic theory is based on a hierarchy of needs that must be met before a person can strive for self-actualization. These needs include (1) physiological needs such as food and sleep, (2) safety needs such as shelter, (3) belongingness and love needs such as relationships, and (4) esteem needs such as respect from others. These four needs are *D-needs*, or deficiency needs; when these needs are not met, the person attempts to fulfill them. Self-actualization, on the other hand, is a *B-need*, or a being need; the person does not have to fulfill this need, but he or she is happier when it is met. One attractive feature of Maslow's theory is that it takes into consideration the fact that social conditions beyond the person's control may prevent the individual from the opportunity to have self-actualization as a goal. For example, people living in poverty may not even have their needs for food, clothing, and shelter satisfied; consequently, they do not have the luxury of worrying about whether or not they are being all that they can be.

Gestalt theory is based on the idea that awareness is the major goal of personality (Perls, 1969). Consequently, problems result when we do not pay enough attention to others, do not express our needs to others, or deny or distort our feelings or perceptions. Gestalt theory emphasizes that the whole is more than the sum of its parts; consequently, the emphasis is not on understanding the person in some compartmentalized fashion such as id, ego, superego, or on focusing on past events that make up the person, but instead on awareness in the present. Gestalt theorists argue that we are alone and ultimately responsible for our behavior and our lives. By becoming more aware of our feelings, we can live a more genuine, *authentic life.* Gestalt therapists promote awareness by encouraging clients to talk about their feelings in an active rather than passive way (e.g., I am upset vs. This bothers me), having them attend to their body language and bodily sensations (e.g., they may ask clients to tap their leg more rapidly), and encouraging clients to role-play different aspects of themselves. One common form of role play is the *empty chair technique,* in which clients take turns speaking to different parts of themselves that they imagine are sitting next to them in an empty chair.

From a multicultural perspective, humanistic and existential theories' focus on phenomenological experiences has advantages over the etic research that characterizes behavioral and social cognitive theories. In addition, feminists like the positive view of human nature and the focus on more egalitarian relationships between therapist and client (Lerman, 1992). Rogers was particularly interested in applying his theory to all cultures and often conducted workshops in other countries.

However, there are some problems with these approaches (Lerman, 1992). First, these theories downplay or neglect external reality factors and place total responsibility for growth on the individual. Consequently, they imply that all one has to do is change one's perception of oneself. This approach may not be useful for women who have been victimized or for minorities who have experienced discrimination (Espin & Gawelek, 1992). Maslow takes into consideration some of the factors involved in discrimination but does not consider the impact of gender on self-actualization. Second, the idea of self-actualization as the goal of life fits individualistic cultures better than collectivist cultures. In the example used for unconditional positive regard, the implication is that persons who try to obtain high academic achievement to please their parents rather than themselves may be in a state of incongruence. This implies that anything other than individually oriented academic achievement is less than ideal. In Asian cultures, academic achievement is more socially oriented; children are encouraged to perform well to please their families (Markus & Kitayama, 1991). Finally, some Asian clients may have difficulty with the nondirective stance of the therapist, because they tend to expect advice and immediate help (Chu & Sue, 1984).

Trait Theories

Traits are characteristics that distinguish one person from another. We often use traits when describing someone's personality; for example, we may describe ourselves as shy or talkative, outgoing or a homebody, intelligent, athletic. We expect that a particular personality trait will have some predictive value, in that we can assume that the person will act the same way across situations and over time. In other words, if we describe someone as shy, this implies that the person has been shy in the past, will be shy in the future, and will be shy in many situations.

Currently, the predominant model in trait theory is the "Big Five," or the Five Factor Model of personality (Wiggins, 1996). These factors are (1) neuroticism/emotional stability, which refers to the extent to which a person can cope with stress; (2) extroversion, which refers to the extent to which a person is reserved or outgoing; (3) openness/culture/intellect, which refers to being original, imaginative, and open-minded; (4) agreeableness, which refers to being cooperative, trusting, and supportive; and (5) conscientiousness, which refers to being hardworking, ambitious, organized, and efficient.

Cross-cultural studies suggest that the Big Five are universal, applying to both Western and non-Western cultures (Morris & Maisto, 1999). However, the factors that emerge across cultures do not always completely coincide. For example, seven personality factors have been identified in Filipino (Church, Katigbak, & Reyes, 1998) and Spanish samples (Benet & Waller, 1995). In addition, the methods used to assess these five factors often focus on individual traits rather than more context-specific measures that are more characteristic of how collectivist cultures describe themselves (Markus & Kitayama, 1991). When participants were given more freedom to choose the terms they wished to use, participants from collectivist cultures were more likely to use terms that reflected situational rather than dispositional responses (Shweder & Bourne, 1994).

Self Theories

Most personality theories either explicitly or implicitly make certain assumptions about the self. For example, both Horney (1950) and Rogers (1959) argue that problems result when people experience a conflict between their real selves and their ideal selves. Eating disorders are a good example of this; even for a woman with anorexia, her perception of her body is that it is still not thin enough. In both of these theories, persons develop this discrepancy because they are trying to live up to some real or fantasized standard that parents have given them of what they need to do to be loved. The psychodynamic perspective of Erikson (1968) and the humanistic perspective of Maslow (1970) both present theories of self that argue that one must accomplish certain tasks before one can have a meaningful relationship with others. For Erikson, persons must form a secure sense of identity before they can have a healthy relationship; for Maslow, persons must have their basic physiological and safety needs met before they can entertain needs for belongingness and love. Kohut and Wolf's (1978) self theory assumes that the goal of personality is to have an integrated, coherent sense of self, which develops from interactions with one's parents that make one feel loved, secure, and important.

Even theories that do not explicitly refer to the self make implicit assumptions about the role of the self in personality (Landrine, 1995; Markus & Kitayama, 1991; Norenzayan & Nisbett, 2000). Most theories assume that the self is independent, self-contained, and autonomous. The self is composed of unique internal attributes that cause our behavior, as we saw in the trait theories. Consequently, those attributes tell us something about what the person has been like in the past and how the person will behave in the future. In addition, we expect the person to act consistently across situations.

Walter Mischel's (1968) research provides some evidence to suggest that personality is not as predictive as we imagine it to be. For example, if a woman describes herself as talkative, we would assume that she was talkative last week, she is talkative today, and that she will be talkative tomorrow. Moreover, she would be talkative around friends, family, and teachers. However, Mischel argues that situational factors are more useful in predicting how someone will behave than are references to presumed internal attributes like talkativeness. In other words, knowing whether the person is in church, at a ball game, with her friends, or meeting strangers for the first time will be more useful in predicting whether this person will be talkative than a self-description of possessing the trait talkativeness. Mischel argues that we see consistency in behavior because of our need to believe that people's motivations are internal rather than external.

Mischel's (1968) research generated considerable controversy in the field of personality; researchers did not want to accept the idea that personality does not predict behavior. The resistance to this idea is understandable, given that it contradicts our basic assumptions about human behavior, which reflect our value of individualism. For members of collectivist cultures, Mischel's findings would be unsurprising. Their view of the self is one that is interdependent, contextual, and relational (Landrine, 1995; Markus & Kitayama, 1991). Behavior should not be consistent across situations and time because what is called for in one situation may not be the appropriate course of action in another situation. Moreover, acting under the influence of others (particularly ingroup members) is not only accepted but required. Thus, acting according to one's own wishes is often viewed as being selfish because it disregards the needs of others.

These differences in the view of the self have major implications for self-knowledge, self-schemas, self-esteem, and affect regulation. For example, in studies in which participants are asked to describe themselves, participants from individualistic cultures are more likely to list abstract personality traits (shy, intelligent, athletic), and participants from collectivist cultures are more likely to describe themselves in relation to other people (with my family, at work, with my boyfriend; Fiske et al., 1998; Markus & Kitayama, 1991). This finding does not mean, however, that members of collectivist cultures do not know themselves or have less insight than members of individualistic cultures; they are simply more likely to have a conceptualization of themselves in connection to other people. Relatedly, American participants are more likely to demonstrate the *false uniqueness effect,* or the tendency to underestimate how similar they are to others, than are Japanese participants, who are more likely to say that they are more like others (Markus & Kitayama, 1991).

Different conceptualizations of self also lead to differences in cognitive processing. For example, gender is an important schema not only for the way in which we understand ourselves, but also for in the way we process and remember information. To illustrate, my husband (Barongan) and I are both big sports fans, but his greater familiarity with the game leads to differences in what we actually perceive when we both watch the same game. My attention to and memory of the game usually involves action near the ball; consequently, I am less likely to see fouls or penalties that occur away from the ball, whereas my husband's attention can cover more of the field or court. This bias in attention and memory is reversed for female gender-related events. A few years ago, my husband attended a wedding of one of his friends, and I asked him to describe the bride's wedding dress, which he was unable to do. I then proceeded to give him some primes (Did it have sleeves? Was it white? Was the skirt puffy or straight?), which did not facilitate his memory of the wedding gown, most likely because he did not attend to it enough to remember the details in the first place.

Culture can affect our cognitive processes in similar ways. It can affect the way we conceptualize time (Landrine, 1995). Americans tend to be future-oriented and think of time as something that can be managed, used wisely, or wasted. Other cultures are less concerned about punctuality (hence, the term CP time, or colored people time) and are less concerned about wasting it, as evidenced by siestas in the middle of the day in some countries, during which businesses actually close down. In addition, biases such as the fundamental attribution error are much more likely to occur among European Americans, who view the cause of behavior as emanating from within the individual, than it is for Japanese, who expect behavior to be regulated by situational factors.

Cultural differences in the view of the self also have implications for the way we try to maintain our self-esteem. In Chapter Three, we discussed the self-serving bias, in which we tend to attribute personal failure to external factors and personal success to internal factors. In collectivist cultures, individuals are more likely to demonstrate a self-effacement bias, in which they attribute their successes to external factors such as luck and their failures to internal factors such as a lack of effort (Kitayama & Markus, 1995). Both biases serve to maintain self-esteem in their respective cultures. Similarly, the tendency to change one's attitude or behavior because of cognitive dissonance reflects the need to be consistent in one's behavior. Individuals from collectivist cultures do not demonstrate cognitive dissonance either, because self-esteem does not occur from behaving consistently, but rather from acting in a manner that will maintain a sense of harmony with others (Fiske et al., 1998).

Differences in the definition of self also have implications for the relevant emotions for a particular culture. In individualistic cultures, there is a high preponderance of ego-focused or socially disengaged emotions (Markus & Kitayama, 1991). These emotions include feelings such as anger, frustration, and pride, and reflect the extent to which the individual's goals and desires have been realized. Collectivist cultures, on the other hand, have a preponderance of other-focused or socially engaged emotions. These emotions include feelings such as indebtedness and guilt, and reflect the extent to which one has successfully participated in or avoided harming another in the relationship. This difference is reflected in the importance of expressing certain emotions. In the West, we assume a hydraulic model of anger: If anger is not expressed as it occurs, it will build up and explode later. Consequently, therapy (particularly with women) is often aimed at helping persons express their anger appropriately. In other cultures, however, anger may not be expressed because it may threaten the interdependent self. Consequently, expressing one's anger may be highly dysfunctional in collectivist cultures such as Japan (Markus & Kitayama, 1991), and perhaps for women as well, who are also more collectivist-oriented.

In fact, whereas some feelings, such as anger and happiness, are universal, other feelings, often referred to as indigenous feelings, appear to be specific to and consistent with the values of certain cultures (Markus & Kitayama, 1991). For example, in Japan, the feeling of *amae* refers to the sense of being lovingly cared for and involves depending on and presuming another person's indulgence. This feeling is probably closest to our understanding of the unconditional positive regard described by Rogers. Its prototypical form involves the bond between mother and infant, but adult forms occur as well, such as the feeling of amae that subordinates may have for their supervisor. This feeling is inherent in forming a mutually reciprocal relationship with someone else and therefore exemplifies an other-focused emotion.

Finally, cultural differences in definitions of self have implications for psychopathology and treatment. Our view of mental health includes descriptors such as being self-actualized, independent, and autonomous. These adjectives reflect the necessity of being separate from others and of acting according to one's own will. Thus, living up to the thin ideal of beauty, being controlled by one's parents as an adult, and allowing one's partner to dictate one's behavior are all potentially abnormal behaviors. People from individualistic cultures may also suffer existential crises in which they experience anxiety and alienation and question the meaning and purpose of life (Landrine, 1995), or narcissistic conflicts due to their need to feel special and to be the best in everything they do. In contrast, people from collectivist cultures are more likely to experience a crisis due to a loss or change of role, such as losing one's job or dropping out of medical school contrary to one's parents' wishes. Landrine points out that there are no diagnoses for these conflicts in the *DSM,* suggesting that we do not take them seriously. She also argues that the biggest error that therapists make is treating clients in isolation, without taking into consideration the impact of family and other members of one's ingroup. This bias toward individual therapy is implicit in all of the theories discussed in this section. Although there is a growing recognition of the value of more social forms of therapy, such as couples, family, and group therapy, graduate schools do not emphasize these forms of treatment to the same extent. Even when these forms of therapy are used, they tend to emphasize individualistic values. For example, in couples therapy, the focus of treatment is often to teach better communication skills; more specifically, partners are often taught to ask for what they want rather than assuming that the other person can read their mind. However, in collectivist cultures, members are expected to "read the mind" of the other person and to anticipate what the other wants without asking for it (Markus & Kitayama, 1991; Rothbaum et al., 2000). Thus, to meet the psychological needs of diverse clients, we must put more effort into understanding views of the self that may differ from our own, for these views can affect the way we define ourselves and conceptualize the world. They dictate the problems that we encounter, the ways we seek to feel better about ourselves, and the treatment that will be most beneficial.

CONCLUSION

Thus far, we have examined multicultural psychology from a scientific perspective and in the context of the various fields of psychology. We have seen that multicultural factors are important to consider in many of our most basic assumptions, such as the nature-nurture debate, our understanding of ourselves and the world, and in understanding the causes and impact of prejudice and discrimination. Different worldviews also affect what we consider normal behavior, how psychological problems are experienced, and what types of treatment are most beneficial. Although research in these areas has improved greatly, especially in the past decade, there is still much to be learned. Although minority groups share many similar experiences, they also differ in important ways, and we are just beginning to explore the nature of some of these differences. In the next chapters, we apply many of the concepts discussed thus far to our understanding of particular ethnic groups.

REFERENCES

American Psychiatric Association. (1994). *Diagnostic and statistical manual of mental disorders* (4th ed.). Washington, DC: Author.

Bailey, J. M., Bobrow, D., Wolfe, M., & Mikach, S. (1995). Sexual orientation of adult sons of gay fathers. *Developmental Psychology, 31,* 124–129.

Banaji, M. R., & Hardin, C. D. (1996). Automatic stereotyping. *Psychological Science, 7,* 136–141.

Bandura, A. (1977). *Social learning theory.* Englewood Cliffs, NJ: Prentice Hall.

Bandura, A. (1978). The self system in reciprocal determinism. *American Psychologist, 33,* 344–358.

Bandura, A. (1986). *Social foundations of thought and action: A social cognitive theory.* Englewood Cliffs, NJ: Prentice-Hall.

Bandura, A., & Walters, R. (1963). *Social learning and personality development.* New York: Holt, Rinehart and Winston.

Baumrind, D. (1989). Rearing competent children. In W. Damon (Ed.), *Child development today and tomorrow* (pp. 349–378). San Francisco: Jossey Bass.

Beck, A. T. (1976). *Cognitive therapy and the emotional disorders.* New York: International Universities Press.

Benet, V., & Waller, N. G. (1995). The Big Seven factor model of personality description: Evidence for its cross-cultural generality in a Spanish sample. *Journal of Personality and Social Psychology, 69,* 701–718.

Blechman, E. (1982). Are children with one parent at psychological risk? A methodological review. *Journal of Marriage and the Family, 44,* 179–195.

Bourne, L. E., Dominowski, R. L., Loftus, E. F., & Healy, A. F. (1986). *Cognitive process* (2nd ed.). Englewood Cliffs, NJ: Prentice Hall.

Bowlby, J. (1951). *Maternal care and mental health.* Geneva, Switzerland: World Health Organization.

Bowlby, J. (1969). *Attachment and loss: Vol. 1. Attachment.* London: Hogarth Press.

Bronstein, P. (1999). Differences in mothers' and fathers' behaviors toward children: A cross-cultural comparison. In L. A. Peplau, S. C. DeBro, R. C. Veniegas, & P. L. Taylor (Eds.), *Gender, culture, and ethnicity* (pp. 70–82). Mountain View, CA: Mayfield.

Buss, A. H., & Plomin, R. (1984). *Temperament: Early developing personality traits.* Hillsdale, NJ: Erlbaum.

Caplan, G. (1989). Parental divorce without harm. *Sexual and Marital Therapy, 4,* 125–126.

Chan, S. F. (2000). Formal logic and dialectical thinking are not incongruent. *American Psychologist, 55,* 1063–1064.

Chao, R. K. (1994). Beyond parental control and authoritarian parenting style: Understanding Chinese parenting through the cultural notion of training. *Child Development, 65,* 1111–1119.

Chisholm, J. (1984). *Navajo infancy.* New York: Aldine.

Chu, J., & Sue, S. (1984). Asian/Pacific-Americans and group practice. In L. E. Davis (Ed.), *Ethnicity in social group work practice* (6th ed., pp. 23–36). Amherst, MA: Human Resource Development Press.

Church, A. T., Katigbak, M. S., & Reyes, J. A. S. (1998). Further exploration of Filipino personality structure using the lexical approach: Do the Big-Five or Big-Seven dimensions emerge? *European Journal of Personality, 12,* 249–269.

Clark, R., Anderson, N. B., Clark, V. R., & Williams, D. R. (1999). Racism as a stressor for African Americans. *American Psychologist, 54,* 805–816.

Coley, R. L. (1998). Children's socialization experiences and functioning in single-mother households: The importance of fathers and other men. *Child Development, 69,* 219–230.

Coll, G. C., Crnic, K., Lamberty, G., Wasik, B. K., Jenkins, R., Garcia, H. V., & McAdoo, H. P. (1996). An integrative model for the study of developmental competencies in minority children. *Child Development, 67,* 1891–1914.

Deater-Deckard, K., Scarr, S., McCartney, K., & Eisenberg, M. (1994). Parental separation anxiety: Relationships with parenting stress, child-rearing attitudes, and maternal anxieties. *Psychological Science, 5,* 341–346.

Derdeyn, A. P. (1994). Parental separation, adolescent psychopathology, and problem behaviors: Comment. *Journal of the American Academy of Child and Adolescent Psychiatry, 33,* 1131–1133.

Diaz, R. M. (1983). Thought and two languages: The impact of bilingualism on cognitive development. *Review of Research in Education, 10,* 23–54.

Eckensberger, L. H. (1994). Moral development and its measurement across cultures. In W. J. Lonner & R. S. Malpass (Eds.), *Psychology and culture* (pp. 71–78). Boston: Allyn & Bacon.

Ellis, A. (1991). Using RET effectively: Reflections and interview. In M. E. Bernard (Ed.), *Using rational-emotive therapy effectively* (pp. 1–33). New York: Plenum Press.

Ellis, A. (1996). *My philosophy of psychotherapy.* New York: Albert Ellis Institute for Rational Emotive Behavior Therapy.

Emmelkamp, P. M. (1994). Behavior therapy with adults. In A. E. Bergin & S. L. Garfield (Eds.), *Handbook of psychotherapy and behavior change* (4th ed., pp. 379–427). New York: Wiley.

Erikson, E. H. (1968). *Identity: Youth in crisis.* New York: Norton.

Espin, O. M., & Gawelek, M. A. (1992). Women's diversity: Ethnicity, race, class, and gender in theories of feminist psychology. In L. S. Brown & M. Ballou (Eds.), *Personality and psychopathology* (pp. 88–107). New York: Guilford Press.

Fergusson, D. M., Horwood, L. J., & Lynske, M. T. (1994). Parental separation, adolescent psychopathology, and problem behaviors. *Journal of the American Academy of Child and Adolescent Psychiatry, 33,* 1122–1131.

Field, T. (1991). Quality infant day-care and grade school behavior and performance. *Child Development, 62,* 863–870.

Fiske, A. P., Kitayama, S., Markus, H. R., & Nisbett, R. E. (1998). The cultural matrix of social psychology. In D. T. Gilbert, S. T. Fiske, & G. Lindzey (Eds.), *The handbook of social psychology* (4th ed., pp. 915–981). New York: McGraw-Hill.

Flaks, D. K., Ficher, I., Masterpasqua, F., & Joseph, G. (1995). Lesbians choosing motherhood: A comparative study of lesbian and heterosexual parents and their children. *Developmental Psychology, 31,* 105–114.

Fordham, S., & Ogbu, J. U. (1986). Black students school success: Coping with the "burden of 'acting white.' " *Urban Review, 18,* 176–206.

Freedman, D. (1974). *Human infancy: An evolutionary perspective.* Hillsdale, NJ: Erlbaum.

Freud, S. (1920). *Beyond the pleasure principle.* London: Hogarth Press.

Gilligan, C. (1982). *In a different voice: Psychological theory and women's development.* Cambridge, MA: Harvard University Press.

Graves, S. B. (1999). Television and prejudice reduction: When does television as a vicarious experience make a difference? *Journal of Social Issues, 55,* 707–725.

Haaga, D. A., & Davison, G. C. (1986). Cognitive change methods. In F. H. Kanfer & A. P. Goldstein (Eds.), *Helping people change: A textbook of methods* (3rd ed., pp. 236–282). New York: Pergamon Press.

Hakuta, K., & Diaz, R. M. (1985). The relationship between degree of bilingualism and cognitive ability: A critical discussion of some new longitudinal data. In K. E. Nelson (Ed.), *Children's language* (Vol. 5, pp. 319–344). Hillsdale, NJ: Erlbaum.

Hall, G. C. N., Bansal, A., & Lopez, I. R. (1999). Ethnicity and psychopathology: A meta-analytic review of 31 years of comparative MMPI/MMPI-2 research. *Psychological Assessment, 11,* 186–197.

Harding, J., Proshansky, H., Kutner, B., & Ghein, I. (1969). Prejudice and ethnic relations. In G. Lindzey & E. Aronson (Eds.), *The handbook of social psychology* (2nd ed., pp. 1–76). New York: McGraw-Hill.

Harlow, H. F., & Zimmerman, R. R. (1959). Affectional responses in the infant monkey. *Science, 130,* 421–432.

Ho, D. Y. F. (2000). Dialectical thinking: Neither Eastern nor Western. *American Psychologist, 55,* 1064–1065.

Holmes, D. E. (1992). Race and transference in psychoanalysis and psychotherapy. *International Journal of Psychoanalysis, 73,* 1–11.

Hong, Y., Morris, M. W., Chiu, C., & Benet-Martinez, V. (2000). Multicultural minds. *American Psychologist, 55,* 709–720.

Horney, K. (1950). *Neurosis and human growth.* New York: Norton.

Horney, K. (1967a). The flight from womanhood: The masculinity complex in women as viewed by men and by women. In H. Kelman (Ed.), *Feminine psychology* (pp. 54–70). New York: Norton.

Horney, K. (1967b). On the genesis of the castration complex in women. In H. Kelman (Ed.), *Feminine psychology* (pp. 71–83). New York: Norton.

Hoyt, L. A., Cowen, E. L., Pedro-Carroll, J. L., & Alpert-Gillis, L. J. (1990). Anxiety and depression in young children of divorce. *Journal of Clinical Child Psychology, 19,* 26–32.

Hyde, J. (1984). Children's understanding of sexist language. *Developmental Psychology, 20,* 697–706.

Kitayama, S., & Markus, H. R. (1995). Culture and self: Implications for internationalizing psychology. In N. R. Goldberger & J. B. Veroff (Eds.), *The culture and psychology reader* (pp. 366–383). New York: New York University Press.

Kochanska, G. (1991). Socialization and temperament in the development of guilt and conscience. *Child development, 62,* 1379–1392.

Koestner, R., Franz, C., & Weinberger, J. (1990). The family origins of empathic concern: A 26-year longitudinal study. *Journal of Personality and Social Psychology, 58,* 709–717.

Kohlberg, L. (1981). *The philosophy of moral development* (Vol. 1). San Francisco: Harper & Row.

Kohut, H., & Wolf, E. S. (1978). The disorders of the self and their treatment: An outline. *International Journal of Psychoanalysis, 59,* 413–425.

Kposowa, A. J. (1998). The impact of race on divorce in the United States. *Journal of Comparative Family Studies, 29,* 529–548.

Krantrowitz, R. E., & Ballou, M. (1992). A feminist critique of cognitive-behavioral therapy. In L. S. Brown & M. Ballou (Eds.), *Personality and psychopathology* (pp. 70–87). New York: Guilford Press.

Lambert, W. E., Genesee, F., Holobow, N., & Chartrand, L. (1993). Bilingual education for majority English-speaking children. *European Journal of Psychology of Education, 8,* 3–22.

Landrine, H. (1995). Clinical implications of cultural differences: The referential versus indexical self. In N. R. Goldberger & J. B. Veroff (Eds.), *The culture and psychology reader* (pp. 744–766). New York: New York University Press.

Lerman, H. (1992). The limits of phenomenology: A feminist critique of the humanistic personality theories. In L. S. Brown & M. Ballou (Eds.), *Personality and psychopathology* (pp. 8–19). New York: Guilford Press.

Levitt, M. J., Guacci-Franco, N., & Levitt, J. L. (1993). Convoys of social support in childhood and early adolescence: Structure and function. *Developmental Psychology, 29,* 811–818.

Levy, S. R. (1999). Reducing prejudice: Lessons from social-cognitive factors underlying perceiver differences in prejudice. *Journal of Social Issues, 55,* 745–765.

Liebert, R. M., & Liebert, L. L. (1998). *Personality: Strategies and issues* (8th ed.). Pacific Grove, CA: Brooks/Cole.

Macedo, D. (1998). English only: The tongue-tying of America. In H. Shapiro & D. E. Purpel (Eds.), *Critical social issues in American education: Transformation in a postmodern world* (2nd ed., pp. 261–272). Mahwah, NJ: Erlbaum.

Markus, H., & Kitayama, S. (1991). Culture and the self: Implications for cognition, emotion, and motivation. *Psychological Review, 98,* 224–253.

Maslow, A. H. (1970). *Motivation and personality* (2nd ed.). New York: Harper & Row.

Mischel, W. (1968). *Personality and assessment.* New York: Wiley.

Norenzayan, A., & Nisbett, R. E. (2000). Culture and causal cognition. *Current Directions in Psychological Science, 9,* 132–135.

Ogbu, J. U. (1999). Beyond language: Ebonics, proper English, and identity in a Black-American speech community. *American Educational Research Journal, 36,* 147–184.

Okun, B. F. (1992). Object relations and self psychology: Overview and feminist perspective. In L. S. Brown & M. Ballou (Eds.), *Personality and psychopathology* (pp. 20–45). New York: Guilford Press.

Pavlov, I. P. (1927). *Conditioned reflexes.* London: Claredon.

Peng, K., & Nisbett, R. E. (1999). Culture, dialectics, and reasoning about contradiction. *American Psychologist, 54,* 741–754.

Perls, F. (1969). *Gestalt theory verbatim.* Lafayette, CA: People Press.

Pettito, L., & Marentetto, P. F. (1991). Babbling in the manual mode: Evidence for the ontogeny of language. *Science, 251,* 1493–1496.

Rogers, C. R. (1959). A theory of therapy, personality, and interpersonal relationship, as developed in the client-centered framework. In S. Koch (Ed.), *Psychology: A study of a science. Formulations of the person and the social context* (Vol. 3, pp. 184–256). New York: McGraw-Hill.

Rogers, C. R. (1961). *On becoming a person.* Boston: Houghton Mifflin.

Rohner, R. P. (1994). Patterns of parenting: The warmth dimension in perspective. In W. J. Lonner & R. S. Malpass (Eds.), *Psychology and culture* (pp. 113–120). Boston: Allyn & Bacon.

Rosch, E. H. (1973). Natural categories. *Cognitive Psychology, 4,* 328–350.

Rothbaum, F., Weisz, J., Pott, M., Miyake, K., & Morelli, G. (2000). Attachment and culture: Security in the United States and Japan. *American Psychologist, 55,* 1093–1104.

Rowe, D. C., Vazsonyi, A. T., & Flannery, D. J. (1994). No more than skin deep: Ethnic and racial similarity in developmental process. *Psychological Review, 101,* 396–413.

Shaw, D. S., Winslow, E. B., & Flanagan, C. (1999). A prospective study of the effects of marital status and family relations on young children's adjustment among African American and European Families. *Child Development, 70,* 742–755.

Shweder, R. A., & Bourne, E. J. (1984). Does the concept of person vary cross-culturally? In R. A. Shweder & R. Levin (Eds.), *Culture theory: Essays on mind, self, and emotion* (pp. 158–199). New York: Cambridge University Press.

Shweder, R. A., Much, N. C., Mahapatra, M., & Park. L. (1997). "The Big Three" of morality (autonomy, community, divinity), and the "Big Three" explanations of suffering. In A. M. Brandt & P. Rozin (Eds.), *Morality and health* (pp. 119–169). New York: Routledge.

Silverstein, L. B., & Phares, V. (1996). Fathering as a feminist issue. *Psychology of Women Quarterly, 20,* 3–38.

Skinner, B. F. (1938). *The behavior of organisms.* New York: Appleton-Century-Crofts.

Sonnek, S. M. (1999). Perception and parenting style: The influence of culture (Hispanic-American, European-American). *Dissertation Abstracts International, 60,* 3021.

Thomas, A., & Chess, S. (1977). *Temperament and development.* New York: Brunner-Mazel.

Thompson, B. (1996). Multiracial feminist theorizing about eating problems: Refusing to rank oppressions. *Eating Disorders, 4,* 104–114.

Triandis, H. C. (1995). The self and social behavior in differing cultural contexts. In N. R. Goldberger & J. B. Veroff (Eds.), *The culture and psychology reader* (pp. 326–365). New York: New York University Press.

Tronick, E. Z., Morelli, G. A., & Ivey, P. K. (1992). The Efe forager infant and toddlers pattern of social relationships: Multiple and simultaneous. *Developmental Psychology, 28,* 568–577.

Victor, S. B., & Fish, M. C. (1995). Lesbian mothers and their children: A review for school psychologists. *School Psychology Review, 24,* 456–479.

Vygotsky, L. S. (1979). *Mind in society: The development of higher mental processes.* Cambridge, MA: Harvard University Press.

Wallerstein, J. S. (1991). The long-term effects of divorce on children: A review. *Journal of the American Academy of Child and Adolescent Psychiatry, 30,* 349–360.

Werker, F. J., & Desjardins, R. N. (1995). Listening to speech in the 1st year of life: Experiential influences on phoneme perception. *American Psychological Society, 4,* 76–81.

Wiggins, J. S. (1996). *The five-factor model of personality: Theoretical perspectives.* New York: Guilford Press.

Wilson, F. L. (1995). The effects of age, gender, and ethnic/cultural background on moral reasoning. *Journal of Social Behavior and Personality, 10,* 67–78.

Wilson, M. N. (1989). Child development in the context of the Black extended family. *American Psychologist, 44,* 380–385.

Yamamoto, J., Silva, J. A., Ferrari, M., & Nukariya, K. (1997). Culture and psychopathology. In G. Johnson-Powell & J. Yamamoto (Eds.), *Transcultural child development* (pp. 34–57). New York: Wiley.

ISSUES FOR DISCUSSION

1. In the recent controversy over whether there should be gay Boy Scout leaders, several assumptions are made regarding how this situation may lead to problems in the development of young boys. What are some of these assumption? What evidence, if any, is there to validate these assumptions?

2. Few theorists explicitly refer to the way that minority status can affect personality development. Erikson is one exception: he believed that minorities were at risk of forming a negative identity because of their devalued status in society. Do you agree with this assumption? How can being a member of a minority group affect the development of personality?

SECTION II

PSYCHOLOGY IN THE CONTEXT OF MULTICULTURAL ISSUES

FIVE

AFRICAN AMERICANS

I am because we are; we are, therefore I am.
—African worldview (Nobles, 1973)

African Americans are currently the largest ethnic minority group in the United States at 35 million, 13 percent of the U.S. population. The term African American is used in this chapter because most African Americans prefer this term (McAdoo, 1998). Ninety-six percent of African Americans' ancestors were brought here from Africa as slaves. A minority of African Americans are recent immigrants, most of whom are persons of African ancestry who have immigrated to the United States from Latin America.

There exists a substantial social psychology literature on European Americans' prejudice and discrimination toward African Americans (Gaines & Reed, 1995; Jones, 1997), some of which was discussed in Chapter Three. The attitudes and behaviors of the majority group certainly affect minority groups; thus, the effects of prejudice and discrimination on African Americans are addressed in this chapter. However, the basis of European American prejudice and discrimination is not emphasized, as the focus of this chapter is on the psychology of African Americans.

HISTORY

February is African American History Month. Although it is important for all Americans to give special recognition to African American history, it is also important to understand that African American history is part and parcel of American history. African Americans have been influenced by and have influenced American history. A synopsis of African American history follows to provide a context for current theory and research in psychology.

1600s–1800s: Slavery and the Civil War

The earliest African immigrants to the United States probably were not slaves. Twenty Africans came to America in 1619 as servants (Takaki, 1993). Similar to many other European immigrants, these Africans were probably indentured servants who were bound by contract for four to seven years to pay for their transportation expenses. Unlike slaves, these servants could eventually earn their freedom.

Black and White servants began to be treated differently during the 1640s (Takaki, 1993). Black servants began to be treated as slaves for life in 1642 in Virginia. In 1648, the children of slaves began to be regarded as slaves. Slavery did not develop in New England because of the absence of a staple crop and a need for slaves. The increase in African slaves in the South decreased the need for White servants, and African labor was less expensive than White labor. The Virginia legislature formally began to define a slave as property in 1669. Later, in 1691, the Virginia legislature denied slaves the right to vote, to hold office, and to testify in court.

The slave trade was abolished by Congress in 1807. However, this did not end slavery. Slavery continued to flourish from 1820 to 1850 in Alabama, Mississippi, and Louisiana because of cotton production. Slave owners depended on slave women to bear children; African American men were used as breeders, and frequent changes of partner were common for African American men and women (Hines & Boyd-Franklin, 1996). Slaves had been prohibited from marrying to prevent family bonds being established that would interfere with the trade of individual slaves. Such destruction of family unity is at odds with African communal traditions. Some White owners raped slave women to produce children (Takaki, 1993).

By the Civil War, 4 million African Americans were enslaved (Takaki, 1993). The Civil War freed African Americans by law from slavery. African Americans played a critical role in the Civil War. Approximately 86,000 African Americans served; by the end of the war, one-third were missing or dead. The pivotal role of African Americans at a time when the Union troops were being depleted is depicted in the popular movie *Glory*. In 1865, near the end of the Civil War, Union Army General William Tecumseh Sherman issued Special Field Order 15, which awarded 40 acres of farmland and a mule to each of the former slaves. This would have been only a token form of reparations for slavery and other forms of oppression, but it would have represented a recognition of the debt owed to African Americans. President Andrew Johnson quickly rescinded this order, returning the land to the former slave owners; no other form of reparations or even an apology has been issued by the U.S. government since then.

Following the Civil War, the vestiges of slavery were prominent. The Civil Rights Act of 1875 gave African Americans the right to equal treatment in public settings, inns, theaters, and public amusement places, but the act was ruled unconstitutional in 1883. The 1896 Supreme Court's "separate but equal" decision in *Plessy v. Ferguson* legalized racial segregation of schools.

1900s–1930s: Racism and Separatism

Racism consists of beliefs, attitudes, institutional arrangements, and acts that tend to denigrate individuals or groups because of phenotypic characteristics or ethnic group affiliation (Clark, Anderson, Clark, & Williams, 1999). Racism can be attitudinal or behavioral. Some individuals may suffer the negative effects of racism without attributing their problems to racism. For example, institutional racism may reduce access to resources (Clark et al., 1999), but individuals may attribute their lack of resources to their own inabilities (Ruggiero & Major, 1998). Although slavery was abolished in the nineteenth century, racism continued in the United States as a legacy of slavery during the twentieth century.

Conflicts between European Americans and African Americans continued during the early 1900s. From 1900 through 1910, anti-Black race riots occurred in the North and lynching and burning in the South (Jones, 1997). In response, the National Association for the Advancement of Colored People was established in New York City in 1909. Between 1910 and 1920, there was a large migration of African Americans north for jobs. However, many European Americans did not want African Americans in their neighborhoods.

The Social Darwinism and Eugenics movements contended that there was an evolutionary basis for the inferiority of African Americans. Natural selection, or "survival of the fittest," favored European Americans. African Americans were viewed as a burden to the progress of European Americans. The field of social psychology, which emphasized the interdependence of individual personality and societal influences, developed in response to the biological emphasis of Social Darwinism (Jones, 1997); race relations problems then were redefined as a problem of European American prejudice rather than African American inferiority. Unfortunately, Social Darwinian thought did not

James M. Jones is professor of psychology at the University of Delaware and director of the Minority Fellowship Program at the American Psychological Association. Dr. Jones earned a BA from Oberlin College (1963); an MA from Temple University (1967); and his PhD in social psychology from Yale University (1970). He was on the faculty of the Social Relations Department at Harvard University (1970–1976), during which time he published the first edition of *Prejudice and Racism* (1972), and spent a year in Trinidad and Tobago on a Guggenheim Fellowship studying Calypso humor. This work led to the development of the TRIOS model of the psychology of African American culture. McGraw-Hill published a second edition of *Prejudice and Racism* in 1997. Professor Jones is currently working on a book on the cultural psychology of African Americans for Westview Press. He is a social psychologist and serves on several editorial boards, including the *International Journal of Intercultural Relations* and *Journal of Black Psychology*, and is past-president of the Society of Experimental Social Psychology. He was awarded the 1999 Lifetime Achievement Award of the Society for the Psychological Study of Ethnic Minority Issues (Division 45) of the American Psychological Association.

Words of Advice to Students:

Find something that interests you in psychology, and try to learn more about it. Be open-minded about the career possibilities because the further you go, the more broadly opportunities will open up for you. And, study hard . . .

cease in the early 1900s, but continues to have proponents, such as Herrnstein and Murray (1994) in *The Bell Curve*.

Separatist movements also developed during the early 1900s. Marcus Garvey made plans for African Americans to return to Africa, but was later deported by the U.S. government. W. E. B. Dubois, the leader of the NAACP, had initially supported integration, but began to support the establishment of a separate African nation. Dubois immigrated to Ghana shortly before his death.

1940s–1970s: Civil Rights

Several landmark civil rights events occurred during the late 1940s and 1950s. President Truman desegregated the military in 1948. One year later, Jackie Robinson became the first African American major league baseball player. In 1954, in the *Brown v. the Board of Education of Topeka* decision, the Supreme Court declared the "separate but equal" doctrine invalid. On

December 1, 1955, Rosa Parks sat at the front of the colored section of a bus in Montgomery, Alabama, and refused to move further back for a White patron when the White section became full. This incident sparked the Montgomery bus boycott, led by Dr. Martin Luther King Jr.

Civil rights activism and legislation continued to blossom during the 1960s. The decade began with four students from North Carolina A&T State University staging a sit-in at a Greensboro lunch counter in February 1960; these students had been refused service because they were African Americans. The Student Nonviolent Coordinating Committee (SNCC) organized in 1960 and coordinated sit-ins. In 1961, an integrated busload of freedom riders traveled south from Washington, D.C.; in Montgomery, Alabama, the riders were beaten and the bus burned, and Attorney General Robert Kennedy sent 600 federal marshals to restore order. The March on Washington for jobs and freedom occurred in 1963, culminating in King's "I have a dream" speech.

The Civil Rights Act of 1964 mandated constitutional rights without discrimination or segregation on the grounds of race, color, religion, or national origin. Affirmative Action legislation was signed by President Lyndon Johnson in 1965. Whereas the Civil Rights Act of 1964 created equal opportunity, the purpose of Affirmative Action was to take proactive steps to include underrepresented groups such that equal outcomes could be achieved. In the equal opportunity approach, employers are able to adopt a passive stance by claiming that they do not actively discriminate against persons or groups; Affirmative Action goes beyond creating opportunities by assessing whether outcomes reflect the goals of diversity (Crosby & Cordova, 1996).

Parallel to these efforts toward integration, the separatist movement that began in the early part of the century continued. Elijah Muhammad and Malcolm X led the Black Muslim movement. Goals of Black Muslims were to replace the negative effects of slavery with positive values and behavior and to develop independence from the dominant culture. Malcolm X broke away from Elijah Muhammad to practice orthodox Islam. In 1965, SNCC moved from its goal of integration to Black power under the leadership of Stokely Carmichael; European American members were informed that their role would be secondary. The Black Panther Party was formed as a protective vigilante group in Oakland, California, in 1966.

The progress of the 1960s spilled over into the early 1970s. The Kwanzaa celebration was established as an integration of African, European American, and Jewish influences (Jones, 1997). Afro-American studies were established at universities, followed by the initiation of women's studies, Asian American studies, Latino studies, and American Indian studies.

The progress of the 1960s and 1970s began to slow near the end of the 1970s. The Supreme Court ruled in the *Bakke* case in 1978 that a separate admissions process for minority groups was illegal. Allan Bakke was initially denied admission to medical school at the University of California at Davis because 16 of 100 slots were allotted to African American, Latino American, and American Indian students who had lower test scores than his; as a result of the Supreme Court decision, Bakke was later admitted to the medical school. Nevertheless, the *Bakke* decision allowed that race could be taken into account in the admissions process.

Psychology in the 1960s and 1970s shifted from individual to cultural and societal explanations of prejudice (Jones, 1997). Childhood socialization and conformity were viewed as causal mechanisms of prejudice. Desegregation, which allowed social contact between African Americans and European Americans, was viewed as the solution to prejudice. However, optimism about solutions to prejudice decreased when the civil rights movement began to focus on institutional racism, including voting rights, jobs, and income disparities that affected both North and South (Jones, 1997).

1980s–1990s: Dismantling of Affirmative Action, but Hope for the Future

Many Americans in the 1980s, led by President Reagan proclaiming that it was "morning in America," contended that racism no longer existed. Although blatant forms of racism may have decreased somewhat, subtle racism continued (Dovidio & Gaertner, 1996; Jones, 1997). Subtle forms of racism include the belief that discrimination no longer exists, and valuing a single way of life. African Americans may be sensitive to subtle racism because of negative personal experiences with racism (Franklin, 1999). What may have been morning for some Americans was dusk for many others. Whereas many Americans would not express overt antagonism toward African Americans, they believed that many gains of African Americans were undeserved. Many of the civil rights gains of the previous four decades began to be dismantled. Because many Americans believed that discrimination was a thing of the past, they believed that fair treatment meant not providing special treatment to African Americans or any other historically disadvantaged group. These critics were not without data to support their arguments. African Americans with college and graduate degrees earned more than their White counterparts from the mid-1970s until 1980. Nevertheless, the reverse occurred from 1981 to 1993, which may reflect changing attitudes concerning Affirmative Action (Jones, 1997). Adversarial relationships between European Americans and people of color continued, resulting in the Hate Crimes Act of 1989. However, those who opposed acts of intolerance were viewed by some as hypersensitive and driven by political correctness.

Despite the belief or wish of some Americans that racism is a thing of the past, nearly all African Americans experience some form of racism during their lifetime (Klonoff & Landrine, 1999). There is also evidence that European Americans have more negative and crystallized attitudes toward African Americans than toward other ethnic minority groups (Sears, Citrin, Cheleden, & van Laar, 1999). Subtle racism may be more prominent for higher SES African Americans, and overt racism may be more prominent for lower SES African Americans (Clark et al., 1999). Nevertheless, there is evidence that overt racism is a problem even for higher SES African Americans.

Discrimination also has negative mental health consequences. Racist discrimination is associated with anxiety, anger, frustration, resentment, somatization, obsessive-compulsive symptoms, interpersonal hypersensitivity, fear, paranoia, helplessness-hopelessness, and depression among African Americans (Clark et al., 1999; Klonoff, Landrine, & Ullman, 1999). These problems occur across social classes, which suggests that higher social class is not a buffer against the effects of racism (Klonoff et al., 1999). However, working-class African Americans may be the targets of discrimination more than middle-class African Americans (Clark et al., 1999; Hughes & Dodge, 1997). Moreover, higher-status African Americans may be more likely to understand the possible role of prejudice when they fail, whereas lower-status African Americans may be more likely to attribute their failures to their own inability (Ruggiero & Major, 1998).

Racism and its negative consequences were overlooked as the dismantling of Affirmative Action continued in the 1990s. The Civil Rights Act of 1991 forbade adjustment of test scores or the use of cutoffs based on race, color, religion, sex, or national origin, which modified the Civil Rights Act of 1964 (Wittig, 1996). However, the 1991 Act pronounced it unlawful for employers to engage in practices that have a disparate impact on racial/ethnic, sex, religious, national origin, or disability groups when not required by business necessity. Thus, qualified applicants from any of these groups should not be discriminated against. Although such legislation may seem fair, the broader issue of how to get qualified ethnic minority applicants into the employment pipeline was not addressed, nor were actions or resources for training potential ethnic minority applicants provided.

Subsequent legislative decisions in education even more directly outlawed Affirmative Action. The 1996 *Hopwood* decision in Texas pronounced the preferential admission of Black and Latino students to the University of Texas law school unconstitutional; this decision overturned the clause from the *Bakke* decision that race could be taken into account during the admissions process. During the same year, Affirmative Action was effectively dismantled by the Board of Regents of the University of California when Proposition 209 was approved. Similar anti-Affirmative Action legislation followed in Washington State.

Is Affirmative Action for women and ethnic minorities still needed? The answer to this question lies in part in whether there continue to be disparities in treatment among European American men, European American women, and ethnic minorities. In 1955, approximately 5 percent of college students age 18 to 24 were African American; this figure increased to approximately 11 percent in 1990 (Murrell & Jones, 1996). Although these college statistics may suggest progress, workplace data suggest that educational opportunities alone do not erase ethnic disparities. Ethnic minority applicants for employment are interviewed less frequently than European American applicants with the same qualifications (Murrell & Jones, 1996). African American men with professional degrees earn 79 percent of what European Americans with the same degrees earn (Murrell & Jones, 1996). The situation is even worse for African American women with professional degrees, who earn only 60 percent of what their European American counterparts earn. Moreover, 97 percent of senior-level managers in Fortune 500 and 1000 companies are European Americans (Murrell & Jones, 1996).

Another criticism is that Affirmative Action policies would take jobs away from European Americans. However, as of 1994, there were 2 million unemployed African Americans and 100 million unemployed European Americans (Plous, 1996). Assuming that less than half of the unemployed African Americans are qualified for existing jobs, even giving these jobs to all the unemployed qualified African Americans would displace fewer than 1 percent of all the unemployed European Americans (Plous, 1996; Sanchez-Hucles, 1997). Thus, Affirmative Action policies would have a relatively minimal impact in displacing European American workers. Moreover, most European

Americans do not perceive ethnic minority groups as a threat to their economic status (Sears et al., 1999).

Some Americans may believe that color-blind approaches that completely disregard racial and ethnic background are the most fair. However, color-blind policies favor European American students because of earlier educational advantages, and European American workers because of experience and seniority (Plous, 1996). For example, if your parents and grandparents have completed college, you are likely to expect to complete college and may have had better preparation to do so than someone who is a first-generation college student. As alumni, your parents may also have greater access to universities than someone whose parents did not attend college.

Despite these political and legal setbacks, psychological theory and research in the 1980s and 1990s offered hope for understanding African American identity and multicultural relations. Against the backdrop of conservativism and the much broader context of centuries of African American oppression, the construct of Afrocentrism was being developed. Afrocentrism espouses African ideals at the center of one's approach to problem solving (Asante, 1987). Another important development in psychology over the past two decades is the multicultural movement (D. Sue, Bingham, Porche-Burke, & Vasquez, 1999; D. Sue & Sue, 1999). This movement emphasizes that different cultural groups have differing worldviews; recognizing and understanding these worldviews allows intercultural communication. Psychology has developed within a Western worldview; however, many persons of color have non-Western worldviews. Multicultural psychology attempts to understand persons within their own cultural context and on their own terms. Psychology in the 1980s and 1990s concluded that social and group influences were not adequate to explain racism (Jones, 1997). The field generally adopted a cognitive perspective, and discrimination came to be viewed as a cognitive process to simplify the complexity of the social world (e.g., stereotyping). It is much easier to perceive people as interchangeable members of a larger group than to go through the effort of understanding them as individuals.

CURRENT DEMOGRAPHICS

African Americans have historically been the largest ethnic minority group in the United States. In the next 50 years, the African American population could increase by 70 percent, from 35 million to 59 million. At this rate, the African

American population would increase from 13 percent to 15 percent of the nation's population. Yet this rate is being surpassed by Latino Americans, who will become the nation's largest ethnic minority group (http://www .census.gov/press-release/www/2000/cb00-05.html). Already in California, African Americans constitute a smaller percentage than Latino Americans or Asian Pacific Americans. The sociopolitical and psychological effects on African Americans of not being the largest group of color remain to be examined.

The African American population is relatively young. Nearly 33 percent of African Americans were under 18 years of age in 1999, compared to 24 percent of European Americans (http://www.census.gov/population/ estimates/nation/intfile3-1.txt). Over 50 percent of African American families do not include a married couple (http://www.census.gov/press-release/www /2001/cb01-34.html): 45 percent of African American families include a female householder with no spouse present, compared to 13 percent of European American families. The absence of African American husbands in families is likely associated with their devalued status in society, as well as with the death rate statistics discussed next.

Average per capita income ($12,957) and household income ($34,139) is lower for African Americans than for European Americans ($22,952 and $54,207, respectively). Part of the reason for this disparity is that fewer African Americans complete college. A slightly higher percentage of African American women than men age 25 and over have earned at least a bachelor's degree (16 percent and 14 percent). For European Americans, the opposite is true: 31 percent of men and 25 percent of women have at least a bachelor's degree. Another reason for the ethnic income disparity is workplace discrimination (Haney & Hurtado, 1994). As discussed above, there are income disparities between African Americans and European Americans even when there are not educational disparities (Murrell & Jones, 1996).

In 1998, 26 percent of African Americans were in poverty, compared to 8 percent of European Americans (http://www.census.gov/hhes/www/poverty .html). Although poverty is often perceived as primarily a problem of ethnic minority groups, these percentages translate to 9 million African Americans and 16 million European Americans in poverty. Thus, although the poverty rate among African Americans is disproportionately high, most poor persons in the United States are European Americans. The popular media often distort this image by portraying the typical African American as poor and the typical poor person as African American.

CULTURAL VALUES AND IDENTITY

Social identity theory suggests that the characteristics of a group need to be distinctive for group membership to be meaningful (Brewer & Brown, 1998). Motives for identification with a social group include a need for inclusion in a group and an opposing need for differentiation from others (Brewer & Brown, 1998). Exclusive groups, such as ethnic minority groups, simultaneously satisfy needs for inclusion and differentiation.

What are the distinctive characteristics of African American cultures? African Americans are sometimes assumed not to have a culture, or if they had one, it is assumed to have been destroyed by slavery (Landrine & Klonoff, 1996). Notwithstanding, many African Americans have a set of core values that are distinct from those of other groups (Boykin & Toms, 1985; Genero, Miller, Surrey, & Baldwin, 1992; Jones, 1997; see Table 5.1). One key African American value is the belief in the *interrelatedness* of nature and the universe. The spiritual and material are also viewed as one, rather than as separate entities. Thus, individual actions and events are not isolated but have a broad impact. Interpersonal relationships are considered to have a bidirectional influence, captured in the saying "What goes around comes around." This cultural emphasis on mutuality and reciprocity has resulted in a flexibility of roles among men and women.

African Americans tend to be more androgynous and tend to have more gender-egalitarian relationships than European Americans (Filardo, 1996; Harris, 1996). African American females may be more active and assertive than European American females in cross-gender interactions (Filardo, 1996). This active, assertive style may cause African American women to be perceived as threatening in relationships with European Americans (Sanchez-Hucles, 1997).

TABLE 5.1   *Core African American Values*

Interrelatedness of nature and the universe

Communalism

Spirituality

Many of the goals of the women's movement, which began in the 1970s and has primarily involved European American women, including egalitarian relationships, assertiveness, and equal employment, had previously been achieved by many African American women. Although African American women may identify as strongly with African American issues as they do with women's issues, they have historically been much more involved in African American issues (Martin & Hall, 1992). For example, in its 27-year history, only two presidents of the American Psychological Association

Dr. Pamela Trotman Reid, a developmental psychologist, is professor of psychology and education at the University of Michigan and a research scientist at the UM Institute for Research on Women and Gender. She has been an educator for more than 25 years, formerly holding faculty positions at Howard University, the University of Tennessee at Chattanooga and at the City University of New York Graduate School, where she also served as interim provost and vice president for Academic Affairs.

She has a BS degree from Howard University, an MA from Temple University, and a PhD from the University of Pennsylvania. Her research has focused on gender and ethnic issues, particularly on the intersections of gender and race as they impact African American women and children. Dr. Reid has numerous publications in journals and books. Her programmatic grants have provided support and mentoring for African American and Latino students to pursue doctoral education in psychology as well as the biomedical sciences. She has recently developed a school-based program to encourage girls to pursue mathematics as a vehicle to addressing social issues.

She has held many elected positions within the American Psychological Association. She was the first woman of color elected to serve on APA Council and the first woman of color elected president of the Division of Psychology of Women. A Fellow of the American Psychological Association, Dr. Reid has been an invited speaker at national and international conferences and the recipient of numerous awards, including being named among the 100 Distinguished Women in the Psychology of Women, Outstanding Professor by the Student Government Association of UT Chattanooga (twice), the Distinguished Leadership Award by the APA's Committee on Women in Psychology, and the Distinguished Publication Award from the Association of Women in Psychology.

Words of Advice to Students:

If you are unsure about your career goals, the best strategy is to learn as much about as many fields as possible. The exciting careers of the future seem to bring together the traditional disciplines in new ways. Those who have trained too narrowly will not be prepared for future opportunities.

Society for the Psychology of Women, Pamela Trotman Reid and Melba Vasquez, have been women of color. The relative lack of participation of African American women in the American women's movement may be more a result of being excluded than of a lack of interest. This issue is discussed in more detail in Chapter Nine.

Another core African American value is *communalism.* African American cultures tend to be more person-centered than object-centered. Thus, personal integrity is as important as possessions and expertise. Communalism is reflected in a strong family orientation. Multiple generations may be part of the same household (Wilson, 1989), and persons need not be blood relatives to be considered family members. Fictive (symbolic) kin not only were part of African cultures, but also served to preserve the concept of family in families that were separated by slavery.

Child-centeredness is also a component of communalism. Child-caretaker attachment and the safety of the child are considered extremely important. Multiple family members may share child care responsibilities (Taylor, Casten, & Flickinger, 1993; Taylor & Roberts, 1995). Such kinship support is associated with self-reliance, better grades, and fewer problem behaviors for African American adolescents (Taylor, 1996). Care is also provided to family elders, and the quality of such care does not differ as a function of whether family elders are blood or fictive kin (Lawton et al., 1992; White-Means & Thornton, 1990). Unfortunately, poverty may prevent some African American families from the cultural tradition of caregiving to family members.

Another central emphasis of African American cultures is *spirituality* (Jones, 1997). Spirituality is an acknowledgment of a higher, nonmaterial power that permeates all forms of life. African American spirituality has its roots in African religious traditions. Common African religious beliefs are that there is a Supreme Being; that particular objects and places are guarded by spirits, who are to be respected; that one's ancestors, although dead, have an interest in the living and should be honored; and that prayers and sacrifices have the ability to inspire the Supreme Being and spirits (Mbiti, 1971). Upon their arrival in America, enslaved Africans were exposed to the Christian religion. Many came to accept Christianity as their faith yet managed to incorporate and develop patterns of worship and expression that differentiated them from their European American counterparts. Some African Americans were able to blend African and European religious traditions (Black, 1996). Through the years, the African American Christian experience frequently served more than strictly spiritual purposes; churches particularly served many roles in the African American community: as schools, town halls, social centers, political headquarters, charitable organizations, and a social support system all at once. Black churches were historically the only institution led and controlled by African Americans.

Islam became influential among African Americans in the early 1900s (Mahmoud, 1996). Early African American Muslim leaders were Noble Drew Ali and Marcus Garvey. Garvey also was the leader of a black nationalist movement. Elijah Muhammad later based his organization on Ali's and Garvey's principles. A contemporary leader who combines Black nationalism and Islam is Louis Farrakhan. Islamic principles impact diet and dress and may limit interactions with non-Muslims. Traditional gender roles are also emphasized. Homosexual behavior is forbidden. The five principles of Islam are (Mahmoud, 1996):

Shadhah: The declaration of faith, the affirmation that there is no god but Allah, and that Muhammad is the Messenger of Allah.
Salah: The five daily prayers.
Zakah: The giving of charity to the needy.
Sawm: Fasting during the month of Ramadan, the month during which the Holy Qur'an was revealed.
Hajj: The pilgrimage to Mecca.

Religiosity has been found to be associated with many positive health outcomes for African Americans. Among these are cohesive family relationships, less parental conflict, fewer psychological problems in adolescents (Brody & Flor, 1998; Brody, Stoneman, & Flor, 1996), high levels of life satisfaction (Levin, Chatters, & Taylor, 1995; St. George & McNamara, 1984; M. E. Thomas & Holmes, 1992), low levels of psychological distress (D. R. Brown, Ndubuisi, & Gary, 1990; D. R. Brown & Gary, 1994), and low levels of mortality among African American elderly (Bryant & Rakowski, 1992). Religious involvement provides African Americans with cognitive and social coping resources (Ellison, 1994).

Although interrelatedness, communalism, and spirituality have been proposed as core African American values, not all African Americans share these values. Ethnic identity theory, as reviewed in Chapter One, suggests that the strength of these values may differ depending on one's stage of ethnic identity (Cross, 1971). Whereas African Americans in the pre-encounter stage of ethnic identity may not share these values, these values are likely to be important for African Americans in other stages.

Consistent with social identity theory, ethnic identity is a source of desirable distinctiveness for many African Americans and results in positive self-esteem (Gray-Little & Hafdahl, 2000). In fact, among children, adolescents, and young adults, African Americans have been found to have greater self-esteem than European Americans (Gray-Little & Hafdahl, 2000). This difference has been attributed to ethnic identity's being a more salient source of positive identity for African Americans than it is for European Americans. Moreover, having close friends with a similar level of ethnic identity is more important for African Americans than it is for Asian American or European American high school students (Hamm, 2000).

Much of the social identity literature has assumed ingroup favoritism to be associated with outgroup derogation. However, ingroup favoritism is not always associated with negative attitudes toward outgroups (Brewer & Brown, 1998). In research among eighth- and eleventh-graders, a positive ethnic identity was found to be associated with positive attitudes toward other groups as a function of contact with other groups (Phinney, Ferguson, & Tate, 1997). Thus, a combination of a strong ethnic identity and experience with other ethnic groups may lead to positive perceptions of one's own ethnic group as well as positive perceptions of other ethnic groups.

Ethnic identity theory also suggests that persons in the internalization stage are comfortable in relating to multiple groups. It appears that one needs to learn about one's own ethnicity and to have experiences with persons in other ethnic groups for effective functioning in a multicultural society. Nevertheless, ethnic groups often remain segregated in multiethnic settings. For example, in ethnically diverse high schools in California and Wisconsin, 81 percent of African Americans and an equal percentage of European Americans nominated persons from their own ethnic group as their best friends (Hamm, 2000).

DEVELOPMENTAL AND FAMILY ISSUES

What is a family? If you thought of the typical family as consisting of a husband, a wife, and two children, think again. The average family size in the United States is approximately three members (http://www.census.gov/population/www/socdemo/hh-fam.html), and 31 percent of U.S. households consist of one member. Fewer than half (49%) of the families in the United States have children under the age of 18 living at home. More than 25 percent of families with children under 18 are headed by a single parent, and 42 percent of mothers in single-parent households with children have never been married. Thus, the "typical" American family across ethnic groups is changing.

Parenting

Attachment theories posit that the quality of parent-child bonds will generalize to other relationships, including adult intimate relationships. This relationship between the quality of parent-child bonds and the quality of adult intimate relationships has been demonstrated among European Americans (Lopez, Melendez, & Rice, 2000). However, parent-child bonds are less predictive of adult intimate relationships among African Americans. Perhaps this is because relationships within African American families are qualitatively different than adult relationships in which African Americans are part of an ethnic minority group (Lopez et al., 2000). Minority status may result in African Americans having difficulty trusting European Americans. In addition, minority status may interfere with African Americans' intimate relationships with other African Americans. African Americans who internalize societal devaluation of African Americans may themselves devalue relationships with African Americans.

Ethnic minority persons may also be socialized in their families to be interdependent, whereas mainstream American society values independence (Rothbaum, Weisz, Pott, Miyake, & Morelli, 2000). An adult who seeks interdependence in intimate relationships may experience difficulties in relationships with other adults who have been socialized to be independent. Most American adults, including ethnic minority persons, have been socialized by society to be independent. Thus, many African Americans may experience conflicts between the expectations of relationships in their families and ethnic communities versus the expectations of mainstream American society.

The failure of some theories of development based on European Americans to explain African Americans may be due to differences between European American and African American family structures. Those who view a nuclear family, consisting of married parents and children, as normative have viewed African American family constellations as deviant (Jones, 1997). African American women have been blamed for being overly dominant or for being inadequate as single parents. Nevertheless, children from families in which the mother gets her way most of the time when the parents disagree compared to families in which the decision making is more egalitarian have been found not to differ on psychopathology or delinquency, whether they are African American or European American (Henggeler, Edwards, Hanson, & Okwumabua, 1988). Thus, not only is wife dominance not pathological in African American families, but it is not pathological in European American families either.

Similarly, no differences have been found between single-mother households and other constellations (both parents, stepparent, mother with extended family, extended family only) in alcohol/substance use, delinquency, school dropout, or psychological distress among African American adolescent males (Zimmerman, Salem, & Maton, 1995). In fact, African American boys in single-mother families reported more parental support than those in other constellations (Zimmerman et al., 1995). It is also inappropriate to assume that all fathers are uninvolved in single-mother families. In a recent study of low-income, unmarried African American mothers of 3-year-olds, half of the fathers were highly involved in raising their child, and half were uninvolved (Coley & Chase-Lansdale, 1999). Paternal involvement may also change over time, as 40 percent of fathers increased or decreased their involvement over three years. Father involvement with African American children in single-mother families may be important. Time spent with father is associated with fewer psychological symptoms, positive psychological well-being, less delinquency, and less marijuana use among African American adolescent males (Zimmerman et al., 1995). The African American community is making efforts to include fathering as part of a positive sense of masculinity (Allen & Connor, 1997). Taking responsibility as husbands and fathers was one of the emphases of the Million Man March.

Racial Socialization

African American parents adopt multiple strategies in socializing their children about their ethnic identity (see Table 5.2). Approximately 33 percent do nothing (Thornton, 1998); other African American parents may emphasize cultural heritage and pride, which tend to have positive effects on ethnic identity. The effects of racism in society are also an important aspect of socialization for many African American parents (Stevenson & Renard, 1993). This emphasis on African American culture and history, including oppression, is known as *racial socialization*. Racial socialization may come from parents, but often comes from other family members (Brega & Coleman, 1999). Racial socialization occurs in African American families across social classes (Hill, 1997). African American parents at the internalization stage of

TABLE 5.2   *African American Parents' Approaches to Socializing Their Children about Ethnic Identity*

No socialization

Racial socialization

Egalitarianism

ethnic identity are most likely to view racial socialization as important for their children (A. J. Thomas & Speight, 1999). Older African American parents often promote views of egalitarianism (Thornton, 1998). However, this mainstream approach that de-emphasizes ethnic group differences may leave African American children ill-equipped to face discrimination (Hughes & Chen, 1999).

African American parents prepare their children to cope with prejudice and discrimination more than other ethnic minority groups do. However, overemphasis on ethnic barriers may undermine children's efficacy (Hughes & Chen, 1999). Indeed, African American college students who are high in ethnic consciousness also have a greater awareness of social inequalities than those lower in ethnic consciousness (L. Brown & Johnson, 1999). Nevertheless, a strong ethnic identity may serve as a buffer against perceived prejudice for African Americans (Branscombe, Schmitt, & Harvey, 1999). To the extent that prejudice represents a rejection by the dominant group, ethnic group identification creates a sense of inclusion and well-being.

Evidence on the effects of racial socialization is mixed. In one study of African American college students, the effects of perceived discrimination on mental health were less for those who received racial socialization from their parents than for those who had not received such socialization (Fischer & Shaw, 1999). Interestingly, self-esteem was negatively associated with mental health among African American college students who perceived discrimination; discrimination may be inconsistent with positive self-esteem and may result in negative mental health effects. Thus, it appears that racial socialization may adequately buffer African Americans against the effects of discrimination, whereas general approaches that increase self-esteem may actually be a set-up for negative mental health consequences.

In a second study of African American college students, a measure of racial socialization was positively correlated with a measure of acculturative stress (Thompson, Anderson, & Bakeman, 2000). The measure of racial socialization assessed the frequency with which individuals received parental messages related to African American culture, racism, the importance of spirituality, and ways to cope with racism. The acculturative stress measure assessed African Americans' psychological discomfort in dealing with European Americans. Racial socialization was positively associated with acculturative stress, whereas racial identity was negatively associated with acculturative stress. This finding means that persons at higher stages of racial identity (e.g., internalization) were less likely to experience acculturative stress. These findings suggest that racial socialization may make some African Americans overly sensitive to perceived injustices (Thompson et al., 2000). In addition, racial socialization alone may be insufficient to create a strong ethnic identity.

Physical Discipline

Social learning theory suggests that children imitate the behavior of adults, including adults' aggressive behavior (Bandura, 1986). Thus, a child who is physically punished is likely to become physically aggressive. A consistent finding in European American families is that harsh physical discipline that is not abusive (i.e., does not result in injury) is associated with children's externalizing behavior, including aggression and teacher-child conflict (Deater-Deckard, Dodge, Bates, & Pettit, 1996). There has been controversy over the use and effects of physical discipline in African American families. However, harsh physical discipline is not associated with externalizing behavior for African American children (Deater-Deckard et al., 1996). It has been contended that harsh physical discipline may be normative among some African American families (Deater-Deckard & Dodge, 1997). However, physical punishment is not normative for all African American families, and may differ as a function of social class and region of the country (J. F. Jackson, 1997). Moreover, the view that physical punishment is normative among African American families could be misused in some settings (e.g., schools) to single out African American children for physical punishment. Spanking in African American families is typically in response to children's antisocial behavior, whereas in European American families, spanking may or may not be in response to children's antisocial behavior (Whaley, 2000). In other words, spanking in some cases in European American families may be driven by the parents' states and behaviors (e.g., anger) rather than the child's misdeeds. Although physical punishment may not necessarily be associated with externalizing behaviors for African Americans, it may be associated with other problems, such as child abuse later in life (Belsky, 1993). Thus, alternatives to physical punishment are as necessary in African American families as they are in families in other ethnic groups.

Academic Achievement

The number of African Americans enrolled in preschool and in college has increased during the past decade (http://www.census.gov/Press-Release/www/1999/cb99-179.html). Nevertheless, many African American children are at risk for academic failure. African Americans are more likely than European Americans to drop out of school (Hammond & Yung, 1994). There have been multiple theoretical explanations of African American academic achievement.

SES has been offered as an explanation of African American academic achievement. Poverty during the first five years of life attenuates children's completed years of schooling more so for African Americans than for European Americans (McLoyd, 1998). African Americans in grades 2 through 7 have lower standardized achievement scores than European American children, regardless of family income level (Pungello, Kupersmidt, Burchinal, & Patterson, 1996). These differences are possibly a result of the effects of racism beyond the effects of SES (Pungello et al., 1996).

Individual expectations about academic performance may be influential. African American high school students are less likely than European Americans or Asian Americans to believe that poor school performance will jeopardize their chances of getting a good job (Steinberg, Dornbusch, & Brown, 1992). Given the income disparities by ethnicity across educational levels presented above, a belief that school performance will not improve one's chances of getting a good job may be factually based for some African Americans.

Parenting style has been another explanation of children's academic performance. African American parents tend to be authoritative. Authoritative parenting involves being responsive to children and demanding, and being supportive of academic achievement (Steinberg et al., 1992). Parenting style, however, is not associated with high school performance among African Americans (Steinberg et al., 1992). It is possible that this lack of influence is because African American parents' unconditional support of their children's academic performance may at times lack credibility (Alexander & Entwisle, 1988).

Consistent parental and peer expectations of academic success are associated with the highest academic performance among African American high school students (Luster & McAdoo, 1994; Maton, Hrabowski, & Greif, 1998; Steinberg et al., 1992). Support from one source was associated with less success, and support from neither source was associated with the least success. These findings of community support being associated with academic success are consistent with the African American cultural emphasis on communalism. Unfortunately, African Americans were found to have limited peer support for academic success (Steinberg et al., 1992).

Negative stereotypes may also affect African American academic performance. The discomfort persons feel when they are at risk of fulfilling a negative stereotype about their group has been termed *stereotype threat* (Aronson, Quinn, & Spencer, 1998; Steele, 1997). Anxiety about poor performance may interfere with performance. For example, an African American student in an elite university in which there are few students of color may believe that African Americans are less capable than other students and less qualified because they are in the university only because of Affirmative Action. Persons do not need to believe the stereotype to be threatened by it; awareness may be sufficient to interfere with performance. An African American who does not believe in negative stereotypes about African American academic performance may nevertheless experience excess pressure to disprove such stereotypes that may also interfere with performance. The more one is invested in a domain (e.g., school), the more vulnerable one may be to stereotypes.

One method of coping with negative group stereotypes is disidentification with the negatively stereotyped domain, which in this case is academics. For some African Americans, academic identification and success is tantamount to "acting White" and must be avoided at all costs (Lazur & Majors, 1995). Another method of coping is to disidentify with the negatively stereotyped group. There is evidence that disidentification with African American identity and peers is associated with better academic performance for African Americans (Arroyo & Zigler, 1995; Steinberg et al., 1992). However, the cost of such disidentification may be anxiety and depression (Arroyo & Zigler, 1995). Moreover, there is also evidence that a strong collectivist orientation and identification with other African American college students is associated with academic success for African Americans (Oyserman, Gant, & Ager, 1995).

MENTAL HEALTH

Psychopathology

Theories of psychopathology suggest that the greater the amount of stress a person experiences, the more vulnerable he or she is to experiencing psychological problems (Monroe & Simons, 1991). Given the many stressors that African Americans have endured both historically and currently, African Americans might be expected to experience greater rates of psychopathology than other ethnic groups. Rates of African American psychopathology, however, do not appear to be substantially different from rates among European Americans. Although some ethnic differences have been reported, these differences are not substantive (Chmielewski, Fernandes, Yee, & Miller, 1995; Hall, Bansal, & Lopez, 1999). For example, there is evidence from the Epidemiological Catchment Area (ECA) community study that African Americans are significantly less likely than European Americans to have Major Depressive Episode, Major Depression, Dysthymia, Obsessive-Complulsive Disorder, drug and alcohol abuse or dependence, antisocial personality, and anorexia nervosa, but significantly more likely to have phobia and somatization (Zhang & Snowden, 1999). However, the large sample size in this study ($N = 18,152$) causes relatively small differences to be statistically significant; differences in rates of disorders of less than 1 percent were statistically significant. Such differences are unlikely to be substantive. Nevertheless, there is other evidence of substantively lower substance abuse and dependence rates among African American than among European American adolescents (Kilpatrick et al., 2000).

Why aren't there differences in psychopathology between African Americans and European Americans, given that African Americans have more stress in their lives? African Americans must cope with racism and its effects more than European Americans do (Clark et al., 1999). The similarities in rates of psychopathology between African Americans and other groups do not preclude the possibility of differences. The finding of minimal differences in rates of psychopathology between African Americans and European Americans may imply that African Americans are engaging in coping strategies to maintain their level of mental health that are not required of European Americans (Hall & Barongan, 1997). This relative lack of ethnic differences in psychopathology also may be explained by the positive effects of ethnic identification. As discussed previously, it has been suggested that

African Americans' greater self-esteem relative to European Americans may be a function of ethnic identity being a more salient source of positive identity for African Americans than it is for European Americans (Gray-Little & Hafdahl, 2000).

Most research on African American psychopathology has compared African Americans to European Americans on measures that were developed by and for European Americans. Communalism, spirituality, and discrimination are experiences that differentiate persons of color in the United States from European Americans (Hall, 2001). These constructs are not typically assessed in clinical research and practice, and cultural contextual influences specific to African American communities have typically not been assessed (Hall et al., 1999). The community impact of psychological problems may be best assessed by community members; however, psychopathology is typically assessed by mental health professionals, most of whom are not persons of color. More careful examination of the types of stress that African Americans experience, the effects of this stress on their mental health, and their coping responses to stress is necessary to determine the validity of stress-induced models of psychopathology for African Americans. If many African Americans are demonstrated to be coping more effectively with stress than other groups, all groups may have something to learn about adaptive coping from African Americans.

Mental Health Services

The amount of stress that African Americans experience as result of discrimination may be reflected in mental health services utilization rates. African Americans are overrepresented in public mental health facilities relative to other groups (S. Sue, Fujino, Hu, Takeuchi, & Zane, 1991). Representation is determined by ethnic group percentages in the local population. For example, if it is assumed that all ethnic groups have approximately the same rates of psychological problems, then if 10 percent of a region's population consisted of African Americans, overutilization would be identified if substantially more than 10 percent of the clients at mental health centers in the area were African Americans. Based on the previous discussion of similar rates of psychopathology among African Americans and other groups, how can the overrepresentation finding be interpreted? The finding that African Americans are overrepresented in public facilities that serve low-income communities suggests that African Americans with fewer resources may experience greater levels of stress that require mental health services than do other groups (Clark et al., 1999). This does not necessarily mean that they have higher rates of psychopathology, but that they are more likely than other groups to seek mental health services to deal with these stressors.

African Americans may use alternative sources of social support. However, controlling for sociodemographic factors, symptom distress, and diagnosis, African Americans are *less* likely to seek help for mental health problems from family members, friends, or religious leaders than are European Americans (Snowden, 1998). Another alternative source of help may be physicians. Depressed African Americans are more likely to see a physician than a mental health professional (D. Brown, Ahmed, Gary, & Milburn, 1995). Thus, educating physicians to know when to refer patients to mental health services may be important for African Americans to receive needed mental health services.

Although African Americans are not necessarily more likely than other ethnic groups to consult a religious leader for help with psychological problems, African Americans are more likely than European Americans or Latino/a Americans to view mental health problems as having a religious or supernatural cause (Alvidrez, 1999). Most African American clergy are comfortable making mental health referrals, and many do so (Williams, Griffith, Young, Collins, & Dodson, 1999). Thus, the church may be an important referral source and partner for the provision of mental health services in African American communities.

Termination from mental health services after a single session has been common among African Americans. Such premature termination may be because African Americans who receive mental health services find them culturally unresponsive (S. Sue et al., 1991; Takeuchi, Sue, & Yeh, 1995). In a large study in Los Angeles, it was found that African Americans attend more psychotherapy sessions in programs whose clients are primarily ethnic minorities than in programs that serve primarily nonminority clients (Takeuchi et al., 1995). Nevertheless, it is unclear whether attending a greater number of psychotherapy sessions is indicative of success. In fact, attending a greater number of psychotherapy sessions could be an indication that psychotherapy is not effective (Hall, 2001).

Clinical psychology has recently emphasized the development of empirically supported psychotherapies, treatments that have been demonstrated to be superior in efficacy to a placebo or another treatment (Chambless & Hollon, 1998). Unfortunately, the empirical support for these therapies has been almost exclusively with European American populations. There is not adequate empirical evidence that any psychotherapy is effective with African Americans or any other groups of color (Matt & Navarro, 1997; Miranda, 1996; S. Sue, 1998, 1999). Therefore, it is unclear whether existing psychotherapy approaches are responsive to the concerns of African Americans. Underutilization and premature termination data from mental health services suggest that they are not. Cultural competence is necessary for mental health providers who serve African Americans or any ethnic minority group (D. Sue et al., 1999).

Violence

African Americans are the ethnic group at highest risk for homicide and nonlethal assault (Hammond & Yung, 1993, 1994). The lifetime risk of death by interpersonal violence is 1 in 27 for African American males, 1 in 117 for African American females, 1 in 205 for European American males, and 1 in 496 for European American females. Since 1978, homicide has been the leading cause of death for both male and female African Americans age 15 to 34. African American males age 15 to 24 are more than eight times more likely than European American males in this age range to be a victim of homicide. Violence is a problem within African American communities, as 90 percent of African American homicide victims are killed by other African Americans.

Why are rates of violence so disproportionately high in certain African American communities (see Table 5.3)? As discussed above, rates of psychopathology are approximately the same across ethnic groups; thus, greater rates of psychopathology are unlikely to explain African American violence. Poverty is one of the strongest predictors of violent behavior, and African Americans have a disproportionately high percentage of poverty (Hammond & Yung, 1994). Some persons in poverty may resort to violent behavior because they do not believe they have the resources to attempt to survive in a conventional, nonviolent manner. However, poverty may have indirect effects on violent behavior. Not everyone who is poor is violent. Family environment and psychosocial characteristics are more strongly associated with violent behavior in African American adolescent males than poverty and other neighborhood characteristics (Paschall & Hubbard, 1998).

The cycle of violence theory suggests that violent victimization, particularly for males, creates a risk for becoming a violent perpetrator (Widom, 1989). This theory would explain the greater rates of violence among African

TABLE 5.3   *Risk and Protective Factors Associated with Violence for African Americans*

Risk Factors
  Poverty
  Violent victimization
  Witnessing violence
  Cool pose
  Aggressive stereotypes
Protective Factors
  Effective discipline
  Parental monitoring of children
  Family cohesion
  Strong belief in the importance of the family

Americans as a result of greater rates of violent victimization. Have Africans been violently victimized at a higher rate than other groups? African American violence may be conceptualized as the legacy of the violence associated with slavery and discrimination (King, 1997). Male victims and witnesses of violence are at risk to become perpetrators of violence (Dodge, Bates, & Pettit, 1990; Grych, Jouriles, Swank, McDonald, & Norwood, 2000; Hammond & Yung, 1993, 1994). It is possible that African American violence is a reaction to the many forms of violence that African Americans have directly and indirectly experienced in society.

But why do African Americans primarily victimize other African Americans if maltreatment by European Americans is at least partially the cause of the problem? Why not retaliate against the perpetrator? African American males may displace their aggression onto other African Americans because they perceive them as less powerful and likely to retaliate than persons outside their community (cf. Comas-Diaz, 1995). Another reason for intraethnic victimization is that violence tends to involve perpetrators and victims who have social contact with one another. Discrimination and segregation has limited the amount of interethnic contact for many African Americans.

African American men have historically been emasculated in American society. The African American community may create a sense of validation and recognition that is not available outside the community (Franklin, 1999). African American ethnic identity has been found to be a protective factor against fighting among adolescents (Arbona, Jackson, McCoy, & Blakely, 1999). A lack of a sense of belonging in the African American community has been demonstrated to be a risk factor for African American men's partner abuse (Rankin, Saunders, & Williams, 2000). However, efforts to create an alternative identity can be taken to extremes. To develop social competence, protection, and a sense of pride, some African American men adopt a "cool pose" (Lazur & Majors, 1995). This is a ritualized form of masculinity that entails behaviors, scripts, physical posturing, impression management, and carefully crafted performances that deliver a single, critical message: pride, strength, and control. Cool pose may interfere with relationships within the African American community because it may foster homicide, drug abuse, and suicide. Cool pose may cause some African American adolescents not to identify with uncool activities, such as academic success.

Social learning theory posits that persons engage in aggressive behavior because it is rewarded in the environment (Bandura, 1986). Aggressive persons believe that aggressive behavior will lead to rewards. Most popular African American boys in high school are prosocial in terms of being above average in academics, affiliative, and physically competent (Rodkin, Farmer, Pearl, & Van Acker, 2000). However, a greater proportion of African American than European American boys who are popular are aggressive. Moreover, a greater proportion of aggressive African American boys are popular in schools in which the majority group is European American than in all-African American schools. These findings suggest that "tough" behavior may be functional for some African American boys in high-risk, low-income environments. The disproportionate number of aggressive African American boys in majority European American schools may suggest that negative stereotypes of African Americans are more prominent in these schools than in African American schools. It is also possible that African American boys in majority European American schools are aggressive in an effort not to conform to European American standards of behavior. Consistent with social learning theory, the rewards of popularity, being perceived as tough, and having a non-White identity may be incentives for some African American boys to engage in aggressive behavior.

The communal nature of African American culture would suggest that solutions to violence are based in the family context. Indeed, family protective factors against African American violence have been identified. These include effective discipline, monitoring of children, family cohesion, and a strong belief in the importance of the family (Gorman-Smith et al., 1996).

Effective parenting may differ according to the child's context. Low maternal control has been found to be optimal in preventing gang activity, drug use, stealing, and fighting with or without weapons for adolescents whose peers engage in low levels of problem behaviors (Mason, Cauce, Gonzales, & Hiraga, 1996). Conversely, those who associate with deviant peer groups benefit from greater maternal control.

Although violence has a disproportionate effect on African American communities, the problem must be considered in context (J. Jackson, 2000). Most violence in the United States involves European American perpetrators and victims. The widespread acceptance and use of violence is a societal problem that affects all ethnic groups and all American communities and must be examined at a societal level (Hall & Barongan, 1997; J. Jackson, 2000). It is important for both African Americans and non-African Americans to recognize that most African Americans are not violent and that it is a stereotype that violence is endemic to the African American community.

CONCLUSION

African Americans and their cultures have survived four centuries of oppression in this country. They have been barred from mainstream American society and have been treated as second-class citizens when they have been allowed citizenship. Despite African Americans' 400-year history in this country and their status as the largest ethnic minority group in the United States, there is surprisingly limited psychological theory and research on African Americans. Psychological theories and research have primarily examined African American deficits. There is a continuing need to understand and prevent social and psychological problems in African American communities. However, there is an equally strong need for psychology to understand the cultural and psychological factors that have contributed to the resilience of African Americans.

REFERENCES

Alexander, K. L., & Entwisle, D. R. (1988). Achievement in the first 2 years of school: Patterns and processes. *Monographs of the Society for Research in Child Development, 53,* 157.

Allen, W. D., & Connor, M. (1997). An African American perspective on generative fathering. In A. J. Hawkins & D. Curtis (Eds.), *Generative fathering: Beyond deficit perspectives* (pp. 52–70). Thousand Oaks, CA: Sage.

Alvidrez, J. (1999). Ethnic variations in mental health attitudes and service use among low-income African American, Latina, and European American young women. *Community Mental Health Journal, 35,* 515–530.

Arbona, C., Jackson, R. H., McCoy, A., & Blakely, C. (1999). Ethnic identity as a predictor of attitudes of adolescents toward fighting. *Journal of Early Adolescence, 19,* 323–340.

Aronson, J., Quinn, D. M., & Spencer, S. J. (1998). Stereotype threat and the academic underperformance of minorities and women. In J. K. Swim & C. Stangor (Eds.), *Prejudice: The target's perspective* (pp. 83–103). San Diego, CA: Academic Press.

Arroyo, C. G., & Zigler, E. (1995). Racial identity, academic achievement, and the psychological well-being of economically disadvantaged adolescents. *Journal of Personality and Social Psychology, 69,* 903–914.

Asante, M. K. (1987). *The Afrocentric idea.* Philadelphia: Temple University Press.

Bandura, A. (1986). *Social foundations of thought and action: A social cognitive theory.* Englewood Cliffs, NJ: Prentice-Hall.

Belsky, J. (1993). Etiology of child maltreatment: A developmental-ecological analysis. *Psychological Bulletin, 114,* 413–434.

Black, L. (1996). Families of African origin: An overview. In M. McGoldrick, J. Giordano, & J. K. Pearce (Eds.), *Ethnicity and family therapy* (2nd ed., pp. 57–65). New York: Guilford Press.

Boykin, A. W., & Toms, F. D. (1985). Black child socialization: A conceptual framework. In H. P. McAdoo & J. L. McAdoo (Eds.), *Black children: Social, educational, and parental environments* (pp. 33–51). Beverly Hills, CA: Sage.

Branscombe, N. R., Schmitt, M. T., & Harvey, R. D. (1999). Perceiving pervasive discrimination among African Americans: Implications for group identification and well-being. *Journal of Personality and Social Psychology, 77,* 135–149.

Brega, A. G., & Coleman, L. M. (1999). Effects of religiosity and racial socialization on subjective stigmatization in African-American adolescents. *Journal of Adolescence, 22,* 223–242.

Brewer, M. B., & Brown, R. J. (1998). Intergroup relations. In D. T. Gilbert, S. T. Fiske, & G. Lindzey (Eds.), *The handbook of social psychology* (4th ed., pp. 554–594). New York: McGraw-Hill.

Brody, G. H., & Flor, D. L. (1998). Maternal resources, parenting practices, and child competence in rural, single-parent African American families. *Child Development, 69,* 803–816.

Brody, G. H., Stoneman, Z., & Flor, D. (1996). Parental religiosity, family processes, and youth competence in rural, two-parent African American families. *Developmental Psychology, 32,* 696–706.

Brown, D. R., Ahmed, F., Gary, L. E., & Milburn, N. G. (1995). Major depression in a community sample of African Americans. *American Journal of Psychiatry, 152,* 373–378.

Brown, D. R., & Gary, L. E. (1994). Religious involvement and health status among African-American males. *Journal of the National Medical Association, 86,* 825–831.

Brown, D. R., Ndubuisi, S. C., & Gary, L. E. (1990). Religion and psychological distress among Blacks. *Journal of Religion and Health, 29,* 55–68.

Brown, L. M., & Johnson, S. D. (1999). Ethnic consciousness and its relationship to conservatism and blame among African Americans. *Journal of Applied Social Psychology, 29,* 2465–2480.

Bryant, S., & Rakowski, W. (1992). Predictors of mortality among elderly African-Americans. *Research on Aging, 14,* 50–67.

Chambless, D. L., & Hollon, S. D. (1998). Defining empirically supported therapies. *Journal of Consulting and Clinical Psychology, 66,* 7–18.

Chmielewski, P. M., Fernandes, L. O. L., Yee, C. M., & Miller, G. A. (1995). Ethnicity and gender in scales of psychosis proneness and mood disorders. *Journal of Abnormal Psychology, 104,* 464–470.

Clark, R., Anderson, N. B., Clark, V. R., & Williams, D. R. (1999). Racism as a stressor for African Americans: A biosocial model. *American Psychologist, 54,* 805–816.

Coley, R. L., & Chase-Lansdale, P. L. (1999). Stability and change in paternal involvement among urban African-American fathers. *Journal of Family Psychology, 13,* 416–435.

Comas-Diaz, L. (1995). Puerto Ricans and sexual child abuse. In L. A. Fontes (Ed.), *Sexual abuse in nine North American cultures: Treatment and prevention* (pp. 31–66). Thousand Oaks, CA: Sage.

Crosby, F. J., & Cordova, D. I. (1996). Words worth of wisdom: Toward an understanding of affirmative action. *Journal of Social Issues, 52* 33–49.

Cross, W. E. (1971). Negro-to-Black conversion experience. *Black World, 20,* 13–27.

Deater-Deckard, K., & Dodge, K. A. (1997). Externalizing behavior problems and discipline revisited: Nonlinear effects and variation by culture, context, and gender. *Psychological Inquiry, 8,* 161–175.

Deater-Deckard, K., Dodge, K. A., Bates, J. E., & Pettit, G. S. (1996). Physical discipline among African American and European American mothers: Links to children's externalizing behaviors. *Developmental Psychology, 32,* 1065–1072.

Dodge, K. A., Bates, J. E., & Pettit, G. S. (1990). Mechanisms in the cycle of violence. *Science, 250,* 1678–1683.

Dovidio, J. F., & Gaertner, S. L. (1996). Affirmative action, unintentional racial biases, and intergroup relations. *Journal of Social Issues, 52,* 51–75.

Ellison, C. G. (1994). Religion, the life stress paradigm, and the study of depression. In J. S. Levin (Ed.), *Religion in aging and health: Theoretical foundations and methodological frontiers* (pp. 78–121). Thousand Oaks, CA: Sage.

Filardo, E. K. (1996). Gender patterns in African American and White adolescents' social interactions in same-race, mixed-gender groups. *Journal of Personality and Social Psychology, 71,* 71–82.

Fischer, A. R., & Shaw, C. M. (1999). African Americans' mental health and perceptions of racist discrimination: The moderating effects of racial socialization experiences and self-esteem. *Journal of Counseling Psychology, 46,* 395–407.

Franklin, A. J. (1999). Invisibility syndrome and racial identity development in psychotherapy and counseling African American men. *Counseling Psychologist, 27,* 761–793.

Gaines, S. O., & Reed, E. S. (1995). Prejudice: From Allport to DuBois. *American Psychologist, 50,* 96–103.

Genero, N. P., Miller, J. B., Surrey, J., & Baldwin, L. M. (1992). Measuring perceived mutuality in close relationships: Validation of the Mutual Psychological Development Questionnaire. *Journal of Family Psychology, 6,* 36–48.

Gorman-Smith, D., Tolan, P. H., Zelli, A., & Huesmann, L. R. (1996). The relation of family functioning to violence among inner-city minority youths. *Journal of Family Psychology, 10,* 115–129.

Gray-Little, B., & Hafdahl, A. R. (2000). Factors influencing racial comparisons of self-esteem: A quantitative review. *Psychological Bulletin, 126,* 26–54.

Grych, J. H., Jouriles, E. N., Swank, P. R., McDonald, R., & Norwood, W. D. (2000). Patterns of adjustment among children of battered women. *Journal of Consulting and Clinical Psychology, 68,* 84–94.

Hall, G. C. N. (2001). Psychotherapy research with ethnic minorities: Empirical, ethical, and conceptual issues. *Journal of Consulting and Clinical Psychology, 69,* 502–510.

Hall, G. C. N., Bansal, A., & Lopez, I. R. (1999). Ethnicity and psychopathology: A meta-analytic review of 31 years of comparative MMPI/MMPI-2 research. *Psychological Assessment, 11,* 186–197.

Hall, G. C. N., & Barongan, C. (1997). Prevention of sexual aggression: Sociocultural risk and protective factors. *American Psychologist, 52,* 5–14.

Hamm, J. V. (2000). Do birds of a feather flock together? The variable bases for African American, Asian American, and European American adolescents' selection of similar friends. *Developmental Psychology, 36,* 209–219.

Hammond, W. R., & Yung, B. R. (1993). Psychology's role in the public health response to assaultive violence among young African-American men. *American Psychologist, 48,* 142–154.

Hammond, W. R., & Yung, B. R. (1994). African Americans. In L. D. Eron, J. D. Gentry, & P. Schlegel (Eds.), *Reason to hope: A psychosocial perspective on violence & youth* (pp. 105–118). Washington, DC: American Psychological Association.

Haney, C., & Hurtado, A. (1994). The jurisprudence of race and meritocracy: Standardized testing and "race-neutral" racism in the workplace. *Law and Human Behavior, 18,* 223–248.

Harris, A. C. (1996). African American and Anglo-American gender identities: An empirical study. *Journal of Black Psychology, 22,* 182–194.

Hawkins, A. J., & Dollahite, D. C. (1997). *Generative fathering: Beyond deficit perspectives.* Thousand Oaks, CA: Sage.

Henggeler, S. W., Edwards, J. J., Hanson, C. L., & Okwumabua, T. M. (1988). The psychosocial functioning of wife-dominant families. *Journal of Family Psychology, 2,* 188–211.

Herrnstein, R. E., & Murray, C. A. (1994). *The bell curve.* New York: Free Press.

Hill, N. E. (1997). Does parenting differ based on social class? African American women's perceived socialization for achievement. *American Journal of Community Psychology, 25,* 675–697.

Hines, P. M., & Boyd-Franklin, N. (1996). African American families. In M. McGoldrick, J. Giordano, & J. K. Pearce (Eds.), *Ethnicity and family therapy* (2nd ed., pp. 66–84). New York: Guilford Press.

Hughes, D., & Chen, L. (1999). The nature of parents' race-related communications of children: A developmental perspective. In L. Balter & C. S. Tamis-LeMonda (Eds.), *Child psychology: A handbook of contemporary issues* (pp. 467–490). Philadelphia: Psychology Press.

Hughes, D., & Dodge, M. A. (1997). African American women in the workplace: Relationships between job conditions, racial bias at work, and perceived job quality. *American Journal of Community Psychology, 25,* 581–599.

Jackson, J. (2000). What *ought* psychology to do? *American Psychologist, 55,* 328–330.

Jackson, J. F. (1997). Issues in need of initial visitation: Race and nation specificity in the study of externalizing behavior problems and discipline. *Psychological Inquiry, 8,* 204–211.

Jones, J. M. (1997). *Prejudice and racism* (2nd ed.). New York: McGraw-Hill.

Kilpatrick, D. G., Acierno, R., Saunders, B., Resnick, H. S., Best, C. L., & Schnurr, P. P. (2000). Risk factors for adolescent substance abuse and dependence: Data from a national sample. *Journal of Consulting and Clinical Psychology, 68,* 19–30.

King, A. E. O. (1997). Understanding violence among young African American males: An Afrocentric perspective. *Journal of Black Studies, 28,* 79–96.

Klonoff, E. A., & Landrine, H. A. (1999). Cross-validation of the Schedule of Racist Events. *Journal of Black Psychology, 25,* 231–254.

Klonoff, E. A., Landrine, H. A., & Ullman, J. B. (1999). Racial discrimination and psychiatric symptoms among Blacks. *Cultural Diversity and Ethnic Minority Psychology, 5,* 329–339.

Landrine, H. A., & Klonoff, E. A. (1996). *African American acculturation: Deconstructing race and reviving culture.* Thousand Oaks, CA: Sage.

Lawton, M. P., Rajagopal, D., Brody, E., & Kleban, M. H. (1992). The dynamics of caregiving for a demented elder among Black and White families. *Journal of Gerontology, 47,* 156–164.

Lazur, R. F., & Majors, R. (1995). Men of color: Ethnocultural variations of male gender role strain. In R. F. Levant & W. S. Pollack (Eds.), *A new psychology of men* (pp. 337–358). New York: Basic Books.

Levin, J. S., Chatters, L. M., & Taylor, R. J. (1995). Religious effects on health status and life satisfaction among black Americans. *Journal of Gerontology: Social Sciences, 50,* 154–163.

Lopez, F. G., Melendez, M. C., & Rice, K. G. (2000). Parental divorce, parent-child bonds, and adult attachment orientations among college students: A comparison of three racial/ethnic groups. *Journal of Counseling Psychology, 47,* 177–186.

Luster, T., & McAdoo, H. P. (1994). Factors related to the achievement and adjustment of young African American children. *Child Development, 65,* 1080–1094.

Mahmoud, V. (1996). African American Muslim families. In M. McGoldrick, J. Giordano, & J. K. Pearce (Eds.), *Ethnicity and family therapy* (2nd ed., pp. 112–128). New York: Guilford Press.

Martin, J. K., & Hall, G. C. N. (1992). Thinking Black, thinking internal, thinking feminist. *Journal of Counseling Psychology, 39,* 509–514.

Mason, C. A., Cauce, A. M., Gonzales, N., & Hiraga, Y. (1996). Neither too sweet nor too sour: Problem peers, maternal control, and problem behavior in African American adolescents. *Child Development, 67,* 2115–2130.

Maton, K. I., Hrabowski, F. A., & Greif, G. L. (1998). Preparing the way: A qualitative study of high-achieving African American males and the role of the family. *American Journal of Community Psychology, 26,* 639–668.

Matt, G. E., & Navarro, A. M. (1997). What meta-analyses have and have not taught us about psychotherapy effects: A review and future directions. *Clinical Psychology Review, 17,* 1–32.

Mbiti, J. S. (1971). *African religion and philosophy.* London: Heinemann.

McAdoo, H. P. (1998). African-American families: Strengths and realities. In H. I. McCubbin, E. A. Thompson, A. I. Thompson, & J. A. Futrell (Eds.), *Resiliency in African-American families* (pp. 17–30). Thousand Oaks, CA: Sage.

McLoyd, V. C. (1998). Socioeconomic disadvantage and child development. *American Psychologist, 53,* 185–204.

Miranda, J. (1996). Introduction to the Special Section on recruiting and retaining minorities in psychotherapy research. *Journal of Consulting and Clinical Psychology, 64,* 848–850.

Monroe, S. M., & Simons, A. D. (1991). Diathesis-stress theories in the context of life stress research: Implications for the depressive disorders. *Psychological Bulletin, 110,* 406–425.

Murrell, A. J., & Jones, R. (1996). Assessing affirmative action: Past, present, and future. *Journal of Social Issues, 52,* 77–92.

Nobles, W. W. (1973). Psychological research and the black self-concept: A critical review. *Journal of Social Issues, 29,* 11–31.

Oyserman, D., Gant, L., & Ager, J. (1995). A socially contextualized model of African American identity: Possible selves and school persistence. *Journal of Personality and Social Psychology, 69,* 1216–1232.

Paschall, M. J., & Hubbard, M. L. (1998). Effects of neighborhood and family stressors on African American male adolescents' self-worth and propensity for violent behavior. *Journal of Consulting and Clinical Psychology, 66,* 825–831.

Phinney, J. S., Ferguson, D. L., & Tate, J. D. (1997). Intergroup attitudes among ethnic minority adolescents: A causal model. *Child Development, 68,* 955–969.

Plous, S. (1996). Ten myths about affirmative action. *Journal of Social Issues, 52,* 25–31.

Pungello, E. P., Kupersmidt, J. B., Burchinal, M. R., & Patterson, C. J. (1996). Environmental risk factors and children's achievement from middle childhood to early adolescence. *Developmental Psychology, 32,* 755–767.

Rankin, L. B., Saunders, D. G., & Williams, R. A. (2000). Mediators of attachment style, social support, and sense of belonging in predicting woman abuse by African American men. *Journal of Interpersonal Violence, 15,* 1060–1080.

Rodkin, P. C., Farmer, T. W., Pearl, R., & Van Acker, R. (2000). Heterogeneity of popular boys: Antisocial and prosocial configurations. *Developmental Psychology, 36,* 14–24.

Rothbaum, F., Weisz, J., Pott, M., Miyake, K., & Morelli, G. (2000). Attachment and culture: Security in the United States and Japan. *American Psychologist, 55,* 1093–1104.

Ruggiero, K. M., & Major, B. N. (1998). Group status and attributions to discrimination: Are low- or high-status group members more likely to blame their failure on discrimination? *Personality and Social Psychology Bulletin, 24,* 821–837.

Sanchez-Hucles, J. V. (1997). Jeopardy not bonus status for African American women in the work force: Why does the myth of advantage persist? *American Journal of Community Psychology, 25,* 565–580.

Sears, D. O., Citrin, J., Cheleden, S. V., & van Laar, C. (1999). Cultural diversity and multicultural politics: Is ethnic balkanization psychologically inevitable? In D. A. Prentice & D. T. Miller (Eds.), *Cultural divides: Understanding and overcoming group conflict* (pp. 35–79). New York: Russell Sage Foundation.

Snowden, L. R. (1998). Racial differences in informal help seeking for mental health problems. *Journal of Community Psychology, 26,* 429–438.

Snowden, L. R. (1999). African American service use for mental health problems. *Journal of Community Psychology, 27,* 303–313.

Steele, C. M. (1997). A threat in the air: How stereotypes shape intellectual identity and performance. *American Psychologist, 52,* 613–629.

Steinberg, L., Dornbusch, S. M., & Brown, B. B. (1992). Ethnic differences in adolescent achievement: An ecological perspective. *American Psychologist, 47,* 723–729.

Stevenson, H. C., & Renard, G. (1993). Trusting ole' wise owls: Therapeutic use of cultural strengths in African-American families. *Professional Psychology: Research and Practice, 24,* 433–442.

St. George, A., & McNamara, P. H. (1984). Religion, race, and psychological well-being. *Journal for the Scientific Study of Religion, 23,* 351–363.

Sue, D. W., Bingham, R. P., Porche-Burke, L., & Vasquez, M. (1999). The diversification of psychology: A multicultural revolution. *American Psychologist, 54,* 1061–1069.

Sue, D. W., & Sue, D. (1999). *Counseling the culturally different: Theory and practice* (3rd ed.). New York: Wiley.

Sue, S. (1998). In search of cultural competence in psychotherapy and counseling. *American Psychologist, 53,* 440–448.

Sue, S. (1999). Science, ethnicity, and bias: Where have we gone wrong? *American Psychologist, 54,* 1070–1077.

Sue, S., Fujino, D. C., Hu, L., Takeuchi, D. T., & Zane, N. W. S. (1991). Community mental health services for ethnic minority groups: A test of the cultural responsiveness hypothesis. *Journal of Consulting and Clinical Psychology, 59,* 533–540.

Takaki, R. (1993). *A different mirror: A history of multicultural America.* New York: Little, Brown.

Takeuchi, D. T., Sue, S., & Yeh, M. (1995). Return rates and outcomes from ethnicity-specific mental health programs in Los Angeles. *American Journal of Public Health, 85,* 638–643.

Taylor, R. D. (1996). Adolescents' perceptions of kinship support and family management practices: Association with adolescent adjustment in African American families. *Developmental Psychology, 32,* 687–695.

Taylor, R. D., Casten, R., & Flickinger, S. M. (1993). Influence of kinship social support on the parenting experiences and psychosocial adjustment of African-American adolescents. *Developmental Psychology, 29,* 382–388.

Taylor, R. D., & Roberts, D. (1995). Kinship support and maternal and adolescent well-being in economically disadvantaged African-American families. *Child Development, 66,* 1585–1597.

Thomas, A. J., & Speight, S. L. (1999). Racial identity and racial socialization attitudes of African American parents. *Journal of Black Psychology, 25,* 152–170.

Thomas, M. E., & Holmes, B. J. (1992). Determinants of satisfaction for Blacks and Whites. *Sociological Quarterly, 33,* 459–472.

Thompson, C. P., Anderson, L. P., & Bakeman, R. A. (2000). Effects of racial socialization and racial identity on acculturative stress in African American college students. *Cultural Diversity and Ethnic Minority Psychology, 6,* 196–210.

Thornton, M. C. (1998). Indigenous resources and strategies of resistance: Informal caregiving and racial socialization in Black communities. In H. I. McCubbin, E. A.

Thompson, A. I. Thompson, & J. A. Futrell (Eds.), *Resiliency in African-American families* (pp. 49–66). Thousand Oaks, CA: Sage.

Whaley, A. L. (2000). Sociocultural differences in the developmental consequences of the use of physical discipline during childhood for African Americans. *Cultural Diversity and Ethnic Minority Psychology, 6,* 5–12.

White-Means, S. I., & Thornton, M. C. (1990). Ethnic differences in the production of informal home health care. *The Gerontologist, 30,* 758–768.

Widom, C. S. (1989). The cycle of violence. *Science, 244,* 160–166.

Williams, D. R., Griffith, E. E. H., Young, J. L., Collins, C., & Dodson, J. (1999). Structure and provision of services in Black churches in New Haven, Connecticut. *Cultural Diversity and Ethnic Minority Psychology, 5,* 118–133.

Wilson, M. N. (1989). Child development in the context of the Black extended family. *American Psychologist, 44,* 380–385.

Wittig, M. A. (1996). Taking affirmative action in education and employment. *Journal of Social Issues, 52,* 145–160.

Zhang, A. Y., & Snowden, L. R. (1999). Ethnic characteristics of mental disorders in five U.S. communities. *Cultural Diversity and Ethnic Minority Psychology, 5,* 134–146.

Zimmerman, M. A., Salem, D. A., & Maton, K. I. (1995). Family structure and psychosocial correlates among urban African-American adolescent males. *Child Development, 66,* 1598–1613.

ISSUES FOR DISCUSSION

1. In what ways might "cool pose" be adaptive for African American men? How might it be maladaptive? Are African Americans and non-African Americans likely to view cool pose differently?

2. Is stereotype threat more likely to be an issue for African Americans in elite private universities than in public universities? What can universities do to reduce stereotype threat? What can African American and non-African American students do to reduce stereotype threat?

SIX

ASIAN PACIFIC AMERICANS

To forget one's ancestors is to be a brook without a source, a tree without a root.

—Chinese proverb

Asian Pacific Americans are immigrants and descendants of immigrants from East and South Asia and the Pacific Islands. They comprise at least 29 different groups whose cultural customs are distinct from most other groups in the United States. The term Asian Pacific American is used in this chapter to include Americans of East Asian (e.g., China, Japan, Korea), Southeast Asian (e.g., Vietnam, Thailand, Cambodia), South Asian (e.g., India), and Pacific Island (e.g., Philippines, Hawaii, Samoa) ancestry, and the term Asian American is used to refer specifically to persons of East Asian ancestry. Chinese, Japanese, and Korean Americans are influenced by Confucian traditions, although each culture has developed these traditions in somewhat unique ways. Over 70 percent of Korean Americans are Protestant Christians as a result of American missionary influences in Korea beginning in the late 1800s (S. Kim, 1997; Kitano & Daniels, 1995; E. Lee, 1997). Hong Kong has been influenced by Chinese culture as well as its former status as a British colony. Vietnamese Americans have been influenced by Chinese culture as well as by French colonization. Vietnamese, Cambodian, and Thai Americans all are likely to have been influenced by Buddhist religion. Indian Americans may have multiple religious influences, including Hinduism, Islam, Sikhism, and Jainism (Min, 1995); British colonization resulted in the adoption of English as the official language in India. Spanish colonization exposed Filipino Americans to Roman Catholic influences; colonization by the United States introduced American influences in the Philippines, including the English language.

These cultural differences obviously qualify Asian Pacific Americans for inclusion in a book on multicultural psychology. The other groups in this book are also regarded as minorities in terms of their status in American society. Should Asian Pacific Americans be regarded as minorities? Asian American psychologist Alice Chang has contended that Asian Pacific Americans are treated as a "minority of convenience." It is convenient for educational institutions to include Asian Pacific Americans as a minority group in statistics concerning recruitment, retention, and graduation. It is also convenient for businesses and communities to tout their diversity by including Asian Pacific Americans. However, it is inconvenient to include Asian Pacific Americans when it comes to funding for ethnic minority programs or Affirmative Action efforts to increase ethnic minority representation. It is also inconvenient for Asian Pacific Americans to be regarded as ethnic minorities when they are perceived by other groups as competing for educational, employment, or other opportunities. Nevertheless, the historical, cultural, and psychological experiences and characteristics of Asian Pacific Americans that are reviewed in this chapter are similar to those of the other minority groups included in this book, and demonstrate that Asian Pacific Americans are a minority group in terms of societal power and discrimination.

HISTORY

Early Immigration

The late 1700s was the first period of Asian Pacific immigration to America, although the total number of immigrants was small. Chinese and Filipino sailors who arrived on Spanish ships founded settlements in Louisiana during this time, and South Asians and Malaysians arrived on English ships on the East Coast as slaves (Agbayani-Siewert & Revilla, 1995).

A cohort of Chinese men came to the United States in the 1820s seeking work in railroads and mines. A larger group came to California following the gold rush in 1849. By the 1860s, there were 24,000 Chinese men working in the mines (Takaki, 1993). Asian miners were subjected to a Foreign Miners Tax that provided European Americans a competitive advantage. Following the gold rush, Chinese farm laborers' agricultural knowledge helped transform California agriculture from wheat to fruit (Takaki, 1993). Over 12,000 Chinese men were hired to build the transcontinental railroad; they received lower pay than the European American workers, and 1,000 died during the railroad construction. The American economy was depressed at the end of the 1800s and Chinese immigrants were often scapegoats. Additional Chinese emigration to the United States ended in 1882 with the Chinese Exclusion Act, motivated in part by perceived competition between Chinese and European American laborers. This was the first law that excluded immigrants on the basis of nationality, and was not repealed until 1942. Most of these immigrants had families in China and intended to eventually return there. However, these men could not have become U.S. citizens even if they had wanted to: A 1790 federal law reserved naturalized citizenship for Whites. Asians were not allowed to become naturalized citizens until 1952 (Takaki, 1993).

Because there were very few Chinese women in California, only 4 percent of Chinese in the United States in 1900 were American-born (Takaki, 1993). Roles for Chinese women were extremely limited in the United States. In 1870, 61 percent of the 3,536 women in California listed their occupation as prostitute (L. Lee, 1998). Chinese men were unable to marry European American women in California as a result of an 1880 California law that prohibited marriage between a White person and a "negro, mulatto, or Mongolian" (Takaki, 1993).

Chinatowns were developed at the end of the 1800s for economic and social support. Many Chinese Americans were forced into self-employment, including stores, restaurants, and laundries, as a result of discrimination and language barriers. Thus, the existence of Chinese restaurants and laundries in the United States is not necessarily the result of a Chinese affinity for these businesses.

Over 6,000 Asian Indian men emigrated to California between 1904 and 1911 (Jensen, 1988). Most of these men worked as farmers. About half were married, but most were unable to bring their wives to the United States until legislation allowed this in 1946. Similar to the Chinese immigration experience, the relative absence of women prevented a lasting Asian Indian presence. Indeed, many of the 1,000 Indian students who came to the United States in the 1920s intended to learn science and technology and to return to India and apply this knowledge (Sheth, 1995). Financial hardships caused by British colonial rule motivated many Indians to emigrate to the United States (Sheth, 1995). However, improved social, political, and economic conditions following India's independence from Great Britain in 1947 curtailed Indian emigration to the United States until 1965.

A wave of immigrants to the United States from Japan followed the Chinese Exclusion Act in 1882. The 1908 Gentleman's Agreement between the United States and Japan allowed Japanese family members to emigrate to the United States. This law allowed many Japanese immigrants to remain with their families in the United States, unlike the Chinese immigrants, whose families remained in China. These immigrants came to seek employment and economic opportunities. Japanese immigrants to California found independent employment in shopkeeping and farming. However, the immigrants' opportunities were restricted by the Alien Land Law of 1913 that prohibited noncitizens from owning land. Nevertheless, their American-born children were able to own land as citizens. By 1940, Japanese Americans grew 95 percent of beans, 67 percent of tomatoes, 95 percent of celery, 44 percent of onions, and 40 percent of green peas in California (Takaki, 1993).

Asian Pacific Americans in Hawaii

The Asian Pacific American diversity in Hawaii is a result of labor force issues. During the early 1900s, many Asian Pacific groups were brought by European Americans to Hawaii to prevent any particular Asian group from becoming the majority (Takaki, 1993). However, the Asian workers in Hawaii united across ethnic groups and eventually became the majority and unionized (Takaki, 1993). Over 60 percent of the current population of Hawaii is Asian Pacific American (U.S. Bureau of the Census, 1993).

The recruitment in Hawaii of Asian laborers resulted in over 7,200 Koreans emigrating from 1903 to 1905 (Min, 1995). Between 1906 and 1923, the primary groups of Korean immigrants to the United States were the wives of the workers, students, and political refugees (Min, 1995). Asian emigration to the United States, other than that of Filipinos, was completely halted in 1924 with the Asian Exclusion Act.

The United States gained possession of the Philippines in 1898 after the Spanish-American war. Between 1906 and 1940, Filipinos were imported to Hawaii and the West Coast of the United States as a cheap source of farm labor (Agbayani-Siewert & Revilla, 1995; Edman & Johnson, 1999). Similar to Chinese immigration, Filipino immigration primarily involved men (Agbayani-Siewert & Revilla, 1995). Many Filipinos served in the U.S. Armed Forces during World War II, and those who served were allowed to become U.S. citizens in 1943. The Philippines gained independence from the United States in 1946.

Japanese American Incarceration during World War II

The largest-scale act of discrimination by the U.S. government against any Asian Pacific American group occurred against Japanese Americans during World War II. Japanese American agricultural productivity was perceived as an economic threat to European American farmers in California and provided much of the impetus for the incarceration of 120,000 Japanese Americans in U.S. internment camps during World War II. David Guterson's novel *Snow Falling on Cedars,* which was made into a movie, has brought attention to Japanese Americans and Europeans during this period.

Two-thirds of the Japanese Americans who were incarcerated were U.S. citizens. The official reason for Japanese American wartime internment was their threat to national security. However, no acts of sabotage against the United States by Japanese Americans were committed before or during World War II (Nakanishi, 1988). Even military leaders debated the actual threat that Japanese Americans posed to national security (Commission on Wartime Relocation and Internment of Civilians, 1982). All Japanese Americans on the West Coast were incarcerated, whereas very few Japanese Americans in Hawaii were similarly incarcerated, nor were Japanese Americans who lived in other parts of the United States. Moreover, the United States was also at war with Germany and Italy, but there were not mass incarcerations of German and Italian Americans. Another irony is that Japanese American men were recruited from the internment camps to serve in the U.S. military in Europe and the Pacific. Somehow, these men's parents and younger siblings constituted a threat to national security, but they did not. It took over 40 years for the U.S. government to apologize to the incarcerated Japanese Americans and provide $20,000 to each camp survivor or the children of those who died. This is a token sum, considering the traumas that Japanese Americans endured in the areas of education, employment, and health.

Repeal of Immigration Restrictions

In 1943, Congress repealed the Chinese Exclusion Act because China had become a U.S. ally (Takaki, 1993). This allowed 105 Chinese persons annually to emigrate to the United States. Many of these Chinese immigrants were women, which resulted in a population of American-born Chinese. Chinese students and professionals who were in the United States after the 1949

Communist Revolution in China and did not wish to return were also permitted to remain in the United States with refugee status. Immigration opportunities were opened for Filipinos and Asian Indians in 1946 in separate congressional acts that allowed the annual immigration of 100 persons from each group (Fong, 1998). The legislation also allowed Filipinos and Asian Indians to apply for U.S. citizenship. However, it was not until the Immigration and Naturalization Act of 1965 that Asians were again allowed to emigrate in large numbers to the United States.

During and following the Korean War in the early 1950s and through 1964, Korean and Japanese women emigrated to the United States as wives of American soldiers. Orphaned Korean children were also part of this wave of immigration. Asian immigrants for the first time became eligible for U.S. citizenship in 1952 with the passage of the McCarran-Walter Act (Nishi, 1995). Exposure to Americans during the Korean War caused over 27,000 Koreans to come to the United States between 1950 and 1964 as nonimmigrant students (Min, 1995). During the 1970s and 1980s, over 3,000 Korean orphans per year were adopted by U.S. citizens (Min, 1995). This wave of adoptions ended, in part, because of negative world publicity during the 1988 Seoul Olympics about Koreans not caring for their own orphans.

The Immigration Act of 1965 repealed the restrictions of the 1924 Asian Exclusion Act. Immigrants from all countries were allowed into the United States if they had valuable occupational skills, were being reunified with family members, or were vulnerable to political or religious persecution. A quota of 20,000 immigrants per country was established.

Asian American identity began to galvanize in the late 1960s in the context of the civil rights movement. The Asian American movement demanded civil and political rights for Asian Americans, created pressure for universities to begin Asian American studies programs, and helped established community services for disadvantaged and poor Asian Pacific Americans (Fong, 1998). The movement was pan-Asian, including Asian Pacific Americans of all ethnic groups. Asian American activists recognized the similarities of their own concerns to those of other ethnic minority groups and the power in uniting with these groups in common struggles. One of the major events of the movement was the Third World Strike in 1968 and 1969 that shut down San Francisco State College for five months. This strike resulted in the establishment of the first School of Ethnic Studies, which included Asian American studies. Permanent Asian American studies programs were also established at major universities in California, including UCLA and the University of California at

Berkeley. Asian American student groups were also formed at universities in other parts of the country, and Asian American studies programs have been established in response to student initiatives.

Southeast Asian Immigration

Following the Vietnam War in 1975, refugees began emigrating from Southeast Asia. These Southeast Asians had become refugees because of the political conflicts resulting from U.S. political and military involvement in Southeast Asia. Many of the first-wave immigrants were Vietnamese and were educated and spoke English (Gold, 1999; Nishio & Bilmes, 1987); this group included Vietnamese government and military personnel (Fong, 1998). The 1975 Indochinese Resettlement Assistance Act was passed by Congress to assist these refugees. The immigration of this initial wave of Southeast Asians was relatively smooth and complete by the time the Resettlement Assistance Act expired in 1977.

After the Immigration Act of 1965, many Asian professionals emigrated to the United States. However, the flow of Asian professional immigrants was severely restricted by the Eilberg Act and the Health Professions Assistance Act in 1976 (Min, 1995). These acts eliminated valuable occupational status as an eligibility criterion for immigration. Thus, a large portion of the Asian immigrants since 1976 have been family members of persons already in the United States and refugees.

From 1979 to 1984, Vietnamese, Cambodian, Laotian, and Hmong refugees were settled across the United States. Many were involuntary immigrants because they had become refugees in their own countries for assisting the U.S. war effort. These groups had been evacuated from their homes, placed in "reeducation camps," forced to labor in rural regions, attacked with bombs and chemical weapons, had family members executed, and were forced to flee to refugee camps in Thailand. At least half of these refugees experienced post-traumatic stress (Sack & Clarke, 1996). Hundreds of thousands of refugees attempted to escape in boats on the South China Sea, with at least 100,000 drowning in these escape attempts (Rumbaut, 1995). Immigrants in this second wave were primarily rural and of lower SES, and did not speak English (Gold, 1999; Nishio & Bilmes, 1987). The 1980 Refugee Act allowed 50,000 refugees to enter the United States annually and initially provided 36 months of assistance, after which time the refugees could become eligible for welfare benefits. The length of assistance was reduced to only 18 months in 1981 under the Reagan administration. Current rates of poverty among Laotians, Cambodians, and Hmong in the United States range from 30 percent to 60 percent (Rumbaut, 1995; U.S. Bureau of the Census, 1993).

Recent Immigration

Over a half million Koreans came to the United States between 1970 and 1990 (Min, 1995). The Korean American community has been highly cohesive because of language barriers and because many immigrants are immersed in the Korean American community, including Korean Christian churches and businesses. Most Korean Americans are either self-employed or work for Korean companies (Min, 1995). Korean businessmen have been described as a middleman minority that distributes products produced by the group in power to the masses (Min, 1995). The 1992 Los Angeles riots, following the not-guilty verdict involving European American police officers who assaulted Rodney King, involved African Americans vandalizing and destroying Korean businesses. However, the coverage of these riots has been perceived by Korean Americans as an attempt by the media to shift public attention from African American–European American conflicts, which may have been the primary source of dissatisfaction in the African American community.

The Asian Pacific American population has continued to change during the past two decades. Since 1971, Filipinos have been the largest group of Asian Pacific emigrants to the United States and will be the largest group of Asian Pacific Americans within 30 years (Fong, 1998). The United States has been particularly attractive to Filipinos because of cultural influences during American colonization and because of intermarriage of Filipinos and U.S. military personnel (Agbayani-Siewert & Revilla, 1995).

CURRENT DEMOGRAPHICS

Asian Pacific Americans currently number 12 million, or 4 percent of the U.S. population. Asian Pacific Americans comprise more than 29 distinct groups, based on their languages, cultural customs, and religions. The largest groups are Chinese Americans (22 percent), Filipino Americans (19 percent), Japanese Americans (12 percent), Asian Indians (11 percent), Korean Americans (11 percent), Vietnamese Americans (8 percent), and Hawaiian Americans (3 percent; U.S. Bureau of the Census, 1993). Even within these groups, there is great variability. For example, there is no single Chinese language, and there are eight major dialects (E. Lee, 1996b), and there are 111 different language dialects in the Philippines (Sustento-Seneriches, 1997).

Before 1965, most of the Asian Pacific American population was born in the United States. Since 1965, when restrictions on Asian immigration were lifted, the population has shifted such that currently, approximately 66 percent of Asian Pacific Americans were born in Asia and the Pacific Islands (U.S. Bureau of the Census, 1993). One in five Asian Pacific Americans cannot communicate in the English language. Japanese Americans are the only Asian Pacific American ethnic group in which the majority (approximately 66 percent) were born in the United States. Modernization and economic prosperity in Japan has not provided the impetus for emigration that is present in many other Asian nations (Nishi, 1995).

Asian Pacific Americans have a higher median household income ($45,248) than European Americans ($40,576). However, this is because 14 percent of European American households have no income earners compared to only 9 percent in Asian Pacific American households (http://www.census.gov/press-release/www/1999/cb99-188.html), and 20 percent of Asian Pacific American households have three or more income earners compared to 12 percent of European American households. Per capita median income for Asian Pacific Americans ($22,398) is somewhat lower than it is for European Americans ($23,191). Moreover, Asian Pacific Americans have more persons living in their households than do other groups. Whereas 47 percent of European Americans have two-member households, only 28 percent of Asian Pacific Americans do (http://www.census.gov/press-release/www/1999/cb99188.html); 48 percent of Asian Pacific American households have four or more members compared to 31 percent for European Americans. Over 90 percent of Asian Pacific Americans live in metropolitan areas, where costs of living are highest (L. Lee, 1998); thus, living expenses are higher for Asian Pacific Americans than for other groups, of whom fewer live in metropolitan areas.

A small percentage of doctoral-level psychologists are Asian Pacific Americans, and among those Asian Pacific Americans with doctoral degrees, a small percentage are psychologists (Commission on Ethnic Minority Recruitment, Retention, and Training in Psychology, 1997). In 1993, 4 percent of bachelor's degrees and fewer than 2 percent of all doctoral degrees in psychology were awarded to Asian Pacific Americans. During the same year, only 4 percent of all Asian Pacific American doctoral degrees were in

Reiko Homma True was born in Niigata, Japan, and emigrated to the United States in 1958. After working as a psychiatric social worker in the San Francisco Bay Area, she returned to school and obtained a doctorate degree in clinical psychology from California School for Professional Psychology Berkeley in 1976.

Early in her career, she was alarmed by the virtual absence or inappropriateness of mental health services for Asian Americans. In spite of strong resistance from the establishment, she mobilized the Asian American community to create the first Asian American community mental health services in California. She expanded her activism to other neglected minority communities when she joined the NIMH, where she helped develop mental health services with a culturally responsive program focus in other states. She was the first female Asian and the first minority to be appointed director of Mental Health and Substance Abuse Services in the San Francisco Department of Public Health. In her leadership role, she further encouraged the development of strong minority-based multicultural services in San Francisco. She was also instrumental in developing a major mental health crisis assistance system following the Loma Prieta earthquake in 1989, which then led to her pioneering work in Kobe helping Japanese professionals develop a disaster assistance system for the victims of the Kobe earthquake in 1995. She is a long-time supporter of the Asian American Psychological Association and served as its president from 1997 to 1999, during which time she tried to increase and expand the participation of Asian American women and emerging Asian American communities.

Words of Advice to Students:

There is much to learn and absorb in the field of psychology. However, there are still large gaps in knowledge and understanding about Asian Pacific Islander and other culturally diverse groups. Reach out to Asian Pacific Islander mentors and students to advance the knowledge base and to create greater resources for our people. Don't hesitate to question and speak up against cultural misconceptions and misinterpretations.

psychology. These percentages are reflected in Asian Pacific American faculty representation at universities and colleges. In 1993, Asian Pacific Americans made up just 2 percent of psychology faculty at American universities and colleges.

Based on birthrates, Asian Pacific Americans are projected to constitute 9 percent of population by 2050 (http://www.census.gov/Press-Release/www /2000/cb00-05.html). An increased Asian Pacific American population will mean increased sociopolitical power. It is also likely that a larger Asian Pacific American population will constitute a threat to other groups. Indeed, there is

Richard M. Suinn started his education at the University of Hawaii, then completed his BA degree at Ohio State University. He then earned his doctoral degree at Stanford University in 1959. He also holds an honorary doctoral degree from the California School of Professional Psychology.

He served as the president of the American Psychological Association in 1999, the first Asian American and the third ethnic minority to be elected in the 107 years of APA. He is also emeritus professor at Colorado State University, where he was head of the Department of Psychology for 20 years. Prior to CSU, he was on appointments at Whitman College, Stanford School of Medicine, and the University of Hawaii.

His varied professional career has involved both science and practice. He has the Diplomate license in behavioral psychology, designed an intervention for anxiety and anger control, was on the Board of Trustees of the American Board of Professional Psychology, was team psychologist for four Olympic Teams, and was mayor of the City of Ft. Collins, Colorado. He has authored over 150 articles, 8 books, and 5 psychological tests—including the Suinn-Lew Asian Self-Identity Acculturation Scale—and served on the editorial boards of nine psychological journals.

His involvement with ethnic minority issues includes being chair of the APA Board of Ethnic Minority Affairs, chair of the APA Commission on Ethnic Minority Recruitment, Retention and Training, organizer of the NIMH Minority Mental Health Services Priorities Workshop, member of the NIMH Center for Minority Studies grant review committee, and on the Board of Directors of the Asian American Psychological Association. As head of the CSU Psychology Department, he significantly increased recruitment of both minority students and faculty, leading to two CSU diversity recognition awards. During his year as APA president, he visited universities with ethnic minority graduate students across the United States, and initiated the annual Suinn Minority Achievement Award that recognizes doctoral programs showing success in recruiting and graduating ethnic minorities.

Words of Advice to Students:

Reach for the summit! This vision had been my watchword during my APA presidency as a theme of my convention and as the theme of my visits with minority students. It is my way of saying that you simply must strive for your goals, whatever are the obstacles. No matter what others say, believe in yourself . . . and engage in whatever is necessary to continue to improve in your competencies and to expand your horizons. Reaching the summit is not meant to be an easy achievement and may seem too distant, especially for an ethnic minority . . . but it is there for everyone who is willing to act on their dreams!

evidence that European Americans, African Americans, and Latino Americans view Asian Americans as a threat in terms of jobs, politics, housing, and economics (Bobo, 1999). Conversely, Asian Americans view African Americans as constituting the greatest threat along these dimensions. It remains to be seen how well the United States will function as an increasingly multicultural society.

CULTURAL VALUES AND IDENTITY

Cultural Values

If several people gave you recommendations for a movie to see, whose recommendation would you be likely to follow: your mother's? your professor's? your friends'? What if you found a movie that you personally would like to see? Would anyone else's recommendation be more influential than your own preference? Asian American elementary school students performed better at word games and liked the games more if their mothers or friends had chosen the games than if they had chosen the games themselves (Iyengar & Lepper, 1999). Conversely, European American elementary school students performed better and liked the games better if they had chosen the games themselves. Asian American adults' behavior is also influenced by their parents and peers. For example, among Asian American men, the belief that sexually aggressive behavior will negatively affect their reputation with their parents and peers is a deterrent against such behavior (Hall, Sue, Narang, & Lilly, 2000). Reputation with parents and peers is generally not a consideration in European American men's sexually aggressive behavior. These studies involving children and adults suggest that Asian Americans' behavior is more influenced by others than European Americans' behavior is.

As discussed in Chapter One, theories of the self make a broad distinction between individualist and collectivist cultures. Many Asian Americans in the United States have emigrated from collectivist cultures and those who are born in the United States often retain collectivist cultural characteristics. In collectivist cultures, loyalty to the group is valued. For example, workers in Japan, which is considered a collectivist culture, often remain with a single company throughout their careers. Efforts to enhance company spirit, such as pep talks, group calisthenics, and company songs, are common. Some workers have even been known to take on the company name as an additional middle name. Thus, if Christy Barongan works for Toyota, she becomes Christy Toyota Barongan. (Although this is a cross-cultural example, collectivist cultural characteristics persist among Americans whose ancestry is in collectivist cultures.) There certainly are parallels in individualist cultures. For example, traditionally, women in the United States have changed their last name to their husband's when they get married. However, about half of marriages in the United States end in divorce, which often means another name change if a woman remarries.

Personal goals in collectivist cultures tend to be subordinated to the goals of the group. Such personal sacrifice for the group is not uncommon in European American contexts, such as the family or sports teams. However, most people in the United States work for more than one organization during their career, and the high divorce rate suggests that even family ties are temporary for many people. Subordination of personal goals may be more pervasive and group membership in collectivist cultures may be viewed as more permanent than in individualist cultures. For example, it is common for elderly parents in the United States to be placed by their children in retirement facilities. For many people having a collectivist orientation, leaving the care of one's parents to non-family members would be an extreme form of disrespect, tantamount to abuse. The expectation for many collectivists is that adult children are responsible for care of their parents in their own home, as they would care for any other family member. Have you had an elderly relative living in your home? If you haven't, would your family expect to have an elderly relative live in your home if he or she couldn't care for himself or herself?

One method of achieving interpersonal harmony in collectivist cultures is to establish clear norms and sanctions for deviant behavior. Having a child out of wedlock in the United States has relatively mild repercussions, and in some circles may even be fashionable. However, the same behavior in Japan may jeopardize a woman's educational, career, and marriage opportunities, and not only hers, but those of her parents and siblings. Family histories are carefully recorded in Japan in a *koseki,* or a formal family tree. The koseki is consulted when one seeks an education, a job, or marriage. Any abnormalities in the koseki may be grounds for disqualification.

Conflicts tend to be hidden in collectivist cultures. The American proverb is "The squeaky wheel gets the grease." The analogous proverb in East Asian cultures is "The nail that sticks out gets hammered." An illustration of this cultural difference involves a lecture that a colleague gave in Japan a few years ago. The colleague is one of the world's experts on the topic he lectured on and following the lecture, he expected to field questions from the audience, as is the custom in most American professional settings. However, there were no questions following his lecture. The colleague later asked his Japanese host why there were no questions from the audience. The host explained that they did not want someone to ask a question that the colleague could not answer. Obviously, the colleague was capable of answering just about any question that the audience could have posed; however, the host's purpose was to avoid any situation in which conflict could arise. This is a stark contrast to many American professional meetings, where discussion is common. Similarly, in classroom settings, college students are often expected to ask questions and participate in discussions. However, direct confrontation in collectivist cultures is usually viewed as an inappropriate method of resolving a conflict. A more viable method is to use a less direct method, such as having a third party (e.g., a mutual friend) as an intermediary, or to wait and discuss the issue in private.

Because of the group orientation in collectivist cultures, there are few internal attributions for failure. Failure is perceived as the responsibility of the group, rather than of the individual, and the coping mechanism for failure is social support. Social support is reassuring to anyone who has had a failure experience—misery loves company. However, to the extent that change is necessary to correct a failure, corrective change in a collectivist context involves the whole group rather than an individual. Even if an individual change might benefit the group, group consensus is usually required for individual change. Thus, at times, the task of changing the whole group's behavior may be burdensome. Conversely, in an individualist context, the responsibility and solution lie within the individual. Change at the individual level may be more easily accomplished than changing a whole group. However, the danger in an individualist context is that change at the individual level may not affect a systemic problem. For example, if you work for a company that has a reputation for being rude to its customers, your politeness to customers as an individual is unlikely to change the company's reputation, and your behavior is likely to be seen as an exception to the rule.

The down side of strong group cohesion is the tendency to make strong distinctions between ingroup and outgroup members. Although cooperation with other ingroup members is highly valued, relationships with outgroup members are not viewed as having a bearing on ingroup relationships; thus, one can mistreat outgroup members with impunity. Although there exist outgroups in individualist cultures (e.g., ethnic minorities), the boundaries between ingroups and outgroups are much more permeable. Thus, ethnic minority persons in the United States are able to enter areas where they had previously been excluded (e.g., some levels of government leadership), whereas such permeability is nearly impossible in collectivist settings (e.g., a Korean in Japanese government). However, it could be argued that the ingroup/outgroup boundaries in individualist cultures seem more permeable because they are more subtle, although they are just as real as the boundaries in collectivist cultures; for example, only European American men have been president of the United States.

Although Asian Pacific American cultures are heterogeneous, across groups there is an emphasis on behaviors that promote interdependence (Uba, 1994; see Table 6.1). As in other collectivist groups, there is a strong emphasis on interpersonal harmony and cooperation with others, in contrast to the competitive emphasis in mainstream American cultures. Blending in with the group is of utmost importance. Indeed, Asian Americans are more susceptible

TABLE 6.1   *Characteristics of Asian American Cultures (Uba, 1994)*

Patience

Gentleness

Being well-mannered

Cooperation

Being accommodating, conciliatory, and cooperative rather than confrontational

Blending in with the group rather than distinguishing oneself for either good or bad behavior

Humility and modesty

Withholding free expression of feelings

Suppression of conflict

Avoiding potentially divisive arguments and debates

Communicating indirectly

Refraining from openly challenging others' perspectives

Nonverbal communication

Conformity to conventional behavior

to embarrassment for their behavior than European Americans are (Singelis & Sharkey, 1995). This emphasis on contextual influences often leads to a belief in fate or karma, compared to a much greater emphasis on personal control of the environment in Western cultures (E. Lee, 1997).

Ethnic Identity

A positive bias toward one's own group being associated with a negative bias toward other groups (outgroups) is consistent with social identity theory (Tajfel & Turner, 1986). However, positive ingroup attitudes are not necessarily associated with negative outgroup attitudes (Brewer & Brown, 1998). A strong ethnic affirmation is associated with positive outgroup attitudes among Asian Americans who have social contact with non-Asians (Phinney, Ferguson, & Tate, 1997; Romero & Roberts, 1998). This positive association among ethnic affirmation, outgroup social contact, and positive outgroup attitudes was also found for other ethnic groups in these studies. Thus, the development of a strong ethnic identity in combination with intergroup contact may result in positive intergroup attitudes for Asian Americans and persons from other ethnic groups (Ponterotto & Pedersen, 1993).

Ethnic identification does not appear to influence Asian Americans' friendships, but does appear to have an influence on intimate relationships. In samples of students in ethnically diverse high schools in California and Wisconsin, ethnic identity among Asian Americans was not associated with choice of same-ethnic or different-ethnic close friends (Hamm, 2000). However, the effect of Asian Pacific American ethnic identification on intimate relationships appears to depend on the amount of contact Asian Pacific Americans have with other groups. Asian Americans who have a strong ethnic identity and a general tendency to affiliate with other Asian Americans are more likely to date Asian Americans than non-Asians (Mok, 1999). Conversely, highly acculturated Asian Americans who affiliate with European Americans are more likely to date European Americans than Asian Americans. These findings appear to imply that having a strong Asian American identity may be associated with negative attitudes toward non-Asians.

Ethnic identity for Asian Pacific Americans is unlikely to be unidimensional. As with other ethnic minority groups in the United States, Asian Pacific Americans face the cultural challenges of two cultures and may adapt their behaviors to particular cultural contexts (LaFromboise, Coleman, &

Gerton, 1993). For example, identification with U.S. culture has been found to be associated with better personal adjustment (i.e., lower depression, lower distress, higher GPA, higher self-esteem) among Vietnamese American junior high and high school students (Nguyen, Messe, & Stollak, 1999). Conversely, involvement in Vietnamese culture was associated with positive family relationships. Thus, exclusive Vietnamese identification could lead to personal adjustment problems, whereas exclusive U.S. identification could lead to family problems. It would be most adaptive for Vietnamese Americans to identify and be involved with both cultures.

Discrimination and Stereotypes

Experiences of discrimination are a component of ethnic identity for many ethnic minority persons in the United States. Proponents of model minority conceptualizations of Asian Pacific Americans might contend that Asian Pacific Americans have overcome discrimination and probably do not experience it. There is some evidence from community samples that Asian Americans are less likely than African Americans or Latino Americans to perceive discrimination (Sears, Citrin, Cheleden, & van Laar, 1999). Nevertheless, there is also evidence that Asian Pacific Americans do experience discrimination. Asian American college students perceive personal disadvantage and discrimination significantly more so than do European American college students (Crocker, Luhtanen, Blaine, & Broadnax, 1994). Moreover, the levels of perceived personal disadvantage and discrimination are not significantly different between Asian American and African American college students. The greater awareness of discrimination in college than in community samples may be a function of education and sensitivity to sociopolitical issues.

A study of Asian Pacific Americans in Hawaii who attended college in the mainland United States illustrates how majority and minority status may affect perceptions of discrimination (Ichiyama, McQuarrie, & Ching, 1996). In Hawaii, Asian Pacific Americans constitute an ethnic majority; issues of ethnic minority status, including discrimination, may be less salient to persons in the majority. Consistent with being part of an ethnic majority, Asian Pacific American newcomers who had left Hawaii for college on the mainland held favorable views of mainland students' attitudes toward them. However, Asian Pacific American students from Hawaii who had spent more time on the mainland had developed more negative views of mainland students' attitudes toward them. These findings appear to mean that Asian Pacific Americans from Hawaii became increasingly aware of their ethnic minority status as a function of time spent on the mainland (Ichiyama et al., 1996).

Are Asian Pacific Americans perceived in a stereotypic manner similar to the manner in which other ethnic minority groups are perceived? A study of commercials during prime-time programming on major television networks suggested that Asian Americans mostly appeared in ads on affluence and work, such as banks, telecommunications, and retail outlets (Taylor & Stern, 1997). Perceived economic and educational competence, however, does not prevent Asian Americans from being disliked by non-Asians (Fiske, Xu, & Cuddy, 1999). Thus, even supposedly positive stereotypes do not prevent ethnic minority groups from discrimination.

Stereotypes of Asian Americans may take on a different meaning if Asian Pacific Americans are perceived as a threat. Non-Asian college students who received feedback that they had performed poorly on a vocabulary test were more likely to generate stereotypes about an Asian American woman in a subsequent word completion task (shy, short, polite, nip) than if they were told they had performed well on the test (Spencer, Fein, Wolfe, Fong, & Dunn, 1998). Stereotypes were not generated about a European American woman in either test performance condition. When people feel threatened, it is possible that stereotypes about others different from themselves may serve to restore their self-esteem (Spencer et al., 1998). It is possible that anti-Asian violence serves this same purpose: If Asian Pacific Americans are perceived as a model minority and as taking opportunities from others, violence against Asian Pacific Americans may be a method, restoring self-esteem (L. Lee, 1998; Min, 1995; Nishi, 1995).

DEVELOPMENTAL AND FAMILY ISSUES

Family Relationships

How close are you to your family? Do you feel that your actions affect your family's reputation? Do you feel that your family members' actions affect your reputation? What would you do if you wanted to make an important decision, such as marrying a particular person, that your family disagreed with? Theories of the self suggest that persons in independent cultures are relatively less concerned about being part of a family and other groups than are persons from interdependent cultures (Markus & Kitayama, 1991).

Asian family relationships tend to be hierarchical and interdependent. Traditional Asian American families are hierarchical, based on age, birth order, and gender (Huang & Ying, 1997; Yee, Huang, & Lew, 1998). There is a patriarchal tradition, with fathers and eldest sons having dominant roles (Wong, 1995). Individuals are expected to conform to their expected role, based on these characteristics (E. Lee, 1996a). Family expectations are that Asian American adult children care for their elderly parents (E. Lee, 1996a). Elderly Asian Americans are much more likely to live with their adult children than is true for other ethnic groups (Burr & Mutchler, 1993; Kamo & Zhou, 1994).

The family structure for many Americans whose background is in East Asia has its origins in Confucian values (Bradshaw, 1994). Confucian ethics prescribe that the father is the undisputed head of the household and that the mother's role is to nurture the father and children. The father is distant, and the mother often intercedes on behalf of the children. Mothers are discouraged from taking on work roles outside the home. First sons are valued above other children (Huang & Ying, 1997). Sometimes, a woman is more strongly attached to her children, particularly her sons, than to her husband (E. Lee, 1996a). In many traditional Asian cultures, women are expected to be in perpetual servitude to men. The three obediences for women in Confucian philosophy are (1) to one's father at home, (2) to one's husband after marriage, and (3) to one's sons in old age (Bradshaw, 1994). Traditional Hindu culture in India prescribes domestic roles for women as well (Almeida, 1996).

Not surprisingly, the value placed on males results in gender double standards. For example, in many Vietnamese American families, a marriage is considered permanent and is breakable only if adultery is committed by the woman but not by the man (Leung & Boehnlein, 1996). In Korean American and Indian American families, a mother is often possessive of her son and has extremely high expectations of her son's wife to care for him (Almeida, 1996; B. Kim, 1996). Conversely, in-law expectations of a husband are that he simply provide for the family and be a faithful husband (B. Kim, 1996). In a recent study of Korean immigrant families in Chicago, two-thirds of the husbands believed that their wives who worked outside the home for economic reasons should be full-time homemakers (K. Kim & Kim, 1998).

Pacific Islander cultures are an exception to the Asian patriarchal tradition. Pacific Island cultures are often a matriarchy (Bradshaw, 1994). Families were traditionally the center of social life, even to the exclusion of friendships outside the family. Women held a powerful position as managers of families. Marital relationships are relatively egalitarian in many Filipino and other Pacific Islander families (Agbayani-Siewert & Revilla, 1995; Espiritu, 1997; Sustento-Seneriches, 1997). Patriarchal values often were introduced into Pacific Island cultures by Western influences, including Christianity (Bradshaw, 1994).

Emotions are suppressed in many Asian American families, and physical and verbal expressions of love are uncommon (Huang & Ying, 1997; E. Lee, 1996a; Nagata, 1997). Communication is often indirect (Huang & Ying, 1997). For example, a family member may express love for another family member by actions, such as helping with a task or giving a gift. Although European American junior high school students indicated more than Asian American junior high students that their mothers let them know that they loved them, Asian American students felt that their mothers understood them more than European American students did (Greenberger & Chen, 1996). Thus, communication may take place in Asian American families even if it is not overt. Another common form of indirect communication is to have an intermediary, such as the mother, older sibling, or trusted family friend, communicate with another family member (E. Lee, 1996a).

Consistent with cultural values of interdependence, the family unit is valued over the individual in many Asian American families. Whereas family relationships are often optional for European Americans, they are often obligatory for Asian Americans (Yee et al., 1998). Obligation to family members typically includes sibling relationships (Cicirelli, 1994). Bringing shame to one's family is to be avoided at all costs (Huang & Ying, 1997); for example, notoriety for deviant behavior (e.g., dropping out of school) may be viewed as a negative reflection on an individual's whole family. What may be considered an individual decision in non-Asian cultures may be a family decision in Asian cultures. For example, marriage in Asian Indian families is viewed as the permanent alliance of the two families, not simply the union of two individuals; thus, marriage decisions are left to elders in the family (Prathikanti, 1997). Although arranged marriages among Asian Indian Americans may not be as common as they are in India, Indian parents in the United States often have a fair amount of control over their children's choice of mate.

The high value placed on the integrity of family relationships may be reflected in divorce rates. Asian Pacific Americans have the lowest divorce rate of any American ethnic group. Only 5 percent of Asian Pacific Americans are divorced, compared to 10 percent of all Americans (http://www.census.gov /prod/2000pubs/p20-529.pdf). Divorce may be viewed among many Asian Pacific Americans as bringing shame to one's family; thus, some spouses may endure much marital conflict and even abuse to avoid the stigma of divorce.

Asian American families may vary as a function of acculturation. E. Lee (1997) has described five types of Asian American families. *Traditional* families usually consist entirely of immigrants. Such families adhere to traditional Asian values, speak native languages, and practice traditional customs. Many live in Asian ethnic enclaves (e.g., Chinatown) and belong to social groups with people from their same background. *Cultural-conflict* families are a blend of immigrant parents and children who are either American-born or who arrived in the United States when they were young. Intergenerational conflicts may involve acculturation, religious, political, and philosophical differences. Children have more status and power in U.S. society than their immigrant parents, which upsets the traditional hierarchy (Yee et al., 1998). *Bicultural* families consist of young adult immigrants who were raised in major Asian cities and exposed to Western influences or adults who were born in the United States, but whose parents were traditional. Many are bilingual but usually do not live in ethnic neighborhoods. Marital relationships in bicultural families tend to be more egalitarian than patriarchal. The difference between cultural-conflict and bicultural families is that the parents in the former adhere to traditional values, whereas the parents in the latter are familiar with both Asian and American values. *American* families consist of members born in the United States. They do not maintain their ethnic identity and adopt an individualistic and egalitarian orientation. *Interracial* families are a growing minority of Asian American families. As in any family, cultural differences may be integrated or may lead to conflict.

Asian American children are typically socialized to respect, honor, and obey their elders (Ho, 1993; Min, 1995). And there may be many elders to respect, honor, and obey, as Asian American families are often extended, with grandparents, aunts, and uncles involved in parenting roles (Das & Kemp, 1997; Hsu, 1981; Sustento-Seneriches, 1997; Wong, 1995). Family members may be influential even if they do not live in the same household (Yee et al., 1998). Asian American children are encouraged to be interdependent; however, these children are also influenced to be independent by European American culture (Ying, Coombs, & Lee, 1999).

Asian values of obedience and respect are not necessarily compatible with American school values of assertiveness and independent thinking (B. Kim,

1996). Thus, Asian American parents who adhere to traditional Asian values may experience difficulties preparing children for the U.S. school system and culture. Indeed, Asian American parents tend to become less restrictive and more encouraging as they become more acculturated to Western values (Uba, 1994).

Academic Achievement

The academic achievements of Asian Americans are well documented. Asian Americans tend to have standardized test scores and grades that equal or exceed those of European Americans at every level in the educational system (Fuligni, 1997; Hsia & Peng, 1998). Eighty-eight percent of Asian American high school graduates go on to college, compared to 64 percent of all high school graduates in the United States (Hsia & Peng, 1998). Among adults 25 years of age and older, 42 percent of Asian Americans have a bachelors degree or higher, compared to 27 percent of European Americans (U.S. Bureau of the Census, 1993).

Many theoretical explanations for Asian American academic success have been offered (see Table 6.2). One is greater intelligence than other groups, with the assumption that intelligence is genetically transmitted. However, the mean IQ scores of Japanese and Chinese American students are approximately 100, which is the mean for other ethnic groups (Flynn, 1991). Moreover, ethnic differences in IQ scores do not have a genetic basis (Neisser et al., 1996).

Another finding has been that SES is associated with academic achievement among Asian Pacific Americans and other immigrant groups (Portes & MacLeod, 1996). There is even evidence that parental SES is more predictive of Asian American children's academic performance than it is for other

---

TABLE 6.2   *Possible Explanations of Asian American Academic Achievement*

Intelligence

Socioeconomic status

Cultural value of education

Peer influences

Limited opportunities in society in nonacademic areas

groups (Sun, 1998). However, SES is positively correlated with parents' own academic achievements; thus, it is possible that because of their own academic achievement, Asian American parents value the academic achievement of their children.

Indeed, Asian Pacific American children's academic performance mirrors that of their parents. In a study of multiple Asian Pacific American ethnic groups, South Asian parents tended to have the highest level of education, followed by Korean, Japanese, Filipino, Chinese, and Southeast Asian parents (H. Kim, Rendon, & Valadez, 1998). South Asian parents tended to have the highest occupational status, followed by Japanese, Korean, Filipino, Chinese, and Southeast Asian parents. South Asian children tended to express the highest educational aspirations, followed by Korean, Japanese, Chinese, Filipino, and Southeast Asian children. South Asian children tended to have the highest math performance, followed by Chinese, Southeast Asian, Korean, Filipino, and Japanese children.

It is possible that the value placed on academic achievement among Asian Americans is culturally based. In Mandarin society, the intellectual elite rose to power by passing stringent tests (Sue & Okazaki, 1990). Asian emigrants to the United States appear to bring these academic achievement values, which they share with their children (Fuligni, 1997). Asian American students do 40 to 50 percent more homework than other students from elementary school on (Steinberg, Dornbusch, & Brown, 1992). It also appears that these values may erode somewhat with acculturation to Western culture. Among college students, recent Asian immigrants also have been found to study more than American-born Asians or Asian immigrants who have been in the United States more than six years (Sue & Zane, 1985). Among Vietnamese Americans, children whose parents spoke Vietnamese at home and were involved in Vietnamese organizations did more homework than those whose parents did not (Bankston, 1998). Although the math achievement of Asian American children is higher than that of European American children, it is lower than that of Taiwanese and Japanese children (C. Chen & Stevenson, 1995). Asian Americans also rate between these groups on parental and peer academic standards for excellence, on believing that success comes from effort, and in having positive attitudes about achievement and studying.

Asian American parents may have higher expectations of their children's academic performance than other parents. Asian American students report that their parents would be angry if they came home with anything less than an A– and react by making them study harder (Steinberg et al., 1992). Asian

American parents are also significantly less happy than other parents with their children's B and C grades (Okagaki & Frensch, 1998). Asian Americans may also expect to be in school longer than other groups. Chinese, Korean, Southeast Asian, and South Asian American parents expect their children to be in school beyond college, whereas European and Filipino American parents expect their children to go to college but not necessarily to complete it (Goyette & Xie, 1999). Children's expectations for amount of education are similar to their parents'.

Despite Asian American parents' high academic expectations of their children, they tend to be *less* involved than other ethnic groups in their children's schooling (Asakawa & Csikszentmihalyi, 1998; Steinberg et al., 1992). This relative lack of parental guidance in the context of Asian American children's academic performance may be additional evidence of unspoken communication. However, it may also suggest other reasons for Asian American academic achievement.

Yet another explanation of Asian American academic performance is peer influence. There is evidence that Asian Americans have more peer support for academic success than other groups (Steinberg et al., 1992). Moreover, Asian Americans who associated with non-Asian peers had lower performance than Asian Americans who associated with Asian peers. Peer involvement also appears to facilitate Asian American academic performance. Vietnamese American high school students who provided help or received help from their peers did better academically than those who did not (Bankston, 1998).

Asian American psychologists Stanley Sue and Sumie Okazaki (1990) have proposed that *relative functionalism* may explain why Asian Americans have focused so heavily on academic achievement. The relative functionalism theory suggests that education becomes increasingly salient as a means of mobility when mobility is blocked in noneducational areas. There is evidence that Asian Americans believe more strongly than other ethnic groups that education will result in success (Steinberg et al., 1992). Success in American society for many Asian Americans has been associated with academic abilities, often in the areas of engineering, computer science, medicine, and business. Two of the more notable Asian Pacific American success stories are Jerry Yang, a former Stanford University student and founder of the Web search engine Yahoo!, and Dr. David Ho, who was named *Time* magazine Man of the Year in 1996 for his developments in medical research on AIDS. There are very few prominent Asian Pacific Americans who have succeeded in nonacademic spheres, such as sports, entertainment, and politics.

For example, only two Asian Pacific American athletes, figure skater Kristi Yamaguchi and golfer Tiger Woods, have appeared on the Wheaties cereal box. Washington State Governor Gary Locke is the only Asian Pacific American governor ever to be elected on the mainland. Margaret Cho was the first Asian Pacific American to star in a weekly television series, only to have it cancelled after one season (see "Issues for Discussion" at the end of the chapter). Successful Asian Pacific American individuals in nonacademic fields may be viewed as exceptions, and to emulate them may be considered extremely risky.

Most Asian Americans are well aware of Asian American academic success stereotypes (Oyserman & Sakamoto, 1997). In fact, simply asking Asian American college women about being an Asian American (e.g., non-English-language knowledge, generation in the United States) resulted in significantly better performance on a quantitative task than when they were not asked about being an Asian American (Shih, Pittinsky, & Ambady, 1999). Although this finding appears to imply that Asian American stereotypes are performance-enhancing, such stereotypes may also be performance-limiting. Interestingly, priming either Asian American or female identity (e.g., Do you live in coed or single-sex living arrangements?) were both associated with decrements in verbal performance relative to a control condition (Pittinsky, Shih, & Ambady, 1999). Thus, Asian American stereotypes of academic success may cause some Asian Americans to focus narrowly on certain quantitative fields and neglect attention to other academic or nonacademic endeavors.

At what price does academic success come? High school senior Jenny Hung described her freshman year in high school as the "Year of Sleepless Nights" in a *Newsweek* essay (September 20, 1999, p. 9). She did not sleep much because she took honors courses, got straight As, and was first in her freshman class. Her usual bedtime was 1 A.M. Her preoccupation with schoolwork resulted in her falling asleep during the day and leaving her room a mess. "I had created my own hell," she said. Her parents applauded her academic success, but her mother was concerned when she inadvertently discovered Jenny awake all night studying. Fortunately, beginning in her sophomore year, Jenny took a more realistic approach to her schoolwork. She took fewer honors courses and became involved in extracurricular activities. Although there is evidence that, similar to Jenny Hung, many Asian American students focus on schoolwork and enjoy it more than other students, Asian American high school students are not more maladjusted than other high school students (Asakawa & Csikszentmihalyi, 1998; C. Chen & Stevenson, 1995).

Stanley Sue is a professor of psychology, director of the Asian American Studies Program, and director of the National Research Center on Asian American Mental Health, an NIMH-funded research center, at the University of California, Davis. He received a BS degree from the University of Oregon (1966) and the PhD degree in psychology from UCLA (1971). From 1981 to 1996, he was a professor of psychology at UCLA, where he was also associate dean of the Graduate Division. Prior to his faculty appointment at UCLA, he served for 10 years on the psychology faculty at the University of Washington and from 1980 to 1981 was director of Clinical-Community Psychology Training at the National Asian American Psychology Training Center in San Francisco, an APA-approved internship program.

His research has been devoted to the study of the adjustment of and delivery of mental health services to culturally diverse groups. The Research Center, which he directs, is engaged in research on assessing the prevalence of mental health problems, determining the factors that predict positive treatment outcomes, and evaluating the effectiveness of mental health services. Dr. Sue is a second-generation Chinese American.

Dr. Sue has been involved in various professional affairs and organizations. He has served as chair of the APA Board of Convention Affairs, was a member of the APA Board of Social and Ethical Responsibility in Psychology, and is founder and executive secretary of the Asian American Psychological Association. He is past-president of the Division of Clinical and Community Psychology for the International Association of Applied Psychology and past-president of the Society for the Psychological Study of Social Issues (APA Division 9). He was a member of the Planning Board for the U.S. Surgeon General's Report on Mental Health. A Fellow of APA and the American Psychological Society, Dr. Sue has held appointments on the editorial boards of various journals, such as *American Psychologist, Journal of Consulting and Clinical Psychology, American Journal of Community Psychology, Journal of Community Psychology, Psychological Assessment,* and *Hispanic Journal of Behavioral Sciences.* For five years, he regularly taught at Zhongshan University in mainland China and is visiting professor of psychology at South China Normal University in Guangzhou.

Words of Advice to Students:

Try to find ways of using psychology, whether through research or practice, to advance the welfare of human beings.

Academic success has not translated into societal success for many Asian Pacific Americans. Nonacademic criteria, such as legacy, athletics, and extracurricular activities, may be used against Asian Pacific Americans in college admission decisions (Fong, 1998). Thus, an exclusive focus on academics, as Jenny Hung initially did in high school, could actually be a deterrent to admission at some colleges. Successful completion of an advanced degree is also not a guarantee of success. Asian Pacific Americans are also underrepresented in supervisory and management positions (P. Kim & Lewis, 1994). Most organizations may not overtly discriminate against Asian Pacific Americans; however, what is considered a "good fit" for a position may be tailored to exclude certain groups. The invisibility of overt discrimination in the face of data that suggest that certain groups are unable to rise to the top of organizations is known as the glass ceiling.

MENTAL HEALTH

Psychopathology

As discussed above, there appear to be personality differences between Asian Pacific Americans and other ethnic groups. How do such differences affect mental health and psychopathology? There appear to be minimal differences in rates of psychopathology between Asian Pacific Americans and other groups (Chmielewski, Fernandes, Yee, & Miller, 1995; Iwamasa & Hilliard, 1999; Uba, 1994; Yamamoto et al., 1985). Nevertheless, there is within-group variability in psychopathology among Asian Pacific Americans. One significant source of variability is levels of acculturation. Social displacement theory suggests that Asian refugees and immigrants may initially have positive feelings on arriving in the United States, but these feelings may be followed by depression and other negative feelings, which could result in more severe psychological disorders. Kinzie et al. (1990) found that up to 54 percent to 93 percent of Southeast Asian refugees may be suffering from Posttraumatic Stress Disorder (PTSD). Intergenerational conflicts may be a source of difficulty, given that younger family members adapt more quickly and may reject many of the traditions of their culture. Acculturation to Western culture has been associated with less psychopathology among Asian Americans (Greenberger & Chen, 1996; Hall & Phung, 2001). Stressors associated with psychological problems for immigrants include cultural barriers, language, lack of social support, and financial strain. Of course, the mental health professionals who determine the criteria for psychopathology usually are not Asian Pacific Americans. Thus, acculturated Asian Pacific Americans' behavior may be consistent with what non-Asian Pacific Americans consider normative. Conversely, some of the characteristics of less acculturated

Asian Pacific Americans could be normative in cultural context; for example, modesty and restraint might be adaptive in some cultural contexts but not in others.

Acculturation to Western values is also associated with Asian Americans' receptiveness to the use of mental health professionals for assistance with psychological problems (Uomoto & Gorsuch, 1984). Perhaps this is because traditional Asian Pacific American beliefs about mental disorders may be incompatible with the use of mental health services. Asian Americans who believe that psychopathology is organically or genetically based may be more likely to seek help from a physician than from a mental health professional (Huang & Ying, 1997). Similarly, those who believe that psychopathology is the result of spiritual causes may be more likely to seek help from a religious leader (Edman & Kameoka, 1997). Psychological problems represent a stigma for some Asian Americans (Iwamasa, Hilliard, & Kost, 1998); thus, disclosing psychological problems would result in loss of face (Huang & Ying, 1997). Earlier research suggested that Asian Americans were underrepresented in public mental health systems relative to their proportion in the population (S. Sue, 1988). More recent studies suggest more proportionate representation of Asian Pacific Americans in the mental health system, possibly because of the greater availability of Asian Pacific American therapists who speak Asian languages (O'Sullivan, Peterson, Cox, & Kirkeby, 1989; Ying & Hu, 1994).

Combining Asian Americans as a single group may obscure important between-group differences in psychopathology. In a study of outpatients in the public mental health system in Seattle, percentages of Asian Pacific Americans and European Americans diagnosed with Schizophrenia and with major affective disorders (e.g., Major Depression, Bipolar Disorder) were approximately the same (see Figure 6.1; Uehara, Takeuchi, & Smukler, 1994). However, an analysis of Asian Pacific American ethnic groups revealed striking differences. Japanese and Chinese American clients were diagnosed with significantly greater rates of schizophrenia than major affective disorders. The opposite was true for Laotian Americans and Filipino Americans. Rates of diagnoses for schizophrenia and major affective disorders for Vietnamese Americans were approximately the same. These findings may reflect a reluctance of Japanese and Chinese Americans to seek public mental health services for major affective disorders. The findings may also suggest that those Japanese and Chinese Americans who do seek public mental health services may be more psychologically disturbed than other groups of Asian Pacific American

FIGURE 6.1   *Percentage of Psychopathology among Mental Health Patients*

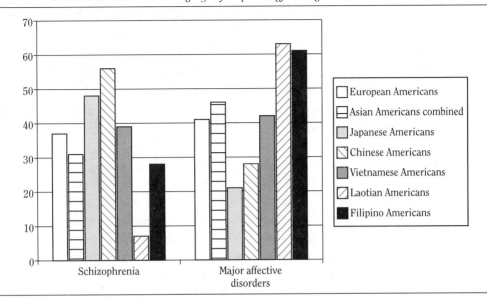

Note: Figures are from outpatient clinics in the Seattle public mental health system.
Source: Adapted from Uehara et al., 1994.

or European American clients. It is possible that Japanese and Chinese Americans who are less psychologically disturbed seek support from family or community sources other than the public mental health system. The Japanese and Chinese American communities in Seattle, and in other areas of the West Coast and Hawaii, have existed longer and are better established than many of the other Asian Pacific American ethnic communities. These well-established communities may be better able to provide alternative sources of support for mental health problems than other, less established Asian Pacific American communities.

Community functioning, which involved a client's ability to meet their basic needs (e.g., hygiene, cooking), community living skills (e.g., grocery shopping), and work/school productivity, was also assessed by case managers for each group (Uehara et al., 1994). Although Chinese American clients had the highest rates of schizophrenia and Laotian Americans the lowest, Chinese Americans had the best community functioning and Laotian Americans the poorest. These findings may reflect the availability of ethnic community resources (Uehara et al., 1994). As discussed above, the Chinese

American community in Seattle is much more established and may be able to provide social support for its members. This well-established community may have been better able to buffer the impact of schizophrenia on community functioning. Conversely, the Laotian American community in Seattle consisted of a large proportion of refugees who may not have had the resources to care for distressed community members. Thus, the impact of psychological disorders on Asian Pacific Americans must be understood in its community context.

Psychotherapy

As with other ethnic minority groups, there is no evidence that empirically supported therapies are valid for Asian Pacific Americans. Moreover, relative to other ethnic minority groups, Asian Americans underutilize mental health services (Sue, Zane, & Young, 1994). Effective psychotherapy for Asian Pacific Americans may involve modifying the assumptions and methods of existing approaches. For many Asian Pacific Americans, the mind and body are considered to be inseparable. Thus, physical problems that appear to have a psychological basis (i.e., somatization) may be viewed as a legitimate reason to seek psychological services (Chin, 1998; Huang & Ying, 1997). Because physical problems may prompt some Asian Pacific Americans to seek psychological services, there may also be an expectation that treatment involves medication. For those Asian Pacific Americans who are open to psychological interventions, the expectation may be that the therapist is an expert who provides information and advice (Chin, 1998). These expectations are consistent with patient-doctor relationships in the medical profession, but are at odds with most approaches to psychotherapy. Therapists must also be careful not to mistake cultural differences for pathology. For example, shame and obligation may be used to encourage responsibility to prescribed roles. In an individualistic culture, this might be perceived as having one's individual freedoms limited, but in a collectivistic culture, this behavior is looked on more favorably. In terms of therapist-client matching, Sue et al. (1991) found that ethnic matching improved treatment outcomes for Asian American clients, although in general, similarities in values and attitudes are usually more important than similarities in race when working with culturally diverse groups.

Psychoeducational approaches emphasize the therapist's expertise and information-providing role, and may have promise with Asian Pacific Americans, who often place a high value on education (E. Lee, 1997). Group therapy might be consistent with Asian Pacific Americans values of interdependence. However, being a member of a group is taken seriously among many Asian Pacific Americans (Nagata, 1997); some may be reluctant to join a therapy group that is temporary.

It would be inappropriate to assume that all Asian Pacific Americans have the same expectations of psychotherapy. Some Asian Pacific Americans are more acculturated than others, and some have expectations that are biculturally based. Thus, it is imperative that therapists have skills in knowing when to generalize across cultures and when to individualize (S. Sue, 1998).

CONCLUSION

Asian Pacific Americans are one of the fastest-growing and most diverse ethnic groups in the United States. The histories of Asian Pacific American groups in the United States are replete with experiences of discrimination similar to those of other ethnic minority groups. Depictions of Asian Pacific Americans as a model minority mask such societal discrimination. For example, the societal emphasis on Asian American academic achievement ignores the possibility that Asian Americans excel in the academic arena because they have been excluded from other arenas. There is an emphasis in Asian Pacific American cultures on interdependence, but many Asian Pacific Americans are bicultural and have both interdependent and independent characteristics. Traditional East Asian American families are hierarchical and paternalistic, whereas other groups, such as Pacific Islanders, have matriarchal traditions. Although rates of psychopathology across Asian Pacific American groups may not be substantially different from those of other groups, there is considerable variability among Asian Pacific American groups.

American psychology has neglected the study of Asian Pacific Americans for a variety of reasons. Among these are limited access to populations, unfamiliarity with Asian Pacific American cultures, and the paucity of Asian Pacific American psychologists who may be most interested in studying Asian Pacific Americans. Nevertheless, 1 in 10 Americans will be of Asian ancestry within the next 50 years. American psychology must become actively involved with Asian Pacific Americans if it is to be relevant for the twenty-first century.

REFERENCES

Agbayani-Siewert, P., & Revilla, L. (1995). Filipino Americans. In P. G. Min (Ed.), *Asian Americans: Contemporary trends and issues* (pp. 134–168). Thousand Oaks, CA: Sage.

Almeida, R. (1996). Hindu, Christian, and Muslim families. In M. McGoldrick, J. Giordano, & J. K. Pearce (Eds.), *Ethnicity and family therapy* (2nd ed., pp. 395–423). New York: Guilford Press.

Asakawa, K., & Csikszentmihalyi, M. (1998). The quality of experience of Asian American adolescents in activities related to future goals. *Journal of Youth and Adolescence, 27,* 141–163.

Bankston, C. L., III. (1998). Sibling cooperation and scholastic performance among Vietnamese-American secondary school students. *Sociological Perspectives, 41,* 167–184.

Barongan, C., Bernal, G., Comas-Diaz, L., Hall, C. C. I., Hall, G. C. N., LaDue, R. A., Parham, T. A., Pedersen, P. B., Porche-Burke, L. M., Rollock, D., & Root, M. P. P. (1997). Misunderstandings of multiculturalism: Shouting fire in crowded theaters. *American Psychologist, 52,* 654–655.

Bobo, L. D. (1999). Prejudice as group position: Microfoundations of a sociological approach to racism and race relations. *Journal of Social Issues, 55,* 445–472.

Bradshaw, C. K. (1994). Asian and Asian American women: Historical and political considerations in psychotherapy. In L. Comas-Diaz & B. Greene (Eds.), *Women of color: Integrating ethnic and gender identities in psychotherapy* (pp. 72–113). New York: Guilford Press.

Brewer, M. B., & Brown, R. J. (1998). Intergroup relations. In D. T. Gilbert, S. T. Fiske, & G. Lindzey (Eds.), *The handbook of social psychology* (4th ed., pp. 554–594). New York: McGraw-Hill.

Burr, J. A., & Mutchler, J. E. (1993). Nativity, acculturation, and economic status: Explanations of Asian American living arrangements in later life. *Journal of Gerontology: Social Sciences, 48,* S55–S63.

Chen, C., & Stevenson, H. W. (1995). Motivation and mathematics achievement: A comparative study of Asian-American, Caucasian-American, and East Asian high school students. *Child Development, 66,* 1215–1234.

Chin, J. L. (1998). Mental health services and treatment. In L. C. Lee & N. W. S. Zane (Eds.), *Handbook of Asian American Psychology* (pp. 485–504). Thousand Oaks, CA: Sage.

Chmielewski, P. M., Fernandes, L. O. L., Yee, C. M., & Miller, G. A. (1995). Ethnicity and gender in scales of psychosis proneness and mood disorders. *Journal of Abnormal Psychology, 104,* 464–470.

Cicirelli, V. G. (1994). Sibling relationships in cross-cultural perspective. *Journal of Marriage and the Family, 56,* 7–20.

Commission on Ethnic Minority Recruitment, Retention, and Training in Psychology. (1997). *Visions and transformations: The final report.* Washington, DC: American Psychological Association.

Commission on Wartime Relocation and Internment of Civilians. (1982). *Personal justice denied.* Washington, DC: Government Printing Office.

Crocker, J., Luhtanen, R., Blaine, B., & Broadnax, S. (1994). Collective self-esteem and psychological well-being among White, Black, and Asian college students. *Personality and Social Psychology Bulletin, 20,* 503–513.

Das, A. K., & Kemp, S. F. (1997). Between two worlds: Counseling South Asian Americans. *Journal of Multicultural Counseling and Development, 25,* 23–33.

Dinh, K. T., Sarason, B. R., & Sarason, I. G. (1994). Parent-child relationships in Vietnamese immigrant families. *Journal of Family Psychology, 8,* 471–488.

Dunbar, E. (1995). The prejudiced personality, racism, and anti-Semitism: The PR scale forty years later. *Journal of Personality Assessment, 65,* 270–277.

Edman, J. L., & Johnson, R. C. (1999). Filipino American and Caucasian American beliefs about the causes and treatment of mental problems. *Cultural Diversity and Ethnic Minority Psychology, 5,* 380–386.

Edman, J. L., & Kameoka, V. A. (1997). Cultural differences in illness schemas: An analysis of Filipino and American illness attributions. *Journal of Cross-Cultural Psychology, 28,* 252–265.

Espiritu, Y. L. (1997). *Asian American men and women.* Thousand Oaks, CA: Sage.

Fiske, S. T., Xu, J., & Cuddy, A. C. (1999). (Dis)respecting versus (dis)liking: Status and interdependence predict ambivalent stereotypes of competence and warmth. *Journal of Social Issues, 55,* 473–489.

Flynn, J. R. (1991). *Asian Americans: Achievement beyond IQ.* Hillsdale, NJ: Erlbaum.

Fong, T. P. (1998). *The contemporary Asian American experience: Beyond the model minority.* Upper Saddle River, NJ: Prentice-Hall.

Fuligni, A. J. (1997). The academic achievement of adolescents from immigrant families: The roles of family background, attitudes, and behavior. *Child Development, 68,* 351–363.

Gold, S. J. (1999). Continuity and change among Vietnamese families in the United States. In H. P. McAdoo (Ed.), *Family ethnicity: Strength in diversity* (2nd ed., pp. 225–234). Thousand Oaks, CA: Sage.

Goyette, K., & Xie, Y. (1999). Educational expectations of Asian American youths: Determinants of ethnic differences. *Sociology of Education, 72,* 22–36.

Greenberger, E., & Chen, C. (1996). Perceived family relationships and depressed mood in early and late adolescence: A comparison of European and Asian Americans. *Developmental Psychology, 32,* 707–716.

Hall, G. C. N., & Phung, A. H. (2001). MMPI/MCMI. In L. Suzuki, J. Ponterotto, & P. Meller (Eds.), *The handbook of multicultural assessment* (2nd ed., pp. 307–330). San Francisco: Jossey-Bass.

Hall, G. C. N., Sue, S., Narang, D. S., & Lilly, R. S. (2000). Culture-specific models of men's sexual aggression: Intra- and interpersonal determinants. *Cultural Diversity and Ethnic Minority Psychology, 6,* 252–267.

Hamm, J. V. (2000). Do birds of a feather flock together? The variable bases for African American, Asian American, and European American adolescents' selection of similar friends. *Developmental Psychology, 36,* 209–219.

Ho, D. Y. F. (1993). Relational orientation in Asian social psychology. In U. Kim & J. W. Berry (Eds.), *Indigenous psychologies: Research and experience in cross-cultural context* (pp. 240–259). Newbury Park, CA: Sage.

Hsia, J., & Peng, S. S. (1998). Academic achievement and performance. In L. C. Lee & N. W. S. Zane (Eds.), *Handbook of Asian American psychology* (pp. 325–357). Thousand Oaks, CA: Sage.

Hsu, F. L. K. (1981). *Americans and Chinese: Passage to differences* (3rd ed.). Honolulu: University of Hawaii Press.

Huang, L. N., & Ying, Y. (1997). Chinese American children and adolescents. In J. T. Gibbs & L. N. Huang (Eds.), *Children of color: Psychological interventions with culturally diverse youth* (pp. 33–67). San Francisco: Jossey-Bass.

Ichiyama, M. A., McQuarrie, E. F., & Ching, K. L. (1996). Contextual influences on ethnic identity among Hawaiian students in the mainland United States. *Journal of Cross-Cultural Psychology, 27,* 458–475.

Iwamasa, G. Y., & Hilliard, K. M. (1999). Depression and anxiety among Asian American elders: A review of the literature. *Clinical Psychology Review, 19,* 343–357.

Iwamasa, G. Y., Hilliard, K. M., & Kost, C. (1998). Conceptualizing anxiety and depression: The older Japanese American adults perspective. *Clinical Gerontologist, 19,* 77–93.

Iyengar, S. S., & Lepper, M. R. (1999). Rethinking the value of choice: A cultural perspective on intrinsic motivation. *Journal of Personality and Social Psychology, 76,* 349–366.

Jensen, J. M. (1988). *Passage from India: Asian Indian immigrants in North America.* New Haven, CT: Yale University Press.

Kamo, Y., & Zhou, M. (1994). Living arrangements of elderly Chinese and Japanese in the United States. *Journal of Marriage and the Family, 56,* 544–558.

Kim, B. C. (1996). Korean families. In M. McGoldrick, J. Giordano, & J. K. Pearce (Eds.), *Ethnicity and family therapy* (2nd ed., pp. 281–294). New York: Guilford Press.

Kim, H., Rendon, L., & Valadez, J. (1998). Student characteristics, school characteristics, and educational aspirations of six Asian American ethnic groups. *Journal of Multicultural Counseling and Development, 26,* 166–176.

Kim, K. C., & Kim, S. (1998). Family and work roles of Korean immigrants in the United States. In H. I. McCubbin, E. A. Thompson, A. I. Thompson, & J. E. Fromer (Eds.), *Resiliency in Native American and immigrant families* (pp. 225–242). Thousand Oaks, CA: Sage.

Kim, P. S., & Lewis, G. B. (1994). Asian Americans in public service: Success, diversity, and discrimination. *Public Administration Review, 54,* 285–290.

Kim, S. C. (1997). Korean American families. In E. Lee (Ed.), *Working with Asian Americans: A guide for clinicians* (pp. 125–135). New York: Guilford Press.

Kinzie, J. D., Boehnlein, J. K., Leung, P. K., Moore, L. J., Riley, C., & Smith, D. (1990). The prevalence of posttraumatic stress disorder and its clinical significance among Southeast Asian refugees. *American Journal of Psychiatry, 147,* 913–917.

Kitano, H. H. L., & Daniels, R. (1995). *Asian Americans: Emerging minorities.* Englewood Cliffs, NJ: Prentice Hall.

LaFromboise, T. D., Coleman, H. L. K., & Gerton, J. (1993). Psychological impact of biculturalism: Evidence and theory. *Psychological Bulletin, 114,* 395–412.

Lee, E. (1996a). Asian American families: An overview. In M. McGoldrick, J. Giordano, & J. K. Pearce (Eds.), *Ethnicity and family therapy* (2nd ed., pp. 227–248). New York: Guilford Press.

Lee, E. (1996b). Chinese families. In M. McGoldrick, J. Giordano, & J. K. Pearce (Eds.), *Ethnicity and family therapy* (2nd ed., pp. 249–267). New York: Guilford Press.

Lee, E. (1997). Overview: The assessment and treatment of Asian American families. In E. Lee (Ed.), *Working with Asian Americans: A guide for clinicians* (pp. 3–36). New York: Guilford Press.

Lee, L. C. (1998). An overview. In L. C. Lee & N. W. S. Zane (Eds.), *Handbook of Asian American psychology* (pp. 1–20). Thousand Oaks, CA: Sage.

Leung, P. K., & Boehnlein, J. (1996). Vietnamese families. In M. McGoldrick, J. Giordano, & J. K. Pearce (Eds.), *Ethnicity and family therapy* (2nd ed., pp. 295–306). New York: Guilford Press.

Markus, H. R., & Kitayama, S. (1991). Culture and the self: Implications for cognition, emotion, and motivation. *Psychological Review, 98,* 224–253.

Min, P. G. (1995). *Asian Americans: Contemporary trends and issues.* Thousand Oaks, CA: Sage.

Mok, T. A. (1999). Asian American dating: Important factors in partner choice. *Cultural Diversity and Ethnic Minority Psychology, 5,* 103–117.

Morishima, J. K. (1973). The evacuation: Impact on the family. In S. Sue & N. N. Wagner (Eds.), *Asian-Americans: Psychological perspectives* (pp. 13–19). Palo Alto, CA: Science and Behavior Books.

Nagata, D. (1993). *Legacy of injustice: Exploring the cross-generational impact of the Japanese American internment.* New York: Plenum Press.

Nagata, D. K. (1997). The assessment and treatment of Japanese American children and adolescents. In J. T. Gibbs & L. N. Huang (Eds.), *Children of color: Psychological interventions with culturally diverse youth* (pp. 68–111). San Francisco: Jossey-Bass.

Nakanishi, D. T. (1988). Seeking convergence in race relations research: Japanese-Americans and the resurrection of the internment. In P. A. Katz & D. A. Taylor (Eds.), *Eliminating racism: Profiles in controversy* (pp. 159–180). New York: Plenum Press.

Neisser, U., Boodoo, G., Bouchard, T. J., Boykin, A. W., Brody, N., Ceci, S. J., Halpern, D. F., Loehlin, J. C., Perloff, R., Sternberg, R. J., & Urbina, S. (1996). Intelligence: Knowns and unknowns. *American Psychologist, 51,* 77–101.

Nguyen, H. H., Messe, L. A., & Stollak, G. E. (1999). Toward a more complex understanding of acculturation and adjustment. *Journal of Cross-Cultural Psychology, 30,* 5–31.

Nishi, S. M. (1995). Japanese Americans. In P. G. Min (Ed.), *Asian Americans: Contemporary trends and issues* (pp. 95–133). Thousand Oaks, CA: Sage.

Nishio, K., & Bilmes, M. (1987). Psychotherapy with Southeast Asian American clients. *Professional Psychology: Research and Practice, 18,* 342–346.

Okagaki, L., & Frensch, P. A. (1998). Parenting and children's school achievement: A multiethnic perspective. *American Educational Research Journal, 35,* 123–144.

Oliver, M. B., & Hyde, J. S. (1993). Gender differences in sexuality: A meta-analysis. *Psychological Bulletin, 114,* 29–51.

Ong, P. (1994). *The state of Asian Pacific America: Economic diversity, issues & policies.* Los Angeles: LEAP Asian Pacific Public Policy Institute and UCLA Asian American Studies Center.

O'Sullivan, M. J., Peterson, P. D., Cox, G. B., & Kirkeby, J. (1989). Ethnic populations: Community mental health services ten years later. *American Journal of Community Psychology, 17,* 17–30.

Oyserman, D., & Sakamoto, I. (1997). Being Asian American: Identity, cultural constructs, and stereotype perception. *Journal of Applied Behavioral Science, 33,* 435–453.

Phinney, J. S., Ferguson, D. L., & Tate, J. D. (1997). Intergroup attitudes among ethnic minority adolescents: A causal model. *Child Development, 68,* 955–969.

Pittinsky, T. L., Shih, M., & Ambady, N. (1999). Identity adaptiveness: Affect across multiple identities. *Journal of Social Issues, 55,* 503–518.

Ponterotto, J., & Pedersen, P. (1993). *Preventing prejudice: A guide for counselors and educators.* Newbury Park, CA: Sage.

Portes, A., & MacLeod, D. (1996). Educational progress of children of immigrants: The roles of class, ethnicity, and school context. *Sociology of Education, 69,* 255–275.

Prathikanti, S. (1997). East Indian American families. In E. Lee (Ed.), *Working with Asian Americans: A guide for clinicians* (pp. 79–100). New York: Guilford Press.

Romero, A. J., & Roberts, R. E. (1998). Perception of discrimination and ethnocultural variables in a diverse group of adolescents. *Journal of Adolescence, 21,* 641–656.

Rotheram-Borus, M. J., Lightfoot, M., Moraes, A., Dopkins, S., & LaCour, J. (1998). Developmental, ethnic, and gender differences in ethnic identity among adolescents. *Journal of Adolescent Research, 13,* 487–507.

Rumbaut, R. G. (1995). Vietnamese, Laotian, and Cambodian Americans. In P. G. Min (Ed.), *Asian Americans: Contemporary trends and issues* (pp. 232–270). Thousand Oaks, CA: Sage.

Sack, W. H., & Clarke, G. N. (1996). Multiple forms of stress in Cambodian adolescent refugees. *Child Development, 67,* 107–116.

Sasao, T. (1994). Using surname-based telephone survey methodology in Asian-American communities: Practical issues and caveats. *Journal of Community Psychology, 22,* 283–295.

Sears, D. O., Citrin, J., Cheleden, S. V., & van Laar, C. (1999). Cultural diversity and multicultural politics: Is ethnic balkanization psychologically inevitable? In D. A. Prentice & D. T. Miller (Eds.), *Cultural divides: Understanding and overcoming group conflict* (pp. 35–79). New York: Russell Sage Foundation.

Sheth, M. (1995). Asian Indian Americans. In P. G. Min (Ed.), *Asian Americans: Contemporary trends and issues* (pp. 169–198). Thousand Oaks, CA: Sage.

Shih, M., Pittinsky, T. L., & Ambady, N. (1999). Stereotype susceptibility: Identity salience and shifts in quantitative performance. *Psychological Science, 10,* 80–83.

Singelis, T. M., & Sharkey, W. F. (1995). Culture, self-construal, and embarrassability. *Journal of Cross-Cultural Psychology, 26,* 622–644.

Spencer, S. J., Fein, S., Wolfe, C. T., Fong, C., & Dunn, M. A. (1998). Automatic activation of stereotypes: The role of self-image threat. *Personality and Social Psychology Bulletin, 24,* 1139–1152.

Steinberg, L., Dornbusch, S. M., & Brown, B. B. (1992). Ethnic differences in adolescent achievement: An ecological perspective. *American Psychologist, 47,* 723–729.

Streltzer, J., Rezentes, W. C., III, & Arakaki, M. (1996). Does acculturation influence psychosocial adaptation and well-being in Native Hawaiians? *International Journal of Social Psychiatry, 42,* 28–37.

Sue, S. (1988). Psychotherapeutic services for ethnic minorities: Two decades of research findings. *American Psychologist, 43,* 301–308.

Sue, S. (1994, November). Asian Americans in psychology. *Focus, 8,* 6–8.

Sue, S. (1998). In search of cultural competence in psychotherapy and counseling. *American Psychologist, 53,* 440–448.

Sue, S., Fujino, D., Hu, L., Takeuchi, D., & Zane, N. (1991). Community mental health services for ethnic minority groups: A test of the cultural responsiveness hypothesis. *Journal of Consulting and Clinical Psychology, 59,* 533–540.

Sue, S., & Okazaki, S. (1990). Asian-American educational achievements: A phenomenon in search of an explanation. *American Psychologist, 45,* 913–920.

Sue, S., & Zane, N. W. (1985). Academic achievement and socioemotional adjustment among Chinese university students. *Journal of Counseling Psychology, 32,* 570–579.

Sue, S., Zane, N., & Young, K. (1994). Research on psychotherapy with culturally diverse populations. In A. E. Bergin & S. L. Garfield (Eds.), *Handbook of psychotherapy and behavior change* (4th ed., pp. 783–817). New York: Wiley.

Sun, Y. (1998). The academic success of East-Asian-American students: An investment model. *Social Science Research, 27,* 432–456.

Sustento-Seneriches, J. (1997). Filipino American families. In E. Lee (Ed.), *Working with Asian Americans: A guide for clinicians* (pp. 101–113). New York: Guilford Press.

Tajfel, H., & Turner, J. (1986). The social identity theory of intergroup behavior. In S. Worchel & W. Austin (Eds.), *Psychology of intergroup relations* (pp. 7–24). Chicago: Nelson-Hall.

Takaki, R. (1993). *A different mirror: A history of multicultural America.* New York: Little, Brown.

Taylor, C. R., & Stern, B. B. (1997). Asian-Americans: Television advertising and the "model minority" stereotype. *Journal of Advertising, 26,* 47–60.

Tsai, D. T., & Lopez, R. A. (1997). The use of social supports by elder Chinese immigrants. *Journal of Gerontological Social Work, 29,* 77–94.

Uba, L. (1994). *Asian Americans: Personality patterns, identity, and mental health.* New York: Guilford Press.

Uehara, E. S., Takeuchi, D. T., & Smukler, M. (1994). Effects of combining disparate groups in the analysis of ethnic differences: Variations among Asian American mental health service consumers in level of community functioning. *American Journal of Community Psychology, 22,* 83–99.

Uomoto, J. M., & Gorsuch, R. L. (1984). Japanese American response to psychological disorders: Referral patterns, attitudes, and subjective norms. *American Journal of Community Psychology, 12,* 537–550.

U.S. Bureau of the Census. (1993). *1990 Census of the Population, Asians and Pacific Islanders in the United States.* Washington, DC: Government Printing Office.

Wong, M. G. (1995). Chinese Americans. In P. G. Min (Ed.), *Asian Americans: Contemporary trends and issues* (pp. 58–94). Thousand Oaks, CA: Sage.

Yamamoto, J., Machizawa, S., Araki, F., Reece, S., Steinberg, A., Leung, J., & Cater, C. (1985). Mental health of elderly Asian Americans in Los Angeles. *American Journal of Social Psychiatry, 5,* 37–46.

Yee, B. W. K., Huang, L. N., & Lew, A. (1998). Families: Life-span socialization in a cultural context. In L. C. Lee & N. W. S. Zane (Eds.), *Handbook of Asian American psychology* (pp. 83–135). Thousand Oaks, CA: Sage.

Ying, Y., Coombs, M., & Lee, P. A. (1999). Family intergenerational relationship of Asian American adolescents. *Cultural Diversity and Ethnic Minority Psychology, 5,* 350–363.

Ying, Y., & Hu, L. (1994). Public outpatient mental health services: Use and outcome among Asian Americans. *American Journal of Orthopsychiatry, 64,* 448–455.

ISSUES FOR DISCUSSION

1. Dr. Alice Chang, the first Asian Pacific American woman to serve on the Board of Directors of the American Psychological Association, has contended that Asian Pacific Americans are a "minority of convenience." Dr. Chang meant that Asian Pacific Americans are counted as minorities when it is convenient, such as when a university or organization wants to tout its efforts in creating a culturally diverse environment; however, such consideration of Asian Pacific Americans as minorities ends when it becomes inconvenient, such as when this involves special programs that cost money. Do you think Asian Pacific Americans are an ethnic minority group in the same sense that other groups of color in the United States are ethnic minority groups?

2. Korean American actress Margaret Cho is the first Asian Pacific American to star in a weekly television comedy television series. The producers of Ms. Cho's 1993–1994 program, *All-American Girl,* told her to lose weight before the program was filmed. Ms. Cho was taken aback by this because she is a comedienne and the program was not necessarily based on her appearance. Do you think the producer's request had something to do with Ms. Cho's being an Asian Pacific American? Is being a comedienne compatible with role expectations for Asian American women? If the star of this program was not Asian Pacific American, do you think the producers would have told the star to lose weight?

3. What are the negative consequences of stereotypes of Asian Americans as academic achievers?

SEVEN

LATINO/A AMERICANS

Things don't change, you change the way of looking, that's all.
—Carlos Castañeda

The terms "Hispanic" and "Latino" are political terms used within a U.S. context (Bernal & Enchautegui-de-Jesus, 1994). Hispanic is an English term and refers to persons having Spanish ancestry, including those from Puerto Rico, Cuba, Central and South America, and Spain. The federal government began to use the term Hispanic in the 1970s for census and federal program purposes (Bernal & Enchautegui-de-Jesus, 1994). Persons having Brazilian ancestry are not considered Hispanic because of the Portuguese influence in Brazil. Latino/a refers to Latin American origins; the term Latino is masculine and Latina is feminine. Those who prefer the term Latino/a may disidentify with Spain and the term Hispanic because of the associations of the latter with colonization (Castro, Proescholdbell, Abeita, & Rodriguez, 1999). Some Mexican Americans prefer the term Chicano/a. Chicano/as view themselves as outsiders to both mainstream U.S. and Mexican cultures (Falicov, 1998). Cuban Americans, Mexican Americans, and Puerto Rican Americans identify more with their particular Latino/a American ethnic group than of Latino/a Americans as a whole (Huddy & Virtanen, 1995).

Latino/as can be from any ethnic group. There are large groups of Latinos having African ancestry, as well as large groups having European ancestry. Alberto Fujimori, former president of Peru, is of Japanese ancestry. Nonetheless, he is Latino/a insofar as part of his cultural identification is Peruvian. Many Latinos are racially mixed. Those having Spanish and Indian ancestry are known as *mestizos*. Those with Spanish and African ancestry are known as *mulattos*.

Mexican Americans constitute 65 percent of the Latino/a American population, Central and South Americans 14 percent, Puerto Rican Americans

10 percent, and Cuban Americans 4 percent (http://www.census.gov/Press -Release/www/2000/cb00-38.html). Because of Spanish influences, most Latino/as speak Spanish and most are Roman Catholics, although the number of practicing Latino/a Catholics may be decreasing (Bernal & Shapiro, 1996).

Within 50 years, Latino/a Americans will be 24 percent of the U.S. population and therefore the single largest ethnic minority group. The population at that time is projected to be approximately 50 percent European American. Insofar as half the European Americans will be men, there will be nearly as many Latino/a Americans as there are European American men.

HISTORY

Highly developed cultures, with achievements in agriculture, textiles, and medical practices, existed in the regions that are now Central and South America long before the Spanish arrived there (Comas-Diaz, Lykes, & Alarcon, 1998). The Mayan, Incan, and Aztec empires were part of these cultures. Much of Central and South America was conquered by the Spanish in the late fifteenth and early sixteenth centuries. The Spanish also conquered the indigenous peoples of what are now New Mexico, Texas, and California in the 1500s.

Mexican Americans

Spanish missions were established throughout what is now California beginning in 1769. Mexican settlers, most of whom were poor, came to live and work at these missions. By 1821, there were 3,000 Mexicans in California. European American settlers were initially welcomed by the Mexicans, although tensions developed between the groups. The Mexicans were viewed by the European Americans as idle and thriftless, and the Mexicans viewed the European Americans as having a sense of entitlement to the land (Takaki, 1993).

The Mexican-American War began in 1846 to gain the Southwest for the United States. Robbery, murder, and rape of Mexicans were common during the war (Takaki, 1993). In 1848, the Treaty of Guadalupe Hidalgo ceded Texas, California, New Mexico, Nevada, parts of Colorado, Arizona, and Utah to the United States. Mexico lost 45 percent of its national territory and over 100,000 of its people (Bernal & Enchautegui-de-Jesus, 1994). The treaty promised citizenship, freedom of religion and language, and maintenance of lands (Garcia-Preto, 1996a). However, similar to the many treaties between the U.S. government and American Indians, Mexicans in the United States were oppressed by these supposed agreements. Mexican landowners lost their land when it was determined in 1851 that land grants under former Spanish and Mexican rule were no longer valid (Takaki, 1993). Those who did not lose their land by legal rulings often lost it because of an inability to pay high taxes.

The gold rush in 1849 resulted in a huge influx of European Americans. Before 1849, Mexicans outnumbered European Americans by 10 to 1 in California (Takaki, 1993). This situation was reversed in 1849, when there were 100,000 European Americans and 13,000 Mexicans in California. Although European Americans learned gold mining methods from Mexicans, foreign miners taxes were imposed on Mexican miners.

Many Mexicans migrated to the United States during the early 1900s for better opportunities. The available work planting cotton, on railroads, and in mining was menial and often dangerous. Mexicans were a cheap source of labor, as they were paid less than European Americans for the same work (Takaki, 1993). Mexican laborers organized strikes in California in the early 1900s. In 1903, Japanese and Mexicans formed the Japanese-Mexican Labor Association, which successfully orchestrated a strike in Oxnard, California, that forced a pay raise. This labor association attempted to join the American Federation of Labor (AFL), but decided not to when the AFL would not accept Japanese members (Takaki, 1993). Anti-Asian immigration laws later caused European American farmers to rely on Mexican labor.

Mexicans in California were faced with segregated public buildings and their children were educated in segregated schools (Takaki, 1993). European American teachers taught Mexican children to be obedient so that they could eventually replace their parents as workers. Mexican children were taught domestic skills and manual labor skills in school.

Mexicans began to be perceived as a source of competition for jobs during the Depression in the 1930s. Approximately 300,000 Mexicans were "repatriated" or deported on trains to Mexico during the early 1930s (Bernal & Enchautegui-de-Jesus, 1994). Many were children who were born in the United States, which made them American citizens. However, the rights of American citizenship have been suspended for ethnic minority groups during times of national emergency, such as when over 120,000 Japanese Americans were incarcerated during World War II.

During World War II, a farm labor shortage in the United States occurred because of involvement in the war effort (Bernal & Enchautegui-de-Jesus, 1994). The United States and Mexico issued Mexicans temporary permits to work in the United States. Mexican immigrants during and following World War II were primarily from rural areas (Bernal & Enchautegui-de-Jesus, 1994).

Puerto Rican Americans

Puerto Rico was colonized by Spain in 1493. Its native Taino Indian inhabitants were enslaved and killed (Comas-Diaz et al., 1998). Taino emphases on tranquility, kinship, and group dependence persist in current Puerto Rican culture (Garcia-Preto, 1996b). Spanish influences included language, the Roman Catholic religion, and patriarchy (Garcia-Preto, 1996b). The Spanish brought African slaves, who also contributed language, religion, and medicine, as well as the fatalism of slavery (Garcia-Preto, 1996b). During the Spanish-American War in 1898, Puerto Rico, Cuba, Guam, and the Philippines were invaded by the United States (Bernal & Enchautegui-de-Jesus, 1994). Puerto Rico has remained a colony of the United States since then. English was mandated as the official language of instruction in Puerto Rican public schools, although few Puerto Ricans, including teachers, spoke English (Garcia-Preto, 1996b). Congress allowed Puerto Ricans to become U.S. citizens in 1917. Nevertheless, many Americans do not regard Puerto Ricans as citizens (Garcia-Preto, 1996a).

Large numbers of Puerto Ricans emigrated to the northeastern United States in the 1940s and 1950s for economic reasons. Puerto Ricans often took menial, low-paying jobs that no one else wanted (Inclan & Herron, 1998). Available employment often involved domestic labor (e.g., housecleaning) that Puerto Rican women were more willing to accept. Thus, women immigrants became more employable than men immigrants, which resulted in a power shift and gender conflicts in many families (Hernandez, 1996).

Puerto Rico became a commonwealth in 1952 and Spanish was reinstituted as the language of instruction in public schools (Garcia-Preto, 1996b). Nevertheless, Puerto Rico still often functions as a colony of the United States (Comas-Diaz et al., 1998). For example, as of this writing, the U.S. military continues aerial bombing practice of Vieques, a populated island that is part of Puerto Rico, despite the protests of the island's inhabitants.

Lillian Comas-Diaz was born in Chicago and at age 6 returned to her parents' native Puerto Rico. Puerto Rico's colonial status and emancipation struggles provided a context for her interest in oppression and liberation. After completing college, Dr. Comas-Diaz worked in Puerto Rico as a science teacher. She later completed a master's degree in clinical psychology at the University of Puerto Rico and moved to Connecticut to work in a community mental health clinic. She then completed her PhD in clinical psychology at the University of Massachusetts at Amherst. After completing her clinical internship at Yale University, she was on the faculty at the Yale School of Medicine, where she directed a Hispanic clinic. In 1984, she became the director of the American Psychological Association's Office of Ethnic Minority Affairs. She currently directs the Transcultural Mental Health Institute in Washington, D.C.

There is virtually no area of ethnic minority psychology that Dr. Comas-Diaz's work has not addressed, including mental health, psychological assessment and diagnosis, psychotherapy, psychopharmacology, mixed ethnic identity, Latino professional identity, feminism and feminist therapy, alcohol abuse, violence against women and child sexual abuse, and political repression. Dr. Comas-Diaz has critically analyzed the interaction of political oppression with gender and race. A combined cultural, historical, and sociopolitical perspective has helped her develop an ethnocultural and gender-sensitive approach to treating victims of political repression and of torture.

Dr. Comas-Diaz is the senior editor of *Women of Color: Integrating Ethnic and Gender Identities in Psychotherapy,* and of *Clinical Guidelines in Cross-Cultural Mental Health.* She is the founding editor of *Cultural Diversity and Mental Health* and continued as editor in chief when this journal became the official journal of the APA Society for the Psychological Study of Ethnic Minority Issues and was renamed *Cultural Diversity and Ethnic Minority Psychology.* She won the APA Award for Distinguished Contributions to the Public Interest in 2000. A clinical professor at the George Washington University Department of Psychiatry and Behavioral Sciences, she infuses cultural diversity into mental health training.

Words of Advice to Students:

Seek out mentors: You can learn something valuable from everyone.

Be grateful, especially to those who help you willingly and unwillingly.

Go back home, learn about yourself, your group, and your circumstances.

Turn your limitations into strengths.

Balance hope with realism, and achievement with serenity.

Alchemize adversity into opportunity.

Develop your inner guidance.

Cuban Americans

Cuba gained its independence from the United States in 1902, but continued to trade with the United States until the Revolution in 1959. The revolutionary government created social, economic, and political changes in Cuba, as well as an economic embargo by the United States (Bernal & Enchautegui-de-Jesus, 1994). Political reasons were the motivation for initial waves of Cuban emigrants to the United States between 1959 and 1965. These initial immigrants were predominantly White and upper and middle class (Bernal & Enchautegui-de-Jesus, 1994). They also received financial assistance from the U.S. government (Garcia-Preto, 1996a). The second wave, from 1965 to 1973, included middle-class, lower-middle-class, and working-class persons, who were allowed to leave to be united with relatives in the United States. The third wave began in 1980, when Fidel Castro allowed anyone who wanted to leave Cuba to do so via boat from the port of Mariel. This third migration wave included a broader spectrum of persons in terms of race, education, gender, and socioeconomic status (Bernal & Enchautegui-de-Jesus, 1994). This third wave also included a greater percentage of Afro-Cubans than had the earlier waves (Bernal & Shapiro, 1996). The higher SES of the first two waves of Cuban immigrants in combination with federal resources that have not been available for other Latino/a groups have placed Cuban Americans in relatively better standing than other Latino/a groups. Indeed, most Cuban Americans, Mexican Americans, and Puerto Rican Americans perceive Cuban Americans as having the highest status among these Latino/a American groups (Huddy & Virtanen, 1995). Although Cuban Americans have been considered by some to be a "model minority," the same stereotypes and disadvantages of being a model minority for Asian Americans that were discussed in Chapter Five apply to Cuban Americans.

A fourth wave of Cuban immigration to the United States occurred in the 1990s (Bernal & Shapiro, 1996). Economic hardships became severe at the end of the Soviet Union, which had been sending aid to Cuba, combined with the U.S. economic blockade. In 1994, thousands of *balseros* attempted to elude coastal police and come to Florida on makeshift rafts. The Cuban government again allowed persons to leave Cuba. The United States and Cuba entered an agreement to allow 20,000 Cubans to legally emigrate each year.

Other Latin Americans

Several waves of emigration to the United States from Latin America have occurred for economic and political reasons. Argentineans and Chileans left their countries for the United States in the 1960s and 1970s because of repressive regimes. Poor economic conditions caused Mexicans from urban areas to come to the United States during the 1970s and 1980s. Political conflicts in Nicaragua, El Salvador, Peru, and Guatemala in the 1980s caused many persons in these countries to leave for the United States. Conflicts have resulted from historic tensions between indigenous peoples and those with Spanish ancestry who have controlled the government. Maoist and Marxist groups have also engaged in guerrilla warfare. Many women joined these guerrilla efforts and participated in changing national politics, which constituted a shift in gender roles (Hernandez, 1996). In an effort to oppose communist influence, the United States has backed the governments of some of these Central American countries (Hernandez, 1996). Hundreds of thousands of civilians, including children and youth, have been murdered and indigenous cultures have been destroyed (Comas-Diaz et al., 1998). Nicaraguans were welcomed in the United States as political refugees of the Sandinistas, whereas Salvadorans and Guatemalans were viewed as emigrating for economic reasons and were often deported (Bernal & Enchautegui-de-Jesus, 1994). In addition to these political and economic motivations for emigration, Latin American countries have been susceptible to the effects of natural disasters, including floods and earthquakes, which has been an additional motivation for emigration to the United States (Hough, Canino, Abueg, & Gusman, 1996).

Refugees to the United States often have had to resort to the services of guides or "coyotes," who bring them to the United States illegally (Hernandez, 1996). The trips may last weeks or months, and the refugees are often taken advantage of by these guides. Many refugees are ultimately captured by immigration officers and deported. Those who remain in the United States often are disappointed at the less than warm welcome they receive. In 1994, Proposition 187 in California denied care to nondocumented immigrants and compelled employers to report undocumented immigrants to immigration officials (Falicov, 1996). Latino/a Americans living in ethnic enclaves are particularly susceptible to investigations and deportation by immigration officials.

Many African Americans may perceive immigration as threatening their job security (Sears, Citrin, Cheleden, & van Laar, 1999). Because many Asian Americans and Latino/a Americans are themselves immigrants, these groups tend to be less likely to perceive immigration as having a negative effect on the economy. Latino/a Americans are more likely than other ethnic groups to support rights for illegal immigrants (e.g., work permits, citizenship for children of illegal immigrants who are born in the United States). Economic threat does not appear to be the reason that European Americans express less support for immigration than Asian Americans and Latino/a Americans do. Prejudice, rather than economic threat, may be the basis of European American opposition to immigration and societal diversity (Bobo, 1999; Sears et al., 1999).

CURRENT DEMOGRAPHICS

How many Latino/a Americans would you guess there are in the United States? Would it surprise you that the Latino/a American population in the United States is nearly as large as the African American population? Whereas African Americans are 13 percent of the population, Latino/a Americans at 32.4 million are approximately 12 percent of the population (http://www.census.gov/population/estimates/nation/intfile3-1.txt). Although there has been evidence of perceived competition between Latino/a Americans and other ethnic groups (Sears et al., 1999), Latino/a Americans could become a very powerful component of a multiethnic coalition of ethnic minority groups that is growing at a faster rate than the European American U.S. population.

Mexican Americans make up the largest percentage of Latino/a Americans because Mexico is adjacent to the United States and because many of their ancestors were native to the areas of the southwestern United States that were ceded to the United States in 1848. California (10.5 million) and Texas (6 million) are home to over half of Latinos in the United States (http://www.census.gov/Press-Release/www/2000/cb00-126.html). Other states with large Latino/a American populations are New York (2.7 million), Florida (2.3 million), Illinois (1.3 million), Arizona (1.1 million), and New Jersey (1.0 million). Latino/a Americans are relatively young, with the median age of the population at 27 years (http://www.census.gov/population/estimates/nation/intfile3-1.txt).

In 1998, approximately 26 percent of Latino/a Americans were poor, which is comparable to the percentage of poor African Americans (http://www .census.gov/Press-Release/www/1999/cb99-188.html). As with African Americans, the majority of Latino/a Americans are not poor. The 1998 poverty rate among Latino/a groups ranged from about 31 percent for Puerto Ricans and Mexicans to 14 percent for Cubans (http://www.census.gov/Press-Release /www/2000/cb00-38.html). The historic reasons for this variability in poverty were reviewed previously.

Fifty-six percent of Latino/a Americans in 1998 had a high school degree or higher (http://www.census.gov/Press-Release/cb98-221.html). As in other groups, many of those who do not graduate from high school may be from lower SES backgrounds. Low-income Latino/a Americans in urban areas may become disengaged from school as they enter high school (Seidman, Aber, Allen, & French, 1996). In 1998, 11 percent of Latino/a Americans had a bachelor's degree (http://www.census.gov/Press-Release/cb98-221.html). College education varies across groups, ranging from 7 percent of Mexican Americans to 25 percent of Cuban Americans (http://www.census.gov /Press-Release/www/2000/cb00-38.html).

Most Latino/a American families are headed by married couples. In 1999, 68 percent of Hispanic families were married-couple families, 24 percent were maintained by a woman with no husband present, and 8 percent by a man with no wife present (http://www.census.gov/Press-Release/www /2000/cb00-38.html). Eighty percent of Cuban families were headed by a married couple, the highest percentage among Latino/a Americans (http://www.census.gov/Press-Release/www/2000/cb00-38.html).

Half (13 million) of the nation's foreign-born residents in 1997 were born in Latin America (http://www.census.gov/Press-Release/www/1999 /cb99-195.html). In 1997, there were four Latin American countries among the top 10 countries of birth of the nation's foreign-born: Mexico, Cuba, the Dominican Republic, and El Salvador (http://www.census.gov/Press-Release /www/1999/cb99-195.html). Unlike the Asian American population in the United States, which is primarily foreign-born, 60 percent of the Latino/a American population was born in the United States.

As of 1998, 10 percent of the adult population of the United States spoke Spanish (http://www.census.gov/Press-Release/www/1999/cb99-238.html). Twenty-seven percent of public high school students in the United States took Spanish courses in 1994 (http://www.census.gov/Press-Release/www

/1999/cb99-238.html). The Spanish language is a resource for cultural heritage (Bernal & Shapiro, 1996). However, California in 1998 voted to ban bilingual education, which had been in place for three decades. Latino/a Americans are more opposed to having English as the official language of the United States than are other ethnic groups (Sears et al., 1999).

Spanglish is a hybridization of the Spanish and English languages. Such language is not acceptable to school systems (Arcaya, 1999). Although Spanglish may create a group identity, it may interfere with opportunities for societal success (Arcaya, 1999).

CULTURAL VALUES AND IDENTITY

Theories of the self posit that interdependent cultures will have cultural traditions that enhance an individual's ability to blend in with the group (Markus & Kitayama, 1991). The characteristics of Latino/a American cultures discussed promote interdependence (see Table 7.1). However, models of acculturation suggest that individuals in the United States having a non-mainstream cultural background are influenced by their culture of origin or the mainstream culture or both (LaFromboise, Coleman, & Gerton, 1993). Among a sample of Puerto Rican American adults, 25 percent were highly immersed in both American and Puerto Rican cultures (Cortes, Rogler, & Malgady, 1994). Another 14 percent considered themselves bicultural but were marginally involved in either culture. Among those who were primarily

---

TABLE 7.1   *Latino American Cultural Values*

Respeto: Respect, deference, and obedience to elders.

Machismo: Courage, family responsibility; also could involve antisocial and narcissistic characteristics.

Marianismo: Spirituality, enduring suffering, sexual purity, placing one's children's welfare above one's own.

Personalismo: Importance of interpersonal relationships and sensitivity.

Familismo: Importance of immediate and extended family.

Religiosity: Belief in and worship of a higher being, fatalism.

monocultural, 27 percent were highly involved in American culture and had low involvement in Puerto Rican culture, and 34 percent exhibited the reverse pattern. Thus, any particular Latino/a American may be more or less influenced by the characteristics as a function of level of acculturation to Latino/a and European American cultures. There also may be variability in adherence to these general cultural values between Latino/a American ethnic groups (e.g., Mexican American, Puerto Rican American, Cuban American), as well as within these groups. Although the cultural characteristics described below may appear similar to those of other traditional cultures, some of these characteristics are not equivalent to those of other cultures.

Respeto is a component of Latino/a American cultures that has been defined as respect, deference, and obedience to elders (Marin & Marin, 1991). Respeto is different from respect in that it connotes additional emotional dependence and dutifulness (Falicov, 1996). Respeto requires that women be respectful and subordinate to men (Bernal & Shapiro, 1996; Ginorio, Gutierrez, Cauce, & Acosta, 1995); failure to show proper respect to a Latino/a American man may be considered an affront (Garcia-Preto, 1996b). Respeto also applies to authority figures outside the community. The emphasis in Latino/a American cultures on respect for elders and authority figures may prevent many parents from questioning their children's teacher or school officials. This may be interpreted as a lack of caring or involvement in the child's education (D. Sue & Sue, 1999).

Children are also expected to demonstrate respeto to elders. For example, many Puerto Ricans believe that it is disrespectful for a child to call adults by their first name without using "Dona," "Don," "Señor," or "Señora" (Garcia-Preto, 1996b). Mexican American elementary school students have been found to rely on authority figures in making decisions more so than African American students (Rotheram-Borus & Phinney, 1990). Although such reliance on others could be viewed as being overly dependent, such behavior may reflect respeto socialization.

A misunderstood Latino/a American cultural tradition is *machismo*. Machismo includes what might be considered positive and negative components. In a positive sense, machismo involves courage and responsibility as a strong protector of the family (Sorenson & Siegel, 1992). In a negative sense, it involves being irresponsible, domineering, jealous, violent, abusing alcohol, being insensitive to women, unfaithful, promiscuous, and abusive and having antisocial and narcissistic characteristics (Castro et al., 1999). Many Latino/a American boys are socialized to be tough and self-reliant and to avoid being weak, disrespected, and taken advantage of or *pendejo* (Arcaya, 1999). Boys may be socialized into a machismo lifestyle by older youths and men (Arcaya, 1999). Women may be viewed as either virtuous or fallen (Arcaya, 1999); fallen women are pursued for pleasure, whereas virtuous women are viewed as ideal mates. Of course, this is a double standard, as men's engaging in extramarital affairs is accepted but not women's (Garcia-Preto, 1996b). It is possible that machismo attitudes lead parents to greater tolerance of aggressive behavior in boys. For example, Puerto Rican American adolescent mothers perceived their sons as having fewer problems than African American adolescent mothers perceived in their sons (Leadbeater & Bishop, 1994). However, it is possible that the Puerto Rican American boys actually did have fewer problems.

There is some evidence from personality studies that Latino/a American men endorse stereotypically masculine preferences in work, hobbies, and other activities more so than European American men do (Hall, Bansal, & Lopez, 1999). However, such ethnic differences in the endorsement of these preferences are relatively minimal. There may exist subgroups of Latino men having a traditionally masculine gender identity, but it is unknown if such subgroups are any larger in Latino/a cultures than in other cultures (Casas, Wagenheim, Banchero, & Mendoza-Romero, 1995).

Some Latina American women are guided by the cultural value of *marianismo.* This value requires that women model themselves after the Virgin Mary, which means that they are spiritually superior to men and capable of enduring much suffering (Ginorio et al., 1995). Sexual purity is required, and sex is viewed as primarily for procreation. One's children's welfare is placed above one's own, and motherly love is considered more important than wifely love (Ramirez, 1998). Although fathers are supposed to enforce discipline, mothers have the primary responsibility for disciplining children (Garcia-Preto, 1996b). Fathers tend to be distant, whereas mothers tend to be involved with their children, as child rearing is viewed as a mother's responsibility. Marianismo may be misinterpreted as dependence by non-Latinos (Vasquez, 1994). Adherence to marianismo may vary as a function of acculturation: More acculturated Latina American women are more egalitarian in their relationships with men (Ginorio et al., 1995).

Personalismo promotes interpersonal harmony by emphasizing the importance of attention to the thoughts and wishes of others and the importance of personal relationships (Bernal & Shapiro, 1996; Falicov, 1996). A related cultural construct is *confianza,* the importance of developing trusting, intimate relationships (Marin & Marin, 1991). An emphasis on interpersonal harmony occurs across contexts for many Latino/a Americans. For example, Mexican American elementary school children have been found to share their money or their lunch more so than children from other ethnic groups (Rotheram-Borus & Phinney, 1990). Similarly, Mexicans and Mexican Americans preferred work groups in which interpersonal harmony was emphasized, whereas European Americans preferred work groups in which task orientation was emphasized (Sanchez-Burks, Nisbett, & Ybarra, 2000).

Similar to the other groups in this book in which the family is emphasized, *familismo* is the importance of immediate and extended family in Latino/a American cultures (Bernal & Shapiro, 1996; Casas & Pytluk, 1995; Comas-Diaz, 1993). The family is more important than the individual. Although family relationships may be emphasized to a certain degree in all cultural groups, Latino/a Americans may perceive their family relationships as more cohesive. Indeed, Mexican American children and their mothers, most of whom were born in the United States, rated their family as more cohesive than did European American children and mothers (Knight, Virdin, & Roosa, 1994). Relative to African Americans, a smaller network of parents, siblings, children, grandchildren, and fictive kin provide support for Latino/a Americans (MacPhee, Fritz, & Miller-Heyl, 1996).

Family members who succeed are expected to help those family members who are less successful (Arcaya, 1999). Family support may be particularly important for immigrants. Mexican emigrants to California having limited family support were found to be more depressed and suicidal than those who had greater family support (Hovey, 2000). Adult family members who are unable to support themselves may be supported by the family (Zea, Mason, & Murguia, 2000). Such practices are likely to be viewed as maladaptive by persons having a more individualistic worldview.

Family support may be provided by relatives as well as nonrelatives. Godparents often have formal economic and personal involvement with godchildren (Garcia-Preto, 1996a). *Hijos de crianza* involves the transfer of children from one nuclear family to another within the extended system during times of crisis (Garcia-Preto, 1996a). Perceptions of the usefulness of family support may vary with acculturation. For example, grandmother involvement was associated with less stress and fewer psychological symptoms for less-acculturated Puerto Rican American adolescent mothers (Contreras, Lopez, Rivera-Mosquera, Raymond-Smith, & Rothstein, 1999). However, for Puerto Rican American adolescent mothers who were more acculturated, grandmother involvement was associated with greater stress and psychological symptoms.

Latino/a American religious beliefs usually include a strong belief in the existence of a higher being and the need to follow prescribed formal practices to worship this being. Latino/a American religiosity may include a belief in folk healing and a tendency not to separate physical from emotional well-being. Another common cultural belief is in fatalism, which is a form of existentialism involving taking life as it comes with a "resigned" mind-set. Many Cuban refugees practice *santeria,* a combination of ritual, magic, and medical beliefs based on Catholic and African folk traditions (Altarriba & Bauer, 1998). African tribal deities and Catholic saints are worshipped. *Santeros* are priests from the santeria religion and may also be involved in folk healing.

Can these interdependent characteristics be adaptive in a society that so highly values individualism? In two studies of Latino/a American college students, identification with Latino/a American culture has been associated with higher self-esteem (Ethier & Deaux, 1994; Lorenzo-Hernandez & Ouellette, 1998). Thus, it may actually be maladaptive for many Latino/a Americans to disidentify with Latino/a American culture or to be expected in educational, business, and other settings to do so.

DEVELOPMENTAL AND FAMILY ISSUES

Independence is the basis of psychological theories of healthy human development. As we discussed in Chapter Four, attachment theories posit that a securely attached person is one who is able to be independent (Rothbaum, Weisz, Pott, Miyake, & Morelli, 2000); an appropriately socialized child is one who is not dependent on parents or others. Autonomy has been conceptualized as part of optimal adolescent adjustment, but strong family ties also appear to be a component of adolescent adjustment even in individualist contexts (Lerner & Galambos, 1998). Theories of adult development are founded on autonomous identity exploration, although it is acknowledged that ethnic minority groups may have fewer opportunities to explore life directions than majority groups (Arnett, 2000). These models of development are based on European Americans and may be less applicable to interdependent cultures (Rothbaum et al., 2000). Based on the Latino/a American cultural characteristics just reviewed, one would expect that interdependence might be the goal of healthy Latino/a American development.

Interdependent, collectivist family patterns could be attributed to SES. Poorer families may need to pool and share resources more than those who are not poor. However, in studies of middle-class European American and Puerto Rican mothers in which resources are more available, it has been found that European Americans place greater emphasis on individualism, whereas Puerto Rican mothers place greater emphasis on the social context (Harwood, Schoelmerich, Schulze, & Gonzalez, 1999; Harwood, Schoelmerich, Ventura-Cook, Schulze, & Wilson, 1996). European American mothers emphasized independence, self-confidence, happiness, and development of personal skills and abilities. Conversely, Puerto Rican mothers emphasized proper demeanor, including being respectful, calm, and polite. For example, European American mothers encouraged their children to actively play with toys in a public situation, whereas Puerto Rican mothers encouraged their children to wait for permission to play with the toys.

Parental conflicts as a result of increasing independence are common among European American adolescents and may be assumed to be normative (Molina & Chassin, 1996). However, there is evidence in Latino/a American families that puberty actually brings parents and their children closer. Latino/a American high school students in California had a greater sense of duty than European American high school students to assist, respect, and support their families (Fuligni et al., 1999). Mexican American teenagers are also less willing to openly contradict their parents and have lower expectations for autonomy than do European American teenagers (Fuligni, 1998). These ethnic differences are most pronounced among boys, possibly because of a greater value placed on the traditional male role in Latino/a American families (Molina & Chassin, 1996).

As discussed previously, interdependent family patterns are not necessarily attributable to SES. Could differences in autonomy between European American and Latino/a American adolescents be a result of parental educational differences? Perhaps better-educated persons have a more independent identity than less-educated persons. However, even when parental educational levels are controlled, Latino/a American families are more interdependent insofar as Latino/a American boys experience more parental support and less parental conflict than do European American boys (Molina & Chassin, 1996).

Ethnic differences in autonomy between European American and Latino/a American adolescents may be explained by parenting patterns in some Latino/a American families. For example, Mexican American parents may be relatively permissive and indulgent with their children until adolescence, when they may begin to expect greater family responsibilities (Ramirez, 1998). Children may be given limited freedom by their parents during adolescence in Mexican American families because Mexican Americans have experienced more risk in the community than European Americans have (Knight et al., 1994). Acculturation may also influence parenting styles and adolescent autonomy; Mexican American teenagers born in the United States are more similar in patterns of autonomy to their European American peers than to those who were born in Mexico (Fuligni, 1998).

An emphasis on family obligations was generally associated with positive family and peer relationships and academic motivation for Latino/a Americans in the California study (Fuligni et al., 1999). However, adolescents who indicated the strongest endorsement of their obligations tended to receive grades as low or lower than those who indicated the weakest endorsement of family obligations. Those having extremely high family obligations may have devoted more attention and effort to their family than to their schoolwork. Similarly, an extreme belief in the importance of family has been found to be associated with violence among inner-city Latino American adolescents (Gorman-Smith, Tolan, Zelli, & Huesmann, 1996). Teens who are extremely involved with their family may find their obligations burdensome and may act out in response. These findings may imply that a bicultural ethnic identification, in which a person balances family commitment with individual concerns, may be most adaptive for Latino American youth. Theories of acculturation posit a bicultural orientation as optimal for ethnic minority persons (LaFromboise et al., 1993).

MENTAL HEALTH

The literature reviewed thus far in this chapter suggests that identification with Latino/a American culture has positive effects on self-esteem, family relationships, and academic motivation. How might cultural identification influence mental health? Theories of psychopathology suggest that social support is associated with mental health (Robinson & Garber, 1995). The strong social support found in many Latino/a American families and communities is likely to be a protective factor against psychopathology. Latino/a American cultural traditions may also deter certain psychological problems. For example, religious involvement has been found to be a protective factor against depression and suicidal ideation for Latino/a immigrants (Hovey, 2000). However, insofar as traditional models of psychological functioning have equated mental health with autonomy, it would appear that some Latino/a American cultural traditions could be an impediment to mental health. Thus, a Latino/a American who is more acculturated to European American culture might be considered to be more psychologically healthy than a person who is less acculturated. Nevertheless, there are many negative behaviors that are relatively common among European Americans, such as smoking, alcohol and drug use, and violence. Acculturation to these mainstream behaviors would be considered psychologically unhealthy. Thus, there are components of Latino/a American and European American cultures that may be adaptive and others that may be maladaptive (Rogler, Malgady, Constantino, & Blumenthal, 1987).

General differences in psychopathology between European Americans and Latino/a Americans have been found to be trivial (Hall et al., 1999). However, most studies of psychopathology have not assessed Latino/a American immigration status or acculturation. Immigrants may be particularly susceptible to depression. Fifty-nine percent of a sample of Mexican immigrants in California exhibited multiple symptoms of depression (Hovey, 2000); most of these immigrants were living at or below the poverty level, which may have contributed to their depression. Eleven percent of this sample experienced suicidal ideation, which is more than three times the rate for other populations (Hovey, 2000). Acculturative stress was associated with both depression and suicidal ideation and also has been found to be associated with alcohol use among Latino/a teens (Gil, Wagner, & Vega, 2000).

Acculturation and Psychopathology

In addition to the stressors of adjusting to a new culture, some traditional Latino/a beliefs may make adjustment difficult to mainstream culture in the United States, which is more individualistic than most Latino/a cultures. For example, unacculturated Mexican Americans may be at greater risk to develop depression than European Americans because of stronger beliefs in fatalism and external control (Roberts, Roberts, & Chen, 1997). Less acculturation has also been associated with adverse parenting beliefs. Spanish-speaking Mexican American mothers were more likely than English-speaking Mexican American mothers to have unrealistic expectations of their children for their level of development, to lack empathic concern, to believe in physical punishment, and to reverse parent-child roles, with the child being expected to comfort the parent during times of distress (Acevedo, 2000).

Acculturation to European American cultures has also been found to be detrimental in some ways for many Latino/a Americans. Acculturation has been found to be associated with drug use (Castro et al., 1999; Zayas, Rojas, & Malgady, 1998) and smoking (Acevedo, 2000; Unger et al., 2000) in Latino/a American samples. Violence has been found to be more common among acculturated than among less-acculturated Latino/a American couples (Caetano, Schafer, Clark, Cunradi, & Raspberry, 2000). Among Latina American women, acculturation has been associated with sexual behavior that creates HIV risk, including oral sex and having multiple sexual partners (Carmona, Romero, & Loeb, 1999; Newcomb et al., 1998).

Being unacculturated and being acculturated both appear to be associated with mental health risks for Latino/a Americans. However, level of acculturation in and of itself is not necessarily a risk factor for psychological problems. It is likely that the context in which a person acculturates will determine the effects of acculturation. For example, acculturation may have indirect effects on delinquency. Acculturation is likely to lead to family conflict between traditional parents and acculturated children, and family conflicts may have a more direct relationship to delinquent behavior than acculturation (Gil et al., 2000; Samaniego & Gonzales, 1999). Delinquent behavior may represent an acculturated child's rebellion against traditional parents' beliefs and restrictions. Conversely, an acculturated child having acculturated parents is less likely to experience family conflicts and may also be less likely to engage in delinquent behavior. Moreover, children who are acculturated to both European American and Latino/a American cultures may experience relatively little family conflict if they are able to adapt to the norms of the family setting (Birman, 1998).

Similarly, the effects of acculturation on Latino/a American smoking behavior may be indirect. English language use has been found to be associated with lifetime risk of smoking among Latino/a American adolescents (Unger et al., 2000). However, the association between language usage and smoking became nonsignificant when access to cigarettes, perceived consequences, friends' smoking, and offers to smoke were controlled; thus, social context was more important in determining cigarette usage than was acculturation. Acculturation may be a risk factor for smoking to the extent that more-acculturated adolescents have more access to cigarettes and perceptions that smoking is not harmful.

A common limitation of the research on acculturation is that proxies, such as country of birth or language use, are used as definitions of acculturation. There are obvious limitations to these proxies. For example, someone who immigrated to the United States during childhood is likely to be much more acculturated than someone who has immigrated during adulthood. Moreover, a person may speak English but retain many Latino/a cultural traditions, and Spanish speakers may become acculturated to mainstream culture on nonlanguage dimensions, such as attitudes.

Another general limitation of the research on acculturation is that acculturation has been regarded as a simple bipolar construct (Cortes et al., 1994; Ryder, Alden, & Paulhus, 2000; Stephenson, 2000): One is acculturated to one culture or the other, but cannot be acculturated to more than one culture. Acculturating to one culture often decreases involvement in a second culture, particularly when one culture is more dominant than the other. Nevertheless, identification with more than one culture is also possible even when one culture is dominant and the other is part of the minority (LaFromboise et al., 1993). Moreover, a person may not be identified with either culture (Felix-Ortiz, Newcomb, & Myers, 1994). Measures to assess both ethnic society identification and dominant society identification within the same individual are being developed (e.g., Stephenson, 2000).

A third limitation of the research on acculturation with Latino/a Americans is a common failure to consider the unique characteristics of individual Latino/a American groups. For example, acculturation has been found to be associated with drinking problems among Cuban Americans and Colombian Americans, but not among Puerto Rican or Dominican Americans (Kail, Zayas, & Malgady, 2000; Vega, Gil, & Zimmerman, 1993). Thus, a general assumption that acculturation is or is not associated with problem drinking among Latino/a Americans would be erroneous.

Mental Health Services

Latino/a Americans have generally been underrepresented in mental health clinics relative to their population in the community (Bui & Takeuchi, 1992). Mexican American immigrants have been found to be less likely to use mental health services than American-born persons of Mexican ancestry (Vega, Kolody, Aguilar-Gaxiola, & Catalano, 1999). Immigrants may seek help more from general practitioner physicians than from mental health centers. It is likely that many mental health centers are not responsive to the language and cultural needs of Latino/a Americans. Such cultural unresponsiveness has been found to be a deterrent to the use of mental health services for Latino/a Americans and for other ethnic minority groups (S. Sue, Fujino, Hu, Takeuchi, & Zane, 1991).

There is some evidence that treatments for depression that have been found to be effective with European Americans are effective with Latino/a Americans. In a study of depressed Puerto Rican adolescents, both cognitive-behavioral therapy and interpersonal therapy reduced depression relative to a control group that did not receive treatment (Rossello & Bernal, 1999). Cognitive-behavioral treatment primarily involves interventions to change a person's thoughts and perceptions that are assumed to be the basis of depression. Interpersonal therapy focuses on problems in interpersonal relationships as the basis of depression. It has been suggested that the interpersonal approach is more consistent with Puerto Rican values and hence is the more culturally sensitive of the two treatment approaches. Culturally responsive treatments may both attract ethnic minority clients to treatment and keep them in treatment for an adequate amount of time for the treatment to be effective (S. Sue et al., 1991).

One critical component of culturally responsive treatment is the therapist's ability to communicate in Spanish with clients for whom Spanish is the primary language (Rogler et al., 1987). However, a basic ability to communicate and understand Spanish is insufficient. A therapist must understand what mental health concepts are equivalent in European American and Latino/a cultures, and what concepts are not. Similarly, translators should have mental health training; those who do not may be biased (D. Sue & Sue, 1999).

One of us (Hall) was offered by the staff of an inpatient psychiatric hospital a Spanish-speaking worker, who did not have mental health training, as a translator for the administration of the Rorschach Inkblot Test to a Spanish-speaking schizophrenic woman. The woman was withdrawn and somewhat uncommunicative and the purpose of administering the Rorschach was to determine how responsive the woman would be to unstructured stimuli that did not have the performance demands of more structured tests, such as IQ measures. The test instructions are simply, "What might this be?" The brief nature of these instructions is intended to make the task ambiguous and to prevent potential biased responding. The translator appeared to translate these brief instructions literally, and the woman gave a one-word response. The translator then began to give what appeared to be an extensive lecture to

Throughout his career, Guillermo Bernal has demonstrated a commitment to multicultural psychology. In 1978, he received his PhD in clinical psychology from the University of Massachusetts at Amherst. He was on the faculty of the University of California Department of Psychiatry at San Francisco General Hospital from 1978 to 1987. He currently is professor of psychology at the University of Puerto Rico, Rio Piedras, where he has been since 1986, and is also director of the University Center for Psychological Services and Research. He is a Fellow of APA Divisions 27 and 45. Dr. Bernal has won the Psychologist of the Year Award from the Asociacion de Psicologos de Puerto Rico and the MENTOR Award from the Section on the Clinical Psychology of Ethnic Minorities of the American Psychological Association Division on Clinical Psychology.

Dr. Bernal's strong commitment to cultural diversity is reflected in his research on Cuban and Latino culture. He has served consecutive terms as president of Division 12, Section VI, as president of APA Division 45, and as vice president for Central America and the Carribbean of the Sociedad Interamericana de Psicologia. One of his major accomplishments as president of Division 45 was the establishment of *Cultural Diversity and Ethnic Minority Psychology* as the official Division journal. In all his professional efforts, he has promoted the strengths of ethnic minorities, increasing our understanding of these groups' social context and behaviors, and he has facilitated access for members of minority groups to resources that are usually inaccessible.

Dr. Bernal is an extremely productive scholar. He has over 80 publications, with a focus on mental health and depression. Many of his publications are coauthored with students whom he has mentored. Dr. Bernal has helped his students gain new knowledge about vulnerability to depression, family therapy, counseling, psychotherapy, Attention Deficit Disorder, and stress in Latino populations. His research has been supported by the National Institute of Drug Abuse. Dr. Bernal has been a member of multiple federal grant panels and currently is a member of the NIMH Treatment Assessment Review Committee. He currently serves on the editorial boards of eight journals and is associate editor of *Cultural Diversity and Ethnic Minority Psychology*. Dr. Bernal initiated the NIMH-funded Hispanic Career Opportunities in Research Program in Puerto Rico, geared toward the development of undergraduate Latino/a researchers.

Words of Advice to Students:

Reach out to other students, faculty, friends, to develop sources of support and organized action. Participation at different levels of the political process is a basic to empowerment. Involvement at any level such as support groups, committees, or professional organizations is a resource that can be invaluable in changing one's context or situation. Organized action at different levels has the potential of shaping social processes.

the woman. When asked what he was saying to the woman, the translator replied that he was telling her to try harder and that he knew that she could do better. The translator was well-intentioned and probably believed that he was helping both me and the woman. However, his intervention obviously compromised the validity of the rest of the test. The purpose was not to create performance pressure, but to determine the woman's baseline ability to respond to the test stimuli. The woman could easily have interpreted the translator's lecture as meaning that she was expected to perform much better than she had. The translator apparently did not understand standardized test administration or that most people give one or two answers in response to the Rorschach stimuli no matter how hard they are trying.

Most traditional psychotherapy approaches involve interventions and solutions at the individual level. Few consider contextual issues. Cultural responsiveness to Latino/a American clients often requires tailoring interventions to the context. For example, encouraging a mother to spend more time on herself than on her family may be counterproductive (Ramirez, 1998); similarly, encouraging an adolescent to develop an independent identity may be at odds with the parents' emphasis on greater family responsibilities. Involving adolescents' parents and respecting their wishes may be critical in therapy with Latino/a American adolescents (Ramirez, 1998). Conversely, helping a client adapt to a maladaptive environment is also unhealthy (Vasquez, 1994). It may be important to help clients balance the demands of family obligations with needs for personal growth. For example, a mother taking time for herself could be conceptualized as helping her become a better mother (Zea et al., 2000).

Cultural responsiveness also involves an understanding of culture-specific syndromes that are not equivalent to disorders that have been identified in European American populations. *Ataques de nervios* involves trembling, heart palpitations, difficulty moving limbs, memory loss, difficulty breathing, dizziness, and fainting spells (Hough et al., 1996); these episodes may be followed by verbal or physical aggressiveness and falling to the ground or convulsions. This syndrome is similar in many ways to Posttraumatic Stress Disorder, but has a different set of symptoms (Ruef, Litz, & Schlenger, 2000). Ataques de nervios may be viewed in some community contexts as an acceptable cry for help, particularly among women. Another culture-specific syndrome is *susto,* a magical fright or soul loss precipitated by a fear-related event (Hough et al., 1996); symptoms include anxiety, increased startle response, sleep problems, worry, and fear. More research is necessary for a better understanding of these culture-specific syndromes and how they do and do not map onto psychological disorders that have been identified in European American populations.

In addition to culture-specific syndromes, there may be culture-specific treatments that differ in important ways from traditional psychological approaches. *Curanderos* are folk healers who combine clinical skills, cultural remedies, and spiritual considerations in their treatments. The goal is to create harmony and balance among the individual, community, and environment, as well as a balance of spiritual, mental, and physical health (Zea et al., 2000). Herbal remedies, candles, religious paraphernalia, and prayer may be employed. The curandero may enter a trance and serve as a medium of a spiritual force (Zea et al., 2000). Treatment may involve ridding the person of an evil spiritual possession. Effective treatment for some Latino/a Americans, particularly those who are unacculturated to the dominant culture, may involve consultation and collaboration with community spiritual healers (Zea et al., 2000).

CONCLUSION

Latino/a Americans are about to become the largest ethnic minority group in the United States. Although most Latino/a Americans were born in the United States, their language and cultural traditions seem foreign to some. Yet, Latino/a American culture has been part of American culture for centuries, and Latino/a American influence is likely to increase, as nearly one in four persons in the United States will be of Latino/a ancestry within 50 years.

Despite the growing size and importance of Latino/a American communities, the psychological literature on Latino/a Americans is striking for its paucity and lack of sophistication. The most common research method involves lumping Latino/a Americans into one group and comparing them with European Americans on some dimension. However, this comparative approach ignores the diversity across Latino/a American groups; moreover, there is much diversity within particular groups of Latino/a Americans. A more sophisticated approach has been to examine the effects of acculturation on behavior. However, most studies of acculturation have typically not examined the possibility of identification with more than one culture. Acculturation is a global construct that may not be directly related to some behavioral outcomes, such as delinquency. In addition, there is a need to examine and measure the effects on behavior of relevant Latino/a American cultural constructs, including respeto, machismo, marianismo, and familismo.

What constitutes culturally competent mental health services for Latino/a Americans has yet to be defined. However, there is some evidence of the effectiveness of established psychological approaches in treating depression. It appears possible to adapt these established approaches to be consistent with Latino/a American cultural values. In addition, the cultural responsiveness of psychological approaches may be enhanced by collaboration with traditional healers in Latino/a American communities.

REFERENCES

Acevedo, M. C. (2000). The role of acculturation in explaining ethnic differences in the prenatal health-risk behaviors, mental health and parenting beliefs of Mexican American and European American at-risk women. *Child Abuse and Neglect, 24,* 111–127.

Altarriba, J., & Bauer, L. M. (1998). Counseling Cuban Americans. In D. R. Atkinson, G. Morten, & D. W. Sue (Eds.), *Counseling American minorities* (5th ed., pp. 280–298). Boston: McGraw-Hill.

Arcaya, J. (1999). Hispanic American boys and adolescent males In A. M. Horne & M. S. Kiselica (Eds.), *Handbook of counseling boys and adolescent males: A practitioner's guide* (pp. 101–116). Thousand Oaks, CA: Sage.

Arnett, J. J. (2000). Emerging adulthood: A theory of development from the late teens through the twenties. *American Psychologist, 55,* 469–480.

Bernal, G., & Enchautegui-de-Jesus, N. (1994). Latinos and Latinas in community psychology: A review of the literature. *American Journal of Community Psychology, 22,* 531–557.

Bernal, G., & Shapiro, E. (1996). Cuban families. In M. McGoldrick, J. Giordano, & J. K. Pearce (Eds.), *Ethnicity and family therapy* (2nd ed., pp. 155–168). New York: Guilford Press.

Birman, D. (1998). Biculturalism and perceived competence of Latino/a immigrant adolescents. *American Journal of Community Psychology, 26,* 335–354.

Bobo, L. D. (1999). Prejudice as group position: Microfoundations of a sociological approach to racism and race relations. *Journal of Social Issues, 55,* 445–472.

Bui, K. T., & Takeuchi, D. T. (1992). Ethnic minority adolescents and the use of community mental health care services. *American Journal of Community Psychology, 20,* 403–417.

Caetano, R., Schafer, J., Clark, C. L., Cunradi, C. B., & Raspberry, K. (2000). Intimate partner violence, acculturation and alcohol consumption among Hispanic couples in the United States. *Journal of Interpersonal Violence, 15,* 30–45.

Carmona, J. V., Romero, G. J., & Loeb, T. B. (1999). The impact of HIV status and acculturation on Latinas' sexual risk taking. *Cultural Diversity and Ethnic Minority Psychology, 5,* 209–221.

Casas, J. M., & Pytluk, S. D. (1995). Hispanic identity development: Implications for research and practice. In J. G. Ponterotto, J. M. Casas, L. A. Suzuki, & C. M. Alexander (Eds.), *Handbook of multicultural counseling* (pp. 155–180). Thousand Oaks, CA: Sage.

Casas, J. M., Wagenheim, B. R., Banchero, R., & Mendoza-Romero, J. (1995). Hispanic masculinity: Myth or psychological schema meriting consideration. In A. M. Padilla (Ed.), *Hispanic psychology: Critical issues in theory and research* (pp. 231–244). Thousand Oaks, CA: Sage.

Castro, F. G., Proescholdbell, R. J., Abeita, L., & Rodriguez, D. (1999). Ethnic and cultural minority groups. In B. S. McCrady & E. E. Epstein (Eds.), *Addictions: A comprehensive guide* (pp. 499–526). New York: Oxford University Press.

Comas-Diaz, L. (1993). Hispanic/Latino/a communities: Psychological implications. In D. R. Atkinson, G. Morten, & D. W. Sue (Eds.), *Counseling American minorities: A cross-cultural perspective* (4th ed., pp. 245–263). Madison, WI: Brown & Benchmark.

Comas-Diaz, L., Lykes, M. B., & Alarcon, R. D. (1998). Ethnic conflict and the psychology of liberation in Guatemala, Peru, and Puerto Rico. *American Psychologist, 53,* 778–792.

Contreras, J. M., Lopez, I. R., Rivera-Mosquera, E. T., Raymond-Smith, L., & Rothstein, K. (1999). Social support and adjustment among Puerto Rican adolescent mothers: The moderating effect of acculturation. *Journal of Family Psychology, 13,* 228–243.

Cortes, D. E., Rogler, L. H., & Malgady, R. G. (1994). Biculturality among Puerto Rican adults in the United States. *American Journal of Community Psychology, 22,* 707–721.

Ethier, K. A., & Deaux, K. (1994). Negotiating social identity when contexts change: Maintaining identification and responding to threat. *Journal of Personality and Social Psychology, 67,* 243–251.

Falicov, C. J. (1996). Mexican families. In M. McGoldrick, J. Giordano, & J. K. Pearce (Eds.), *Ethnicity and family therapy* (2nd ed., pp. 169–182). New York: Guilford Press.

Falicov, C. J. (1998). *Latino/a families in therapy: A guide to multicultural practice.* New York: Guilford Press.

Felix-Ortiz, M., Newcomb, M. D., & Myers, H. (1994). A multidimensional measure of cultural identity for Latino/a and Latina adolescents. *Hispanic Journal of Behavioral Sciences, 16,* 99–115.

Fuligni, A. J. (1998). Authority, autonomy, and parent-adolescent conflict and cohesion: A study of adolescents from Mexican, Chinese, Filipino, and European backgrounds. *Developmental Psychology, 34,* 782–792.

Fuligni, A. J., Burton, L., Marshall, S., Perez-Febles, A., Yarrington, J., Kirsh, L. B., & Merriwether-DeVries, C. (1999). Attitudes toward family obligations among American adolescents with Asian, Latin American, and European backgrounds. *Child Development, 70,* 1030–1044.

Garcia-Preto, N. (1996a). Latino/a families: An overview. In M. McGoldrick, J. Giordano, & J. K. Pearce (Eds.), *Ethnicity and family therapy* (2nd ed., pp. 141–154). New York: Guilford Press.

Garcia-Preto, N. (1996b). Puerto Rican families. In M. McGoldrick, J. Giordano, & J. K. Pearce (Eds.), *Ethnicity and family therapy* (2nd ed., pp. 183–199). New York: Guilford Press.

Gil, A. G., Wagner, E. F., & Vega, W. A. (2000). Acculturation, familism and alcohol use among Latino/a adolescent males: Longitudinal relations. *Journal of Community Psychology, 28,* 443–458.

Ginorio, A. B., Gutierrez, L., Cauce, A. M., & Acosta, M. (1995). Psychological issues for Latinas. In H. Landrine (Ed.), *Bringing cultural diversity to feminist psychology: Theory, research, and practice* (pp. 241–263). Washington, DC: American Psychological Association.

Gorman-Smith, D., Tolan, P. H., Zelli, A., & Huesmann, L. R. (1996). The relation of family functioning to violence among inner-city minority youths. *Journal of Family Psychology, 10,* 115–129.

Hall, G. C. N., Bansal, A., & Lopez, I. R. (1999). Ethnicity and psychopathology: A meta-analytic review of 31 years of comparative MMPI/MMPI-2 research. *Psychological Assessment, 11,* 186–197.

Harwood, R. L., Schoelmerich, A., Schulze, P. A., & Gonzalez, Z. (1999). Cultural differences in maternal beliefs and behaviors: A study of middle-class Anglo and Puerto Rican mother-infant pairs in four everyday situations. *Child Development, 70,* 1005–1016.

Harwood, R. L., Schoelmerich, A., Ventura-Cook, E., Schulze, P. A., & Wilson, S. P. (1996). Culture and class influences on Anglo and Puerto Rican mothers' beliefs regarding long-term socialization goals and child behavior. *Child Development, 67,* 2446–2461.

Hernandez, M. (1996). Central American families. In M. McGoldrick, J. Giordano, & J. K. Pearce (Eds.), *Ethnicity and family therapy* (2nd ed., pp. 214–224). New York: Guilford Press.

Hough, R. L., Canino, G. J., Abueg, F. R., & Gusman, F. D. (1996). PTSD and related stress disorders among Hispanics. In A. J. Marsella, M. J. Friedman, E. T. Geritty, & R. M. Scurfield (Eds.), *Ethnocultural aspects of posttraumatic stress disorder: Issues, research, and clinical applications* (pp. 301–338). Washington, DC: American Psychological Association.

Hovey, J. D. (2000). Acculturative stress, depression, and suicidal ideation in Mexican immigrants. *Cultural Diversity and Ethnic Minority Psychology, 6,* 134–151.

Huddy, L., & Virtanen, S. (1995). Subgroup differentiation and subgroup bias among Latinos as a function of familiarity and positive distinctiveness. *Journal of Personality and Social Psychology, 68,* 97–108.

Inclan, J. E., & Herron, D. G. (1998). Puerto Rican adolescents. In J. T. Gibbs & L. N. Huang (Eds.), *Children of color: Psychological interventions with culturally diverse youth* (pp. 240–263). San Francisco: Jossey-Bass.

Kail, B., Zayas, L. H., & Malgady, R. G. (2000). Depression, acculturation, and motivations for alcohol use among young Colombian, Dominican, and Puerto Rican men. *Hispanic Journal of Behavioral Sciences, 22,* 64–77.

Knight, G. P., Virdin, L. M., & Roosa, M. (1994). Socialization and family correlates of mental health outcomes among Hispanic and Anglo American children: Consideration of cross-ethnic scalar equivalence. *Child Development, 65,* 212–224.

LaFromboise, T. D., Coleman, H. L. K., & Gerton, J. (1993). Psychological impact of biculturalism: Evidence and theory. *Psychological Bulletin, 114,* 395–412.

Leadbeater, B. J., & Bishop, S. J. (1994). Predictors of behavior problems in preschool children of inner-city Afro-American and Puerto Rican adolescent mothers. *Child Development, 65,* 638–648.

Lerner, R. M., & Galambos, N. L. (1998). Adolescent development: Challenges and opportunities for research, programs, and policies. *Annual Review of Psychology, 49,* 413–446.

Lorenzo-Hernandez, J., & Ouellette, S. C. (1998). Ethnic identity, self-esteem, and values in Dominicans, Puerto Ricans, and African Americans. *Journal of Applied Social Psychology, 28,* 2007–2024.

MacPhee, D., Fritz, J., & Miller-Heyl, J. (1996). Ethnic variations in personal social networks and parenting. *Child Development, 67,* 3278–3295.

Marin, G., & Marin, B. V. (1991). *Research with Hispanic populations*. Newbury Park, CA: Sage.

Markus, H. R., & Kitayama, S. (1991). Culture and the self: Implications for cognition, emotion, and motivation. *Psychological Review, 98*, 224–253.

Molina, B. S. G., & Chassin, L. (1996). The parent-adolescent relationship at puberty: Hispanic ethnicity and parent alcoholism as moderators. *Developmental Psychology, 32*, 675–686.

Newcomb, M. D., Wyatt, G. E., Romero, G. J., Tucker, M. B., Wayment, H. A., Carmona, J. V., Solis, B., & Mitchell-Kernan, C. (1998). Acculturation, sexual risk taking, and HIV health promotion among Latinas. *Journal of Counseling Psychology, 45*, 454–467.

Ramirez, O. (1998). Mexican American children and adolescents. In J. T. Gibbs & L. N. Huang (Eds.), *Children of color: Psychological interventions with culturally diverse youth* (pp. 215–239). San Francisco: Jossey-Bass.

Roberts, R. E., Roberts, C. R., & Chen, Y. R. (1997). Ethnocultural differences in prevalence of adolescent depression. *American Journal of Community Psychology, 25*, 95–110.

Robinson, N. S., & Garber, J. (1995). Social support and psychopathology across the life span. In D. Cicchetti & D. J. Cohen (Eds.), *Developmental psychopathology: Risk, disorder, and adaptation* (Vol. 2, pp. 162–209). New York: Wiley.

Rogler, L. H., Malgady, R. G., Constantino, G., & Blumenthal, R. (1987). What do culturally sensitive mental health services mean? *American Psychologist, 24*, 565–570.

Rossello, J., & Bernal, G. (1999). The efficacy of cognitive-behavioral and interpersonal treatments for depression in Puerto Rican adolescents. *Journal of Consulting and Clinical Psychology, 67*, 734–745.

Rothbaum, F., Weisz, J., Pott, M., Miyake, K., & Morelli, G. (2000). Attachment and culture: Security in the United States and Japan. *American Psychologist, 55*, 1093–1104.

Rotheram-Borus, M. J., & Phinney, J. S. (1990). Patterns of social expectations among Black and Mexican-American children. *Child Development, 61*, 542–556.

Ruef, A. M., Litz, B. T., & Schlenger, W. E. (2000). Hispanic ethnicity and risk for combat-related posttraumatic stress disorder. *Cultural Diversity and Ethnic Minority Psychology, 3*, 235–251.

Ryder, A. G., Alden, L. E., & Paulhus, D. L. (2000). Is acculturation unidimensional or bidimensional? A head-to-head comparison in the prediction of personality, self-identity, and adjustment. *Journal of Personality and Social Psychology, 79,* 49–65.

Samaniego, R. Y., & Gonzales, N. A. (1999). Multiple mediators of the effects of acculturation status on delinquency for Mexican American adolescents. *American Journal of Community Psychology, 27,* 189–210.

Sanchez-Burks, J., Nisbett, R. E., & Ybarra, O. (2000). Cultural styles, relationship schemas, and prejudice against out-groups. *Journal of Personality and Social Psychology, 79,* 174–189.

Sears, D. O., Citrin, J., Cheleden, S. V., & van Laar, C. (1999). Cultural diversity and multicultural politics: Is ethnic balkanization psychologically inevitable? In D. A. Prentice & D. T. Miller (Eds.), *Cultural divides: Understanding and overcoming group conflict* (pp. 35–79). New York: Russell Sage Foundation.

Seidman, E., Aber, J. L., Allen, L., & French, S. E. (1996). The impact of the transition to high school on the self-esteem and perceived social context of poor urban youth. *American Journal of Community Psychology, 24,* 489–515.

Sorenson, S. B., & Siegel, J. M. (1992). Gender, ethnicity, and sexual assault: Findings from a Los Angeles study. *Journal of Social Issues, 48,* 93–104.

Stephenson, M. (2000). Development and validation of the Stephenson Multigroup Acculturation Scale (SMAS). *Psychological Assessment, 12,* 77–88.

Sue, D. W., & Sue, D. (1999). *Counseling the culturally different: Theory and practice* (3rd ed.). New York: Wiley.

Sue, S., Fujino, D. C., Hu, L., Takeuchi, D. T., & Zane, N. W. S. (1991). Community mental health services for ethnic minority groups: A test of the cultural responsiveness hypothesis. *Journal of Consulting and Clinical Psychology, 59,* 533–540.

Takaki, R. (1993). *A different mirror: A history of multicultural America.* New York: Little, Brown.

Unger, J. B., Cruz, T. B., Rohrbach, L. A., Ribisl, K. M., Baezconde-Garbanti, L., Chen, X., Trinidad, D. R., & Johnson, C. A. (2000). English language use as a risk factor for smoking initiation among Hispanic and Asian American adolescents: Evidence for mediation by tobacco-related beliefs and social norms. *Health Psychology, 19,* 403–410.

Vasquez, M. J. T. (1994). Latinas. In L. Comas-Diaz & B. Greene (Eds.), *Women of color: Integrating ethnic and gender identities in psychotherapy* (pp. 114–138). New York: Guilford Press.

Vega, W. A., Gil, A. G., & Zimmerman, R. S. (1993). Patterns of drug use among Cuban-American, African-American, and White non-Hispanic boys. *American Journal of Public Health, 83,* 257–259.

Vega, W. A., Kolody, B., Aguilar-Gaxiola, S., & Catalano, R. (1999). Gaps in service utilization by Mexican Americans with mental health problems. *American Journal of Psychiatry, 156,* 928–934.

Zayas, L. H., Rojas, M., & Malgady, R. G. (1998). Alcohol and drug use, and depression among Hispanic men in early adulthood. *American Journal of Community Psychology, 26,* 425–438.

Zea, M. C., Mason, M. A., & Murguia, A. (2000). Psychotherapy with members of Latino/Latina religions and spiritual traditions. In P. S. Richards & A. E. Bergin (Eds.), *Handbook of psychotherapy and religious diversity* (pp. 397–419). Washington, DC: American Psychological Association.

ISSUES FOR DISCUSSION

1. The English-only movement seeks to make English the official language of the United States, which would eliminate bilingual education for Spanish speakers. It has been argued that Spanish is part of the cultural heritage of Latino/a Americans. Based on acculturation theories, what psychological effects could the English-only movement have on Latino/a Americans?

2. Given the tremendous pressure to acculturate to the dominant culture in the United States, is a bicultural identity a viable option? Which Latino/a Americans are most likely to acculturate? Which are most likely to develop a bicultural identity? Which are most likely to maintain their Latino/a American identity without acculturating?

EIGHT

AMERICAN INDIANS

This we know—we do not own the world, we are part of it.

This we know—we did not weave the web of life, but we are simply a
strand in it.

—Chief Seattle

The current existence of American Indians and their cultures is a tribute to
their resilience. Indians have survived outsiders' attempts of extermination,
relocation, and destruction of their language, culture, and religion (Norton
& Manson, 1996; Trujillo, 2000). Indians could not escape this oppression
because it was occurring in their own homeland (E. Duran, Duran, Brave
Heart, & Yellow Horse-Davis, 1998). The oppression that Indians have experienced in this country has been conceptualized as hate crimes (Herring,
1999), although American Indians receive limited attention as hate crime
victims. Yet, American Indians remain a vibrant and growing group in the
United States.

Despite being one of the smallest ethnic groups discussed in this book,
American Indians are among the most diverse, comprising over 250 federally
recognized tribes (Norton & Manson, 1996). Most of these tribes also have
their own languages. The two largest tribes are the Navajo and Cherokee, each
with over 200,000 members. The Bureau of Indian Affairs (BIA) defines an Indian as an enrolled or registered member of a federally recognized Indian
tribe, or someone who is at least one-fourth Indian or more in blood quantum
and can legally demonstrate that to BIA officials (Trimble, Fleming, Beauvais,
& Jumper-Thurman, 1996). However, being an American Indian involves not
only ancestry but also cultural identity (Herring, 1999). Because many Indian
tribes are sovereign nations, many Indians have dual citizenship in their tribal
nation and in the United States (Castro, Proescholdbell, Abeita, & Rodriguez,

Joseph E. Trimble earned a baccalaureate degree from Waynesburg College in 1961 and pursued graduate studies at the University of New Hampshire, Harvard University, and the University of Oklahoma; he received his doctorate from Oklahoma in social psychology in 1969. In addition, he pursued postdoctoral studies at the University of Colorado, Ohio University, and the East-West Center in Honolulu, Hawaii. For the 2000–2001 academic year, he was a Fellow at Harvard University's Radcliffe Institute for Advanced Study. Additionally, he is professor of psychology at Western Washington University in Bellingham and a visiting senior scholar at the Tri-Ethnic Center for Prevention Research at Colorado State University.

Throughout his 30-year career, he has focused his efforts on promoting psychological and sociocultural research with indigenous populations, especially American Indians and Alaska Natives. For the past 20 years, he has been working on drug abuse prevention research models for American Indian youth. He is collaborating on a series of studies concerning the etiology of drug abuse among American Indian youth, and is involved in promoting drug use research among America's ethnic minority populations. In 1991, he received a Certificate of Appreciation from the National Institute on Drug Abuse (NIDA) for his outstanding contribution to the development and implementation of NIDA's Special Populations Research Programs. In addition, recently he completed a term as a review committee member of NIDA's Subcommittee on Epidemiology and Prevention Research, for which he received a Certificate of Appreciation in 1999. Most recently, Dr. Trimble served as a member of the Risk, Prevention, and Health Behavior Initial Review Group for the Center for Scientific Review at the National Institutes of Health.

Dr. Trimble has held offices in the International Association for Cross-Cultural Psychology and the American Psychological Association; he holds Fellow status in three divisions in the APA. He is the past president of the Society for the Psychological Study of Ethnic Minority Issues (1999–2000), Division 45 of the American Psychological Association. In 1994, he received a Lifetime Distinguished Career Award from the APA's Division 45 for his research and dedication to cross-cultural and ethnic psychology. In 2001, he received the eleventh annual Janet E. Helms Award for Mentoring and Scholarship in Professional Psychology, presented at the Teachers College, Columbia University, eighteenth annual Roundtable on Cross-Cultural Psychology and Education. He has presented over 150 papers, invited addresses, and invited lectures at professional meetings, and has generated over 130 publications and technical reports on cross-cultural topics in psychology and higher education research. He is the recipient of three awards from Western Washington University: the Outstanding Teacher-Scholar Award in 1985, the Excellence in Teaching Award in 1987, and the Paul J. Olscamp Outstanding Faculty Research Award in 1999.

Words of Advice to Students:

Let me pass along three moving and inspiring quotations to students. The words of those who offered the following advice have served me well over many decades.

"The chief cause of failure and unhappiness is trading what we want most for what we want at the moment." (Author unknown)

"Refuse to fall down.
If you cannot refuse to fall down,
refuse to stay down.
If you cannot refuse to stay down,
lift your heart toward heaven,
and like a hungry beggar,
ask that it be filled,
and it will be filled.
You may be pushed down.
You may be kept from rising.
But no one can keep you
from lifting your heart
toward heaven." (Clarissa Pinkola Estés, *Women Who Run with the Wolves*)

"Whatever you can do or dream you can, begin it. Boldness has genius, power, and magic in it. Begin it now." (Johann Wolfgang von Goethe, German poet, novelist)

1999). Indians display a range of phenotypic characteristics in terms of body size, skin and hair color, and facial features (Pewewardy, 1999). At least half of Indian youth have nonnative ancestry (Herring, 1999).

The designation "American Indian" is accepted by many Indians themselves (LaFromboise & Graff Low, 1998; Trimble et al., 1996) and will be the term used in this chapter. However, the term "Indian" is a misnomer, coined by Europeans who, when they reached this country, believed that they had reached India. The term "Native American" is confusing, insofar as many who are not American Indians consider themselves native Americans.

Media images of Indians have been created by and for European Americans (Bird, 1999). Indian men have been portrayed as primitive, sexually aggressive savages who are stoic and lack emotion. Indian men's purported sexual brutality became a rationale for European Americans to destroy them. Recent stereotypes of Indian men as wise elders or lovers are ostensibly more benign; however, both are stereotypes and restrict Indian roles and are not acceptable to Indians themselves (Bird, 1999). The Indian princess stereotype represented the virgin land to be possessed by European American men. An even more degrading female stereotype has been the squaw, who endlessly has sex and bears children. The term squaw is derived from the Iroquois language and refers to a female's genitalia in a very offensive and pejorative way (Joseph Trimble, personal communication, March 2000); this term began to be used by European Americans. Indian relationships with other Indians are rarely portrayed in the popular media (Bird, 1999); Indians are defined in the media by their relationships with the dominant culture.

There is some evidence that non-Indians' attitudes toward Indians are generally positive (Ancis, Choney, & Sedlacek, 1996). However, this may be because Indians are such a numerically small group that they are not viewed as a threat to resources. Under conditions of threat, however, negative stereotypes of Indians may be more readily expressed. For example, following a procedure to place them in a negative mood, English Canadians expressed a greater number of negative stereotypes of native Canadian Indians than of Chinese, English Canadians, Arabs, or Jews (Esses & Zanna, 1995). More generally, American Indians are ignored by much of society and issues that concern them are not viewed as having relevance beyond the Indian context. As an example, see the first exercise at the end of this chapter on Indian sports team names.

Indian tribes are very diverse. Nine major geographic areas in which Indian nations have shared an ecological environment have been identified (Hodge & Fredericks, 1999): the Northeast, Southeast, Southwest, Northern Plains, Northwest Coast, Plateau/Great Basin/Rocky Mountains, Oklahoma, California, and Alaska. Although different tribes have shared the same geographic environment, their cultures and languages are not necessarily shared.

HISTORY

Indian cultures were highly developed by the time European explorers first reached this continent (Hodge & Fredericks, 1999). Many tribes had sophisticated systems of agriculture, government, and commerce with other tribes. Knowledge in medicine, astronomy, and the arts was also developing. There was more cultural and linguistic diversity on this continent when Columbus arrived than there was in Europe (B. Duran & Duran, 1999).

Indian tribes treated the environment with respect. Agriculture, hunting, and fishing were primarily for subsistence purposes. The land was not misused or polluted, nor were animals killed except for food. Indian attempts to maintain a balance between the land's resources and their own survival needs were consistent with spiritual values of harmony within nature (Hodge & Fredericks, 1999). Non-Indians have desecrated the land by polluting the air, water, and soil, creating health hazards for many Indians (Hodge & Fredericks, 1999). Pollution and industrialization have also limited farming and fishing opportunities; for example, Indians can no longer hunt buffalo, which were exterminated by settlers.

Displacement by Europeans

Despite the existence of advanced Indian cultures, European explorers viewed Indians as savages dominated by passions, especially sexuality (Takaki, 1993). Indians initially viewed the unfamiliar White explorers as gods. They soon learned, however, that Europeans were very human and out to exploit them, their land, and their possessions.

Within 50 years of Columbus's arrival on this continent, European settlers began to displace Indians in the southeastern area of this country (Hodge & Fredericks, 1999). English settlers in Virginia during the early 1600s believed that the Indians, who grew corn, were not using the land properly; thus, confiscating Indian land was not considered robbery (Takaki, 1993). Although the Indians had initially assisted the English settlers, English attacked Indians in 1608 and destroyed their villages to get food supplies. The European settlers' need for land increased in 1613 when they began exporting tobacco to England. In 1622, the Indians attempted to forcibly drive them out. Migration from the East to the Plains began in 1650, when European settlements drove Indians west (Hodge & Fredericks, 1999).

The Indian population decreased dramatically between 1610 and 1675 because of the introduction of European diseases (e.g., smallpox) to which they were not immune (Takaki, 1993). For example, the Abenakis decreased from 12,000 to 3,000, and the southern New England tribes decreased from 65,000 to 10,000. Many colonists interpreted Indian deaths as divine intervention and confirmation that they should take the land (Takaki, 1993). Wars were another cause of Indian deaths. In 1637, 700 Pequots were killed by colonists, and 6,000 Indians died from combat and disease from 1675 to 1676 in King Philip's War (Takaki, 1993). Violence against Indians was justified by Europeans as driving out the Devil.

Early American History

American statesman and founding father Thomas Jefferson's view of Indian culture mirrored that of the early European settlers. In 1776, Jefferson believed that Indians should either be civilized, which meant adopting European methods of farming, or exterminated (Takaki, 1993). "Civilizing" the Indians would limit their needs for hunting lands. Jefferson contended that lands had been fairly and legally purchased from Indians. He blamed Indian cultural practices for the decline in their numbers. Ironically, he publicly stated that both Indians and colonists were Americans, born in the same land, and hoped the two could be friends. Such duplicity was not unknown to Jefferson, who publicly opposed slavery but personally owned hundreds of slaves who were never freed.

The U.S. government, not long after it was established, began a repeated pattern of removing Indians from their lands and marginalizing them from American society. Even the leftover lands that Indians were given were often eventually taken from them. The Northwest Ordinance of 1783 and the 1790 Trade and Intercourse Acts gave Indian tribes sovereignty and protection in exchange for their lands (Carson & Hand, 1999). Although sovereignty and protection might appear to be at least somewhat beneficial, the Naturalization Act of 1790 excluded non-White immigrants and Indians from citizenship (Takaki, 1993). Indian land in the South became valuable for cotton production, and the government forced Indians to sell their land in Alabama, Mississippi, and Louisiana between 1814 and 1824. The BIA was created within the U.S. War Department in 1824 to oversee relationships with tribes.

Andrew Jackson was elected president of the United States in 1828 in part because he had been a hero in wars against the Indians (Takaki, 1993). Jackson believed that efforts to civilize Indians had failed and that they should be removed. In 1830, the Indian Removal Act moved 70,000 Indians to west of the Mississippi (Carson & Hand, 1999). Most of the Indians in Oklahoma settled there because they were removed from other areas, primarily the South (Hodge & Fredericks, 1999). In 1829 and later, over 10,000 Cherokee, Choctaw, Chickasaw, Creek, and Seminole Indians were forced to leave their sacred homelands and burial grounds in the South without their belongings, often during winter; 4,000 Indians died in transit (Takaki, 1993). This forced exodus is known as the "Trail of Tears." Throughout American history, over 600 treaties were made with Indian tribes, often by force or with subgroups of Indians who did not represent tribal wishes (Duran et al.,

1998; Takaki, 1993). Ancestral tribal lands are considered sacred by Indians (Trujillo, 2000); thus, the government's removal of Indians from their ancestral tribal lands is analogous to a church being seized by the government and the prohibition of its members from worshipping there.

Indians in California were also exploited during Spanish colonization during the nineteenth century. Spanish settlers sought to turn these Indians into laborers and to convert them to Christianity. Diseases introduced by Europeans and violence from non-Indian settlers and the U.S. military completely exterminated some tribes.

Government Interventions

Banishing Indians to previously uninhabited regions of the nation did not end government interference. To connect parts of the country for commerce, railroads through Indian territories were needed (Takaki, 1993). The Indian Appropriation Act of 1871 stated that "no Indian nation or tribe within the territory of the United States shall be acknowledged or recognized as an independent nation, tribe or power with whom the United States may contract by treaty." This Act allowed railroads to be built through the Plains and buffalo, which were the Plains Indians' sustenance, to be killed by non-Indians.

A major provision of the Indian Appropriation Act was the establishment of Indian reservations. The purpose of these reservations was to be a temporary support to help Indians make the adjustment to assimilate into U.S. society (Takaki, 1993). Because Indians were federally mandated to live on reservations, those who refused could be attacked with impunity. Children were taken from their families and forced to live in boarding schools beginning in 1879 in Pennsylvania (Brucker & Perry, 1998; EchoHawk, 1997). Church attendance was mandatory at boarding schools, and Indian traditions and religions were regarded as pagan and uncivilized (LaFromboise, Berman, & Sohi, 1994). Federal policy in the late 1800s outlawed traditional Indian religion and spirituality (Trujillo, 2000).

Sixteen years after reservations were established, Congress passed the Dawes Act, which sought to discontinue reservations and help Indians become property owners and U.S. citizens (Takaki, 1993). Individual landownership was encouraged, and each Indian family was given 160 acres for 25 years. Large areas of land from the reservations were also taken from the Indians and sold to non-Indians. Ironically, the 1906 Burke Act nullified the

25-year trust provision of the Dawes Act. "Last arrow" pageants that marked the transition to American citizenship were established (Takaki, 1993). In these pageants, Indians wore a traditional costume and shot an arrow; they then entered a teepee and changed into "civilized" clothing, emerging to receive a plow and an American flag.

Despite the oppression that Indians suffered as non-Indians began to occupy their lands, many were undaunted and maintained their ancestral traditions. In 1890, Wovoka of the Paiutes claimed to be the messiah and believed that Indian customs, lands, and buffalo would be restored. The time when the White man would leave Indian lands was celebrated with the tradition of ghost dancing (Takaki, 1993). Ghost dancers wore muslin shirts decorated with sacred symbols that they believed would protect them from their enemies. To quell this growing Indian nationalism, Sitting Bull, a Ghost Dance leader, was arrested and then killed by Indian policemen who worked for the U.S. government. Sioux Indians were also arrested and taken to the Wounded Knee camp, where hundreds were massacred when they attempted to escape.

Civil Rights

Indians gained some civil rights during the early twentieth century. They became official U.S. citizens in 1924. The 1934 Indian Reorganization Act allowed tribal land acquisition and self-government. Nevertheless, these rights were in many ways empty to people whose residence on this continent predated those who were offering these rights. Also, as with many other government treaties and laws involving Indians, the apparent freedom that these acts provided proved to be temporary. From 1933 through 1945, the federal government reorganized Indian groups into councils that adopted Western structures (Hodge & Fredericks, 1999). Beginning in 1946, the government sought to terminate tribes by taking their land, Indian status, and services and relocating them from reservations to urban areas (Hodge & Fredericks, 1999; Norton & Manson, 1996).

During the 1960s, a supratribal identification as Indians began to develop (Nagel, 1995). The Indian Civil Rights Act that allowed Indian self-governance was passed in 1968, and self-determination became the government's policy toward Indians (Hodge & Fredericks, 1999). In 1969, Indian students from San Francisco State University took over Alcatraz Island, a former penitentiary in the San Francisco Bay (Nagel, 1995), reclaiming the island in the name of all Indians. The purpose of the occupation was to establish cultural and training centers on the island. The protesters were removed from Alcatraz in 1971 by local and federal authorities. Although the cultural and training centers were not established, Alcatraz spawned other Indian protests and became a rallying point for Red Power activism during the 1970s, which saw the passage of the Indian Self-Determination Act (1975), the Indian Child Welfare Act (1978), and the Religious Freedom Act (1978). These acts all provided increased authority and autonomy to Indian tribes. Federal funding for Indian tribes declined in the 1980s, but Indians continue to work for control over reservation government and industry (Hodge & Fredericks, 1999).

CURRENT DEMOGRAPHICS

There are approximately 2.4 million American Indians in the United States (http://www.census.gov/Press-Release/www/1999/cb99-101.html), constituting approximately 0.9 percent of the U.S. population. The Indian population in 2050 is expected to be 4.4 million or 1.1 percent of the total population (http://www.census.gov/Press-Release/fs97-11.html). Mirroring these population percentages, fewer than 1 percent of psychologists are American Indians (Thomason, 1999). Although American Indians constitute one of the nation's smallest ethnic minority groups, the group's existence and its current growth is remarkable, given the oppression Indians have coped with.

There is not a single geographic area in which Indians have a strong cultural and political base, although nearly half of the nation's American Indians, Eskimos, and Aleuts live in Western states. In 1996, the metropolitan areas with the largest American Indian, Eskimo, and Aleut populations were the greater Los Angeles area; the greater Phoenix area; the greater New York City area; Tulsa, Oklahoma; the San Francisco Bay area; Oklahoma City; the greater Seattle area; Albuquerque; the Flagstaff, Arizona area; and the greater Minneapolis-St. Paul area (http://www.census.gov/Press -Release/cb98-226.html). Twenty-eight percent of the population of Flagstaff is American Indian, and Flagstaff is the only metropolitan area in which Indians constitute greater than 10 percent of the total population. Alaska's population of Indian, Eskimo, and Aleuts is 16 percent; Alaska is the only state in which the Indian population is at least 10 percent. The states with the largest American Indian, Eskimo, and Aleut populations are

California (309,000), Oklahoma (263,000), Arizona (256,000), New Mexico (163,000), Washington (103,000), Alaska (100,000), North Carolina (98,000), Texas (96,000), New York (76,000), and Michigan (60,000). The Indian population is growing fastest in Arizona.

American Indians tend to be younger and are more likely to have single-parent households and larger families than other groups. The nation's American Indian, Eskimo, and Aleut resident population is relatively young, with an estimated median age of 27.6 years, which is nearly eight years younger than the median for the population as a whole. Among Indian families, 65 percent are maintained by married couples, 26 percent by women with no husband present, and 9 percent by men with no wife present (http://www.census.gov/population/projections/nation/hh-fam/table4n.txt). The figures for European American families are 82 percent, 13 percent, and 5 percent, respectively. The typical American Indian, Eskimo, and Aleut family was made up of 3.59 people, larger than the average 3.12 people for families of all groups.

American Indians tend to be unaffected by national economic cycles, as their unemployment tends to be chronically high (LaFromboise, 1988). From 1997 to 1999, 26 percent of the nation's American Indian, Eskimo, and Aleut households had incomes that placed them below the poverty line (http://www.census.gov/Press-Release/www/2000/cb00-158.html). Poverty is associated with multiple health and mental health problems.

CULTURAL VALUES AND IDENTITY

Do you consider yourself a competitive person? Are you punctual and do you watch the clock? Do you feel that you must assert yourself in most situations? Do you believe that religion is just a set of superstitions for the gullible? If your answer is yes to any of these questions, you might have a difficult time in an Indian community. As with other groups discussed in this section of the book who have interdependent cultural traditions, traditional American Indian values include communal values of sharing, cooperation, emphasis on the group and extended family, and respect for elders (see Table 8.1; Garrett & Garrett, 1994; Wise & Miller, 1983). In contrast to non-Indian estimation of personal worth based on what one has acquired, ritual gift-giving between families is a way of gaining honor and respect in many Indian cultures (Wise & Miller, 1983). An extended family may consist of as many as 200 members, including fifth-degree relatives (Wise & Miller,

TABLE 8.1   *Indian Cultural Values*

Sharing

Cooperation

Group orientation

Extended family

Respect for elders

Harmony

Noninterference

Spirituality of all things

Being

Present-time orientation

1983). A brother is "one who feels like a brother," regardless of biological relationship, and is treated as a family member (Manson et al., 1996). Competition is discouraged, as is self-serving behavior. Nevertheless, there is much diversity across Indian tribal groups. For example, Pueblo and Southwest tribes typically have a strong family and community orientation, whereas individual achievement is often emphasized in Northern Plains tribes (Novins, Beals, Roberts, & Manson, 1999).

Other Indian values are harmony with nature and noninterference. These values are consistent with a belief that there is a natural order guided by supernatural spirits. Noninterference includes respect for the rights of others (Wise & Miller, 1983). Tendencies to silently observe, rather than to react, out of respect for others may be interpreted by non-Indians as passivity (Wise & Miller, 1983).

This value of noninterference may be associated with the acceptance of multiple sexual orientations. American Indians may be more flexible in sexual orientation than other groups. Homosexuality has traditionally been accepted among many tribes, and many, including the Zuni, Navajo, and Crow, recognize a third homosexual gender (Herring, 1999). At least 168 of the 250 native languages have terms for persons not identified as male or female (Tafoya, 1997). Gays and lesbians have been considered to have both male and female spirits (Tafoya, 1997). In a large study of reservation and rural adolescents, 5 percent of Indians and 6 percent of European Americans considered themselves exclusively homosexual (Saewyc, Skay, Bearinger, Blum,

& Resnick, 1998). However, only 49 percent of Indians considered themselves exclusively heterosexual, compared to 78 percent of European Americans. Most of the Indians who were not homosexual or heterosexual considered themselves unsure of their sexual orientation (29 percent); only 12 percent of European Americans were unsure of their sexual orientation. Indian lesbians are more active than other groups in the lesbian community, which may be another reflection of greater flexibility in sexual orientation in the American Indian community (Morris & Rothblum, 1999). Nevertheless, non-Indian homophobic attitudes also influence some tribal groups (Tafoya, 1997).

There is an intimate connection between Indian culture and religion, and all aspects of life have religious significance for American Indians (Harrison, Wilson, Pine, Chan, & Buriel, 1990). However, there is no single dominant religion. There is a common quest for a guardian spirit that helps persons cope with stress. The belief that all of nature is connected is a component of Indian spirituality (Garrett & Garrett, 1994); thus, plants, animals, rocks and minerals, the land, the winds, the sky, the sun, the moon, and thunder are all imbued with personhood. Tribal lands are considered sacred, and even Indians who live off the reservation may return to tribal lands to reinforce their religious and cultural identity (Trujillo, 2000). All life is valued and part of the intricate balance of nature; for example, the death of a wild animal during hunting is accompanied by a ritual, ceremony, and prayer that acknowledge the balance between the animal's death and the life it gives to people (Trujillo, 2000). The interconnectedness of life is represented as a circle, with East representing the spirit, South representing nature, West representing the body, and North representing the mind (Garrett & Garrett, 1994). Ancestral spirits from each of these directions are summoned during Indian ceremonies. Non-Indians may never completely understand Indian spirituality, as it is viewed by many Indians as the domain of the tribal membership that should not be made available to outsiders (Trujillo, 2000). For many tribes, a shaman is responsible for keeping this sacred knowledge and passing it from generation to generation (Trujillo, 2000). Most Indian spiritual and religious practices have been passed from generation to generation via oral tradition, as such practices were illegal until the Indian Religious Freedom Act of 1978.

Another Indian value is being. This value is illustrated in the importance placed on who a person's family is and where they are from. This information is more important than what a person does for a living (Garrett & Garrett, 1994). Many Indians are also oriented toward living in the present. Indian time means that things begin when everyone has arrived and is ready, and things end when they are finished, rather than at a particular time of day (Garrett & Garrett, 1994). Indeed, there is a lack of concern about the passage of time for many Indians (Wise & Miller, 1983). Just as non-Indians might have a difficult time living in a community with Indian values, Indians may also experience difficulties living in a society that has many values that are diametrically opposed to Indian values.

One might conclude that adherence to Indian culture could be detrimental in the context of a mainstream American culture that is so vastly different. However, Indian cultural identification, as measured by cultural pride and interest, family cultural activities, and view of self as an American Indian, is associated with self-esteem among youth in the Odawa and Ojibwa tribes (Zimmerman, Ramirez-Valles, Washienko, Benjamin, & Dyer, 1996). In a large sample of Indian adolescents, involvement in cultural activities, including living by the Indian way, speaking a tribal language, and participating in traditional activities, was associated with better school performance, interpersonal competency, and helping elders in the community (Mitchell & Beals, 1997).

There is a generation of urban Indians who have never seen a reservation or experienced tribal culture and language (Hodge & Fredericks, 1999). Nevertheless, many Indian adolescents may have a bicultural identification in that they are identified with both the Indian and White ways of life (Moran, Fleming, Somervell, & Manson, 1999). Strength of ethnic identity may depend on contact with the Indian community. For example, American Indians were found to have a relatively weak ethnic identity in a community in Colorado in which Indians were a small group (Martinez & Dukes, 1997), whereas ethnic identity among Indians at a Navajo college in New Mexico was as strong as the ethnic identity of other ethnic minority groups in a previous study at UCLA (McNeil, Kee, & Zvolensky, 1999).

DEVELOPMENTAL AND FAMILY ISSUES

Family Structures

Across tribes, Indian family structures are diverse. There are patriarchal, matriarchal, and egalitarian family structures (Brucker & Perry, 1998). Although ties to the extended family may be less common among American Indians than they once were, the extended family is still important in many communities. American Indians have been found to have more contact than European Americans and Latino Americans with extended family and to have more family network members who know each other (MacPhee, Fritz, & Miller-Heyl, 1996). Moreover, American Indians tend to have more contact with extended family than with friends.

As with other ethnic groups discussed in this book, Indian family patterns may vary in the manner in which they interface with the dominant society and culture (Herring, 1999). *Traditional* families attempt to maintain their cultural lifestyle, including Indian language and customs, and prefer isolation from non-Indians. *Transitional* families prefer to live within mainstream culture, retaining only rudimentary elements of Indian culture; however, transitional families do not identify with either culture. *Bicultural* families practice both Indian and mainstream cultures and are accepted by the mainstream society. *Assimilated* families are also accepted by the mainstream society but practice only mainstream culture.

Divorce has traditionally been an option in most Indian tribes (LaFromboise et al., 1994). However, family pressures against divorce in Indian families may be similar to those in non-Indian families; for example, a conflicted couple may be encouraged to stay together for the sake of the children. Moreover, Christian religious influences also discourage divorce in Indian families (LaFromboise et al., 1994). Intertribal divorces may be complicated in that a woman's children may lose their inheritance in their father's tribe (LaFromboise et al., 1994).

Elder abuse appears to be relatively rare in Navajo and Plains tribes (Carson & Hand, 1999). Respect for elders and for life in general may be reasons for this finding. However, it is also possible that in close-knit Indian communities, such abuse is not reported out of fear of incriminating family members.

Strong family ties may also lead to a lack of contact with persons outside the family. Indeed, there is evidence that American Indians have less interest than other ethnic groups in communicating with people from other cultures (Lattimore & Borgen, 1999). Another reason for the insularity of American Indians may be the prejudice that they have faced outside the Indian community (MacPhee et al., 1996).

Parenting

As discussed in Chapter Four, theories of the self, interdependent cultures are posited to place less emphasis on independence and competition, which may interfere with group harmony (Markus & Kitayama, 1991). American

Teresa D. LaFromboise, associate professor of counseling psychology at Stanford University, is a descendant of the Miami tribe of Indiana. She received her PhD from the University of Oklahoma in 1980.

Dr. LaFromboise is a counseling psychologist concerned about stress-related problems of ethnic minority youth. Her research topics include interpersonal influence in multicultural counseling, bicultural competence, and ethnic identity and adolescent health. Dr. LaFromboise is currently investigating parental drinking, parenting, and alcohol use among American Indian adolescents. She teaches seminars on counseling theories and interventions from a multicultural perspective, education and American Indian mental health, and racial and ethnic identity development and is the faculty sponsor for the Stanford Counseling Institute.

Her publications include "American Indian Mental Health Policy" in *Counseling American Minorities* (1998 with D. Sue et al.), *American Indian Life Skills Development Curriculum* (1996), "Psychological Impact of Biculturalism: Evidence and Theory" (with H. Coleman and J. Gerton) in *Psychological Bulletin* (1993), "Help-Seeking Behavior of Native American Indian High School Students" (with D. Bee-Gates, B. Howard-Pitney, & W. Rowe) in *Professional Psychology: Research and Practice* (1996), and "American Indian Women and Psychology" (with S. Choney, A. James, and P. Running Wolf) in H. Landrine (Ed.), *Bringing Cultural Diversity to Feminist Psychology* (1995).

Dr. LaFromboise is an American Psychological Association Council Representative for Division 45: Society for the Psychological Study of Ethnic Minority Issues. She received an Outstanding Contribution Award from the Mental Health/Social Service Program of the Indian Health Service in 1996 and a Women of Color Psychologies Award from the Association of Women in Psychology in 1992. Dr. LaFromboise was previously on the faculty at the University of Nebraska-Lincoln and the University of Wisconsin-Madison.

Words of Advice for Students:

Multicultural Psychology is a burgeoning, multifaceted area of study. There are many different areas within this field that are important to investigate that can quickly become an area of concentration. Don't be afraid to explore and find your niche. However, connect your academic exploration to your own life experiences. Make it relevant to your own family and friendship contexts. Connect it with your other concerns for society. Multicultural Psychology has much to offer—but it must join with other movements for social change, both to serve them and be served by them.

Indian parents have been found to be less likely than European Americans or Latino Americans to emphasize independence and achievement (MacPhee et al., 1996). Moreover, American Indians tend to be less punitive and more indulgent with their children than other groups. Many Indian parents view themselves as responsible for preserving their culture by transmitting traditional cultural values to their children (LaFromboise et al., 1994). These parenting values and behaviors may place American Indian children at a disadvantage in competitive European American environments and may be a reason for isolation from non-Indian communities.

Grandparents often are involved in rearing children, and in some tribes the primary responsibility of parents is economic support (Garrett & Garrett, 1994). In some tribes, a child is named after another person; the child is expected to emulate that person, and that person is expected to be involved in the care of the child, particularly if the child's parents are unable to do so (LaFromboise et al., 1994). Children may live in different households at various times during their development. Grandparents, uncles, and aunts often nurture, discipline, and teach infants in a home separate from the nuclear family (McPhee et al., 1996). Eighty percent of American Indian adolescents report that their family cares about them a great deal (Bagley, Angel, Dilworth-Anderson, Liu, & Schinke, 1995). In many Indian communities, persons of all ages are included in community activities and ceremonies (Castro et al., 1999).

Patterns of socialization of children vary from tribe to tribe. However, a general principle is that Indian children are socialized to be attached to the family, the tribe, and spiritual realms, rather than to individuate (LaFromboise et al., 1994). Traditional socialization for boys involves learning to hunt and playing games that involve endurance, strength, and the ability to withstand pain (Herring, 1999). Traditional socialization for girls involves domestic responsibilities and caring for younger siblings in preparation for motherhood (LaFromboise et al. 1994). However, certain tribes, including the Hopi, do not emphasize gender differences, and girls are involved in active sports, such as swimming, horse racing, and snow sledding (LaFromboise et al., 1994).

MENTAL HEALTH

If you were a member of a group who had endured repeated attempts of extermination for hundreds of years, do you think that your mental health would be affected? Theories of psychopathology posit that it is stress-induced at the individual level (Monroe & Simons, 1991); however, if one is identified with a group that has endured centuries of suffering, it is likely that stressors experienced by the group will also affect individual psychopathology. The historical trauma that American Indians have experienced has been termed a "soul wound" (E. Duran et al., 1998). Such trauma is intergenerational and cumulative. Psychological disturbance among American Indians is a reaction to an environment that offers few viable options (LaFromboise, 1988). Indians are more likely to be exposed to traumatic events that may trigger psychological problems than are other groups (Robin, Chester, Rasmussen, Jaranson, & Goldman, 1997). For example, 22 percent of a Southwestern tribe (Robin et al., 1997), 27 percent of a sample of Indian teenagers, and over 50 percent of a sample of Northern Plains Vietnam veterans (Manson et al., 1996) were diagnosed as experiencing Posttraumatic Stress Disorder. Common traumatic experiences were injury or violent death of a loved one and physical assault.

Psychopathology

Mental illness is viewed by many American Indians as a result of overly individualistic behaviors (LaFromboise, 1988). Other causes of mental illness include an imbalance in one's body, mind, or spirit, the breaking of taboos, and witchcraft (LaFromboise et al., 1994). Individual problems are considered to be problems of the whole community. Thus, it is critical for accurate assessment to determine the community's perspective on an Indian's psychological functioning (Hall, Bansal, & Lopez, 1999; LaFromboise et al., 1994).

Depression, suicide, and alcoholism are the most common mental health problems among American Indians (Beals, Manson, Keane, & Dick, 1991). Nevertheless, overall rates of mental disorders do not differ between Cherokee Indians and European Americans in the Appalachians (Costello, Farmer, & Angold, 1999; Costello, Farmer, Angold, Burns, & Erkanli, 1997). Indian adolescents are not at greater risk to develop depression than European American adolescents (Roberts, Roberts, & Chen, 1997). Rates of depression in elderly Great Lakes American Indians were similar to those in other groups (Curyto, Chapleski, & Lichtenberg, 1999). However, certain problems may occur at greater rates for Indian populations. Parental violence, substance abuse, and crime rates are greater among Cherokee than among European American families in Appalachia (Costello et al., 1997, 1999). Substance abuse disorders and Attention-Deficit/Hyperactivity Disorder among

Northern Plains Indian adolescents occur at higher rates than in non-Indian populations (Beals et al., 1997). If alcohol-related crimes (e.g., public drunkenness and its effects) are excluded, Indian crime rates are comparable to the crime rates of other ethnic groups (Lester, 1999).

There is evidence that American Indian youth engage in risky behaviors at greater rates than do European Americans. These include unhealthy weight loss (i.e., via vomiting, laxatives, diet pills, diuretics), unprotected sexual intercourse, smoking at least monthly, alcohol use at least monthly, marijuana use at least monthly, and suicide attempts (Neumark-Sztainer et al., 1996). Engaging in risk behaviors may also persist into adulthood, as 80 percent of a sample of Indian women in New York City had unprotected sex (Walters & Simoni, 1999). Indian family connectedness may be a protective factor against risk taking, particularly in urban settings away from tribal communities (Machamer & Gruber, 1998). Indian students who reported that their parents and family cared about them were less likely to skip school or to drink or use marijuana before school.

It is possible that there are psychological disorders that are culturally specific to American Indians. For example, there may be several types of disorders similar to depression that do not map onto non-Indian conceptualizations of depression. These include worry, sickness, unhappiness, heartbreak, drunken-like craziness with or without the use of alcohol, and disappointment/pouting (Allen, 1998). Ninety-three percent of a sample of Hopi Indians believed that there was no word or phrase for depression in the Hopi language.

Alcohol Use

In the history of most Indian tribes, alcoholic beverages were introduced by Spanish and other European settlers (Taylor, 2000). In 1832, the Indian Intercourse Act made it illegal to trade or sell alcohol to Indians (Abbott, 1998). This ban was lifted by Congress in 1953 because of its lack of success. Tribes currently can regulate and control the use of alcohol and other controlled substances because of sovereignty rights legislation (Daisy, Thomas, & Worley, 1998). Over half of Indian tribes prohibit alcohol use, but this has not prevented alcohol use and in some cases may have inadvertently encouraged alcohol abuse by making it a forbidden fruit (Abbott, 1998).

As with other characteristics, the percentage of Indian drinkers varies widely across tribes, ranging from 30 percent of the Navajo nation to 84 percent of the Ojibwa (Abbott, 1998); the overall percentage of Americans who drink is 67 (see Table 8.2). Although the overall percentage of Indians who abuse alcohol may be higher than among the non-Indian population, the percentage of Indians who abstain is also greater (Castro et al., 1999). Urban Indian populations have higher drinking rates than reservation populations, primarily because of easier access to alcohol in urban areas (Castro et al., 1999). Fewer Indian women than men drink, although the percentage of Indian women who do drink may be increasing. The alcoholism death rate among Indians is 37.2/100,000 compared to 6.8/100,000 for the general U.S. population. Alcohol abuse is also associated with other problems, including fetal alcohol syndrome, motor vehicle accidents, suicide, homicide, family violence, and other criminal behavior. However, alcohol abuse could just as easily be an effect of some of these problems rather than a cause (Taylor, 2000).

Many Indians who drink do so excessively (Abbott, 1998; Taylor, 2000). For example, in a Navajo population, the lifetime rates of alcohol dependence were estimated to be 70 percent for males and 30 percent for females (Kunitz et al., 1999). The greatest proportion of Indian drinkers are between the ages of 15 and 29 (Abbott, 1998). By the twelfth grade, 82 percent of all Indians have used alcohol and half are at risk for developing alcohol problems. Drinking is modeled by family members for many Indians. Indians who have drinking problems often begin drinking during adolescence, develop alcohol dependence during early adulthood, and do not seek treatment until much later. In a study of adults from seven tribal groups in Anchorage who were in residential treatment, the men first got drunk at age 13 and the women first got drunk at age 14 (Hesselbrock, Segal, & Hesselbrock, 2000). Men developed alcohol dependence at age 18 and women at age 20. The first treatment the men received was at age 25; women first received treatment at age 28. These data

---

TABLE 8.2   *American Indian Alcohol Use*

Tribal rates of use range from 30 percent to 84 percent.

Urban Indians have higher rates of drinking than reservation Indians.

Most drinkers are between 15 and 29 years of age.

Drinking decreases after age 40.

Indian heritage is not associated with alcohol sensitivity.

suggest that interventions during preadolescence and adolescence may do much to mitigate the later negative effects of alcohol abuse.

There tends to be a reduction in drinking after age 40 (Abbott, 1998), with a rate of 27 percent of a sample of older Navajo, Apache, Choctaw, Cherokee, Chickasaw, Creek, Seminole, and Sioux Indians in Los Angeles reporting that they drank (Barker & Kramer, 1996). There is also evidence that drinking among Indians is associated with the belief that they can control their use of alcohol (Taylor, 2000). Perhaps many older Indians who stop drinking feel that they are no longer able to control their alcohol use. Indeed, personal alcohol-related illnesses or those of family members and friends may be associated with this decrease in drinking among older Indians (Taylor, 2000).

The "firewater myth," that American Indians are more sensitive than other groups to the effects of alcohol, is the most common misconception about Indian alcohol use (Taylor, 2000). The myth had its origins among European American frontiersmen and explorers who, ironically, also exhibited rapid intoxication and boisterous behavior from small amounts of alcohol (Taylor, 2000). Nevertheless, physiological evidence suggests that Indian heritage is not associated with alcohol sensitivity (Garcia-Andrade, Wall, & Ehlers, 1997).

Most treatment interventions for alcohol abuse require commitment to complete abstinence. However, programs in which reducing and controlling drinking is the goal are applicable to a broader range of persons having alcohol problems (Daisy et al., 1998). Such treatment programs that are accepting rather than punitive of persons having alcohol problems are consistent with Indian models of helping, such as the Talking Circle, in which community members are heard and not criticized (Daisy et al., 1998).

Substance Use

Ethnicity does not appear to be a general risk factor for drug use among European American, Mexican American, and American Indian adolescents (Beauvais, Chavez, Oetting, Deffenbacher, & Cornell, 1996; Kilpatrick et al., 2000). However, American Indians may have a somewhat greater use of inhalants than other groups (Beauvais et al., 1996). There is evidence of American Indian children as young as 4 years using inhalants (LaFromboise, 1988). Inhalant use is particularly prominent among school dropouts, ranging from 38 percent to 40 percent (Beauvais et al., 1996). Unfortunately, 91 percent of Indian high school students on reservations use alcohol, 78 percent use marijuana, and 37 percent use stimulants (Beauvais et al., 1996; Oetting & Beauvais, 1990). Marijuana use slows around age 16 (Mitchell, Novins, & Holmes, 1999). Between 1975 and 1994, drug use rates among Indian seventh- through twelfth-graders generally decreased, which is a trend that also has occurred in non-Indian populations (Beauvais, 1996). However, psychedelic drug use did not decrease, nor did general drug use among heavy users, who make up about 20 percent of those who use drugs. Given the poor prospects for life success for many Indians, it is not surprising that many become depressed. Alcohol and drug use may be methods, albeit maladaptive ones, of coping with depression.

Cultural identification has been proposed as a protective factor against alcohol and substance use, in that these behaviors are not part of the traditional Indian lifestyle (Zimmerman et al., 1996). Nevertheless, there is limited evidence for a link between cultural identification and drug use among Indians (Beauvais, 1998; Howard, Walker, Walker, Cottler, & Compton, 1999; Novins & Mitchell, 1998). Moreover, traditional values were also not linked to other forms of psychopathology among Indian adolescents (Fisher, Storck, & Bacon, 1999). These findings do not necessarily mean that cultural identification has no impact on Indian mental health problems. The relationship between culture and behavior may be subtle (Beauvais, 1998). For example, peers influence drinking and inhalant use among Indian adolescents (Bates, Beauvais, & Trimble, 1997; Howard et al., 1999). Such peer influences may be greater among Indian than non-Indian adolescents (Jung & Rawana, 1999). This greater degree of peer influence among Indians may be an indirect reflection of Indian cultural values that emphasize interdependence. Thus, the effects of cultural identification may be subtle and influenced by other factors. There is a need for the study of substance-abuse-related attitudes and behaviors specific to cultural groups (Beauvais, 1998).

Tobacco Use

American Indians have the highest rate of smoking of any ethnic group in the United States. Unlike alcohol, tobacco has had a role in Indian history. Tobacco is used in some Indian ceremonies, but it is not smoked in these ceremonies in the form of cigarettes (Kegler et al., 1999). Tobacco has also been a cash crop for some tribes (Hodge & Fredericks, 1999). Over 33 percent of American Indians have smoked cigarettes or used smokeless tobacco during their lifetime compared to 26 percent of European Americans

(Kegler et al., 1999; Moncher, Holden, & Trimble, 1990). Lung cancer is the leading cause of cancer deaths among Indians (Bagley et al., 1995). Reasons for smoking among Indians include modeling by family members, projecting a cool, mature image for boys, and countering a "goody-two-shoes" image for girls (Kegler et al., 1999). Tobacco use is also strongly associated with the use of other substances (Moncher et al., 1990). Unfortunately, smoking cessation interventions with Indians have been minimally effective. In a large study in four urban Indian health clinics, only 7 percent of those who underwent a treatment intervention involving advice from physicians had remained abstinent at a one-year follow-up compared to 5 percent who had not received the treatment (Johnson, Lando, Schmid, & Solberg, 1997). Quit rates with a similar program for non-Indians were 20 percent (Solberg, Maxwell, Kottke, & Gepner, 1990).

Mental Health Services

According to the cultural responsiveness hypothesis, ethnic and cultural minority groups are more likely to utilize mental health services that are culturally sensitive and less likely to use those that are not (Sue, Fujino, Hu, Takeuchi, & Zane, 1991). A dearth of American Indian mental health professionals and a general lack of understanding of Indian culture is likely to render most available mental health services culturally unresponsive for Indians. Seeking professional assistance may be a last resort for American Indians when community-based helping is not effective or available (Herring, 1999; LaFromboise, 1988). Because there are so few Indian psychologists, most Indians who seek help in the mental health system will not receive services from an Indian mental health professional. American Indians are over-represented in inpatient psychiatric services (Snowden & Cheung, 1990). This finding in combination with the reluctance of Indians to seek mental health services may mean that only the most severely disturbed Indians are seen in the mental health system. Moreover, a cultural value of noninterference may make many Indians reluctant to refer others for services (LaFromboise et al., 1994).

Zuni high school students have been found to be more likely to seek help for personal problems from a friend, parent, or relative than from professional sources (Bee-Gates, Howard-Pitney, LaFromboise, & Rowe, 1996). When Zuni students did seek professional help, it was primarily for academic and career problems (Bee-Gates et al., 1996). Thus, academic and career counselors should be alert to potential psychological problems among American Indian youth, as these problems are not likely to come to the attention of mental health clinicians.

Indians who seek mental health services may be bicultural or nontraditional, recognizing that the answer to their problems may not reside in a single culture (LaFromboise et al., 1994; Trujillo, 2000). However, seeking mental health services may not necessarily mean that Indians are seeking to change their way of life. Thus, it is important for clinicians to respect that Indian traditions may dictate a particular way of living that may not coincide with mainstream American prescriptions for mental health.

Most psychotherapy approaches focus on the individual client. Such approaches may not adequately address the sociocultural context that may be important for the psychological health and psychopathology of many American Indians. Cognitive-behavioral therapy holds promise because of the emphasis on person-environment interactions; it can therefore lend itself to cultural adaptation (LaFromboise & Jackson, 1996). Nevertheless, most cognitive-behavioral approaches focus on individual interventions and do not attempt to change contextual influences on psychopathology, such as discrimination (Hall, 2001).

Indians may seek alternative sources of help, such as traditional healers, for less severe problems. Traditional healers function as doctor, counselor, priest, and historian (LaFromboise, 1988). They may use spiritual legends to help explain human problems. Treatment goals are to restore harmony, balance, and integration into the community (Garrett & Garrett, 1994). Culturally sensitive interventions may be particularly critical for culturally specific disorders, such as the many depression-like syndromes discussed above (Allen, 1998). Traditional healing practices have also been applied to the treatment of alcohol abuse. These healing practices have included the use of peyote; sacred dances, including the Ghost Dance described above; a form of group therapy known as the Talking Circle in which participants speak without interruption, telling of traditional Indian stories and legends; and the sweat lodge, in which persons are exposed to steam and engage in fasting and prayer (Abbott, 1998; Herring, 1999; LaFromboise & Graff Low, 1998). Collaborative treatment approaches involving traditional healing and non-Indian psychologists have been recommended (E. Duran et al., 1998; Herring, 1999). However, Western psychology has traditionally been hostile to the spirituality that characterizes much of Indian cultures (LaFromboise, Choney, James, & Running Wolf, 1995).

Network therapy has been developed by American Indians to mobilize extended family support and draw a person out of individual isolation. Sessions are conducted in the home and may involve multiple members of an intervention team, the extended family, and other nonrelatives known to the family (LaFromboise et al., 1994). The family system is engaged to help heal relationships. Occasionally, a person suffering from a psychological disorder may be adopted into a new clan group.

CONCLUSION

American Indians and their culture continue to thrive, and the Indian population is rapidly growing. As with all groups discussed in this book, much more psychological research is necessary to understand American Indians (LaFromboise et al., 1995). There is relatively less psychological research on American Indians than there is on African Americans, Asian Americans, and Latino Americans. Unfortunately, the history of maltreatment and abuse of American Indians by non-Indians has characterized the relationship between Indians and non-Indian researchers. Thus, American Indians have been justifiably suspicious of researchers and have often restricted or prevented research projects (Norton & Manson, 1996). Data on Indians are easily misinterpreted by outsiders. Solutions to this conflict include tribal review and approval of research projects and the recruitment and training of American Indian researchers, who may have cultural awareness and understanding (Norton & Manson, 1996). Research that is perceived as beneficial to Indian communities is more likely to elicit participation. Yet, even when researchers are culturally sensitive, misinterpretations of findings may still occur on the part of the media and the public. This is a broader problem that requires attitudinal changes at the societal level concerning Indians.

The intricate relationships among individuals, families, tribes, and non-Indians all impact behavior. Traditional individual psychology is not adequate to fully understand Indian cultures. Ecological approaches that comprehensively examine intrapersonal, interpersonal, institutional, community, and public policy influences may be useful because they consider the context of Indian behavior (B. Duran & Duran, 1999).

REFERENCES

Abbott, P. J. (1998). Traditional and Western healing practices for alcoholism in American Indians and Alaska Natives. *Substance Use and Misuse, 33,* 2605–2646.

Allen, J. (1998). Personality assessment with American Indians and Alaska Natives: Instrument considerations and service delivery style. *Journal of Personality Assessment, 70,* 17–42.

Ancis, J. R., Choney, S. K., & Sedlacek, W. E. (1996). University student attitudes toward American Indians. *Journal of Multicultural Counseling and Development, 24,* 26–36.

Bagley, S. P., Angel, R., Dilworth-Anderson, P., Liu, W., & Schinke, S. (1995). Panel V: Adaptive health behaviors among ethnic minorities. *Health Psychology, 14,* 632–640.

Barker, J. C., & Kramer, J. (1996). Alcohol consumption among older urban American Indians. *Journal of Studies on Alcohol, 57,* 119–124.

Bates, S. C., Beauvais, F., & Trimble, J. E. (1997). American Indian adolescent alcohol involvement and ethnic identification. *Substance Use and Misuse, 32,* 2013–2031.

Beals, J., Manson, S. M., Keane, E. M., & Dick, R. W. (1991). Factorial structure of the Center for Epidemiologic Studies: Depression Scale among American Indian college students. *Psychological Assessment, 3,* 623–627.

Beals, J., Piasecki, J., Nelson, S., Jones, M., Keane, E., Dauphinais, P., Red Shirt, R., Sack, W. H., & Manson, S. M. (1997). Psychiatric disorder among American Indian adolescents: Prevalence in Northern Plains youth. *Journal of the American Academy of Child and Adolescent Psychiatry, 36,* 1252–1259.

Beauvais, F. (1996). Trends in drug use among American Indian students and dropouts, 1975 to 1994. *American Journal of Public Health, 86,* 1594–1599.

Beauvais, F. (1998). Cultural identification and substance use in North America: An annotated bibliography. *Substance Use and Misuse, 33,* 1315–1336.

Beauvais, F., Chavez, E. L., Oetting, E. R., Deffenbacher, J. L., & Cornell, G. R. (1996). Drug use, violence, and victimization among White American, Mexican American, and American Indian dropouts, students with academic problems, and students in good academic standing. *Journal of Counseling Psychology, 43,* 292–299.

Bee-Gates, D., Howard-Pitney, B., LaFromboise, T., & Rowe, W. (1996). Help-seeking behavior of Native American Indian high school students. *Professional Psychology: Research and Practice, 27,* 495–499.

Bird, S. E. (1999). Gendered construction of the American Indian in popular media. *Journal of Communication, 49,* 61–83.

Brucker, P. S., & Perry, B. J. (1998). American Indians: Presenting concerns and considerations for family therapists. *American Journal of Family Therapy, 26,* 307–319.

Carson, D. K., & Hand, C. (1999). Dilemmas surrounding elder abuse and neglect in Native American communities. In T. Tatara (Ed.), *Understanding elder abuse in minority populations* (pp. 161–184). Philadelphia: Brunner/Mazel.

Castro, F. G., Proescholdbell, R. J., Abeita, L., & Rodriguez, D. (1999). Ethnic and cultural minority groups. In B. S. McCrady & E. E. Epstein (Eds.), *Addictions: A comprehensive guide* (pp. 499–526). New York: Oxford University Press.

Costello, E. J., Farmer, E. M. Z., & Angold, A. (1999). Same place, different children: White and American Indian children in the Appalachian Mountains. In P. Cohen, C. Slomkowski, & L. N. Robins (Eds.), *Historical and geographical influences on psychopathology* (pp. 279–298). Mahwah, NJ: Erlbaum.

Costello, E. J., Farmer, E. M. Z., Angold, A., Burns, B. J., & Erkanli, A. (1997). Psychiatric disorders among American Indian and White youth in Appalachia: The great Smoky Mountains study. *American Journal of Public Health, 87,* 827–832.

Curyto, K. J., Chapleski, E. E., & Lichtenberg, P. A. (1999). Prediction of the presence and stability of depression in the Great Lakes Native American elderly. *Journal of Mental Health and Aging, 5,* 323–340.

Daisy, F., Thomas, L. R., & Worley, C. (1998). Alcohol use and harm reduction within the Native community. In G. A. Marlatt (Ed.), *Harm reduction* (pp. 327–350). New York: Guilford Press.

Duran, B. M., & Duran, E. F. (1999). Assessment, program planning, and evaluation in Indian country: Toward a postcolonial practice. In R. M. Huff & M. V. Kline (Eds.), *Promoting health in multicultural populations: A handbook for practitioners* (pp. 291–311). Thousand Oaks, CA: Sage.

Duran, E., Duran, B., Brave Heart, M. Y. H., & Yellow Horse-Davis, S. (1998). Healing the American Indian soul wound. In Y. Danieli (Ed.), *International handbook of multigenerational legacies of trauma* (pp. 341–354). New York: Plenum Press.

EchoHawk, M. (1997). Suicide: The scourge of Native American people. *Suicide and Life-Threatening Behavior, 27,* 60–67.

Esses, V. M., & Zanna, M. P. (1995). Mood and the expression of ethnic stereotypes. *Journal of Personality and Social Psychology, 69,* 1052–1068.

Fisher, P. A., Storck, M., & Bacon, J. G. (1999). In the eye of the beholder: Risk and protective factors in rural American Indian and Caucasian adolescents. *American Journal of Orthopsychiatry, 69*, 294–304.

Garcia-Andrade, C., Wall, T. L., & Ehlers, C. L. (1997). The firewater myth and response to alcohol in Mission Indians. *American Journal of Psychiatry, 154*, 983–988.

Garrett, J. T., & Garrett, M. W. (1994). The path of good medicine: Understanding and counseling Native American Indians. *Journal of Multicultural Counseling and Development, 22*, 134–144.

Hall, G. C. N. (2001). Psychotherapy research with ethnic minorities: Empirical, ethical, and conceptual issues. *Journal of Consulting and Clinical Psychology, 69*, 502–510.

Hall, G. C. N., Bansal, A., & Lopez, I. R. (1999). Ethnicity and psychopathology: A meta-analytic review of 31 years of comparative MMPI/MMPI-2 research. *Psychological Assessment, 11*, 186–197.

Harrison, A. O., Wilson, M. N., Pine, C. J., Chan, S. Q., & Buriel, R. (1990). Family ecologies of ethnic minority children. *Child Development, 61*, 347–362.

Herring, R. (1999). Helping Native American Indian and Alaska Native male youth. In A. M. Horne & M. S. Kiselica (Eds.), *Handbook of counseling boys and adolescent males* (pp. 117–136). Thousand Oaks, CA: Sage.

Hesselbrock, V. M., Segal, B., & Hesselbrock, M. N. (2000). Alcohol dependence among Alaska Natives entering alcoholism treatment: A gender comparison. *Journal of Studies on Alcohol, 61*, 150–156.

Hodge, F. S., & Fredericks, L. (1999). American Indian and Alaska Native populations in the United States: An overview. In R. M. Huff & M. V. Kline (Eds.), *Promoting health in multicultural populations: A handbook for practitioners* (pp. 269–289). Thousand Oaks, CA: Sage.

Howard, M. O., Walker, R. D., Walker, P. S., Cottler, L. B., & Compton, W. M. (1999). Inhalant use among urban American Indian youth. *Addiction, 94*, 83–95.

Johnson, K. M., Lando, H. A., Schmid, L. S., & Solberg, L. I. (1997). The GAINS project: Outcome of smoking cessation strategies in four urban Native American clinics. *Addictive Behaviors, 22*, 207–218.

Jung, S., & Rawana, E. P. (1999). Risk and need assessment of juvenile offenders. *Criminal Justice and Behavior, 26*, 69–89.

Kegler, M. C., Kingsley, B., Malcoe, L. H., Cleaver, V., Reid, J., & Solomon, G. (1999). The functional value of smoking and nonsmoking from the perspective of American Indian youth. *Family and Community Health, 22*, 31–42.

Kilpatrick, D. G., Acierno, R., Saunders, B., Resnick, H. S., Best, C. L., & Schnurr, P. P. (2000). Risk factors for adolescent substance abuse and dependence: Data from a national sample. *Journal of Consulting and Clinical Psychology, 68,* 19–30.

LaFromboise, T. D. (1988). American Indian mental health policy. *American Psychologist, 43,* 388–397.

LaFromboise, T. D., Berman, J. S., & Sohi, B. K. (1994). American Indian women. In L. Comas-Diaz & B. Greene (Eds.), *Women of color: Integrating ethnic and gender identities in psychotherapy* (pp. 30–71). New York: Guilford Press.

LaFromboise, T. D., Choney, S. B., James, A., & Running Wolf, P. R. (1995). American Indian women and psychology. In H. Landrine (Ed.), *Bringing cultural diversity to feminist psychology: Theory, research, and practice* (pp. 197–239). Washington, DC: American Psychological Association.

LaFromboise, T. D., & Graff Low, K. (1998). American Indian children and adolescents. In J. T. Gibbs & L. N. Huang (Eds.), *Children of color: Psychological interventions with minority youth* (pp. 112–142). San Francisco: Jossey-Bass.

LaFromboise, T., & Jackson, M. (1996). MCT theory and Native-American populations. In D. W. Sue, A. E. Ivey, & P. B. Pedersen (Eds.), *A theory of multicultural counseling and therapy* (pp. 192–216). Pacific Grove, CA: Brooks/Cole.

Lattimore, R. R., & Borgen, F. H. (1999). Validity of the 1994 Strong Interest Inventory with racial and ethnic groups in the United States. *Journal of Counseling Psychology, 46,* 185–195.

Lester, D. (1999). *Crime and the Native American.* Springfield, IL: Charles C. Thomas.

Machamer, A. M., & Gruber, E. (1998). Secondary school, family, and educational risk: Comparing American Indian adolescents and their peers. *Journal of Educational Research, 91,* 357–369.

MacPhee, D., Fritz, J., & Miller-Heyl, J. (1996). Ethnic variations in personal social networks and parenting. *Child Development, 67,* 3278–3295.

Manson, S., Beals, J., O'Nell, T., Piasecki, J., Cechtold, D., Keane, E., & Jones, M. (1996). Wounded spirits, ailing hearts: PTSD and related disorders among American Indians. In *Ethnocultural aspects of posttraumatic stress disorder: Issues, research, and clinical applications* (pp. 255–283). Washington, DC: American Psychological Association.

Markus, H. R., & Kitayama, S. (1991). Culture and the self: Implications for cognition, emotion, and motivation. *Psychological Review, 98,* 224–253.

Martinez, R. O., & Dukes, R. L. (1997). The effects of ethnic identity, ethnicity, and gender on adolescent well-being. *Journal of Youth and Adolescence, 26,* 503–516.

McNeil, D. W., Kee, M., & Zvolensky, M. J. (1999). Culturally related anxiety and ethnic identity in Navajo college students. *Cultural Diversity and Ethnic Minority Psychology, 5,* 56–64.

Mitchell, C. M., & Beals, J. (1997). The structure of problem and positive behavior among American Indian adolescents: Gender and community differences. *American Journal of Community Psychology, 25,* 257–288.

Mitchell, C. M., Novins, D. K., & Holmes, T. (1999). Marijuana use among American Indian adolescents: A growth curve analysis from ages 14 through 20 years. *Journal of the American Academy of Child and Adolescent Psychiatry, 38,* 72–78.

Moncher, M. S., Holden, G. W., & Trimble, J. E. (1990). Substance abuse among Native-American youth. *Journal of Consulting and Clinical Psychology, 58,* 408–415.

Monroe, S. M., & Simons, A. D. (1991). Diathesis-stress theories in the context of life stress research: Implications for the depressive disorders. *Psychological Bulletin, 110,* 406–425.

Moran, J. R., Fleming, C. M., Somervell, P., & Manson, S. M. (1999). Measuring bicultural ethnic identity among American Indian adolescents: A factor analysis study. *Journal of Adolescent Research, 14,* 405–426.

Morris, J. F., & Rothblum, E. D. (1999). Who fills out a "lesbian" questionnaire? The interrelationship of sexual orientation, years "out," disclosure of sexual orientation, sexual experience with women, and participation in the lesbian community. *Psychology of Women Quarterly, 23,* 537–557.

Nagel, J. (1995). American Indian ethnic renewal: Politics and the resurgence of identity. *American Sociological Review, 60,* 947–965.

Neumark-Sztainer, D., Story, M., French, S., Cassuto, N., Jacobs, D. R., & Resnick, M. D. (1996). Patterns of health-compromising behaviors among Minnesota adolescents: Sociodemographic variations. *American Journal of Public Health, 86,* 1599–1606.

Norton, I. M., & Manson, S. M. (1996). Research in American Indian and Alaska Native communities: Navigating the cultural universe of values and process. *Journal of Consulting and Clinical Psychology, 64,* 856–860.

Novins, D. K., Beals, J., Roberts, R. E., & Manson, S. M. (1999). Factors associated with suicide ideation among American Indian adolescents: Does culture matter? *Suicide and Life-Threatening Behavior, 29,* 332–346.

Novins, D. K., & Mitchell, C. M. (1998). Factors associated with marijuana use among American Indian adolescents. *Addiction, 93,* 1693–1702.

Oetting, E. R., & Beauvais, F. (1990). Adolescent drug use: Findings of national and local surveys. *Journal of Consulting and Clinical Psychology, 58,* 385–394.

Pewewardy, C. (1999). Culturally responsive teaching for American Indian students. In E. R. Hollins & E. I. Oliver (Eds.), *Pathways to success in school* (pp. 85–100). Mahwah, NJ: Erlbaum.

Roberts, R. E., Roberts, C. R., & Chen, Y. R. (1997). Ethnocultural differences in prevalence of adolescent depression. *American Journal of Community Psychology, 25,* 95–110.

Robin, R. W., Chester, B., Rasmussen, J. K., Jaranson, J. M., & Goldman, D. (1997). Prevalence and characteristics of trauma and posttraumatic stress disorder in a southwestern American Indian community. *American Journal of Psychiatry, 154,* 1582–1588.

Saewyc, E. M., Skay, C. L., Bearinger, L. H., Blum, R. W., & Resnick, M. D. (1998). Demographics of sexual orientation among American-Indian adolescents. *American Journal of Orthopsychiatry, 68,* 590–600.

Snowden, L. R., & Cheung, F. K. (1990). Use of inpatient mental health services by members of ethnic minority groups. *American Psychologist, 45,* 347–355.

Solberg, L. I., Maxwell, P. L., Kottke, T. E., & Gepner, G. J. (1990). A systematic primary care office-based smoking cessation program. *Journal of Family Practice, 30,* 647–654.

Sue, S., Fujino, D. C., Hu, L., Takeuchi, D. T., & Zane, N. W. S. (1991). Community mental health services for ethnic minority groups: A test of the cultural responsiveness hypothesis. *Journal of Consulting and Clinical Psychology, 59,* 533–540.

Tafoya, T. (1997). Native gay and lesbian issues: The two-spirited. In B. Greene (Ed.), *Ethnic and cultural diversity among lesbians and gay men* (pp. 1–10). Thousand Oaks, CA: Sage.

Takaki, R. (1993). *A different mirror: A history of multicultural America.* New York: Little, Brown.

Taylor, M. J. (2000). The influence of self-efficacy on alcohol use among American Indians. *Cultural Diversity and Ethnic Minority Psychology, 6,* 152–167.

Thomason, T. C. (1999). Improving the recruitment and retention of Native American students in psychology. *Cultural Diversity and Ethnic Minority Psychology, 5,* 308–316.

Trimble, J. E., Fleming, C. M., Beauvais, F., & Jumper-Thurman, P. (1996). Essential cultural and social strategies for counseling Native American Indians. In P. B. Pedersen, J. G. Draguns, W. J. Lonner, & J. E. Trimble (Eds.), *Counseling across cultures* (4th ed., pp. 177–209). Thousand Oaks, CA: Sage.

Trujillo, A. (2000). Psychotherapy with Native Americans: A view into the role of religion and spirituality. In P. S. Richards & A. E. Bergin (Eds.), *Handbook of psychotherapy and religious diversity* (pp. 445–466). Washington, DC: American Psychological Association.

Walters, K. L., & Simoni, J. M. (1999). Trauma, substance use, and HIV risk among urban American Indian women. *Cultural Diversity and Ethnic Minority Psychology, 5,* 236–248.

Wise, F., & Miller, N. B. (1983). The mental health of American Indian children. In G. J. Powell, J. Yamamoto, A. Romero, & A. Morales (Eds.), *The psychosocial development of minority group children* (pp. 334–361). New York: Brunner/Mazel.

Zimmerman, M. A., Ramirez-Valles, J., Washienko, K. M., Benjamin, W., & Dyer, S. (1996). The development of a measure of enculturation for Native American youth. *American Journal of Community Psychology, 24,* 295–310.

ISSUES FOR DISCUSSION

1. American Indian names abound as nicknames and mascots for college and sports teams. Indians, Braves, Illini, Redskins, and Black Hawks are names for teams that often compete against teams with animal names, such as Bears, Lions, and Tigers. Many Indians find the use of these names offensive and a desecration of their culture. A few institutions have attempted to be sensitive to Indian concerns and have changed the offensive names. For example, Stanford University changed its team nickname from Indians to the Cardinal over 25 years ago. Most institutions and teams, however, refuse to change these Indian names. An example of this is the Cleveland Indians professional baseball team, which also has a caricature of an Indian as a mascot and contends that the team name honors an early Indian player and that changing the name would ruin the team's tradition. Do you believe that the use of Indian names for sports teams is harmful? What should the criteria be for changing sports team names from Indian names? Why are other ethnic group names (e.g., Notre Dame Fighting Irish) so rarely used in this context?

2. Traditional American Indian values are at odds with many of those of the mainstream U.S. population. Discuss the potential advantages and disadvantages for Indians of being raised in a traditional, assimilated, and bicultural family.

NINE

EMERGING ISSUES

The emphasis in this book has been on areas in which there is a substantive body of empirical research. We have covered the substantial body of psychological research on persons of color in the United States. Nevertheless, there are some important gaps in the literature that we discuss in this concluding chapter.

Persons of color often have multiple identities. Many of these individuals share similar issues such as prejudice and discrimination from both the majority and their own minority group, identity issues, risk of internalizing negative stereotypes, and potentially increased risk for psychological problems. However, other issues are unique to the interaction of multiple minority statuses, as we will see. Although the focus of multicultural psychology is to value individual differences, in practice, many minorities within the minority (such as gay men and lesbians of color) have been ignored in the research. Part of the reason for this invisibility is a prevailing belief among minority group members that individuals who deviate from the homogeneous group will weaken the cause of the group as a whole. Consequently, people with multiple minority statuses are often pressured to select which identity is more important to them (such as being a woman or being an African American). In addition, minority group members can also exhibit an ethnocentric bias in assuming that all members of their group will be similar in certain ways. In the following sections, we explore the research on sexual identity, multiethnic identity, feminism and women of color, disabled individuals, and older adults.

SEXUAL IDENTITY OF PERSONS OF COLOR

Gays and lesbians of color are in the unfortunate position of being rejected by many groups. First, they are often rejected by mainstream society for their double (triple for women) minority status. Second, the gay community often does not accept them because of its own racist and anti-Semitic beliefs (Savin-Williams, 1996). European American gays and lesbians may hold stereotypes of gay minorities, such as the "Madame Butterfly" role and that of the "good oriental" for Asian men (Savin-Williams, 1996). Finally, they may also be rejected by their own ethnic group, given that most minority groups are homophobic. Many minorities perceive being gay as a "White disease," a product of being too assimilated (Fukuyama & Ferguson, 2000; Savin-Williams, 1996; Walters, 1998). They may interpret the person's coming out as weakening the movement of their ethnic group and as an attack on the group's survival (Greene, 1994; Walters, 1998). Consequently, gays and lesbians of color are asked to pick where their loyalties lie. Coming out is further complicated by the fact that most minority groups place a strong emphasis on family and extended family, and being gay is perceived as a threat to the family community. Most minority families have the expectation that their children will get married and have children, and being gay is perceived as interfering with those expectations as well. Although some cultures tolerate homosexual behavior if it is not labeled as such, coming out may result in disgracing the family (Greene, 1994; Walters, 1998). Many ethnic groups do not even have names for gays and lesbians, and when they do, these names are usually derogatory (Greene, 1994). Facing multiple sources of oppression, discrimination, and negative stereotypes can sometimes lead gays and lesbians of color to internalize these negative beliefs about their identity (Greene, 1994; Walters, 1998).

Specific cultural pressures can also add to the formation of a gay/lesbian identity. In the African American community, the fact that gender roles have been more egalitarian is important to consider. Historically, African American women have worked outside the home as well as being primarily responsible for domestic tasks. The matriarchal focus in the African American community has led to a stereotype of African American women as masculinized, which fits the stereotype of lesbians in general (Greene, 1994, 1997). In addition, they are portrayed as being sexually promiscuous and morally loose, as are most lesbian minority females (Greene, 1994). The influence of Christianity also contributes to homophobic attitudes in the African American community.

American Indians have historically had more fluid ideas about gender (Fukuyama & Ferguson, 2000; Greene, 1994, 1997). American Indian writings suggest the existence of cross-gender role behaviors, such as males acting like females and vice versa. Indians believed that "two-spirited people" possessed both a male and a female spirit, and a wide range of behaviors were deemed appropriate for these individuals. Women were also allowed to have roles of power and make important decisions in their communities. Unfortunately, the effects of colonization resulted in forcing American Indians to conform to the values of a patriarchal society; as a result, American Indians are more homophobic currently than they were in the past.

Asian Americans place great importance on obedience to one's parents and concern for one's ancestors. Consequently, there is great concern among Asian Americans about duty to one's family and avoiding bringing shame not only upon one's family but one's ancestors as well (Greene, 1994; Fukuyama & Ferguson, 2000). Most Asian groups are patriarchal in that women are considered second-class citizens; their primary roles are to get married and to have children. They are not supposed to talk about or enjoy sex, although stereotypes for Asian American women include both being sexy/exotic and being asexual. Thus, coming out for a woman implies that she is a sexual being, she is choosing to shame her family and ancestors, and she is losing her Asian heritage.

Latino Americans also value traditional gender roles (Fukuyama & Ferguson, 2000; Greene, 1994, 1997; Savin-Williams, 1996). Men are expected to exhibit machismo (manliness, virility) and sexual activity is expected. In fact, sexual activity with other men is tolerated as long as the person assumes the active role in the sexual act rather than the passive role. Women are expected to exhibit marianismo, meaning that they are submissive, self-sacrificing, and pure; thus, they are expected to remain virgins until they are married and are not supposed to be interested in sex. Latino Americans are strongly influenced by Catholicism, which also contributes to their negative views about homosexuality. Homosexual activity may be tolerated, but an open acknowledgment of one's sexual orientation is viewed as an act of treason against the culture and family.

Asian Indian Americans share many of the aspects of other minority cultures, including a patriarchal focus, emphasis on obedience to one's parents, and the taboo against talking about or desiring sex (Greene, 1994). Arranged marriages are still common due to women's economic dependence on men; consequently, there are intense pressures on Asian Indian American women to marry and have children. Those who are well-educated and financially secure can avoid being forced into an unhappy heterosexual relationship by moving to the United States or Great Britain, but this is an option available to a small number of women. The imposition of British morals has also reinforced homophobia in that homosexuality was considered a legal offense.

Theoretical models of lesbian and gay identities have described a developmental coming-out process. The sequence typically involves awareness of same-sex attractions around 8 to 11 years of age, same-sex sexual behaviors at 12 to 15 years, identification as a gay or lesbian at 15 to 18 years, disclosure to others at 17 to 19 years, and the development of same-sex romantic relationships at 18 to 20 years (Dube & Savin-Williams, 1999). Latino American male youths have been found to have an earlier awareness of same-sex attraction than in other ethnic groups. It is unknown if this difference is culturally based because of a cultural intensification of gender roles or because of a greater cultural acceptance of gay identity. Asian American male youth engaged in same-sex sexual behavior later than other ethnic groups. This may be because of cultural restrictions on sexual activity and a general tendency to engage in less sexual behavior than other groups (McLaughlin, Chen, Greenberger, & Biermeier, 1997).

Bisexual individuals also face unique conflicts, as they are often forced to choose a single sexual orientation. The number of jokes over actress Anne Heche's announcement that she was a lesbian during her relationship with Ellen Degeneres and subsequent announcement that she was interested in men again after their breakup illustrates the pressure that bisexuals may feel to pick a single orientation. Part of the reason for this pressure to choose is that some gays and lesbians feel that these individuals are simply trying to deny that they are, in fact, homosexual. In addition, bisexuals may be considered too mainstream; therefore, they weaken the position of the gay movement (White & Langer, 1999). Furthermore, being bisexual is an affront to our tendency to categorize people into groups because they do not fit into our classification system of gay versus straight. Collins (2000) argues that for this reason, bisexual and biracial individuals share much in common and may go through similar processes in forming and accepting an identity.

Although the body of literature on ethnic minorities and gays and lesbians is growing, the literature on the intersection of these identities is considerably smaller. Most of the research on ethnic minorities assumes that individuals are heterosexual, and most of the research on gays and lesbians assumes that the person is White and from the middle class. In fact, the need to specify gays and lesbians of color suggests that such terms are usually reserved for members of the majority (Walters, 1998). Similarly, other minority statuses, such as being a feminist, a bisexual, and/or biracial minority, are given little attention in the literature.

MULTIETHNIC IDENTITY

In the following, we often refer to race in describing multiethnic individuals in order to be consistent with the literature, which uses the terms "mixed race" and "biracial" to describe those with a multiethnic identity. In addition, the term race reflects the fact that the primary focus is usually on the person's salient physical characteristics, such as hair and skin color, more so than on a shared common culture. However, we also discuss bicultural individuals in this section. Research on these groups is limited, and most of the literature on multiethnic identity primarily focuses on biracial individuals (rather than multiracial individuals or bicultural individuals) whose heritage is a racial mix of minority group (usually African American) and European American (rather than two minority groups).

As we have seen from the previous chapters, the existence of multiracial individuals is not a new phenomenon. In times of slavery, it was not uncommon for slave owners to have children who were biracial as a result of sexual relations with female slaves (Greene, 1994), in spite of the fact that sexual relations between African Americans and European Americans were officially prohibited until 1967 (Wardle, 1992). Since antimiscegenation laws were outlawed, the number of interracial marriages has increased considerably, although some people still have negative attitudes toward these unions (Root, 1994). In addition, sexual relations between U.S. soldiers in Vietnam and Vietnamese women have resulted in biracial children, often referred to as Amerasians (Bemak & Chung, 1998). Because of changing views about interracial relationships and the ease with which people can cross geographic barriers that once led to more homogeneous groups of individuals, multiethnic individuals are increasingly becoming a larger segment of our population.

Interethnic friendship and intermarriage rates suggest acceptance of Asian Americans into American society. Whereas 19 percent of European American and 19 percent of African American students in ethnically diverse high schools reported that their closest friends were from other ethnic groups, 41 percent of Asian Pacific Americans reported non-Asians as their closest friends (Hamm, 2000). Asian Pacific Americans are more likely to date or marry European Americans than any other ethnic minority group (Lee &

Yamanaka, 1990). If Asian Pacific Americans do not marry someone from their specific ethnic group (e.g., Japanese American), they are more likely to marry a European American than an Asian Pacific American from another ethnic group (e.g., Chinese American; Fujino, 1992; Lee & Yamanaka, 1990). Asian Pacific American women date and marry European American men at a higher rate than Asian Pacific American men date and marry European American women (Fujino, 1992; Mok, 1999). This difference is not a result of Asian Pacific American women being more acculturated to Western values. Perhaps it is because Asian Pacific American women have fewer sexist and racist attitudes than Asian Pacific American men do (Liu, Pope-Davis, Nevitt, & Toporek, 1999). Racist attitudes may prevent some Asian Pacific American men from considering non-Asian partners, and those Asian Pacific American men who have sexist attitudes may be viewed as unattractive by many women from all ethnic groups. The greater acceptance of Asian American women than men into interethnic relationships may also reflect negative stereotypes of Asian American men as "nerdy" or effeminate (Espiritu, 1997).

Although the existence of multiracial individuals can certainly be viewed as a positive outcome of our increased tolerance and value of diversity, this group of individuals brings its own unique issues in multicultural psychology. First, there is the dilemma of how to classify such individuals. Recall from Chapter Three that humans have a natural tendency to categorize, with one of the unfortunate results of this tendency being the formation of stereotypes. Given this tendency, multiracial individuals' ambiguous appearance often creates discomfort in people who cannot place them in a particular group. Historically, census forms have not had a category for multiracial individuals—an example of our resistance to individuals who defy classification. As a result, multiracial individuals have been forced to choose a particular identity, and it is usually the minority identity. This is illustrated in the one-drop rule: If a person has one drop of African American blood, that person is African American. In reality, many African Americans are actually multiracial (Bowles, 1993). The rationale for such a perspective is that the person has to identify as a minority because this is the way that society will categorize him or her (Kerwin, Ponterotto, Jackson, & Harris, 1993). Moreover, including racially mixed individuals presumably strengthens the power of the minority group by increasing the number of individuals who can be classified as a minority. An illustration of this phenomenon is the reaction of some African Americans to Tiger Woods's self-identification as Caublasian. Woods chooses to identify himself as being part Caucasian, African American, and

Asian, but some members of the African American community feel that he should stop pretending that he is not an African American. To avoid this conflict, some biracial individuals compartmentalize their identities into public and private components; they may label themselves as African American to others, but they identify as being mixed (U. Brown, 1995).

Unfortunately, there are also times when multiracial individuals are not accepted by the minority group either. Recall our discussion of horizontal

Christine C. Iijima Hall received her PhD and MA from UCLA; her BA from California State University, Long Beach; and her AA from Los Angeles Harbor Community College. Dr. Hall has worked at University of California, Irvine; been the director of the Office of Ethnic Minority Affairs for the American Psychological Association; and served as the associate vice provost for Academic Affairs at Arizona State University West. In 1998, Dr. Hall decided to return to the higher education system where she had originally planned to work: the community college system. She is currently the director of employment with the Maricopa Community College District (AZ), one of the largest community college districts in the United States.

Dr. Hall is the youngest child of Roger and Fumiko Hall, an African American retired Army master sergeant and a Japanese warbride nurse. They have been married for over 50 years. Christine's life was very influenced by her mixed-race heritage. As a psychology student, she read much about the negative effects of mixed-race and mixed-culture children but knew many well-adjusted biracial individuals. She discovered that the past research had been conducted on biracials who had been institutionalized!—a very biased sample. Thus, her life's work was to conduct research on "average" biracial individuals and share the results of her work with others. Dr. Hall's dissertation was the first large-scale research on biracial individuals in the United States. She has spent the past 20 years continuing her research and her writing on mixed-race issues. In addition to this research, Dr. Hall also writes and lectures on the need for diversity in psychology, on ethnic women and beauty issues, and overall political issues of race and diversity in the United States.

Words of Advice to Students:

Be true to yourself. Work and strive for what you believe in. You will be much happier with yourself if you do.

Work hard and keep your promises to others.

Take time for your family and yourself.

Know about your culture(s). Be proud of it and learn from your ancestors.

hostility in Chapter Three, in which a light-skinned African American woman, for example, may be resented by other African Americans for not being Black enough. White and Langer (1999) argue that this occurs because multiracial individuals weaken the position of African Americans as a whole and are resented for being aligned with the mainstream group. Another reason for this animosity may be due to the fact that light-skinned African Americans are usually accepted more easily into mainstream society because of their greater similarity to European Americans in their physical characteristics (Clark, Anderson, Clark, & Williams, 1999). Root (1990) argues that there is a hierarchy of color in the United States based on a group's similarity to middle-class, European American structure and values. Whereas minority groups are low in this hierarchy, individuals who are mixed with European Americans are necessarily higher in this hierarchy and will therefore be more accepted by the majority. Consequently, a multiracial individual may be resented by other minority group members because of this greater acceptance.

There has also been concern about the psychological impact on the individual of being forced to choose to identify with the disenfranchised group, particularly in terms of identity development and risk for psychopathology. Historically, it has been assumed that racially mixed individuals necessarily develop marginal identities (Collins, 2000). Many theorists refer to Erikson's psychodynamic theory in conceptualizing how being multiracial may contribute to problems (Bowles, 1993; Lyles, Yancey, Grace, & Carter, 1985; Poston, 1990). Erikson argues that one of the major tasks of adolescence is to form a positive identity. This task is often conflictual for adolescents, as it requires them to form an identity that may be different from their parents and peers. Identity formation is further complicated for an ethnic minority because the individual must identify with a group that is not valued and may even be scorned in our society. In addition to these dilemmas, the multiracial individual must also deal with issues involving ambiguous status, the pressure to identify with the minority group, and rejection by both minority and majority groups. Erikson argues that the problems that ethnic minorities face may put them at risk for developing a negative or less fully formed identity, which may put them at risk for other psychological problems, given how important our identities are to our sense of well-being. Bowles argues that biracial children may be forced to disidentify with one of their parents because of parents' and/or society's encouragement. The child may disidentify with either the parent who is a minority or the one from the majority group. In either case, disidentifying with an aspect of one's identity leads to anxiety because it creates a conflict between the way one thinks one should be and what one actually is (a common assumption in many insight-oriented theories). As a result, identifying as anything other than biracial may lead to psychological problems, because it is necessarily not congruent with reality.

More recent research on identity development in multiethnic individuals assumes that a positive identity can be attained. For example, Poston (1990) argues that biracial individuals go through five stages of identity development: (1) personal identity, in which one's sense of self is independent of one's ethnic background; (2) choice of group categorization, in which the individual is usually forced to choose a minority identity; (3) enmeshment/denial, in which the person may experience confusion and guilt over having to choose one identity; (4) appreciation, in which the person still identifies with one group but begins to appreciate aspects of the other group; and (5) integration, in which the person recognizes and values all identities. Poston's theory suggests that a healthy identity is a biracial identity, which is consistent with psychodynamic theory (Bowles, 1993) and with empirical research (U. Brown, 1995; Tizard & Phoenix, 1995).

Root (1990) offers a different model of development from that of Poston, suggesting that there are several ways in which a biracial individual can have a positive resolution of identity. First, individuals can accept the identity that society assigns them, as long as this identity is consistent with their self-identification. Second, individuals can identify with a single race group; this solution is different from the first alternative in that persons choose their identity rather than agree to the identity assigned to them. Finally, individuals can identify as members of a new racial group. This resolution is similar to stage 5 in Poston's theory. Such a resolution makes it more likely that the biracial individual will feel a sense of kinship to other biracial individuals because of the common struggle with a marginal status. (See Table 9.1.)

Although most of the theories about being racially mixed posit that multiracial individuals are at increased risk for psychological problems, much of the research in this area does not support this assumption. Empirical studies indicate that multiracial individuals are not necessarily at increased risk for maladjustment and do not see their mixed identity as a source of conflict (Grove, 1991; Henriksen, 1997; Johnson & Nagoshi, 1986; Kerwin et al., 1993). There has been some empirical evidence to suggest that Amerasians may be at risk for maladjustment, in part because of the greater likelihood that they have also experienced traumatic events (Bemak & Chung, 1998; McKelvey & Webb, 1995, 1996). In addition, some racially mixed individuals

TABLE 9.1 *Stages of Biracial Identity*	
Poston (1991): Stages of Identity Development	Root (1990): Positive Resolutions of Identity Development
1. Personal Identity: Sense of self is independent of one's ethnic background.	1. Acceptance of identity assigned to them by society.
2. Choice of Group Categorization: The individual is forced to choose a minority identity.	2. Identification with a chosen single race group.
3. Enmeshment/Denial: Confusion and guilt over choosing one identity.	3. Identification as a member of a new racial group (biracial identity).
4. Appreciation: The person begins to appreciate aspects of the majority group.	
5. Integration: The person recognizes and values all identities.	

may suffer from problems with anxiety and depression as a result of identity crises (Root, 1994). Root also suggests that they may internalize negative stereotypes about themselves or may push themselves to excel to overcompensate for their presumed inferiority. Root argues that their unique appearance can often be a double-edged sword; mixed-race individuals may receive compliments for being attractive and unique, but they are also constantly reminded of their differentness through (sometimes rude) inquiries, such as "What are you?" She suggests that although multiracial individuals usually have high self-esteem, one potentially negative outcome of their uniqueness is that they may present in therapy with narcissistic-like conflicts such as self-entitlement, feeling like an imposter, and self-doubt.

Mixed-race women may also have the added complication of dealing with gender stereotypes in addition to being a minority among minorities. For example, multiracial women are often presented as being exotic and sexy because of their unique appearance, and this stereotype is exemplified in the pornography and modeling industries (Root, 1994). Multiracial women may internalize this stereotype and act in ways to make their presumed sexuality a self-fulfilling prophecy. In addition, women in general face pressures to

Maria P. P. Root, a psychologist in Seattle, Washington, has researched and published extensively on the topic of identity development and related topics, such as minority mental health, gender, and trauma. Dr. Root has edited and authored six books. She has two award-winning books, *Racially Mixed People in America* (1992) and *Multiracial Experience: Racial Borders as the New Frontier* (1996). These books were used by the U.S. Bureau of the Census to facilitate deliberations on a historical change to the Census for the year 2000. Dr. Root has received several career contribution and research awards from the Washington State Psychological Association, American Psychological Association, Asian American Psychological Association, and the Filipino American National Historical Society. Her forthcoming book, *Love's Revolution: Racial Intermarriage,* discusses open and closed families, the ways the business of family operates when race is a commodity, stages of family development in the introduction of a racially different member, and an analysis of the intersections of race, gender, and class in society's reception of interracial relationships.

Words of Advice to Students:

Travel to countries where people who are considered racial or ethnic minorities in the United States are the majority and observe how people act. If you travel to a place where you are considered part of the majority by phenotype, observe how this feels. Read interdisciplinarily to obtain different theoretical frameworks for understanding the issues or phenomena you study: sociology, political science, literature, ethnic studies, philosophy.

focus heavily on their physical appearance; consequently, the unique appearance of multiracial women is of particular concern for them. Although they may be perceived as attractive by some individuals because of their lighter skin and more Caucasoid features, they may also be resented by other minorities. They may struggle with wanting to look either more mainstream or more ethnic, which is often exemplified through concerns about their hair. In fact, Root argues that because hair is so ethnically distinctive, concern about one's hair often symbolizes a more pervasive concern about identity issues. Although all individuals want to feel a sense of belonging and acceptance, these issues may be of particular concern to multiracial women because of their collectivist orientation. Thus, they may be even more sensitive to the fact that they may not fit into and may not be completely accepted by any particular group. Some biracial women describe themselves as being "liked by all but dated by none" because they are too White for African Americans and too Black for European Americans (Root, 1994).

It is important to keep in mind, however, that most of the research in this area is limited to individuals who are mixed with African American or Asian ancestry and does not examine other ethnicities. Nor are there studies examining individuals who are a mixture of two minority groups or are from multiple minority groups. In addition, selection procedures such as the snowball technique are commonly used, which limits the generalizability of the findings (see Chapter Two). Moreover, participants who volunteer in a study concerning multiracial identity may vary in important ways from those individuals who did not wish to participate. Perhaps well-adjusted individuals are more interested and motivated to participate than the less well adjusted, for example. Finally, most of the research on multiracial individuals has been conducted on children and adolescents, most likely because they are in the process of forming a sense of identity. Nevertheless, research needs to focus on identity issues/resolution as they occur across the life span (Root, 1994).

Bicultural individuals belong to two cultures. These individuals share many of the same issues that biracial individuals face, and many of the same theories are used to understand them. For example, historically, theorists have argued that bicultural individuals will also develop a marginal identity, and those individuals who act too White are perceived by the minority group in a negative ways, as indicated by terms such as "oreo," "banana," and "apple" (LaFromboise, Coleman, & Gerton, 1995). Indeed, biracial individuals are bicultural individuals, but the reverse is not necessarily true, in that immigrants who live in America are not always biracial.

As discussed in Chapter One, LaFromboise et al. (1995) present several models of second-culture acquisition: assimilation, accommodation, alternation, multicultural, and fusion. In the *assimilation model,* individuals attempt to absorb into the dominant culture. Although this strategy may lead to greater acceptance by members of the target culture, it poses several dangers, including the potential of being rejected by members of the majority culture and by members of their culture of origin, as well as the stress of learning new behaviors and unlearning old ones. The *acculturation model* is similar to the assimilation model; the only difference is that in this model, the person is still identified as a minority. As a minority, the person is often viewed as a second-class citizen, which often leads to negative economic and psychological effects. In the *alternation model,* the person knows and understands two different cultures. This competency is evident in behaviors such as code-switching in people who are bilingual. An advantage of this model is that it does not assume that one culture is better than the other. In the *multicultural model,* several cultures can live together in harmony and maintain a positive identity. However, it is likely that over time, each culture might not be able to maintain a separate identity but instead form a new cultural group. The *fusion model* is akin to the melting pot theory, where cultures fuse and form a new culture. The psychological impact of this model is unclear, and there are few successful examples of such a new culture.

LaFromboise and colleagues (1995) argue that the alternation model encourages bicultural competence, which is an important key to psychological well-being, as we have seen in Chapters Five to Eight. To develop bicultural competence, one needs a sense of self-sufficiency and a cultural identity. Moreover, the more integrated the identity, the healthier one will be. This idea is reflected in many models of identity, where the highest stage is usually one in which the person internalizes the values of both cultures. Other important factors in cultural competence are knowledge of cultural beliefs and values, positive attitudes toward both groups, and bicultural efficacy, or the belief that one can live effectively in a satisfying manner within two groups without compromising one's sense of cultural identity. Other important skills include communication ability in both cultures, role repertoire (the greater the range of roles, the higher the cultural confidence), and groundedness, or stable social networks in both cultures. Although further empirical evidence on the concept of cultural competence is needed, there is some preliminary support for its importance. Fiske, Kitayama, Markus, and Nisbett (1998) have found that people can learn the skills necessary to go back and forth between different cultures, which is increasingly necessary not only for bicultural individuals, but for people who must communicate with individuals from other cultures to conduct business, conduct research, and share ideas with one another. Similarly, Hong, Morris, Chiu, and Benet-Martinez (2000) cite empirical evidence indicating that bicultural individuals have internalized constructs unique to each culture and engage in frame switching, depending on which set of constructs is primed.

FEMINISM AND WOMEN OF COLOR

Most of the literature on feminism and women of color has focused primarily on the reluctance of African American women to join the feminist movement. Consequently, many of the issues discussed refer specifically to

African American women; some of these issues may also apply to other women of color, but more research in this area is needed.

There has been considerable discussion about whether African American women support the feminist movement. Although African American women support feminist goals, they participate less in the feminist movement than European American women do (Martin & Hall, 1992; Reid, 1984, 1993). One reason for their reluctance to embrace feminism is the belief that racism is the more pervasive problem in their lives. Those who hold this belief feel that African American men and women need to unite to fight for freedom of oppression from the dominant society. Indeed, Martin and Hall found that some African American women do, in fact, feel that their identity as an African American is more important than their identity as a woman.

Moreover, some researchers argue that the term "sexism" cannot be applied in the same way to the African American community because of the structural inequality between the African American community and the dominant society (Reid, 1984, 1993; Staples, 1979). Lewis (1977) points out that historically, African American men and women have both been denied power and authority. Moreover, because African American women were less threatening than African American men, they had easier access to education and better jobs. Therefore, the gender role relationships between African American men and women cannot be attributed to the differential participation of men and women in the public sphere as it can be for European American men and women. In addition, African American men also have less power in the domestic sphere than do European American men due to absence, lack of financial support, and the slavery system (Frazier, 1939; Moynihan, 1965). These historical factors suggest that the power relationship between African American men and women has been more egalitarian or one in which African American women dominate, in contrast to the power relationship between European American men and women.

Unfortunately, the lack of male dominance and female subordination in the African American community has been interpreted to suggest that African American women, rather than racist institutions, are to blame for the oppression of African American men (Greene, 1994). Some African American men feel that African American women's gains as women are limiting their ability to prevail in a patriarchal society (Reid, 1993). Such an interpretation highlights the assumption that a patriarchal society is the ideal and anything that deviates from this ideal is abnormal (Boyd, 1990; Jackson, 1973; Reid, 1984). Moreover, critics argue that there is no empirical support for the dominant role of the African American woman within the family structure (Boyd, 1990; Gutman, 1976) and that African American women do not have the power to oppress African American men because they do not have authority positions in society and within the job market (Hooks, 1984). Nevertheless, this myth has been internalized by some African Americans (Greene, 1994).

In addition to the problems that African American women have faced within their own community, they have also encountered difficulties in their relationships with European American women that have affected their willingness to participate in the feminist movement. Some feminists have feared that concerns with racism in the feminist movement will weaken the fight for women's rights (Reid, 1984). Historically, there has been a great deal of discrimination against African American women in the feminist movement (E. Brown, 1989; Dill, 1983; Martin, 1984). European American feminists have also accepted principles that were in opposition to the interests of African Americans in order to gain advances for themselves. For example, European American women have historically supported the lynch law (Dill, 1983). In her efforts to fight for women's rights, Susan B. Anthony purposely neglected African Americans to ensure the vote for European American women (Terborg-Penn, 1985). European American women have even feared that African American women are surpassing them in job opportunities because of their double minority status (Reid, 1984; Zinn, Cannon, Higginbotham, & Dill, 1986).

In addition to these examples of overt discrimination, status differences also make it difficult for African American women to embrace feminist goals. European American feminists are usually in the middle class, whereas African American women are more concentrated in the lower class. As a result, African American women have not felt that the goals of European American feminists are comparable to their own goals as a group. For example, European American feminists have fought for the right to work outside the home as part of the paid labor force, but African American women have traditionally been required to participate in the labor force; in fact, many African American women consider it a luxury to be a housewife and have a man who provides all of the economic support for the family.

In addition, European American women are necessary to the existence of European American men; consequently, they can have power because of their sexual desirability to European American men (Reid, 1993). Lewis (1977) suggests that African American women have less access to deference, power, and authority. European American women receive deference because they have some roles that are highly valued, such as helpmate, sex object, and the "driving force behind every man." European American women have also been given special treatment in terms of chivalry because they have been viewed as helpless and therefore in need of rescue and aid on the part of men. Although many feminists reject this treatment of women, it is a situation from which many African American women have not benefited.

Even standards of attractiveness for African American women are often based on European American women. Light skin color and Caucasoid features are seen by both European American and African American people as being more attractive and are associated with higher status because they are taken as evidence of European American ancestry (Neal & Wilson, 1989). When women of color are used in advertising, they usually have long straight hair, light skin, and thin lips and nose—characteristics that make them look less African American and more like European American women (Boyd, 1990). In fact, some African American men prefer to date European American women because they are the standard of what is beautiful and they fit the model of femininity better than African American women do (Staples, 1979). Thus, oppression on the basis of sex means different things for African American and European American women. Hurtado (1989) argues that European American women's oppression consists of seduction by European American men, but African American women's oppression consists of rejection by African American men. Because rejection by African American men is partly a result of European American standards of comparison, many African American women resent the European American women to whom they are compared.

Furthermore, the lack of research in women's studies on minorities indicates that feminists have not been interested in African Americans as women. According to Zinn et al. (1986), part of the problem is that African Americans are not members of the prestigious academic institutions in which such literature is published. For minorities, just completing college can be an obstacle. They are more likely to attend public schools and, as faculty, are more likely to have positions in public institutions that do not grant doctorates and do not have the resources of the more prestigious institutions. Consequently, they have few opportunities to become a part of networks that control the distribution of knowledge in women's studies. Moreover, because the women who hold positions in these privileged institutions are usually European American and are from the middle class, they have little exposure to people of different races and classes; hence, they develop and teach concepts that do not represent the experiences of minorities and women from the lower class. When European American feminists try to include women of color in feminist theory, their point of view is often rejected because it does not reflect the issues and concerns that relate to women of color. Even in courses taught on women's studies, material concerning minority women is not given much significance. The feminist literature by women of color that does exist often goes untranslated and is therefore ignored (Espin & Gawelek, 1992). Zinn et al. (1986) found that even in feminist journals that claim to have an interest in minorities and working-class women, those who hold the gatekeeping positions are predominantly European American. Similarly, Reid and Kelly (1994) found that few articles in the *Psychology of Women Quarterly* included women of color and participants other than college students. Thus, many European American women have been subject to the same ethnocentric bias of assuming that what is true for White, middle-class women is true for all women (Espin & Gawalek, 1992).

In the few articles in which women of color have been included, important differences have been found that reflect their unique experiences. For example, in U.S. culture, an emphasis on a thin ideal of beauty is related to eating disorders because women strive to live up to this ideal. In addition, the majority of eating disorders begin around adolescence, a time when girls' bodies change considerably. In contrast, Thompson (1992, 1996) found that many women of color reported having eating disorders for half of their lives, and their reasons for developing eating disorders had less to do with appearance; eating disorder symptoms are often a coping strategy for dealing with issues such as trauma, sexual abuse, poverty, heterosexism, racism, and classism. Moreover, she did not find evidence for the stereotype that obesity is more an issue for women of color and that anorexia is only a concern for European American women; the specific types of eating problems did not correlate with race, class, sexuality, or nationality.

In spite of the numerous reasons for African American women to dismiss the feminist movement altogether, many of them have expressed interest in feminist goals (Martin, 1984; Martin & Hall, 1992; Reid, 1984). One reason for this interest in sexism is the increasing awareness of the ways in which sexual discrimination has affected the African American community. For example, the Black Power movement in the 1960s and the Black Is Beautiful movement in the 1960s and 1970s, both of which were attempts to promote African American standards of beauty and self-worth, were primarily male-inspired and male-led; African American women helped mainly by supporting the men (Lewis, 1977). Consequently, these movements represented the needs and problems of African American men, and little discussion was given to the problems, objectives, or concerns of women. In addition to these changes, the fact that African American women are, in comparison to European American women, more often single, employed, head of the household, and self-supporting are other reasons why African American women are supportive of the feminist movement. More recent issues such as equal pay for equal work, child care, shared household responsibilities, reproductive rights, and no-fault divorce are more in line with concerns of women of color (Comas-Diaz, 1991).

The fact that African American women are showing increasing support for the feminist movement does not mean, however, that they have chosen to fight sexism rather than racism. On the contrary, African American women have demonstrated their commitment to fighting both forms of discrimination by forming organizations that tackle both issues, such as Black Women Organized for Action (BWOA) and the National Black Feminist Organization (NBFO). Thus, many African American women feel the need to fight for the liberation of all oppressed people, not only women or African Americans. This ability to identify with the oppression of all people is consistent with the internalization stage of racial identity discussed in Chapter One (Cross, 1971). In fact, the idea of making African American women choose between the two identities is, in many respects, a false choice and has been interpreted as a product of the patriarchal strategy to divide the interests of these two groups, thereby weakening the efforts of both (Dill, 1983).

Thus far, we have primarily discussed problems related to African American women's participation in the feminist movement because most of the literature has focused specifically on this ethnic group. Unfortunately, there is even less research focusing on the concerns and feelings that other women of color have about the feminist movement. Chow (1987) suggests that feminist issues may be relevant to Asian American women in that they are also a part of a patriarchal system in which men dominate, yet they have often been neglected because of their relatively small numbers, the diversity among Asian groups, the fact that many Asian American women are foreign-born and therefore less aware of the feminist movement, and because of experiences with racism and classism. As with African American women, Asian American women are concerned that affiliation with the feminist movement will be interpreted as a threat to Asian concerns.

Poor women have also been neglected by most feminists. Poverty is of particular concern for women in general in that the strongest predictor of poverty is being a female householder with no spouse (Reid, 1995). Reid also points out that poor women are a diverse group that includes minorities, the elderly, and teen mothers. Yet, despite the number of women who face poverty (an issue particularly relevant to women), few research studies focus on the experiences of poor women (Reid, 1995; Saris & Johnston-Robledo, 2000).

DISABLED PERSONS OF COLOR

Historically, our view of people with disabilities has changed in ways that parallel the changes that have taken place in our views of diversity (Prilleltensky, 1995). Atkinson and Hackett (1998) indicate that initially, we viewed people with disabilities as being a burden; our first human ancestors were nomadic, and those individuals who could not keep up with the group or participate in the hunting and gathering were left to survive on their own. Even today, some individuals still view people with disabilities as a burden rather than as productive members of society. This perspective is similar to the inferiority model of minorities, which assumed that ethnic minorities' lower level of education and employment were due to biological inferiorities. We then moved to a charitable view of people with disabilities, which emerged as a forceful theme when Jesus Christ focused on this population through his teachings (Atkinson & Hackett, 1998). Although this view encourages more empathic treatment of people with disabilities, it can also translate into sympathy, pity, and paternalistic attitudes toward them. This model corresponds to the deficit model in multicultural psychology, in which there is a recognition that the difficulties that minority groups encounter are due to environmental factors rather than biological factors, but European American culture was still the standard of comparison. Finally, Atkinson and Hackett argue that the civil, women's, and gay rights movements also helped to foster a more egalitarian view of people with disabilities rather than viewing them as individuals with a deficit in need of our help. Consequently, laws that ensure that people with disabilities will not be discriminated against in federal programs, the workforce, and the education system have been passed to protect their rights. This view corresponds to the multicultural model, in which differences between groups are not viewed as deficits but as equivalent perspectives. (See Table 9.2.)

TABLE 9.2   *Theories of Disability and Diversity*

Disability (Atkinson & Hackett, 1998)	Diversity (Prilleltensky, 1995)
1. Disabled individuals as a burden rather than productive members of society.	1. Inferiority model: Minorities as less intelligent and less capable than European Americans.
2. Disabled individuals as in need of charity, sympathy, and pity.	2. Deficit model: Minority members' lower achievement attribute to cultural disadvantage.
3. Disabled individuals as different but equal.	3. Multicultural model: Different but equal perspective of diverse groups.

Although the treatment of people with disabilities has improved, these individuals still face many obstacles. Psychologists and other helping professionals often have stereotypes about people with disabilities that prevent them from attaining the assistance they need for job placement. These include beliefs that people with disabilities are not motivated to work and that they have little training or work experience. Atkinson and Hackett (1998) argue that blaming people with disabilities for their lack of training and work experience is yet another example of blaming the victim. Employers may also have negative biases about them, such as that they are accident-prone, will frequently miss work, and have low rates of productivity. They are also reluctant to make adjustments to the work setting to accommodate people with disabilities because they fear that it will be too expensive. As a result of these biases, people with disabilities have difficulty finding jobs, and when they do work, their average annual income is less than those without disabilities. The discrepancy in income is even worse for minorities with a disability. Consequently, many people with disabilities live in poverty.

Atkinson and Hackett (1998) argue that negative attitudes toward people with disabilities is also fostered by the Bible, which suggests that their disability is punishment for not obeying God's laws, and by the media, which often foster negative portrayals of people with disabilities. In addition, they point out that the language used when speaking with people with disabilities, such as the use of "motherese" speech, which is often used with children, differs from the language used with nondisabled persons. Even though most people support the rights of people with disabilities in the abstract, they oppose them whenever such rights affect them personally, such as when a group home for people with disabilities will be opening in their neighborhood (another example of symbolic racism). Many physical barriers, transportation barriers, and communication barriers still exist as well. People with disabilities are also frequently targets of physical, sexual, and emotional abuse.

In addition to these problems, minorities with disabilities often face other unique obstacles. Hanna and Rogovsky (1993b) found that women with disabilities are less likely to participate in social relations, educational institutions, and the labor force than are men with disabilities. They propose that this discrepancy occurs for three reasons. First, attributions for disability differ for males and females; whereas people are likely to attribute disabilities in men to situational factors such as war injuries, sports injuries, and car accidents, they are more likely to make internal attributions for women's disabilities, such as carelessness or being accident-prone. Second, women with disabilities are perceived as being unable to fulfill their role as caretaker, as people assume that they cannot take care of themselves, cannot adequately take care of a husband, and should not raise children. These biases rob many women with disabilities of an important source of self-esteem and identity, given society's expectations for women as caregivers. Finally, women with disabilities cannot live up to the standard of beauty expected of them. Many women suffer body image and self-esteem problems because of their inability to live up to unrealistic standards of beauty, and this problem is compounded even further for women with disabilities. This has both social and economic consequences because of the value we place on attractiveness, which can negatively affect self-concept and self-image.

African American women often have a higher incidence of physical disabilities than do African American men (Hanna & Rogovsky, 1993a). Hanna and Rogovsky argue that this occurs for many of the reasons discussed above as a result of being female, but these women also face some unique stressors because of their ethnicity. First, because there are fewer single African American males than females (a phenomenon that is sometimes referred to as the endangered Black male), and because those African American males who are available often date non-African American women, these men can be more selective in choosing partners and are therefore less likely to choose a woman with a disability. Second, African American women are not able to fulfill the matriarchal expectation of being a strong presence in the workforce and in the home because of the perception that people with disabilities are helpless. Finally, their limited spatial mobility prevents them from seeking jobs in the suburbs, given that minorities are often more concentrated in the city. Mobility also limits their dating choices. They may also be discouraged from moving outside of the city because of the loss of social support systems such as church, family, and friends.

Disabled lesbians also face unique obstacles because of their multiple minority status. O'Toole and Bregante (1993) argue that disabled lesbians have less access to socially sanctioned roles, few role models to emulate, and a lack of family support. They are often targets of violence (especially assault) and often receive negative attention from health care workers, which can lead to neglect and maltreatment. In addition, their partners often have no automatic rights because their relationship is not legally recognized in the way that heterosexual unions are, they are discouraged from motherhood, and the assumption that people with disabilities are asexual makes it difficult for them to find partners and to accept their sexuality.

As with other minority groups, there is little research on people with disabilities in general. Consequently, research on disabled individuals who are also members of other minority groups is even more scarce. Given that people with disabilities face many of the same issues as other minority groups, such as prejudice and discrimination, they, too, should be included more frequently in research and theory on diverse populations.

OLDER PERSONS OF COLOR

Historically, the treatment of older adults has also been negative. In our nomadic ancestry, elders were often treated in the same way that people with disabilities were because of their limited mobility, although some elderly persons whose knowledge was valued were supported by the group for as long as possible (Atkinson & Hackett, 1998). In the United States, the elderly were treated with more respect because of their position as property owners. However, the value of the elderly changed, particularly during the Industrial Revolution, when youth was considered more important because young people were believed to be more productive and to learn more quickly.

Psychologists have also neglected to examine the experiences of the elderly (Atkinson & Hackett, 1998). Until fairly recently, limited research was conducted to explore their experiences and to validate assumptions about the elderly. Mental health professionals often were not trained in working with elderly clients, nor did they have a desire to work with this population. Negative stereotypes among laypeople and health professionals include the belief that older people are not sexual (and when they are, they are dirty old men and women), not useful members of society, and that they are poor, rigid, sick, and isolated. Even the language used by geriatric advocates conveys the belief in their frailty and dependence (e.g., bedridden, chair-bound, dependent). Not surprisingly, older adults have underutilized mental health services, despite the fact that mental health problems do not decrease with age and therapy is effective with older people.

However, this neglect of the elderly is changing because of the growing segment of the population that constitutes older adults, a process that has been referred to as the "graying of America." This is due in part to the projected growth of the "baby boomers" into older age groups and to gains in life expectancy. Increases in the number of older adults are expected in all segments of the population, and minorities in particular are expected to increase dramatically; by 2030, it is expected that older minorities will have increased by 328 percent (Haley, Han, & Henderson, 1998).

Older adults constitute both the wealthiest and the poorest segments of the population (Atkinson & Hackett, 1998). The affluent status results from rising salaries, pension plans, and a growing economy. Unfortunately, this increase in wealth among the elderly has created negative stereotypes of older adults as "greedy geezers" and "fat cats," which has created public opinion that government funding and programming designed to benefit the elderly should be cut. However, these stereotypes do not hold true for many older adults, particularly single women, ethnic minorities, the seriously ill, and the old old (over 85). Older adults are often the first to lose their job in economic downsizings, and when they lose their job, it is more difficult for them to obtain new employment. In addition, the security of some pension plans and other federal and state programs is now threatened.

Older adults are likely to be the victims of violent crimes and abuse (Atkinson & Hackett, 1998). Property crimes are particularly common, as well as home repair fraud and health care fraud. In addition, older adults live in fear of violent crime, which can also have a negative effect on their well-being. Rates of elder abuse are similar to the rates for child abuse. Abuse includes physical battering, threats of physical assault, physical constraint, overmedicating, psychological abuse, and sometimes sexual abuse. Perpetrators are most often family members, particularly a child caring for his or her parent, but may also include staff in institutional settings. Elder abuse is often underreported because of the fear that reporting that their child is abusing them will bring shame to their family, as well as the fear that they will lose what limited support they are receiving. Evidence of abuse such as bruises and cuts is often ignored and attributed to ambulation problems, and self-report of abuse is attributed to senility.

Older minority adults face other unique problems as well (Haley et al., 1998). Members of minority groups often have lower levels of income and education, with poverty being highest among minority older women. Older African Americans have the highest level of vulnerability and disease, followed by Latino Americans. Lifetime experiences with prejudice and discrimination can lead to minority older adults' mistrust of health care workers, which may lead to avoidance or delay in seeking treatment. Lower levels of acculturation are often associated with negative results such as adjustment disorders, depressive symptoms, and less utilization of both medical and mental health services. Different levels of acculturation can create conflict among family members; younger family members are often more acculturated than older members, which can cause conflicts such as less respect for authority, communication problems, and lower preference for minority traditions. However, on the positive side, living with negative experiences may have led to the development of coping strategies that will help them in difficult times.

Special considerations may also need to be made when treating minority older adults for mental problems (Haley et al., 1998). Although older adults have lower rates of major depression than younger people do, they have higher rates of milder depressive symptoms, usually due to impairments in physical health. Older minority adults who are less acculturated may experience depression, and symptoms are usually physical rather than psychological. African Americans appear to experience higher rates of chronic diseases but not depression. Dementia is at least as common in minorities, if not more common, because dementia is related to low educational attainment, which is more prevalent among older minorities. Dementia is not as commonly detected among older minorities because they often do not go to specialized clinics and are less likely to seek help for memory problems because they assume that these are a natural part of aging. Consequently, more research needs to be conducted that will facilitate the utilization, assessment, and treatment of this population.

One example of an assessment strategy for working with diverse older adults has been proposed by Hays (1996). She outlines a specific assessment strategy that will help clinicians pay attention to multicultural factors, which she labels ADRESSING: Age and generational influences, Disability, Religion, Ethnicity, Social status, Sexual orientation, Indigenous heritage, National origin, and Gender. This assessment strategy incorporates all of the factors examined in this text and requires that clinicians become educated about how these factors can potentially impact the mental health of clients.

MULTICULTURAL CONTEXTS

Although this is a book on multicultural psychology, there is a dearth of literature in psychology on multiple cultural groups in the same context. The literature on interethnic contact has primarily focused on European American–African American relations. However, interethnic contact often does not include European Americans. There is a dearth of literature on relations among non-European American ethnic groups. Moreover, the focus has typically been on the influence of the dominant European American group on ethnic minority groups. As ethnic minority groups increase in size and power, the influence of non-European American ethnic groups on European Americans will become increasingly important.

The increasing size of the ethnic population will not automatically shift the power structure in the United States, however. Indeed, an increasing non-European American population may cause some European Americans to feel threatened and to become more prejudiced and exclusive of ethnic minority persons (Brewer, 1999). Even when there is not a direct threat to economic security, old prejudices against ethnic minority groups are hard habits to break (Bobo, 1999; Sears, Citrin, Cheleden, & van Laar, 1999).

Classic social psychology experiments have demonstrated that common goals facilitate cooperation between competing groups (Sherif, 1966). However, even when groups have common goals, the ingroup may continue to engage in social comparison with the outgroup on characteristics or achievements on which they perceive themselves as superior to the outgroup (Brewer, 1999). A potential alternative to strong ingroup-outgroup distinctions is an emphasis on the multiple group memberships that people identify with (Brewer, 1999). Most people are able to generate four or five important group identities, including gender, religion, ethnicity, political party, college major, and region of residence. Multiple group identities tend to be positively correlated, such that one identity does not necessarily compete with another.

However, it is unknown whether these results are applicable to persons of color. Whereas persons of color may seek multiple group identities, they may not have equal access to all groups; historic and current exclusion from certain groups may cause persons of color to identify with those groups that are most inclusive. Even when persons of color are included in a group, the politics of majority group dominance may persist.

Whose responsibility is it to create groups with multicultural memberships? It could be argued that because European Americans occupy positions of power, it is incumbent on them to become more inclusive. However, persons in power are unlikely to become motivated to change a system that has favored them (Bobo, 1999). Persons of color could be called on to include European Americans in their groups. For example, several Fellows of the American Psychological Association Society for the Psychological Study of Ethnic Minority Issues are European Americans; these persons are viewed as allies, although they are not themselves persons of color. However, many persons of color may be legitimately concerned that because of their lack of societal power, European Americans may attempt to take over their organizations if they are allowed to join. Moreover, many European Americans may be reluctant to join groups in which they are the minority for the same reasons that persons of color are reluctant to join groups in which they are the minority. Nevertheless, because many persons of color are bicultural, insofar as they have been socialized in the dominant culture as well as in their ethnic culture, persons of color may be in a better position to understand the dynamics of intergroup contact than those European Americans who have not had experiences in cultures other than the dominant one.

REFERENCES

Atkinson, D. R., & Hackett, G. (1998). *Counseling diverse populations* (2nd ed.). Boston: McGraw-Hill.

Bemak, F., & Chung, R. C. (1998). Vietnamese Amerasians: Predictors of distress and self-destructive behavior. *Journal of Counseling and Development, 76,* 452–458.

Bobo, L. D. (1999). Prejudice as group position: Microfoundations of a sociological approach to racism and race relations. *Journal of Social Issues, 55,* 445–472.

Bowles, D. D. (1993). Bi-racial identity: Children born to African American and European American couples. *Clinical Social Work Journal, 21,* 417–428.

Boyd, J. A. (1990). Ethnic and cultural diversity: Keys to power. In L. S. Brown & M. P. Root (Eds.), *Diversity and complexity in feminist therapy* (pp. 151–167). New York: Hawthorne Press.

Brewer, M. B. (1999). The psychology of prejudice: Ingroup love or outgroup hate? *Journal of Social Issues, 55,* 429–444.

Brown, E. B. (1989). Women's consciousness: Maggie Lena Walker and the independent order of Saint Luke. *Signs, 14,* 610–633.

Brown, U. M. (1995). African American/European American interracial young adults: Quest for a racial identity. *American Journal of Orthopsychiatry, 65,* 125–130.

Chow, E. N. (1987). The development of feminist consciousness among Asian American women. *Gender and Society, 1,* 284–299.

Clark, R., Anderson, N. B., Clark, V. R., & Williams, D. R. (1999). Racism as a stressor for African Americans. *American Psychologist, 54,* 805–816.

Collins, J. F. (2000). Biracial-bisexual individuals: Identity. *International Journal of Sexuality and Gender Studies, 5,* 221–253.

Comas-Diaz, L. (1991). Feminism and diversity in psychology. *Psychology of Women Quarterly, 15,* 597–609.

Cross, W. E. (1971). The Negro to Black conversion experience. *Black World, 20,* 13–17.

Dill, B. T. (1983). Race, class, and gender: Prospects for an all-inclusive sisterhood. *Feminist Studies, 9,* 131–150.

Dube, E. M., & Savin-Williams, R. C. (1999). Sexual identity development among ethnic sexual-minority male youths. *Developmental Psychology, 35,* 1389–1398.

Espin, O. M., & Gawelek, M. A. (1992). Women's diversity: Ethnicity, race, class, and gender in theories of feminist psychology. In L. S. Brown & M. Ballou (Eds.), *Personality and psychopathology* (pp. 88–107). New York: Guilford Press.

Espiritu, Y. L. (1997). *Asian American men and women.* Thousand Oaks, CA: Sage.

Fiske, A. P., Kitayama, S., Markus, H. R., & Nisbett, R. E. (1998). The cultural matrix of social psychology. In D. T. Gilbert, S. T. Fiske, & G. Lindzey (Eds.), *The handbook of social psychology* (4th ed., pp. 915–981). New York: McGraw-Hill.

Frazier, E. F. (1939). *The Negro family in the United States.* Chicago: University of Chicago Press.

Fujino, D. (1992). *Extending exchange theory: Effects of ethnicity and gender on Asian American heterosexual relationships.* Unpublished doctoral dissertation, University of California, Los Angeles.

Fukuyama, M. A., & Ferguson, D. (2000). Lesbian, gay, and bisexual people of color: Understanding culture complexity and managing multiple oppressions. In R. M. Perez, K. A. DeBord, & K. J. Bieschke (Eds.), *Handbook of counseling and psychotherapy with lesbian, gay and bisexual clients* (pp. 81–105). Washington, DC: American Psychological Association.

Greene, B. (1994). Lesbian women of color: Triple jeopardy. In L. Comas-Diaz & B. Greene (Eds.), *Women of color: Integrating ethnic and gender identities in psychotherapy* (pp. 389–427). New York: Guilford Press.

Greene, B. (1997). Ethnic minority lesbians and gay men. In B. Greene (Ed.), *Ethnic and cultural diversity among lesbians and gay men* (Vol. 3, pp. 216–239). Thousand Oaks, CA: Sage.

Grove, K. J. (1991). Identity development in interracial Asian/European American late adolescents: Must it be so problematic? *Journal of Youth and Adolescence, 20,* 617–628.

Gutman, H. G. (1976). *The Black family in slavery and freedom, 1750–1925.* New York: Vintage Books.

Haley, W. E., Han, B., & Henderson, J. N. (1998). Aging and ethnicity: Issues for clinical practice. *Journal of Clinical Psychology in Medical Settings, 5,* 393–409.

Hamm, J. V. (2000). Do birds of a feather flock together? The variable bases for African American, Asian American, and European American adolescents' selection of similar friends. *Developmental Psychology, 36,* 209–219.

Hanna, W. J., & Rogovsky, B. (1993a). On the situation of African-American women with physical disabilities. In M. Nagler (Ed.), *Perspectives on disability* (2nd ed., pp. 149–160). Palo Alto, CA: Health Markets Research.

Hanna, W. J., & Rogovsky, B. (1993b). Women with disabilities: Two handicaps plus. In M. Nagler (Ed.), *Perspectives on disability* (2nd ed., pp. 109–120). Palo Alto, CA: Health Markets Research.

Hays, P. A. (1996). Culturally responsive assessment with diverse older clients. *Professional Psychology: Research and Practice, 27,* 188–193.

Henriksen, R. C. (1997). Counseling mixed parentage individuals: A dilemma. *Texas Counseling Association Journal, 25,* 68–74.

Hong, Y., Morris, M. W., Chiu, C., & Benet-Martinez, V. (2000). Multicultural minds. *American Psychologist, 55,* 709–720.

Hooks, B. (1984). *Ain't I a woman: Black women and feminism.* Boston: South End Press.

Hurtado, A. (1989). Relating to privilege: Seduction and rejection in the subordination of White women and women of color. *Signs: Journal of Women in Culture and Society, 14,* 833–855.

Jackson, J. J. (1973). Black women in a racist society. In C. Willie, B. Kramer, & B. Brown (Eds.), *Racism and mental health* (pp. 185–268). Pittsburgh, PA: University of Pittsburgh Press.

Johnson, R., & Nagoshi, C. (1986). The adjustment of offspring of within-group and interracial/intercultural marriages: A comparison of personality factor scores. *Journal of Marriage and Family, 48,* 279–284.

Kerwin, C., Ponterotto, J. G., Jackson, B. L., & Harris, A. (1993). Racial identity in biracial children: A qualitative investigation. *Journal of Counseling Psychology, 40,* 221–231.

LaFromboise, T. D., Coleman, H. L. K., & Gerton, J. (1995). Psychological impact of biculturalism: Evidence and theory. In N. R. Goldberger & J. B. Veroff (Eds.), *The culture and psychology reader* (pp. 489–535). New York: New York University Press.

Lee, S. M., & Yamanaka, K. (1990). Patterns of Asian American intermarriage and marital assimilation. *Journal of Comparative Family Studies, 21,* 287–305.

Lewis, D. K. (1977). A response to inequality: African American women, racism, and sexism. *Signs, 3,* 339–361.

Liu, W. M., Pope-Davis, D. B., Nevitt, J., & Toporek, R. L. (1999). Understanding the function of acculturation and prejudicial attitudes among Asian Americans. *Cultural Diversity and Ethnic Minority Psychology, 5,* 317–328.

Lyles, M. R., Yancey, A., Grace, C., & Carter, J. H. (1985). Racial identity and self-esteem: Problems peculiar to biracial children. *Journal of the American Academy of Child Psychiatry, 24,* 150–153.

Martin, J. K. (1984). *Racial differences in gender role orientation and attitudes about feminism: Correlates with self-esteem.* Unpublished master's thesis, Kent State University, Kent, OH.

Martin, J. K., & Hall, G. C. N. (1992). Thinking African American, thinking internal, thinking feminist. *Journal of Counseling Psychology, 39,* 509–514.

McKelvey, R. S., & Webb, J. A. (1995). A pilot study of abuse among Vietnamese Amerasians. *Child Abuse and Neglect, 19,* 545–553.

McKelvey, R. S., & Webb, J. A. (1996). A comparative study of Vietnamese Amerasians, their non-Amerasian siblings, and unrelated, like-aged Vietnamese immigrants. *American Journal of Psychiatry, 153,* 561–563.

McLaughlin, C. S., Chen, C., Greenberger, E., & Biermeier, C. (1997). Family, peer, and individual correlates of sexual experience among Caucasian and Asian American late adolescents. *Journal of Research on Adolescence, 7,* 33–53.

Mok, T. A. (1999). Asian American dating: Important factors in partner choice. *Cultural Diversity and Ethnic Minority Psychology, 5,* 103–117.

Moynihan, D. P. (1965). *The Negro family: The case for national action.* Washington, DC: U.S. Department of Labor, Office of Police Planning and Research.

Neal, A. M., & Wilson, M. L. (1989). The role of skin color and features in the Black community: Implications for Black women and therapy. *Clinical Psychology Review, 9,* 323–333.

O'Toole, C. J., & Bregante, J. L. (1993). Disabled lesbians: Multicultural realities. In M. Nagler (Ed.), *Perspectives on disability* (2nd ed., pp. 261–272). Palo Alto, CA: Health Markets Research.

Poston, W. S. C. (1990). The biracial identity development model: A needed addition. *Journal of Counseling and Development, 69,* 152–155.

Prilleltensky, I. (1995). The politics of abnormal psychology: Past, present, and future. In N. R. Goldberger & J. B. Veroff (Eds.), *The culture and psychology reader* (pp. 652–673). New York: New York University Press.

Reid, P. T. (1984). Feminism versus minority group identity: Not for African American woman only. *Sex Roles, 10,* 247–255.

Reid, P. T. (1993). Women of color have no "place." *Focus, 7,* 2.

Reid, P. T. (1995). Poor women in psychological research: Shut up or shut out. In N. R. Goldberger & J. B. Veroff (Eds.), *The culture and psychology reader* (pp. 184–204). New York: New York University Press.

Reid, P. T., & Kelly, E. (1994). Research on women of color: From ignorance to awareness. *Psychology of Women Quarterly, 18,* 477–486.

Root, M. P. (1990). Resolving "other" status: Identity development of biracial individuals. *Women and Therapy, 9,* 185–205.

Root, M. P. (1994). Mixed-race women. In L. Comas-Diaz & B. Greene (Eds.), *Women of color: Integrating ethnic and gender identities in psychotherapy* (pp. 455–478). New York: Guilford Press.

Saris, R. N., & Johnston-Robledo, I. (2000). Poor women are still shut out of mainstream psychology. *Psychology of Women Quarterly, 24,* 233–235.

Savin-Williams, R. C. (1996). Ethnic- and sexual-minority youth. In R. C. Savin-Williams & K. M. Cohen (Eds.), *The lives of lesbians, gays, and bisexuals* (pp. 152–165). Fort Worth, TX: Harcourt Brace.

Sears, D. O., Citrin, J., Cheleden, S. V., & van Laar, C. (1999). Cultural diversity and multicultural politics: Is ethnic balkanization psychologically inevitable? In D. A. Prentice & D. T. Miller (Eds.), *Cultural divides: Understanding and overcoming group conflict* (pp. 35–79). New York: Russell Sage Foundation.

Sherif, M. (1966). *In common predicament: Social psychology of intergroup conflict and cooperation.* New York: Houghton Mifflin.

Staples, R. (1979). The myth of African American macho: A response to angry African American feminists. *African American Scholar, 10,* 24–32.

Terborg-Penn, R. (1985). Has poverty been feminized in Black America? *Black Scholar, 16,* 14–24.

Thompson, B. (1992). "A way outa no way": Eating problems among African-American, Latina, and White women. *Gender and Society, 6,* 546–561.

Thompson, B. (1996). Multiracial feminist theorizing about eating problems: Refusing to rank oppressions. *Eating Disorders, 4,* 104–114.

Tizard, B., & Phoenix, A. (1995). The identity of mixed parentage adolescents. *Journal of Child Psychology and Psychiatry, 36,* 1399–1410.

Walters, K. L. (1998). Negotiating conflicts in allegiances among lesbians and gays of color: Reconciling divided selves and communities. In G. P. Mallon (Ed.), *Foundations of social work practice with lesbian and gay persons* (pp. 47–75). New York: Haworth Press.

Wardle, F. (1992). Supporting biracial children in the school setting. *Education and Treatment of Children, 15,* 163–172.

White, J. B., & Langer, E. J. (1999). Horizontal hostility: Relations between similar minority groups. *Journal of Social Issues, 55,* 537–559.

Zinn, M. B., Cannon, L. W., Higginbotham, E., & Dill, B. T. (1986). The costs of exclusionary practices in women's studies. *Signs: Journal of Women in Culture and Society, 11,* 290–303.

ISSUES FOR DISCUSSION

1. In this chapter, we have discussed the impact of being a minority member on more than one dimension. Have you ever experienced a conflict from having to choose among different aspects of your identity? What was this experience like?

2. How has what you have learned in this text affected your understanding of psychology? Will this information change the way you think, feel, and act in your daily life?

About the Authors

Gordon C. Nagayama Hall is professor of psychology at the University of Oregon. He received his MA in theology in 1979 and his PhD in clinical psychology in 1982 from Fuller Theological Seminary. He worked as a psychologist at Western State Hospital in Washington State and was professor of psychology at Kent State University before going to Penn State in 1998. In 2001, he moved to the University of Oregon. Dr. Hall has taught undergraduate and graduate courses on multicultural psychology since 1988. He is a Fellow of the American Psychological Association and was president of the APA's Society for the Psychological Study of Ethnic Minority Issues. He is the coeditor with Sumie Okazaki of *Asian American Psychology: Scientific Innovations for the 21st Century.* His research interests are in cultural risk and protective factors associated with psychopathology, particularly sexual aggression.

Christy Barongan is an assistant professor of psychology at Mary Baldwin College. She was trained as a clinical psychologist at Kent State University. Before coming to Mary Baldwin College, she was an assistant professor at the University of Pittsburgh at Johnstown. She has taught introduction to psychology, personality, abnormal psychology, counseling and psychotherapy, behavior modification, and assessment. Dr. Barongan's experiences as a female and as a Filipino have fostered her interest in issues of diversity. She is a member of the American Psychological Association, Division 35 (Psychology of Women) of APA, and Division 45 (Society for the Psychological Study of Ethnic Minority Issues) of APA. Her research has focused on sexual aggression and body image/eating disorders.

Author Index

Subject Index

ABAB design, 43–44
Academic achievement, 176–177, 216–221
  African Americans, 176–177
  Asian Pacific Americans, 216–221
  parenting style/expectations and, 176,
    217–218
  peer support and, 218
  poverty and, 176
  relative functionalism, 218
  socioeconomic status and, 176, 216–217
Acculturation, 21–24, 132, 175, 215, 222,
  251–253, 308–309, 320
  conflict among family members due to
    different levels of, 320
  models, 21–24, 308–309
  proxies, and limitation of research on, 253
  psychopathology and (Latino/a Americans),
    251–253
  stress of, and racial socialization, 175
Adaptive behavior, 78–79
Affirmative action, 162–165, 177
African Americans, 18–20, 48, 54, 63, 157–193,
  242, 298, 301–303, 309–315, 317
  academic achievement, 176–177
  Afrocentrism, 165
  attachment theories, 172
  child-centeredness, 169
  communalism, 167, 169, 170, 179
  "cool pose," 182, 183, 193
  cultural values and identity, 167–171
  demographics, 157, 165–166
  developmental and family issues, 171–177
  with disabilities, 317
  discipline, 175–176, 182
  discrimination, 179
  ethnic identity theory, 170–171
  family issues, 171–177, 182
  history, 157–165
  identity development model (Cross), 18–20
  immigration, attitudes toward, 242

  ingroup favoritism, 171
  interrelatedness (of nature and the universe),
    167, 170
  mental health, 63, 178–184
  multiethnic identity, 301–303
  parenting, 172–173, 175–176, 182
  physical discipline, 175–176
  poverty, impact of, 166, 176, 181, 182
  psychopathology, 63, 178–179
  racial socialization, 173–175
  services, 179–181
  "sexism," 310
  sexual identity, 298
  social support, 180
  spirituality, 167, 169–170, 179, 180
  stereotypes, 48, 177, 182
  violence, 181–184
  women/feminism, 309–315, 317
Aggression/aggressive behavior, 76–77, 79,
  99–102
  authoritarian personality (group violence),
    101
  cultural differences in condoning, 101–102
  factors contributing to, 100
  gender/sex differences in, 79
  genocidal violence, 101
  toward groups/individuals, 101
  intention and, 99–100
  sexual, 79, 100, 206
  See also Violence
Alcohol/alcoholism, 84, 282–284
Alpha bias, 45–46
Alternation (acculturation model), 22, 23–24,
  308–309
American(s):
  defining, 3–4
  family type, 215
American Indians, 265–295
  alcohol use by, 282–284
  "being," 276–277

341